RACHMANINOFF AND HIS WORLD

THE BARD MUSIC FESTIVAL

LEON BOTSTEIN AND CHRISTOPHER H. GIBBS,
SERIES EDITORS

RACHMANINOFF
AND HIS WORLD

EDITED BY PHILIP ROSS BULLOCK

THE UNIVERSITY OF CHICAGO PRESS
CHICAGO AND LONDON

The University of Chicago Press, Chicago 60637
The University of Chicago Press, Ltd., London
© 2022 The Bard Music Festival
All rights reserved. No part of this book may be used or reproduced in any
manner whatsoever without written permission, except in the case of brief quotations
in critical articles and reviews. For more information, contact the University of
Chicago Press, 1427 E. 60th St., Chicago, IL 60637.
Published 2022
Printed in the United States of America

31 30 29 28 27 26 25 24 23 22   1 2 3 4 5

Cloth ISBN-13: 978-0-226-82074-3
Paper ISBN-13: 978-0-226-82375-1
E-book ISBN-13: 978-0-226-82374-4
DOI: https://doi.org/10.7208/chicago/9780226823744.001.0001

This publication has been produced by the Bard College Publications Office:
Irene Zedlacher, project director
Karen Spencer, design
Text edited by Paul De Angelis and Erin Clermont
Music typeset by Christopher Deschene
Indexed by Scott Smiley

This publication has been underwritten in part by a grant from
Roger and Helen Alcaly

Library of Congress Control Number: 2022934268

♾ This paper meets the requirements of ANSI/NISO Z39.48-1992
(Permanence of Paper).

Contents

Introduction

PHILIP ROSS BULLOCK

In 1939, a CBS poll of listeners asked which living composers would still be performed in a century's time. The resulting list is prescient: "the public gave Rachmaninoff third place in a list of ten names. Only Jean Sibelius and Richard Strauss were ahead of him; those after him included Stravinsky, Prokofieff, and Shostakovich."[1] Of the six figures named here, five have been the subject of previous Bard Music Festivals, so it is fitting that Rachmaninoff's time has come at last. If the directness and accessibility of his music have long appealed to audiences worldwide, then the story of his life satisfies an equal fascination with some of the most vivid pages of twentieth-century history. Born in Russia in 1873, he established himself as one of the most famous composers, conductors, and pianists of the turn of the century, not just in Russia, but in Europe and America too. After he emigrated to the United States in the wake of the Bolshevik Revolution of 1917, he became the most prominent symbol of the fate of Russian culture in exile. His music nourished the nostalgia that many émigrés felt for their lost homeland, and for non-Russian audiences, his aristocratic bearing and seemingly old-fashioned music evoked the values of a society and a culture that had been swept away by warfare and revolution. His death in Los Angeles in 1943 marked the passing of "the world of yesterday," to draw on the title of Stefan Zweig's memoirs of pre-war Austro-Hungary, which first appeared in English that same year.

Yet for all that Rachmaninoff continues to top audience polls, and his solo piano pieces, concertos, and symphonic works are central to the modern concert and recording repertory, other works—notably his three operas and his many songs—are less familiar. And despite—or perhaps because of—his great popularity, Rachmaninoff has had perhaps more detractors than any other major composer. Even in his lifetime, he was dismissed by many as the embodiment of conservatism and anachronism, and ever since he has been judged—and found wanting—by the arbiters of taste and progress. In 1954, Eric Blom, editor of the fifth edition of *Grove's Dictionary of Music and Musicians*, offered an infamously condescending view of Rachmaninoff's claim on posterity:

> As a pianist Rakhmaninov was one of the finest artists of his time; as a composer he can hardly be said to have belonged to his time at all. . . . His music is well constructed and effective, but monotonous in texture, which consists in essence mainly of artificial and gushing tunes accompanied by a variety of figures derived from arpeggios. The enormous popular success some few of Rakhmaninov's works had in his lifetime is not likely to last, and musicians never regarded it with much favour.[2]

In a preface to an earlier biography by Victor Seroff, Virgil Thomson enumerated what he saw as the characteristic features of his style—"his passionless melancholy, his almost too easy flow of melody, his conventional but highly personal harmony, the loose but thoroughly coherent structure of his musical discourse"—and suggested that they amounted to "a retreat from battle, an avoidance of the contemporary problem."[3] The most withering judgment belonged to Theodor Adorno, whose avant-garde credentials precluded any understanding or acceptance of Rachmaninoff's music or its popularity. Writing about the C-sharp Minor Prelude, he declared: "it sounds tremendously difficult and at all events very loud. But it is comfortingly easy to play: the child knows that the colossal effect cannot misfire and that he is assured in advance of a triumph that has been achieved without effort." It was, he pronounced, a "triumph for infantile adults."[4]

Even more influential than Rachmaninoff's critics were his admirers. In 1946, a group of friends compiled a series of vignettes and reminiscences of the composer. Edited by the artist Mstislav Dobuzhinsky and published by the composer's sister-in-law Sofiya Satina, *Pamyati Rakhmaninova* (In Memory of Rachmaninoff) may not have been a scholarly work, yet in curating his image so assiduously, it established a set of myths that have proved hard to shake off.[5] Take, for instance, Mark Aldanov's brief essay, which sees Rachmaninoff as fundamentally conservative in spirit:

> In the field of art, the nineteenth century in Russia was an extraordinary phenomenon, to be compared only with the seventeenth century in France—"le grand siècle." . . . Rachmaninoff was a man of the nineteenth century. Fame

came to him in the twentieth century, but only thanks to and on account of what he was given by the nineteenth—the only truly civilized century in the history of the world.[6]

Rachmaninoff himself was complicit in perpetuating such an interpretation of his music. In an interview published posthumously in 1959, he reportedly claimed: "I reflect the philosophy of old Russia—White Russia—with its overtones of suffering and unrest, its pastoral but tragic beauty, its ancient and enduring glory." "I am," he concluded, "a Victorian-Edwardian—actually the last of the romantic composers."[7] In another interview, seemingly given in 1939 but held back for publication until a week after his death, he expressed feelings of loss and regret. "I feel like a ghost wandering in a world grown alien," he confessed to Leonard Liebling, editor of *The Musical Courier*.[8]

His estrangement from the world was not just the result of exile, but of his inability to come to terms with musical modernism:

> I cannot cast out the old way of writing, and I cannot acquire the new. I have made intense effort to feel the musical manner of today, but it will not come to me. Unlike Madame Butterfly with her quick religious conversion, I cannot cast out my musical gods in a moment and bend the knee to new ones. Even with the disaster of living through what has befallen the Russia where I spent my happiest years, yet I always feel that my own music and my reactions to all music, remained spiritually the same, unendingly obedient in trying to create beauty. . . . [9]

Statements such as these—and there are plenty of them—have given rise to a view of the works that Rachmaninoff wrote before his emigration as static, almost pictorial evocations of the lost world of tsarist Russia. Similarly, his long periods of creative silence after his emigration have been interpreted as manifestations of debilitating homesickness, and the works he did compose during his long exile in Western Europe and North America have been reduced to nostalgic testaments of loss.

The term "nostalgia" was invented by a seventeenth-century Swiss medical student, Johannes Hofer, to describe the symptoms he identified in individuals who had been displaced from their homelands.[10] The idea was not a new one, of course, but what Hofer did was translate the German *Heimweh* and French *maladie du pays* into the more scholarly sounding *nostalgia*. Comprising two Greek words—*nostos* (return to one's native country) and *algos* (suffering or grief)—his neologism externalized irreducible and individual human experience into hard and universal scientific fact. If nostalgia has long clung to Rachmaninoff's reputation, so too has another word from the medicalized language of the emotions: melancholy. One of the four temperaments originally proposed by the Greek physician Hippocrates (the others were the sanguine, the choleric, and the phlegmatic), melancholy was central to the early modern vocabulary of the emotions, before being repurposed by Sigmund Freud in his 1915 essay *Mourning and Melancholy*. Here, Freud contrasts two differing reactions to loss. The first is a normal, even healthy process, in which the individual comes to terms with the absence of someone or something beloved ("one's country, liberty, an ideal").[11] The other reaction is that of melancholy, whose symptoms include "profoundly painful dejection, cessation of interest in the outside world, loss of the capacity to love, inhibition of all activity, and the lowering of the self-regarding feelings."[12]

These histories and etymologies may not come consciously to mind when we listen to Rachmaninoff, describe our reactions to his music, or read the criticism of others, yet they have implicitly shaped the reception of his works. The story of the botched premiere of the First Symphony in St. Petersburg in March 1897 has been often told, as has the story of Rachmaninoff's slow recovery from the depression it provoked in him. The therapy that he underwent with Nikolai Dahl in early 1900 has given rise to the idea of his music as an outward projection of inward psychological suffering. As Virgil Thomson put it: "his depressive mentality has come to represent to the Western world a musical expression both specifically Russian and specifically attractive."[13] Yet the work that Rachmaninoff dedicated in gratitude to Dahl—the Second Piano Concerto—affirms psychological recovery and revels in the return of creativity and inspiration. Similarly, the works that Rachmaninoff composed in emigration represent hardy resilience and a vital will to express himself in new surroundings and to new audiences. They are decidedly not the debilitating symptoms of an unconquerable nostalgia for a world to which he knew he would never return. Rachmaninoff may have mourned the Russia of his birth, yet he was more able to understand, accommodate, and savor the modern world than has often been appreciated.

Here, the house that Rachmaninoff had built in the early 1930s at Hertenstein on the banks of Lake Lucerne provides a framework for reassessing the place of his music in the twentieth century. In one sense, he was seeking to recreate the atmosphere of Ivanovka, the estate in the Tambov region that originally belonged to his wife's family, and whose practical management he oversaw with notable efficiency. Certainly the gardens at Villa Senar (named after the composer and his wife—i.e. *Se*rgei and *Na*talya *R*achmaninoff) were designed to evoke the Russian countryside: "Natalya Aleksandrovna constantly teased Sergei Vasilyevich

Figure 1. Architectural sketch for Rachmaninoff's home, Hertenstein, Switzerland, 30 December 1930.

that in preparing such a level, flat area for a meadow and a garden, he wanted to turn Switzerland into Ivanovka."[14] Yet the house itself comes as something of a surprise. Designed by Alfred Möri and Karl-Friedrich Krebs, it is a starkly beautiful, elegantly rational building, very much in the spirit of the Bauhaus movement (see Figure 1). Rachmaninoff paid great attention to every detail of its construction, creating nothing less than a modernist *Gesamtkunstwerk*, whose confident feeling for contemporary design reveals something unexpected about his tastes. Sebastian Jacobi enumerates its contents:

> a small, plain fold-out bureau with its original frame painted over in light grey, in the style of Josef Frank; a larger writing desk veneered in walnut, reminiscent of Erich Dieckmann's furniture designs from his time at the institution Bauhochschule in Weimar. A tubular-steel sofa in the style of Le Corbusier unexpectedly confronts the visitor in the cellar and, one room further on, in the former laundry, a large extending table with a sophisticated extension mechanism, presumably a custom-made item, also brings Le Corbusier to mind. Other pieces of original garden and kitchen furniture, as well as original free-standing cabinets, all of which have been painted over

many times and used for purposes other than those originally intended, are also to be found in other rooms. For instance, there is also a small wall-mounted sideboard in the gardener's house. The evidently reconstructible historical kitchen fit-out has the look and feel of a combination of Margarete Schütte-Lihotzky's "Frankfurt Kitchen" and the kitchen furniture that Mies van der Rohe designed for residential buildings. Many of the surviving pieces of furniture blend to form a collective in terms of design, enabling a symbiosis between the architecture and the interior space.[15]

As Villa Senar amply demonstrates, Rachmaninoff was entirely able to respond to the modern world. That was true enough in his daily life, as suggested by his love of fast cars, transatlantic liners, speedboats, and the latest comforts of Möri and Krebs's Bauhaus architecture. And beneath its lush surface, Rachmaninoff's music has more sinew and energy than its reputation suggests. His genius was to sound the grandeur of the nineteenth century—whether as a composer or as one of the world's most feted piano virtuosos—and repurpose it for a new era and a new world.

Why, then, does the image of Rachmaninoff as belated, conservative, nostalgic, and even sentimental persist? The use of his music in films such from *Brief Encounter* (1945) to *Shine* (1995) is certainly one factor, as is a performance tradition that has often emphasized lushness over the *pudeur* to be heard in his own recordings. But the most significant factor is surely our understanding of the nature and origins of Russian musical modernism. In many respects, our narratives are indebted to the city of St. Petersburg, which produced not only composers such as Prokofiev and Stravinsky, but also influential catalysts and mediators such as Serge Diaghilev and the coterie of artists and writers associated with the *Mir iskusstva* (World of Art) movement and later the Evenings of Contemporary Music. In turn, they went on to shape Western European perceptions of modern Russian music, not least through the work of the Ballets Russes. As Rachmaninoff's first "biographer," Oskar von Riesemann, observed:

> The attitude of Paris audiences towards Russian music is well known. They have always upheld St. Petersburg. The "Nouvelle Ecole Russe," chiefly represented by Rimsky-Korsakov, Borodin, Moussorgski, and Glazounov, and recently also by Stravinsky and Prokofyeff, is counted as the only movement worth considering. All works originating from there are sure of a friendly reception. Moscow, on the other hand, had a hard fight for popularity in France, even in the person of its greatest

representative, Tchaikovsky, and has never won the same appreciation there as in Germany, where the exact opposite is the case. . . . Owing to this attitude shown by public opinion in Paris, the St. Petersburg composers during Diaghilyeff's "Russian Season" had a much easier success than their Moscow colleagues, as, for instance, Rachmaninoff, because he was considered a follower of Tchaikovsky, and Scriabin, because his nebulous world-philosophy was not congenial to the sharp, crystal-clear intellect and the straightforward musical hedonism of the French.[16]

There is no gainsaying the importance of turn-of-the-century St. Petersburg and interwar Paris as crucibles for a distinct form of Russian modernism, yet their histories can overshadow other, equally important responses to modernity.

Rachmaninoff's career is a case in point. The brief period he spent in St. Petersburg in the early 1880s was as unhappy as it was unproductive, and his relationship with the city was subsequently tainted by César Cui's withering attack on his First Symphony. His relationship with Diaghilev's Ballets Russes was equally fleeting and inconclusive.[17] By contrast, Moscow proved to be a city in which Rachmaninoff not only established himself as the heir to Tchaikovsky, but also formed part of a younger generation of composer-pianists, most notably Nikolai Medtner and Aleksandr Scriabin. Broadly speaking, the myth of Moscow is that of a more traditional, more authentic, more conservative older sibling to the younger and more iconoclastic St. Petersburg, yet it too experienced its own form of modernity in the early twentieth century. With their strong investment in German Romantic idealism, tinged with decadence, messianism, and fin-de-siècle ennui, intellectual and artistic circles in Moscow fashioned Rachmaninoff's pre-revolutionary works every bit as much as Western European and American interwar modernism shaped his émigré compositions. Writing of his First Symphony shortly after its disastrous premiere in St. Petersburg in March 1897, for instance, he confessed that "this Symphony, even if it is not decadent, as this word is normally used and understood, is really rather 'new.'"[18] To hear the First Symphony as an innovative work—even one in dialogue with aspects of decadence (as modernism was often called in Russia in the 1890s)—is a first step in seeing Rachmaninoff less through the prism of late Romanticism than through that of a nascent modernism associated above all with Moscow, and which was pursued yet further during the time he spent in Dresden between 1906 and 1909. As he stated in an interview that appeared shortly after his first American tour in 1909–10:

> While we must respect the traditions of the past, which for
> the most part are very intangible to us because they are only
> to be found in books, we must, nevertheless, not be bound
> down by convention. Iconoclasm is the law of artistic prog-
> ress. All great composers and performers have built on the
> ruins of conventions that they themselves have destroyed.[19]

Although that iconoclasm did not obviously manifest itself in Rachmaninoff's
art, it nonetheless opens up a new way of thinking about his place in twentieth-
century music.

As with other volumes in the Bard Music Festival series, *Rachmaninoff
and His World* does not aim to be a complete companion to the composer's life and works. Instead, its three subsections and afterword explore
his music by focusing on his interaction with the artistic and intellectual worlds in which he lived and worked. Throughout, the image that
emerges is not that of a composer airily disengaged from contemporary
debates, but one of a figure who reacted thoughtfully, creatively, and
individually to a strikingly wide range of stimuli. His career was that of
a busy, successful professional musician, shaped by the new cultural and
social institutions that came into being in Russia in the second half of the
nineteenth century. He may have sought peace and isolation as a composer, but as a pianist and conductor, he traveled extensively throughout
the Russian Empire, Western Europe, and North America, even before
his emigration in 1917. The twenty-five and a half years he lived outside
the land of his birth were just as dynamic and driven. His busy concert
life took him to the most important cultural centers in Europe and the
United States, as well as many smaller and more easily overlooked towns
and cities. Interviews with the press allowed him to spread his renown
with the large audiences for classical music that emerged between the
wars, and recording offered new possibilities for cultivating his artistic
celebrity. Keeping up with his extended family and circles of friends
entailed lengthy journeys across countries and continents. And even if
he was unable to return to his homeland, he maintained an energetic
correspondence with those friends and colleagues who had remained
behind. Despite his antipathy toward communism, he provided financial
support to the Red Army during the Second World War, and his works—
even those composed in emigration—came to enjoy a central place in the
Soviet repertoire.

The volume's opening section focuses primarily on cultural life in
Moscow in the final decades of the Russian Empire. It was here that
Rachmaninoff studied and first made his name, and where he developed into the musician—composer, pianist, and conductor—whom we
know now. Peter Franklin's essay—which ranges beyond Moscow to St.

Petersburg, Dresden, and even the composer's émigré years—sets forth a reading of Rachmaninoff's orchestral music that moves beyond his acknowledged debt to Tchaikovsky, finding instead parallels with Mahler and Reger, and proposing a genealogy of modernism that runs contrary to narratives associated with Schoenberg and Stravinsky. Rebecca Mitchell focuses on turn-of-the-century Moscow and its musical institutions, illustrating how Rachmaninoff—even while he never associated himself with any particular clique or movement, and shied away from the kind of manifestos and programmatic statements that were so characteristic of modernism—was a dynamic presence in the city. Mitchell's appeal here is not, in fact, to artistic modernism, but to the broader and more productive concept of modernity, a term that captures the energetic transformation of urban life in early twentieth-century Russia. Mitchell's reading of modernity is catholic and capacious, incorporating elite musical institutions (the Moscow Conservatory, Russian Music Society, private concert series), as well as facets of popular culture (gypsy singers, the café chantant). Similarly Marina Frolova-Walker emphasizes Rachmaninoff's kinship with aspects of early twentieth-century culture that have not always figured in classic accounts of Russian modernism. Evoking the notion of the "middlebrow," Frolova-Walker situates Rachmaninoff's music at the intersection between high art and popular culture and proposes an interpretation of his songs that reveals affinities with the work of a number of early twentieth-century writers, many of them women, who have not always been accorded a place in the literary canon. This literary focus extends to my own close reading of the "Vocalise," which has long stood as an archetypical example of Rachmaninoff's characteristic lyricism, but which is here interpreted as a response to contemporary literary aesthetics.

The centrality of opera to the Russian musical canon is well attested, yet Rachmaninoff's three one-act operas are unfamiliar to many music lovers and have often been seen as failures, even by sympathetic scholars. Emily Frey examines Rachmaninoff's graduation piece, *Aleko*, demonstrating its subtle refraction and reconfiguration of Russian musical realism. Frey also illustrates how the opera encodes Rachmaninoff's productive relationship with a number of turn-the-century Moscow's leading theatrical innovators—Chaliapin, Nemirovich-Danchenko, and Stanislavsky. Caryl Emerson and Simon Morrison explore the pair of operas whose premiere Rachmaninoff himself conducted at Moscow's Bolshoi Theatre in January 1906. As interpreted by Emerson, *The Miserly Knight* becomes not just the last of Pushkin's "little tragedies" to be set to music (coming after Dargomyzhsky's *Stone Guest*, Rimsky-Korsakov's *Mozart and Salieri*, and Cui's *Feast in Time of Plague*), but a commentary on the nature of creativity and the vocation of the artist in an era of increasing mercantilism. As well as its social and biographical relevance, *The Miserly Knight* also deals with the theology of sin. As such, it makes an ideal pairing with *Francesca da Rimini*, based on Dante's *Commedia*, and constituting one of European culture's most durable evocations of adulterous love. Morrison, like Emerson, notes the Wagnerian quality of the score, and shows Rachmaninoff's evolving—and often innovative—approach to the musical treatment of eroticism.

Rachmaninoff's experience of displacement after 1917 has given rise to a sense of him as the archetypal Russian émigré, and it is not hard to find evidence of his abiding attachment to his lost homeland. The music of this period has come to embody what Edward Said sees as the exile's divided self:

> Exile is strangely compelling to think about but terrible to experience. It is the unhealable rift forced between a human being and a native place, between the self and its true home: its essential sadness can never be surmounted. And while it is true that literature and history contain heroic, romantic, glorious, even triumphant episodes in an exile's life, these are no more than efforts meant to overcome the crippling sense of estrangement. The achievements of exiles are permanently undermined by the loss of something left behind for ever.[20]

There are, though, other ways of hearing Rachmaninoff's final works. Accordingly, this volume's third section dwells less on a sense of loss than on the achievements of his American years (which began even before he settled in the United Stated in 1918). A selection of his interviews with the American press reveals him to have been adept at conveying a highly marketable image to his new audience, and belies a reputation for dour taciturnity (to one editor he coyly claimed: "I mostly keep my opinions to myself, and in consequence I am generally regarded as a silent man. So be it. In silence lies safety").[21] Steve Swayne's study of the eighteenth variation from the *Rhapsody on a Theme of Paganini* reveals a knowing dialogue between Rachmaninoff's own brand of lush Romanticism and aspects of interwar modernism (not least Schoenberg's serial technique), as well as celebrating its evergreen emotional appeal. Christopher H. Gibbs and Marina Raku explore contrasting aspects of Rachmaninoff's reception around the mid-century. Gibbs focuses on the festival of Rachmaninoff's music that was given by his beloved Philadelphia Orchestra in 1939, which represents the culmination of his canonization as the most popular living classical composer in America. Raku reminds us that despite his emigration, Rachmaninoff enjoyed equal popularity in the Soviet Union, and that his music came to represent a point of continuity between the nineteenth-century Russian classics and the aspirations of socialist realism, both as a musical style, and as a form of cultural appreciation. Leon Botstein's essay traces Rachmaninoff's career as a one of a number composer-pianists to have brought the grand tradition of European art music to modern America, contrasting his legacy with the very different styles of Busoni and Paderewski.

Published to coincide with the 2022 Bard Music Festival, *Rachmaninoff and His World* anticipates the celebrations of the hundred-and-fiftieth anniversary of the composer's birth in 1873 (not to mention the eightieth anniversary of his death in 1943). Viewed from the vantage point of the present day, Rachmaninoff seems ever less a relic of the nineteenth century, and more and more the quintessential composer of the first half of the twentieth. After all, scholarship has moved on from the tenets of high modernism that once denigrated or ignored altogether composers such as Rachmaninoff on the grounds of their supposed conservatism and commercial appeal. Equally, we have learned to be less anxious about the enormous pleasure that his music affords and to celebrate—or at least not dismiss—its enduring expressive appeal. Each of the essays here reveals a reflective, undogmatic individual, who saw his music not as a vehicle for conveying a nationality, an ideology, an aesthetic, or a philosophy, but as the articulation of his own, highly personal and irreducible emotional constitution. As Rachmaninoff himself wrote in December 1941:

> In my own compositions, no conscious effort has been made to be original, or Romantic, or Nationalistic, or anything else. I write down on paper the music I hear within me, as naturally as possible. I am a Russian composer, and the land of my birth has influenced my temperament and outlook. My music is the product of my temperament, and so it is Russian music; I never consciously attempted to write Russian music, or any other kind of music. I have been strongly influenced by Tchaikovsky and Rimsky-Korsakov; but I have never, to the best of my knowledge, imitated anyone. What I try to do, when writing down my music, is to make it say simply and directly that which is in my heart when I am composing. If there is love there, or bitterness, or sadness, or religion, these moods become a part of my music, and it becomes either beautiful or bitter or sad or religious.[22]

NOTES

1. "Rachmaninoff Festival: Series Marks 30th Anniversary of his Debut in U.S.," *Newsweek*, 4 December 1939, 40.

2. "Rakhmaninov, Sergey Vassilievich," in *Grove Dictionary of Music and Musicians*, ed. Eric Blom, 5th ed., 10 vols. (London: Macmillan, 1954), 7:27–29, at 27.

3. Virgil Thomson, "Foreword," in Victor I. Seroff, *Rachmaninoff* (New York: Simon and Schuster, 1950), xi–xiv, at xii.

4. Theodor W. Adorno, "Commodity Music Analyzed," in *Quasi una Fantasia: Essays on Modern Music*, trans. Rodney Livingstone (New York: Verso, 1998), 37–52, at 38.

5. M. V. Dobuzhinkskiy, ed., *Pamyati Rakhmaninova* (New York: Izdaniye S. A. Satinoy, 1946).

6. M. Aldanov, untitled essay in ibid., 1–5, at 4.

7. Glenn Quilty, "Rachmaninoff—The Last Romantic Composer," *HiFi Review* 3/4 (October 1959): 26 and 28, at 26. The whole of this interview is reproduced later in this volume, 212–14.

8. Leonard Liebling, "Variations," *Musical Courier*, 5 April 1943, 16–17, at 17.

9. Ibid.

10. Johannes Hofer, "Medical Dissertation on Nostalgia," trans. Carolyn Kiser Anspach, *Bulletin of the Institute of the History of Medicine* 2/6 (1934): 376–91.

11. Sigmund Freud, "Mourning and Melancholy" in *The Standard Edition of the Complete Works of Sigmund Freud*, trans. and ed. James Strachey et al., 24 vols (London: Hogarth Press, 1953–74), 14:243–58, at 243.

12. Ibid., 244.

13. Thomson, "Foreword," xi.

14. S. A. Satina, "Zapiska o S. V. Rakhmaninove," in *Vospominaniya o Rakhmaninove*, ed. Z. Apetyan, 5th ed., 2 vols (Moscow: Muzïka, 1988): 1:12–115 at 86.

15. Sebastian Jacobi, "From the Architecture to the Interior Design: An Investigative Search at Villa Senar," in *Villa Senar: Dream of a House* (Hertenstein: Serge Rachmaninoff Foundation, 2016), 16–17. For a richly documented and illustrated study of the villa, see Baptiste Berrut-Maréchaud and Federica Grande, "Senar: Un passé, un présent et un futur: La villa de Sergei Rachmaninoff à Hertenstein" (MA thesis, École polytechnique fédérale de Lausanne, 2018).

16. Oskar von Riesemann, *Rachmaninoff's Recollections*, trans. Dolly Rutherford (New York: Macmillan, 1934), 147–48.

17. Rachmaninoff's only brush with Diaghilev was in 1907, when he took part in the first of the impresario's Russian seasons in Paris, conducting his cantata, *Spring*, and taking the solo part in his Second Piano Concerto. Much later, his *Rhapsody on a Theme of Paganini* was choreographed by Mikhaïl Fokine and staged in London in 1939 and New York in 1940, long after the novelty of Diaghilev's enterprise had faded into something more conventional.

18. Rachmaninoff to A. V. Zatayevich, 6 May 1897, in S. V. Rakhmaninov, *Literaturnoye naslediye*, ed. Z. A. Apetyan, 3 vols (Moscow: Sovetskiy kompozitor, 1978–80), 1:262.

19. S. V. Rachmaninoff, "Ten Important Attributes of Beautiful Pianoforte Playing," *Etude* 28:3 (1910): 153–54, at 154.

20. Edward W. Said, "Reflections on Exile," in *Reflections on Exile and Other Essays* (Cambridge, MA: Harvard University Press, 2000), 173–86, at 173.

21. Liebling, "Variations," 17.

22. David Ewen, "Music Should Speak from the Heart: A Conference with Sergei Rachmaninoff, the World-Famous Composer-Pianist," *The Etude* 59:12 (1941): 804 and 849, at 849. The whole of this interview is reproduced later in this volume, pp. 209–12.

Permissions and Credits

The following copyright holders, institutions, and individuals have graciously granted permission to reprint or reproduce the following materials:

Serge Rachmaninoff Foundation for Figure 1 in Bullock, "Introduction."

Russian National Museum of Music for Figure 1 (RNMM F211.258) in Franklin, "Reading the Popular Pessimist"; for Figures 5 (RNMM No. N-6105) and 6 (RNMM No. 3511-V) in Mitchell, "Sergei Rachmaninoff and Moscow Musical Life"; for Figures 1 (RNMM F380.2227) and 2 (RNMM F380.1467) in Frey, "Tchaikovsky's Echoes, Chaliapin's Sobs"; for Figure 1 (RNMM No. 1986/V) in Emerson, "Rachmaninoff's Miserly Knight"; and Figure 1 (RNMM No. N-15325) in Morrison, "Burning for You"; for Figure 1 (RNMM F18.1424) in Swayne, "The Eighteenth Variation."

Wikimedia Commons for Figure 1 in Mitchell, "Sergei Rachmaninoff and Moscow Musical Life."

Wikipedia https://en.wikipedia.org/wiki/GUM_(department_store) for Figure 2 in Mitchell, "Sergei Rachmaninoff and Moscow Musical Life."

The Moscow State Conservatory, RussiaSputnik/Bridgeman Images for Figure 3 in Mitchell, "Sergei Rachmaninoff and Moscow Musical Life."

Moscow State Tchaikovsky Conservatory for Figure 4 in Mitchell, "Sergei Rachmaninoff and Moscow Musical Life."

Ogonyok **19 (1901): 152, courtesy of East View Information services, Inc.** for Figure 7 in Mitchell, "Sergei Rachmaninoff and Moscow Musical Life."

Rusneb.ru open resource, from I. E. Bondarenko, *Arkhitekturnïye pamyatniki Moskvï*, 2 vols (Moscow: K. A. Fisher, 1904-6), vol. 1, plate 16 for Figure 8 in Mitchell, "Sergei Rachmaninoff and Moscow Musical Life."

The British Library Board © The British Library Board, *Yezhegodnik Moskovskogo arkhitekturnogo obshchestva*, 2 (1910/11): 105-6 / X.415/2281) for Figures 9a and 9B in Mitchell, "Sergei Rachmaninoff and Moscow Musical Life."

Boosey & Hawkes for permission to reprint examples from Rachmaninoff's *Aleko* and *The Miserly Knight* in Frey, "Tchaikovsky's Echoes, Chaliapin's Sobs."

Digital Commons @ Gardner-Webb University, Boiling Springs, NC, https://digital-commons.gardner-webb.edu/etude/662 for Figure 1 in Bullock, "Rachmaninoff and the Celebrity Interview."

Carl Fischer Music for permission to reprint "Rachmaninoff Is Reminiscent," from *The Musical Observer* in Bullock, "Rachmaninoff and the Celebrity Interview."

Theodor Presser Company for permission to reprint "Music Should Speak from the Heart," from *The Etude*, in Bullock, "Rachmaninoff and the Celebrity Interview."

Ziff-Davis for "Rachmaninoff—The Last Romantic Composer," in Bullock, "Rachmaninoff and the Celebrity Interview."

Philadelphia Orchestra Archive for Figures 1 and 2 in Gibbs, "'One of the Outstanding Musical Events of All Time."

G. Schirmer for permission to print the two music examples by Dmitry Shostakovich in Raku, "The Case of Rachmaninoff"

The authors, editor, and publisher have made every effort to trace holders of copyright. They much regret if any inadvertent omissions have been made.

Acknowledgments

Since I was first invited to be scholar-in-residence at the Bard Music Festival and to edit *Rachmaninoff and His World* for its accompanying publication series, I have greatly depended on the advice, kindness, and generosity of many individuals. Leon Botstein, Christopher H. Gibbs, and Irene Zedlacher have helped shape the contents of this volume, as well as of the festival itself (where Byron Adams also shared his expertise). Paul De Angelis, Erin Clermont, Christopher Deschene, Scott Smiley, and Karen Spencer have guided this book through to publication with deft professionalism. Margaret Frainier provided crucial research assistance, and I am grateful to the following colleagues and friends for stimulating conversations, bibliographical sources, and creative insights along the way: Iain Burnside, Clément Dessy, Stefano Evangelista, Annegret Fauser, Christoph Flamm, Daniel M. Grimley, Nick Hearn, Martin Holmes, Aleksandr Komarov, Elizabeth Macfarlane, Grigory Moiseev, Elger Neils, Geoffrey Norris, Marsha Seifert, Emma Smith, Laura Tunbridge, Ronald de Vet, Ettore Volontieri, and Wouter de Voogd.

Philip Ross Bullock, Oxford and London, February 2022

Note on Transliteration and Dating

The transliteration system used in this book is based on that devised by Gerald Abraham for the *New Grove Dictionary of Music and Musicians* (1980), with modifications introduced by Richard Taruskin in *Musorgsky: Eight Essays and an Epilogue* (1993). The principal exceptions to this system concern commonly accepted spellings of names and places (most notably, Sergei Rachmaninoff rather than Sergey Rakhmaninov) and suffixes (-*sky* rather than -*skiy*). In bibliographic citations, however, the transliteration system is respected without exception (i.e. Sergey Rakhmaninov). Surname suffixes are presented intact, and hard and soft signs preserved.

Russia used the Julian calendar until 1 February 1918, when the Gregorian calendar was adopted. Both systems are used in this book—the Julian calendar for events pertaining to Rachmaninoff's life in Russia before his emigration, and the Gregorian calendar thereafter (as well as during Rachmaninoff's trips outside of Russia before 1918). Since the Gregorian calendar was in use in Europe and America long before 1918, Russians often double-dated their letters when traveling or communicating abroad, and this practice is respected here.

Moscow and Modernity

Reading the Popular Pessimist:
Thought, Feeling, and Dance in
Rachmaninoff's Symphonic Narrative

PETER FRANKLIN

> I believe it is possible to be very serious, to have something to
> say, and at the same time to be popular, I believe that.
> —Sergei Rachmaninoff

In October 2019 film director Martin Scorsese revived a century-old argument about the supposed inadequacies of mass-cultural entertainment. He aimed some exasperated words at Marvel Comics–based superhero movies, which he denounced as "not cinema": "The closest I can think of them, as well made as they are . . . is theme parks. It isn't the cinema of human beings trying to convey emotional, psychological experiences to another human being."[1] He subsequently elaborated: "We need cinemas to step up and show film that is narrative film." We understand him, but there has to be a problem about clearly distinguishing between narratives and theme-park rides. After all, the simplest roller-coaster theme-park ride relies upon a kind of experienced narrative: anticipation, shock, pleasure, crisis, and, we hope, relieved arrival. And do not real, "serious" literary or cinematic narratives communicate best when they have some of those imaginatively involving theme-park elements of anticipation, surprise, and closure (whether they leave us feeling satisfied or sad)? Beyond Scorsese's despairing discrimination between good and bad narrative "rides," we might ask whether it is possible to conceive of the aesthetic, emotional, and even physical pleasure he associates with "low" kinds of popular entertainment embracing the "serious" attempt to confront what Sergei Rachmaninoff would call "soul states" in a 1939 interview. He was delivering a broadside of his own, not at the popular so much as the fashionably serious.[2] "Classical" symphonies, too (his own not least), were then in the firing line. Much depends upon how, and how *closely*, we read them.

I.

It was Rachmaninoff's misfortune to have been misunderstood, in quite different ways, by self-appointed arbiters of taste at both ends of his career. As a young composer in Russia, he was harassed by conservative critics who willfully failed to understand what he was doing. Later, as a celebrity pianist in Europe and America, his orchestral works in particular fell foul of a different breed of critics: stern proponents of Stravinskian modernism (including Stravinsky himself) or of the new music associated with Schoenberg and his pupils. Rachmaninoff's triumph was to survive both scorn and incomprehension with outwardly good grace, a degree of taciturn equanimity, and, against all odds, a determination to hold on to an oft-shaken belief in himself and what he was doing. His later opponents were critics who celebrated precisely those qualities in artists who did things the way *they* wanted them to: pathbreakers and stylistic innovators who were reckoned to be pushing heroically at boundaries over which Rachmaninoff roamed with the unfashionable ease of an aristocrat who had, however, lost everything. It is hardly surprising that he often felt, as he put it himself, "like a ghost wandering in a world grown alien."[3]

There was, of course, a specific sociopolitical dimension to Rachmaninoff's later sense of historical and geographical uprootedness and alienation, but so too one defined by that tough critical debate about modernism and the nature and role of the artist in society, both before and after the First World War. To understand how Rachmaninoff began less as a conservative than a misunderstood innovator in late nineteenth-century Russia, we might turn to his early Fantasy for Orchestra, Op. 7. It came to be known as *The Crag* (*Utyos*, also known as *The Rock*), in light of the score's poetic epigraph from Lermontov:

> Ночевала тучка золотая
> На груди утёса-великана

> A little golden cloud spent the night
> On the breast of a giant crag

There will be more to say about this and other such epigraphs that link symphonic with literary culture, but *The Crag* was composed in the summer of 1892; it was the year after Rachmaninoff's graduation from the Moscow Conservatory, with a rarely awarded gold medal. It was also the year that saw the first Bolshoi performance of his opera *Aleko*, whose relative success was sealed, he believed, by the support it received from Russia's foremost living composer, Tchaikovsky, in the year before his untimely death in

1893. With his student contemporary Aleksandr Scriabin, Rachmaninoff was one of the second generation of "star" composers to come out of the still relatively new conservatory system. Tchaikovsky had been one of the first students of the St. Petersburg Conservatory in the 1860s, and subsequently taught at its Moscow cousin from 1866 until 1877.

Tchaikovsky figured significantly in Rachmaninoff's student years. The determinants of the older man's equivocation about publishing explanatory "programs" for orchestral works (be they personal or literary) probably influenced the young composer's preference initially to conceal the Fantasy's "private" program, derived from an 1886 story by Anton Chekhov, "On the Road'" ("Na puti"), which opens with the same Lermontov epigraph as Rachmaninoff's Opus 7 Fantasy. The story describes a snowy Christmas Eve encounter between travelers temporarily marooned in a wayside inn. A big, ruggedly "Russian" man—Grigory Petrovich Likharyov, his broad features awkward, yet "harmonious and even handsome"—is trying to pass the night at one of its tables while his eight-year-old daughter sleeps fitfully on a bench. [4] A storm rages outside; tomorrow they will go to a potentially failing coal mine that he plans to manage. They are joined by an elegant and resourceful young woman who is traveling to her father and brothers on a farmstead owned by their estate, which *she* feels obliged to manage, given the irresponsible ways of the men. But was she a golden cloud? Chekhov's description of Marya Mikhaylovna Ilovayskaya is satirical: "she had a habit of fluttering her fingers in front of her spiky face as she spoke, and she licked her lips with her pointed little tongue after every phrase." She is nevertheless transfixed by Grigory's account of his spiritual and intellectual journey through Russian philosophy, religion, politics, and science. He feels himself to be on a passionate but goalless quest, even responsible for the death of his wife after he had foolishly impoverished his family; he believes that women alone, however flawed and malleable, can redeem the failed world of Russian masculinity. Following his Faustian tirade, she seems about to offer herself as his redeemer, but after toying with the idea of giving him some money, she simply departs on her sledge the next morning. In the most recent English translation of "On the Road," Lermontov's "crag" has disappointingly shrunk into a mere "boulder," but the story's end, as Grigory gazes at her sledge's tracks in the falling snow, remains stark: "Soon the tracks left by the runners disappeared, and he himself was covered in snow and beginning to look like a white boulder, but his eyes were still seeking something in the snowclouds."[5]

Rachmaninoff's Fantasy has never quite recovered from the redoubtable César Cui's dismissive, "could do better" review in 1896:

> As a musical composition the *Fantasy* presents a kind of mosaic,
> consisting of small pieces without organisational relationship
> among themselves; the composer is always going somewhere
> but getting nowhere . . . . Rachmaninoff is undoubtedly a
> talented man, he has taste and considerable technique but at
> the moment he has neither a sense of scale nor the ability to
> concentrate on an idea and its natural development.[6]

Citing this, Barrie Martyn notes that *The Crag* is generally discussed as
"an immature work," in spite of the fact that the composer programmed
it alongside *The Isle of the Dead* and *The Bells* in his last Moscow concert
in 1917. It is infrequently heard and rarely celebrated. Indeed, my own
vinyl recording, bought long ago, has Yevgeny Svetlanov conducting the
USSR Symphony Orchestra, in 1978. Its period style and sound quality
emphasize the wayward and fragmentary nature of the work that Cui had
dismissed, with its shifts of character and gendered cinematic cuts from
the flute-dominated flightiness of "her" music to the rather obsessive
heaviness of "his"—appropriately enough "going somewhere but getting
nowhere." The effect is that of a rather striking operatic or balletic *scena*.
In Svetlanov's reading it sounds like nothing so much as the flexible and
subtly nuanced underscore to a never-made film of the 1920s or '30s.
Was Rachmaninoff perhaps experimenting with a completely new kind
of symphonic drama that went far beyond the evocative or pictorial implications of the mid-nineteenth-century European "programmaticism" of
Berlioz or Liszt?

The form of the work alludes to the "fatal" ABA structure of Tchaikovsky's
Francesca da Rimini (1876), but somehow dissolved into naturalistic expressive fluidity, marked by shifting subject positions and occasional illustrative
markers of silences or unseen gestures. The little rising flutters of trem-
olando strings seem to call attention to themselves as isolated effects
demanding interpretation. Might they illustrate the snowflakes that land
on the windows, immediately to vanish, "carried away by the wind"? The
whirling tarantella at the center of Grigory's monologue certainly mirrors
what Chekhov describes as the "wild, inhuman music of the storm." Such
music firmly establishes the credentials of a young composer with ideas of
his own.

A photograph of Rachmaninoff, taken in the1890s, shows him sitting,
elegantly dressed in a bow tie and comfortable velvet frockcoat with wide
lapels (Figure 1). He is reading a paperback book, his hair cut short in
a startlingly modern style. His head leans on his right hand, the elbow
supported on a side table bearing more books and some candles beneath

Figure 1. Rachmaninoff in the 1890s with his dog, Levko (photograph: V. Chekhovsky).

a large draped and framed portrait of Tchaikovsky; Levko the dog lies mournfully gazing at the camera at the composer's feet. It was, as we shall see, a bad time for Rachmaninoff, but the photograph seems to show him "at home" in a rather revealing, slightly decadent pose, the portrait emphasizing his early debt to Tchaikovsky. As a student he had made four-handed piano arrangements of both the *Manfred* Symphony and the ballet *The Sleeping Beauty*. Might he also have been aware of Tchaikovsky's own ideas about the social character and role of symphonic as opposed to theatrical music in the Russia in which he had grown up?

Tchaikovsky's rueful belief was that in the Moscow and St. Petersburg of his day symphonic music played to "an elite audience that is small in number."[7] In 1885 he wrote to his publisher about *Manfred*: "Even if it is a work of genius, [it] is the kind of symphony that because of its unusual complexity and difficulty can be played only once every ten years; for this reason it cannot make any money for you."[8] From a European perspective at that time this would have been surprising, given the ostensibly crowd-pleasing programmatic and dramatic nature of *Manfred*. But for Tchaikovsky, opera was the form in which to engage the widest public. In an 1879 letter about *The Maid of Orleans*, he had remarked: "Opera has the great advantage that it gives one the opportunity of addressing the masses through the language of music."[9] The idea that music might be a medium through which "the masses" might be addressed is in itself a significant reflection of the period and place. That opera should have been Tchaikovsky's preferred genre for this contrasts with evidence that European audiences were, if anything, witnessing a rebalancing of "social reach" between the forms. Tchaikovsky's own last three symphonies were soon to become staples of a rapidly expanding audience for symphonic music. Gustav Mahler, writing from Hamburg in 1893 (the year of Tchaikovsky's death), significantly put it that music was becoming "more and more common property—the listeners and players becoming ever more numerous . . . in our over-large concert-halls and opera-houses."[10] Another mark of the impending popular appropriation of the dramatic or "programmatic" symphony was the care with which its spurious validation as "absolute" (read: intellectually and spiritually significant "high culture") was already being policed by stern critics and self-censoring composers. Tchaikovsky was an example, disavowing the programmatic implications of his Fourth Symphony (minutely explained to Mme. von Meck) when faced with critical put-downs like Sergei Taneyev's 1878 claim to have discerned "something that recalls ballet-music" in all of its movements (a criticism that Mahler later received in response to his Third Symphony).[11] Tchaikovsky's nonetheless angry response to Taneyev was interesting: "I simply cannot understand why there should be anything at all *reprehensible* about the expression *ballet music*! . . . I still cannot grasp why a dance melody cannot appear episodically in a symphony, if only with a deliberate shade of vulgar, coarse humor."[12] Tchaikovsky inadvertently reveals here the answer to his own question: because it was deemed "vulgar, coarse"—in the way that ballet music might well have been regarded in comparison with opera or more tastefully "correct" forms of the symphony, as the elite genre Tchaikovsky would regretfully come to consider it.

The respective forms of symphony and opera stood at a significant juncture in terms of reception and audience appeal at the end of the 1870s in Russia, but we can see from this how for a time the symphony—its expressive range and dramatic, narrative implications becoming more complex even as cultural politics required them to be veiled or disavowed—grew ever more elaborately referential, drawing intertextually upon literary, operatic, and indeed *balletic* modes of dramatic expression. One can imagine why a refined, Tchaikovsky-worshipping young composer like Rachmaninoff might utilize a displaced literary allusion to Chekhov's "The Crag," using the same Lermontov epigraph employed by Chekhov at the beginning of that story. He would similarly dedicate his *Elegiac Trio*, Op. 9, to the recently deceased Tchaikovsky by adopting the precise formula, in French, employed by Tchaikovsky for his own Piano Trio, dedicated not quite by name to Nikolai Rubinstein, but *A la mémoire d'un grand artiste*.

Ballet, as a source of referential gesture for the serious composer of modern, Tchaikovskian symphonies in Russia at that time, might illuminate a work like *The Crag*, and the "cinematic" fluidity of its narrative manner. It could also lead us toward a more fruitful way of hearing and understanding Rachmaninoff's crushingly misunderstood First Symphony in 1896. Given the young composer's close familiarity with Tchaikovsky's *The Sleeping Beauty*, in the dramatic tradition of "ballet-pantomime," we might recall that Tchaikovsky's masterpiece opens with music of chaotic turmoil that anticipates the party-wrecking arrival of Carabosse, before giving way to a lyrical melody (of the Lilac Fairy) that comforts with a vision of bliss.[13] When the curtain rises, a march takes shape to accompany the arrival of the courtiers before going on to music that is rhetorically categorized by the heading "Récit de Catalabutte": a danced "recitation" or "narrative" preparing us for the drama to come. We would do well to bear in mind this dramatic underscoring of narrative dance and spectacle, composed to Petipa's precise instructions, which Wilfrid Mellers long ago described as "hardly less exacting than the mathematically measured schedule of the modern film score."[14]

The First Symphony

The Moscovites hated and did not know Wagner, disliked the Russian national school in the persons of Borodin, Rimski-Korsakoff and Musorgski (especially the last), maintained a skeptical attitude towards Liszt and Berlioz, considered Brahms a nonentity and worshipped Chaykovski as the people of St. Petersburg never worshipped him either before that or later.[15]

Leonid Sabaneyev's essay on Rachmaninoff in his 1927 *Modern Russian Composers* localizes the young composer's taste and affiliations in a very specific musical culture dominated by Nikolai Rubinstein and Tchaikovsky. He goes on to characterize the city's bourgeois bohemianism:

> Moscow's musicians gave themselves up to life's amusements considerably more than the musicians of St. Petersburg. The famous Moscow restaurants, the no less famous gypsy choruses, the atmosphere of continuous dissipation. . . . Music here was a terrible narcosis, a sort of intoxication and oblivion, a going off into irrational planes. Drunken mysticism, ecstatic sensations against a background of profound pessimism permeating existence.[16]

Sabaneyev entertainingly prepares his positioning of Rachmaninoff as a Tchaikovskian decadent, a "profound and passionate, self-enclosed and pessimistic soul [who] was will-less, just as was his great teacher, Chaykovski."[17] As a result, he implies, his career was spasmodic, dogged by self-criticism and the fatalism expressed in his famous early C-sharp Minor Prelude. Almost inevitably, it seems, Sabaneyev records that his First Symphony "composed for a large orchestra on themes from Russian ecclesiastical melodies, ended in failure. Symphonic style still baffled the young composer."[18]

Sabaneyev, although a Muscovite himself and one, like Rachmaninoff, who had studied piano with Nikolai Zverev, might have formed a different impression of the First Symphony if he had had a chance to become acquainted with it. At the age of sixteen, he would be unlikely to have attended its fateful first performance in St. Petersburg in March 1897, which, conducted badly by Aleksandr Glazunov, was almost set up to be a disaster. The time and place had been wrong, and Cui's famous critical hatchet job played its part in causing its distraught composer to lock the score away in his desk, never to be heard again in his lifetime (its posthumous premiere was the result of the score being reassembled from surviving orchestral parts).[19] It deserves to be reckoned a masterpiece of advanced, post-Tchaikovskian symphonic form, its dramatic narrative considerably more ambitious, subtle, and innovative than that of *The Crag*.

Once again, however, we encounter that anxiety about Lisztian or Berliozian programmaticism that had plagued Tchaikovsky and led Rachmaninoff to displace direct admission of referential intent onto an oblique allusion to a piece of high-grade contemporary literature in an appropriated epigraph. Any reader of Tolstoy could have recognized it as having appeared in more or less the same form on the title page of *Anna Karenina* (1878):

Мне отмщение, и Аз воздам.

Vengeance is mine, and I will repay.[20]

We need not, I think, try to reconstruct a consistent program based on the events of Tolstoy's novel, nor make assumptions about the relevance of the symphony's cryptic dedication to "A. L." (the wife of a friend of Rachmaninoff). We might put it that the symphony is sufficiently articulate in its stylistic, structural, and gestural manners for us to "read" its depicted tension between private and public modes of address and representation and be struck by its stern opening motif derived from the "Dies irae" chant beloved of Liszt and other Romantic composers (it remains the only "ecclesiastical" melody recognized in the work, although Rachmaninoff had apparently referred to "themes taken from the Oktoechos").[21] Most of the significant material of all four of the symphony's movements is derived from the first phrase of this melody, marked by the gloomy portent of the fanfare-like "Fate" motif that dominates Tchaikovsky's Fourth Symphony. Here, however, the protean power of the figure to generate new material has narrative significance beyond the melodramatic interventions of the initial angry "turn" figure and the following six-note proclamation derived from the chant's opening phrase (Example 1).

As a precociously innovative "first symphony" to set alongside that of Mahler in 1888, Rachmaninoff's easily accommodates some of the critical categories devised by Theodor Adorno (to whose later scorn of Rachmaninoff we will return) to elucidate how Mahler's symphonies function like novels. Rachmaninoff's arresting opening gestures even conclude with a G-major-to-minor chord anticipating Mahler's Sixth Symphony. The conventionally modeled structure of the first movement has a first subject derived straightforwardly from the opening motto, its magisterial presence turned into an ostensibly good musical citizen going about its business and defining an image of what Adorno called the *Weltlauf*—the "way the world goes." Energetically bustling forward in D minor it spawns subsidiary motifs, while being open to momentary distraction by B-flat-major arpeggios that mysteriously rise in the lower strings just before rehearsal number 1, where the *Weltlauf* resumes. A sense of busyness and increased embattlement overtakes the music before it drifts away into silence and a meandering cello line that ushers in what

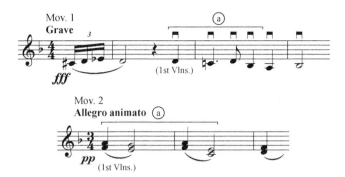

Example 1. Rachmaninoff, First Symphony, initial statement of the Dies irae–derived figure, generative of subsequent material, like the opening of the second movement.

clearly presents itself as a "second subject"—contrasted to the first, as second subjects are supposed to be in late nineteenth-century symphonies. Expressively lyrical, they typically model subjective inwardness that might suggest a "feminine" counterpart to the "masculine" purposefulness of the first-subject material. Here it halts the flow of the latter, replacing regular metrical drive with an intimately improvisatory, lightly accompanied string melody, its meter flexibly shifting from $\frac{4}{4}$ to $\frac{3}{4}$ and back before it generates a $\frac{7}{4}$ bar of woodwind "sighs" (*Meno mosso*) and a more compressed version of its initial figure that rises like an intake of breath and falls in a sighing exhalation, always descending via the augmented second of the "gypsy scale" (here B♭–A—G♭–F etc.).[22] Before long the motif is adopted with urgent expressive commitment by the full string orchestra, supported by wind and brass in a moment of Tchaikovskian lyrical expostulation, aspiring even as it falls away into the depths, shortly to be dismissed by an *fff* scream—a cinematic "stinger" if ever there was— before the first subject takes up where it had left off, ever more urgently. It now conventionally assumes the contrapuntal bustle of a post-Beethovenian "development" section of the kind that always seems to model strife and the approach of a climactic crisis. It arrives here with a grandiose and overwhelmingly "public" *Maestoso* march derived from the first subject's parent motto figure. Fanfares accompany the grand-operatic procession, which subsequently falls away in a version of what, in Mahler, Adorno might have called a "dissolution field." We eventually tumble straight into a recapitulation in which all the elements of the exposition are heightened by an urgent forward momentum that has little room for the second subject's lyrical reflection. There is, however, a final eruption of its climactic expressive gesture (see Example 2), now in a form recalling the rising

Example 2. Rachmaninoff, First Symphony, first movement, second subject, the aspiring and sighing gesture in initial and then more concentrated form.

arpeggio figure, in two great sighing arcs, each weighed down by darkly reiterated brass chords, before the *Più vivo* dash to a noisy close.

The following Scherzo (the title is not actually employed) continues the first movement's narrative, *Allegro animato*. The continuity is stressed in a fascinating manner. After the reused initiating "turn" in the violas, muted strings create a texture that might have suited an intimate slow movement, but this is a Tchaikovskian dance in which the symphony's motto-theme is presented in major-key form (we are now in the relative F major) as a lilting motif that might be characterized by Tolstoy's depiction of Kitty being drawn straight into a waltz at the ball in chapter 22 of *Anna Karenina*: "Her little feet in their rose-colored slippers began to glide swiftly and lightly over the polished floor in time with the music."[23] We hardly notice the horns reiterating an insistent falling and returning major third (F–D♭–F) that will come to sound like the distant echo of a battle threatening the ball and the dance. Ever darker murmurings in the strings, like a looming storm, underpin the dancing figures in a brief middle section (*Meno mosso*) where the calls take on the explicit shape of the motto theme's main four notes and more clearly reassume the character of the Dies irae. This is a dance on the edge of a precipice. At rehearsal number 29, a solo violin detaches itself from the texture to play an odd little variation of its own, accompanied by pizzicato strings for some twenty bars. Like "Freund Hein" in the Scherzo of Mahler's Fourth Symphony, it is a spectral presence in the music, perhaps anticipating the second Scherzo of Mahler's Tenth Symphony where the Devil is present among the dancers—"Der Teufel tanzt es mit mir!" Mahler wrote on the movement's title page.[24]

What is clear about Rachmaninoff's Scherzo, apart from its position-ing *before* the Larghetto (following Borodin?), is precisely that it overlays and sets in dialogue with each other the first movement's *Weltlauf* ("pub-lic" in its rhetorical manner and inclusiveness) and the expressive subject who might experience it as fatal or coercive, seeking escape into inward-ness and dream. The subject is consistently represented here by the Dies irae motto in re-spelled rhythmic and modal form (the initial third now major, see Example 1). This emphasizes its complex involvement with the *Weltlauf* as communal dance. In keeping with Romantic symphonic prece-dent, the narrative thread is strengthened by the fact that the material of the Larghetto's third-movement "song" is derived from the second-subject material of the first movement. The rhythm of the halting oscil-lation that had preceded the rising and falling wave of its main lyrical gesture, at the *Meno mosso* (twenty-eight bars after rehearsal number 3; see Example 2), seems to have suggested the lilting rhythm of the Dies irae–derived dance figure introduced at the start of the second move-ment; it is also heard at the outset of the third. The Larghetto's unfolding, almost improvisatory melodic line also incorporates the little dropping and returning third figure with which the horns had threatened the sec-ond movement's dance. We might indeed hear the Larghetto itself as a kind of *dance*, intimate and sensual, in the manner of a *pas de deux* for the prima ballerina and her partner—or a solo for the prima ballerina alone, dreaming of what *might* have been.

Dance is unequivocally evoked in the Finale, whose initial energetic flourishes, *"con fuoco,"* are succeeded by onstage theatrical fanfares that seem to summon an entire *corps de ballet* in the manner of the first and last acts of Tchaikovsky's *Sleeping Beauty*. A grand procession ensues with a march that is brilliantly derived from the Dies irae theme and rep-resents the most theatrically "public" music of the symphony, anticipated at the climax of the first movement's development. As if maintaining the allusion to a balletic ball scene, it soon gives way to a wildly energetic dance that seems designed for male performers, a kind of *trepak* even. It is shadowed by warning interruptions from hand-stopped horns; their three-note falling and returning figure, already heard in the previous two movements, had terminated the opening march, which it recalls, as if from a distance, with now familiar darkening intent. A clear and fore-grounded statement of the four-note Dies irae figure (trombones and tuba) marks a climax and expressive release into what Martyn describes as the "first 'big tune'" in Rachmaninoff's output.[25] The upper strings, in Tchaikovskian triple octaves, swing into a *"con anima"* theme that dips and swoops with urgent emotional energy.

But is it quite the "big tune" that Martyn suggests? It undoubtedly wants to be, yet with its over-exuberant octave leaps it seems set to fly apart and disintegrate. Clearly incorporated elements of the first movement's second subject complex—not least its focal "aspiring sigh" gesture—with some of the second movement's dance figures and their synthesis in the Larghetto, clarify the material's relationship to the implicitly "feminine" expressive subject of the entire symphony. It disintegrates into violently frenetic sequences that are abruptly cut off by an *sfff* chord that leave shocked cellos and basses to introduce a quite new metrical pulse that takes us across a key-signature change (from two to four sharps) and a shift from $\frac{4}{4}$ to $\frac{3}{4}$ in an extended allusion to the second movement's dance. The chromatic oboe line, which incorporates the "aspiring sigh," constantly crosses the bar line in swaying syncopation. It ultimately achieves only a return to the original key signature of two sharps (the relative major of the symphony's key of D minor). Before long the energetic *trepak*-like dance resumes, as in a kind of recapitulation in which the contrasting lyrical theme makes a last, desperate reappearance. Just after rehearsal number 57, its climactic rising and falling arc—the "aspiring sigh" initially encountered in the first movement's second subject—leads to a now irrevocable sequential collapse into extended insistence on the angry dotted-rhythm figure, with its wild initiating flourishes, that had opened the movement and now lead to a final catastrophic hiatus, seven bars after rehearsal number 60. Another fortissimo *sf* chord (a B–D–F–G♭ diminished seventh) brings about a silence that is broken by one of the most chilling of tam-tam strokes.

Shortly, in the *Largo* coda, the strings (now only in double octaves) offer a lamenting version of the presiding Dies irae figure. A full orchestral climax, *ffff*, is reached before a slow chromatic descent in the heavy brass toward a ninefold reiteration of the fatal descending and rising third from the Scherzo. Now minor, it eventually stretches to a fourth in the final dominant-tonic insistence, repeatedly attached to the somber "turn" that had opened the symphony—which closes in a merciless D major. It would not, I think, be over-imaginative to glimpse a little peasant muttering as he works near the tracks on which roll the great iron wheels of a slowly passing steam train—wheels between which Anna Karenina has deliberately positioned herself before the candle illuminating the book of her life will flicker, grow dim, and then go out forever.[26]

II.

In all corners of the hall could be heard nothing but criticism, indignation, bewilderment, even rude language. Some

shrugged their shoulders in astonishment at how so decadent
a composition could have penetrated the polite programmes
of the Belyayev concerts.

—Aleksandr Ossovsky
after the premiere of the First Symphony[27]

I had a very high opinion of my work.... I was convinced that I
had discovered and opened up entirely new paths in music.
—Rachmaninoff as reported by Riesemann[28]

It is one of the tragedies of music history that Rachmaninoff was subsequently led by its critics to lose faith in his First Symphony and in himself:
"There are serious illnesses and deadly blows from Fate which entirely
damage a man's character. This was the effect of my own symphony
on myself."[29] I venture to suggest that he had indeed opened up new
paths in the First Symphony, not least in the remarkably coherent presentation of all of its foregrounded "expressive" material as tracing the
dramatic development of a single character or persona. It did this in a
manner far more subtle that any recurring "idée fixe" or "Leitmotiv" in
the mid-nineteenth-century European manner. This symphony repurposed the form's conventional four-movement structure to unusually
complex ends, representing a high point of the notionally elite Russian
symphony—literate, even explicitly "literary," dramatic, and allusive
of theatrical models like Tchaikovsky's ballets as much as that composer's symphonies. But we recall Tchaikovsky complaining that the latter
addressed only a privileged, and implicitly conservative, perhaps imaginatively limited, audience in the Moscow of his day. Rachmaninoff was
almost certainly expecting too much of the rather different, but no more
sympathetically inclined St. Petersburg audience at the premiere. The key
elements in Ossovsky's recollection of the premiere of Rachmaninoff's
First are found in his allusions to the normally "polite programmes" of
the Belyayev concerts that its audience considered violated, not so much
by the ineptness of the new work as by its "decadence." Here they may
well have spotted something of significance beyond the richness and
luxuriance of the work's textures, or the chromaticism of its harmonies,
colored by use of the so-called "gypsy" scale. The directness of its dramatic character might well have defined the "impolite" way in which it
seemed to address its audience. The story of Rachmaninoff's shattered
self-confidence after that 1897 premiere and how the damage was com-
pounded by a visit, made with his friend Fyodor Chaliapin, to the home
of the author of *Anna Karenina* in 1900 has often been told. Tolstoy had

in fact disapproved of Rachmaninoff's song "Fate," Op. 21, No. 1 (alluding to Beethoven's Fifth Symphony) and held forth on the pointlessness of Beethoven, Pushkin, and Lermontov: "It was awful. . . . I never went back. . . . And just think, the first time I went to him I went as to a God."[30] There followed the therapeutic sessions with Charcot pupil Dr. Nikolai Dahl, which finally seemed to have had a beneficial effect that in some way facilitated the composition of the Second Piano Concerto. Dedicated in French "To Dr. N. Dahl," it was the first of his works (after the famous Prelude in C-sharp Minor, that is) successfully to address "the masses," as Tchaikovsky might have put it. The concerto seems to have been successful from its very first performance. Its clear structure utilized undeniably "big tunes," whose deployment facilitated emotionally heightened moments of arrival and return, of storm and stress rewarded by gratifyingly "public" and passionately triumphant resolution. Such a description is not intended to be dismissive. It is certainly not intended to prepare the way for a negative evaluation of Rachmaninoff's subsequent works, like that distilled by Adorno in his later references to Eastern European music of merely "nationalistic" intent:

> The national moment is represented by themes that either were or seemed to have been borrowed from folk music. . . . The sole remaining organizing factor is the schema, not work from within. The structures approximate the medley form. Song hits have become the heirs of nationally tinged thematics: the legitimate successor of Rachmaninoff was Gershwin.[31]

There was Rachmaninoff, pinned scornfully between the mass-entertainment industry and sham symphonics that mirrored the way in which "mankind breaks up into a potentially hostile multiplicity of nations and so do the symphonic movements split into single themes and the connection slapped on them."[32] It is here that we encounter the later misunderstanding of Rachmaninoff that contrived to match, in its quite different way, the scorn of Cui and other St. Petersburg critics of the First Symphony.

Modernisms

If Adorno's dismissal of Tchaikovsky and Rachmaninoff (he included Dvořák too) was a function of European modernist aesthetics, mediated by Marxian criticism, we would do well to remember that before the First World War there were various and often conflicting ways of being "modern." In Mahler's Vienna, still officially dominated by Romantic (read: Beethovenian-Brahmsian) classicism, other modernisms flourished, sometimes welcoming as much as shocking the bourgeois audience for symphony concerts (as much as for opera), on whose continuing expansion Mahler had commented in 1893.

Modernism in turn-of-the-century Vienna was perhaps most tangibly encountered in the architecture, decorative work, and paintings of the Secession associated with Gustav Klimt, Joseph Hoffmann, and others, whose work was positioned as "seceding" from the officially established manners (framed as conservative and hidebound) of the Akademie der bildender Künste and the Künstlerhausgenossenschaft.[33] Classical historical studio painting still held sway there. It is often forgotten that a precise musical equivalent to the painters' and sculptors' Secession was briefly constituted, under Mahler's invited presidency, in the earnestly named Vereinigung schaffender Tonkünstler in Wien (Association of Creative Composers in Vienna).[34] The title was precisely modeled on the official name of the graphic artists' Secession: Vereinigung bildender Künstler Österreichs (Association of Austrian Graphic Artists), while implying a more welcoming approach to those not specifically "Austrian." The manifesto-like pamphlet of May 1904 announcing the new association is thought to have been written by the young Arnold Schoenberg. As the artists sought emancipation from academic tradition and the dealers who sold it (and them), "so too, do composers need to close their ranks and act together." The new association sought to circumvent the journalistic power of conservative critics and form "a direct relation between itself and the public," as well as "to give modern music a permanent home in Vienna . . . and to keep the public constantly informed about the current state of musical composition."[35] The venture foundered after a single season for lack of financial backing, but the single full-scale orchestral concert it sponsored in November 1904 had Mahler directing Strauss's *Symphonia Domestica* in a program that had started with Zemlinsky conducting Siegmund von Hausegger's symphonic poem *Dionysische Fantasie*. This was not the "modern" music that would dominate Schoenberg's post–First World War Society for the Private Performance of New Music, shunning both critics *and* applause and implicitly hostile to the popular audience. It was, however, just the kind of music that Rachmaninoff was writing and would continue to refine in Germany in 1906 when he made his first temporary escape from Russia, taking his wife and young daughter, in the wake of the "failed" 1905 Revolution.

Rachmaninoff in Dresden and Leipzig

The works Rachmaninoff would write during his European sojourn between 1906 and 1909 were as modern as the symphonies of Mahler and the tone poems of Richard Strauss: complex, serious, and yet audience-friendly in their mode of address. Such works should have been set to join the late symphonies of Tchaikovsky as they began to reach the masses that their composer felt he had failed to communicate with in Moscow or even St. Petersburg. But Rachmaninoff's self-critical nervousness was reawakened by European music in the current modern manner that he encountered in Dresden, where he was living, and in Leipzig (its Gewandhaus concerts a relatively easy train journey away). It was in Dresden that he saw Strauss's *Salome* in 1906:

> There were many things in the music itself I liked, whenever it didn't sound too discordant. Yet Strauss is a very talented man. And his instrumentation is amazing. As I sat there in the theatre . . . I suddenly imagined, if an opera of mine should be played here, how ashamed I should feel. A feeling exactly as if I had appeared undressed before the audience. That Strauss certainly knows how to dress up.[36]

The letter from which this is taken eloquently testifies to his sense of the dominant international power of the German tradition at that time, and to Strauss's position within it. Rachmaninoff, who in the very next year would defiantly describe chromaticism as "the source of all the wretched modernism," clearly felt the backward provincial in the presence of such things in 1906.[37] His developing attitude toward "wretched modernism" proves on closer inspection to have been contextually complex, and the *Salome* letter reveals the extent to which Rachmaninoff was able to recognize Strauss's music for what it was and identify with its aims. As individuals, both composers merit the term "conservative" in the broad sense of social manners and political attitudes, but given differences in the nature of their musical backgrounds, each was arguably as thoroughly modern as could be in his art during the first decade and a half of the twentieth century. Indeed, as recently as 1904, in a private tirade about the "absurd cacophony" of decadent modernism in the Straussian manner, Cui had confessed a suspicion (from his St. Petersburg viewpoint) that "Moscow harbours more of these Skryabins and Rachmaninoffs, just as they have more houses in *le style nouveau*."[38]

To consider in what manner modernist sympathies continued to manifest themselves in Rachmaninoff's music, modified perhaps by his experience of Strauss and others of his European contemporaries, we need to turn to the remarkable series of works written during his Dresden period. In those four years he produced the Second Symphony, his first Piano Sonata (based on

Faust), part of an opera on Maurice Maeterlinck's *Monna Vanna*, the Third Piano Concerto, and a fine and surely very well "dressed-up" symphonic poem *The Isle of the Dead* (1909).[39] Piano concertos, of course, were by their very nature and history theatrically performative and popu-lar. The Second Symphony arguably achieves in its own way a brilliant balance between late-Romantic popularism, with its Finale's idiosyncratic "big tune" and "happy ending," and a post-Tchaikovskian seriousness of expressive symphonic purpose. As a successor to the First Symphony, it displays a similar richness and clarity while engaging unapologetically with the still growing audience for such symphonic entertainments, and on a high level of complexity in its expressive eloquence and integrated dramatic structure.[40]

More succinctly considered in the present context is the symphonic poem, not least because it affords the opportunity to make a direct comparison with a nearly contemporary German musical treatment of the same subject, a symbolist painting by Arnold Böcklin. Rachmaninoff saw a monochrome illustration of it before encountering the genuine article (or one of its versions) in the Leipzig Museum der bildenden Künste. In the painting an open boat carries an oarsman and a white-shrouded attendant standing before a draped coffin; they are arriving at a craggy island whose cliff-like rock faces are studded with tomb entrances, sheltered by tall cypresses against a lowering sky; on one of the entrances the artist's name is visible.

Max Reger, born near Bayreuth in the same year as Rachmaninoff, was a composer, pianist, and organist, whose works with their complex contrapuntal textures and chromatic harmony were interpreted as signaling the Bachian intentions of a German known to have "resolutely flown the banner of absolute music."[41] Like Rachmaninoff, he scorned the "wretched modernism" soon to be associated with Schoenberg and his pupils. Reger would become a neighbor of the Russian in Leipzig in 1907 (they seem never to have met); he also found himself confronting a reversed form of the same audience problem sensed by Rachmaninoff (and Tchaikovsky before him) when called to take up the position of Hofkapellmeister in Meiningen in 1911. Now in charge of a high-quality orchestra with a regular audience, Reger pragmatically chose to shelve absolutism in favor of works that sought more directly to communicate with the middle-class "masses" attending orchestral concerts. An early product of this policy was the suite of *Four Tone-Poems After Böcklin*. The first three are based on specific paintings, the third being *The Isle of the Dead* (*Die Toteninsel*), referring to the same version of the painting that Rachmaninoff saw in Leipzig. In a letter to his new employer, Duke Georg II, about the tone poems' first performance in Essen in 1913, Reger was happy to report on the suite's success, while expressing surprise that the two more obviously (as he thought) audience-pleasing "scherzo" movements (particularly the final *Bacchanale*) received less applause than the two "eerie" (*schauerlich*) movements, *Der geigende Eremit* (The Hermit Fiddler) and *Die Toteninsel*. The latter he characterized as "bleak, utterly inconsolable despair" alternating with "tempestuous outbursts of pain before the great final transfiguration."[42] Present in the audience was Strauss, the unofficial leader of the New German School. Strauss is reported to have joked to Reger, after the performance, "Noch einen Schritt und Sie sind bei uns" (Another step in this direction and you'll be one of us).[43]

A comparison between Reger's *Isle of the Dead* and Rachmaninoff's earlier work with the same title will serve not to facilitate value judgment on their respective merits (both are very fine in their different ways) so much as to demonstrate how complex and rich the possibilities and technologies of musical representation were at this time, once the carping of conservative critics and their various, tendentiously mocking caricatures of "program music" have been set aside. Reger's letter to Duke Georg appropriately characterized his "eerie" essay in expressive subjectivity— implicitly that of a *viewer* of Böcklin's painting, contemplated in a kind of orchestrally voiced soliloquy, comprising a series of short poetic strophes or stanzas. It opens like the preludial underscore to one of Wotan's monologues in the *Ring* cycle. Failing to sustain the reverential calm to which it aspires, a series of agonized outbursts give way to the poem's "final transfiguration," whose tragically accepting benediction in D-flat major might well remind us more of late Mahler than Reger would have wished.

By contrast, Rachmaninoff's longer work is elaborately "immersive" in effect. Its underlying $\frac{5}{8}$ rhythmic ostinato evokes the sight and sensation of being slowly rowed across the dark waters from a point in the coffin's journey set well *before* the moment recorded in Böcklin's painting. Rachmaninoff evokes *movement through* a musical structure that again references the "fatal" ABA form of Tchaikovsky's *Francesca da Rimini*, but delays the expected lyrical subjectivity of a B section until the work is almost over, our expectation of consolation apparently frustrated. At the last possible moment—perhaps when the vessel has moored and the coffin is being carried toward its resting place—a Tchaikovskian grand melody detaches itself from sepulchral iterations of the funereal Dies irae figure on whose gloomy surface we have floated thus far. The ostensibly final achievement of E major (as dominant to the closing tonic of A minor?) suddenly drops into E-flat major, and an aspiring, salvation-seeking theme begins to wind its way heavenward (Rachmaninoff described it as representing "life").[44] However, it repeatedly degenerates into sequentially writhing chains of aspiring and falling chromatic figures. In the climax at rehearsal number 16, the heroic-funereal manner gives way to music that seems to allude to the redeeming conclusion of *Götterdämmerung*, until its silvery ascent meets a low ceiling of sulfurous cloud, from which it recoils. Its fate is apocalyptically sealed by rehearsal number 22. A melodramatic series of shattering death-blows shortly weaponizes the Dies irae figure. The "expressive" subject is again consigned to the waters of oblivion as the oarsman continues on his journey, the coffin safely delivered. With him, we and the music disappear into a final darkness.

III.

> Claude Debussy may frighten the bourgeois, sitting in his tower of ivory, but somewhere, sometime, there is a public to be astonished. With superb, unassumed superiority, Rachmaninoff, self-absorbed, contemplates a great picture, then takes an immense modern orchestra, improvises upon it, talks to himself, quite regardless. It is by fortune, not design, and the grace of an enormous technique as well as an imagination that turns notes to gold, that this music has many qualities which appeal to audiences at large.[45]

Olin Downes excelled himself in his review of Rachmaninoff's December 1909 concert in Boston's Symphony Hall, in which he had conducted *The Isle of the Dead* and played his Second Piano Concerto. The critic mediates the iconic image of an autonomous and self-absorbed "great composer" for a potential mass audience of musical consumers who might well, on Downes's reading, have been flattered by Rachmaninoff's performance of *The Isle of the Dead*. Aligning himself with that audience, Downes seems to have been moved by the Russian composer speaking so directly, but not "down to," an American audience prepared to self-identify more as a "general public" than a privileged bourgeois one. These were no mockable "middlebrows"; Downes seems struck by genuine artistic communication having been achieved, to the credit of both the communicator and his audience.

By the time he finally bade farewell to his homeland and his beloved Ivanovka estate in 1917, Rachmaninoff had apparently discovered how to be serious, having "something to say" while addressing a popular audience without condescension and in a language it, and he, understood. Since his return to Russia he had produced, among other things, another big "public" symphonic work, *The Bells*, described as a "Poem for Soprano, Tenor, and Baritone Soli, Chorus and Orchestra," unambiguously programmatic in its setting of all four sections of Konstantin Balmont's Russian translation of Edgar Allan Poe's poem of the same name (the four movements change from sleigh bells to wedding bells to alarm bells and, finally, the tolling bells of death and mourning). Rachmaninoff's recent work as a conductor left time for no other large-scale orchestral projects, apart from the revised First Piano Concerto, before his final departure from Russia to give a series of invited concerts in neutral Scandinavia in December 1917, at the height of the First World War and in the wake of the October Revolution.

By November 1918 he had his family settled in New York, after which his career of necessity became that of a celebrity pianist. The three big orchestral works of the later American years (with the Fourth Piano Concerto) all represented significant achievements, revealing elements of both retrospection and renewal. The 1934 *Rhapsody on a Theme of Paganini*, for piano and orchestra, successfully married his most outgoing manner as a composer with a tribute to the virtuoso tradition of the nineteenth century, of which he was himself a late product. The brilliantly dark and edgy *Symphonic Dances* of 1940 effectively closed his career as a composer with a highly original three-movement essay in dance-rooted symphonic style of the kind he had first explored long ago in the ill-fated First Symphony. No less interesting and significant (and initially misunderstood) was the other late three-movement work: the Third Symphony of 1936.

Stravinsky sought waspishly to sum up Rachmaninoff as immortalized by his dour manner—"He was a six-and-a-half-foot-tall scowl"—yet the Third Symphony proved no less rich in variety of mood and color than its predecessors.[46] While hardly neoclassical in any useful sense, the Third Symphony utilizes its form-driven balancing of contrasting moods and manners in an often more playful way than had earlier been the case. Even less than in the Second Symphony is the repeated exposition of the first movement apologetic about rerunning its rhetorical trajectory, from the controlled melancholy of the first subject through its attempts to skip and jump before giving way to one of Rachmaninoff's last "big tunes." This second-subject theme is first sung by the cellos, *dolce cantabile* at rehearsal number 5. The falling sighs of the first subject are replaced by brighter, upward-arcing phrases that owe a certain "American" quality not just to their apparent allusion to *Shenandoah*, but also to the way in which the theme is "dressed up," as he might once have put it. First, as so often before, Rachmaninoff prepares for the arrival of such a theme by clearing the stage and pushing back the chairs from three bars before rehearsal number 4. Most striking perhaps is its fullest, second presentation, which sets in motion an ever more determined aspirational flight. This is eventually celebrated by an energized brass choir of trumpets and trombones that seem to have defected from a Paul Whiteman-style big band: its joyous final contribution to the festivity almost demands that the players stand up to reinforce the performative energy of their contribution—the subsequent fall-away, too, is appropriately pure Hollywood.

It is small wonder that Rachmaninoff was proud of this work, which he famously and most revealingly recorded, along with *The Isle of the Dead*. Stravinsky may have implied another witticism when he commented on the curious fact that he had never met Rachmaninoff in Russia, first encountering him only in Hollywood.[47] Another Stravinsky joke had it that, at the age of twenty-five, Rachmaninoff "became a very old composer indeed." Listening to the latter's fleet-footed and passionate recording of his Third Symphony, however, one is impressed by the extent to which he was saying new things in the "old" tonal language that might still engage Olin Downes's "audiences at large"—those masses, perhaps, that had earlier eluded Rachmaninoff and Tchaikovsky. The influence of both composers on mass entertainment movies of the 1930s and '40s, in Hollywood and beyond, is found not just in stylistic echoes in the scores of a new generation of film composers, but also in direct quotation of their works, whether in actual concert sequences or in the underscore: one thinks of Tchaikovsky's Sixth Symphony in *Now, Voyager* in 1942, or the Rachmaninoff Second Piano Concerto in *Brief Encounter* in 1945, or even—in parodic form—*The Seven-Year Itch* in 1955. What Rachmaninoff still had to say to that audience is part of the unwritten history of twentieth-century music, as we liberate ourselves from the endlessly rehearsed narrative of the once fashionable modernism that Rachmaninoff perhaps needlessly confessed to being unable to grasp in the interview in which he had implicitly claimed to deal in "soul states," feeling "like a ghost wandering in a world grown alien":

> I have made intense effort to feel the musical manner of today, but it will not come to me . . . The new kind of music seems to come not from the heart but from the head. Its composers think rather than feel. They have not the capacity to make their works "exult," as Hans von Bülow called it. . . . It may be, too, that the spirit of the times does not call for expression in music.[48]

Surely Rachmaninoff demonstrably *thought* while exulting and lamenting—constantly experimenting with ways of nuancing and moving between those modes of expression. As we more closely read his works, we might find very much more to feel and think about than cultural politics or stylistic fashion once permitted us to admit.[49]

The epigraph is a quote from Olin Downes, as reported in Sergei Bertensson and Jay Leyda, *Sergei Rachmaninoff: A Lifetime in Music* (Bloomington and Indianapolis: Indiana University Press, 2001), 220.

1. The debate arose out of an interview Scorsese had given to *Empire* magazine; it was summarized, with quotations, in the *New York Times*, 4 November 2019.

2. Bertensson and Leyda, *Sergei Rachmaninoff*, 351–52.

3. Ibid.

4. All quotations are taken from the translation by Rosamund Bartlett in Anton Chekhov, *About Love and Other Stories* (Oxford: Oxford University Press, 2004), 8–23.

5. Ibid., 23. In the Lermontov epigraph quoted, I have replaced "boulder" with "crag" to clarify the source of Rachmaninoff's title.

6. Barrie Martyn, *Rachmaninoff: Composer, Pianist, Conductor* (Aldershot, UK: Scolar Press, 1990), 79.

7. Philip Ross Bullock, *Pyotr Tchaikovsky* (London: Reaktion, 2016), 120.

8. Ibid., 143.

9. Ibid., 120.

10. Knud Martner, ed., *Selected Letters of Gustav Mahler* (London: Faber & Faber, 1979), 148. Mahler performed a number of Tchaikovsky's works as well as the operas *Evgeny Onegin*, *The Queen of Spades*, and *Iolanta*; he conducted the Second, Fifth, and Sixth symphonies and the First Suite, Op. 43.

11. Bullock, *Pyotr Tchaikovsky*, 94. On Mahler, see Peter Franklin: *Mahler Symphony No. 3* (Cambridge: Cambridge University Press, 1991), 32.

12. Bullock, *Pyotr Tchaikovsky*, 94.

13. Rachmaninoff had plans for ballet projects of his own, albeit never realized.

14. Wilfrid Mellers, "Romanticism and the 20th Century," part 4 of Alec Harman and Wilfrid Mellers, *Man and His Music: The Story of Musical Experience in the West* (London: Barrie & Rockliff, 1962, 2nd ed., 1964), 869.

15. Leonid Sabaneyeff, *Modern Russian Composers* (London: Martin Lawrence, c. 1927), 104.

16. Ibid., 104–5.

17. Ibid., 106.

18. Ibid., 107.

19. The most quoted passage of Cui's review runs: "If there were a conservatoire in Hell, if one of its talented students were instructed to write a programme symphony on 'The Seven Plagues of Egypt,' and if he were to compose a symphony like Mr. Rachmaninoff's, then he would have fulfilled his task brilliantly and delighted the inmates of Hell." Cited in Martyn, *Rachmaninoff*, 97.

20. Translations from the Russian differ slightly, and some sources suggest that Rachmaninoff continued the biblical quotation from Romans XII ". . . saith the Lord."

21. A possibly unreliable source for this claim is *Rachmaninoff's Recollections Told to Oskar von Riesemann*, trans. Dolly Rutherford (London: George Allen & Unwin, 1934), 98.

22. The "gypsy scale" is essentially a minor scale with sharpened fourth and flattened sixth. See Example 2.

23. L. N. Tolstoy, *Anna Karenin*, trans. Rosemary Edmonds (London: Penguin, 1954), 92.

24. "Freund Hein" was a folkloristic German representation of Death the Fiddler. The suppressed title of the second movement of Mahler's Fourth Symphony began "Freund Hein spielt zum Tanz auf. . . ." See Bruno Walter, *Briefe 1894–1962* (Frankfurt-am-Main: S. Fischer, 1969), 52. For a facsimile of the inscribed title page of Mahler's draft of the

Tenth Symphony, fourth movement, see Peter Franklin, *The Life of Mahler* (Cambridge: Cambridge University Press, 1997), 196, Fig. 19a.

25. Martyn, *Rachmaninoff*, 102.

26. The words of the last two lines here closely follow those of the final sentence of Tolstoy's *Anna Karenin*, Part 7, chap. 30, 802.

27. Martyn, *Rachmaninoff*, 97.

28. Riesemann, *Rachmaninoff's Recollections*, 98.

29. Ibid.

30. Bertensson and Leyda, *Sergei Rachmaninoff*, 89.

31. Theodor Adorno, *Introduction to the Sociology of Music*, trans. E. B. Ashton (New York: Seabury Press, 1976), 166–67.

32. Ibid.

33. See Peter Vergo, *Art in Vienna 1898–1918: Klimt, Kokoschka, Schiele and Their Contemporaries* (Oxford: Phaidon, 1975), 18–26. The two terms might be translated as "Academy of Fine Arts" and "Exhibiting Artists' Association."

34. More information can be found in Franklin, *The Life of Mahler*, 150–54.

35. The source is Willi Reich, *Schoenberg, A Critical Biography*, trans. Leo Black (London: Longman, 1971), 19.

36. Bertensson and Leyda, *Sergei Rachmaninoff*, 130.

37. Ibid., 139.

38. Ibid., n72.

39. The composition of the lengthy piano sonata occasioned a revealing admission that he was "lured into such length by the programme. . . . Of course there will be no programme given, although it does occur to me that if I revealed the programme, the sonata would be clearer." See Martyn, *Rachmaninoff*, 188.

40. I have written at greater length about the Second Symphony in Peter Franklin, *Reclaiming Late-Romantic Music: Singing Devils and Distant Sounds* (Berkeley: University of California Press, 2014), 35–43.

41. Suzanne Popp, Introduction to the revised score of Max Reger, *Vier Tondichtungen nach Arnold Böcklin* (London: Edition Eulenburg, 1990), Eulenburg No.8020, vii.

42. Ibid., ix.

43. Ibid., vi.

44. See Martyn, *Rachmaninoff*, 205.

45. Olin Downes, *Olin Downes on Music: A Selection of His Writings During the Half-Century, 1906–1955*, ed. Irene Downes (New York: Simon & Schuster, 1957), 21.

46. Stravinsky's quote can be found in *Stravinsky in Conversation with Robert Craft* (London: Penguin Books, 1962; US ed. 1958), 55.

47. Ibid.

48. Cited in Bertensson and Leyda, *Sergei Rachmaninoff*, 351–52.

49. John Culshaw recalled in 1973: "It proved highly undesirable even to mention the name of Rachmaninov in London musical circles in 1946, let alone admit that one was trying to write a book about him. Then as now . . . certain works would fill a concert hall." See Culshaw, "Rachmaninov Revisited," *Soundings* 3 (1973): 2–6, at 2.

Sergei Rachmaninoff and
Moscow Musical Life

REBECCA MITCHELL

In 1912, the idealistic young writer Marietta Shaginyan (1888–1982) dashed off a fiery philosophical defense of Sergei Rachmaninoff's music. Refuting attacks on the composer's allegedly traditional musical language, she argued that Rachmaninoff's compositions expressed not merely music's struggle "to preserve itself as an art," but a fundamental battle of the "human self" to preserve its true nature against the dangers of modern life.[1] Perhaps bemused by her youthful passion when she later penned her 1955 reminiscences, Shaginyan felt it necessary to stress "the unique situation" in which her friendship with Rachmaninoff had flourished. "In the environment in which I grew up and interacted from childhood, music was not considered just an isolated 'art form,'" she reflected, but "an inalienable composite part of all culture."[2] A mandatory subject in school, music had been a vital pastime for those who considered themselves part of educated society, and an obsession among artistically inclined students and cultural elites. Far from a mere hobby, music was "discussed philosophically not in its separate manifestations (one or another composer, one or another composition), but in its essence, in connection with its epoch, with [one's] worldview [*mirosozertsaniye*], with fundamental questions of life and death."[3]

Rachmaninoff's place within the development of twentieth-century music is still surprisingly contentious. Both during his lifetime and after, Rachmaninoff's popular success with audiences contrasted with an oft-dismissive attitude toward his compositional accomplishments by music critics and theorists. At the same time, calls for a reevaluation of Rachmaninoff's compositional legacy have long been a recurring feature of scholarly discussion of the composer.[4] However, as musicologist Richard Taruskin has noted, reevaluations have often subscribed to the very same "modernist argument that traditional styles had been exhausted."[5] Employing examples of Rachmaninoff's harmonic, melodic, or formal innovation to disprove claims of his irrelevance ultimately adopts the basic modernist assumption that stylistic innovation is inherently good. In this essay I propose a different approach: rather than taking a stance in the debate over how "modern" Rachmaninoff's compositional style was, I instead place Rachmaninoff into the inherently modern context in which most of his compositions were written, the context described by Shaginyan in her reminiscences. Regardless of whether one concludes Rachmaninoff's music should be understood within a compositional style definable as "modern," it is an indisputable reality that he and his music were shaped by the strains and the opportunities of a rapidly changing social, political, and cultural world. In this broader sense, Rachmaninoff's music is unequivocally a product of *modernity*.

Though modernism has typically referred to a particular artistic style and attitude about art (the specific characteristics of which have been the subject of heated debate among both artists and critics), "modernity" as a concept has a broader meaning. In his classic work of cultural history, Marshall Berman defined "modernity" as a "way of being" in the world, arguing that "to be modern is to find ourselves in an environment that promises us adventure, power, joy, growth, transformation of ourselves and the world—and, at the same time, threatens to destroy everything we have, everything we know, everything we are. . . . To be modern is to be part of a universe in which, as Marx said, 'All that is solid melts into air.'"[6] Whether framed as a shift in mentality traced to the French Revolution, or the cultural transformation wrought by the Industrial Revolution and related urbanization in the nineteenth century, "modernity" thus emphasizes the lived experience of uncertainty and the loss of a sense of solid mooring in a system of governing moral codes. In recent years, cultural historians of Russia have drawn renewed attention to the contingency, flux, and transformation that was an inherent aspect of urban life in late Imperial Russia. Attention has been given to the impacts of rapid urbanization and industrialization, the breakdown of traditional social structures and rise of professional rather than estate (*sosloviye*)-based identities, renewed interest in political reform, and accompanying experimentation in the realms of art, literature, theater, and music as aspects of Russia's confrontation with modernity.[7] Building on this literature, this essay discusses the ways in which the complex and multifaceted nature of the experience of modernity in late Imperial Moscow affected Rachmaninoff and his creative milieu.

The philosophical significance that Shaginyan granted to the composer might well give a contemporary reader familiar with Rachmaninoff's biography pause. In contrast to fellow Muscovite Aleksandr Scriabin, scholars seldom frame Rachmaninoff's significance in explicitly meta-physical terms. Nevertheless, Rachmaninoff's early career was shaped by a subculture in which music was conceived as a powerful artistic form with the ability to transform human experience. Musicians, art-ists, poets, and philosophers gathered alongside wealthy entrepreneurs, white-collar professionals (professors, doctors, lawyers, teachers, state bureaucrats), students, and nobles in an intimate world of private socie-ties and circles (*kruzhki*) where music was performed, discussed, and debated alongside other pressing political, social, and philosophical ques-tions. Rachmaninoff's creative career thus took root in an aesthetic world where musical style and interpretation were often believed to portend the future of Russia itself. Positioned within a changing urban space and appealing to a growing public seeking to make sense of the dramatic changes they were experiencing, Rachmaninoff's music resonated with the complex, modernizing society from which it sprang.

The musical world of Rachmaninoff's youth retained echoes of the once intense divide between the nationalist style of the *moguchaya kuchka* (Balakirev, Borodin, Cui, Musorgsky, and Rimsky-Korsakov) and the con-servatory tradition (the Rubinstein brothers, Tchaikovsky). Nonetheless, the emergence of both a wealthy entrepreneurial elite independent of state and nobility and a growing educated society (*obshchestvennost'*) made Moscow a natural hothouse for exploring new images of Russianness. This search found expression in architectural projects that transformed Moscow's urban landscape and in the formation of private performance groups, whose programming differed from that of the Russian Music Society (RMO, founded 1859), a voluntary organization that enjoyed Imperial patronage and was generally associated with the state. Rachmaninoff's direct interactions with two such institutions—the Moscow Private Opera (MPO) and the Circle for Lovers of Russian Music (*Kruzhok lyubiteley russ-koy muziki*)—shaped his early creative profile and broadly framed musical Russianness in practice.

The discussion here then turns to Moscow's changing social milieu. Seeking to emphasize the importance of their profession to society, Russian musicians joined other cultural elites in proclaiming music's social mission to provide moral and spiritual uplift to a population con-fronting the ills of urban modernity, while also assailing the deleterious effects of popular music. Particularly after the Revolution of 1905, which shook the foundations of autocracy, music was seen as a potential means of healing social divisions wrought by the modern age. The final section of this essay assesses how Rachmaninoff and his music were positioned within these broader social and philosophical trends after 1905. Regular comparisons drawn between Rachmaninoff and his contemporary Scriabin were framed around questions of "tradition," "modernity," and "humanity," echoing widespread concerns about the impact of modernity on Russian society. While anxiety within educated society found expression in debates over the impact of Rachmaninoff's evocation of pessimistic emotions, a broader audience found a consoling echo of their own experiences in Rachmaninoff's music.

Moscow's Modernization and the Search for "Russian" Music

I think that Moscow harbors more of these Scriabins and Rachmaninoffs, just as they have more houses there in *le style nouveau*.

—César Cui to Mariya Kerzina

Moscow, where Rachmaninoff arrived in 1885 to begin his studies under the tutelage of famed piano pedagogue Nikolai Zverev, was a city in the midst of dramatic social and cultural changes.[8] Abandoned by Peter the Great for St. Petersburg, his newly-founded European-style capital in the swamps of the north, Moscow was later devastated during Napoleon's 1812 invasion. By the late nineteenth century, Moscow was home to a small entrepreneurial elite that emerged from a unique confluence of successful Old Believer peasants who had purchased their freedom from their former lords, a merchant class that had remained to rebuild the city after its wartime devastation, and a noble class that preferred a quiet provincial life over the prestige of state service in St. Petersburg. Their investment in such areas as vodka tax farming, textile manufacturing, banking, and railroad construction proved financially successful, particularly as Alexander II's Great Reforms restructured Russian society. Seeking a conceptual language through which to express their own image of Russian society, entrepreneurs supported a vision of Russia that combined strands of Pan-Slavism, Slavophilism, and religious sectarianism with a forward-looking assertiveness befitting their envisioned role as key figures in the emergence of a modern culture and society.[9] As European-style education added a cosmopolitan flair to the worldview of the younger generation of entrepreneurs, they turned their financial resources to supporting art, theater, and music, and encouraged the development of an explicitly Russian (yet socially modern) style in painting, architecture, and music.[10] Rejecting earlier notions of Russia as inherently backward and inferior to Europe, these wealthy entrepreneurs gathered with culturally-minded nobility, liberal intelligentsia, and

Figure 1. Modernist façade of the Ryabushinsky House, architect Fyodor Schechtel, constructed 1900–1902.

artistic elites in private societies and circles to debate music, philosophy, art, and the problems confronting a rapidly modernizing Russia. Moscow was thus positioned as a cultural center whose perceived "Russianness" might complement rather than contradict the emergence of a modern culture in direct connection with European artistic trends.[11]

A self-confident exposition of a modern Russian identity—informed by Europe but with a dominant place for Russian art broadly defined— took physical shape in museums, theaters, churches, schools, hospitals, concert stages, and grand private houses financed by this entrepreneurial elite. The Ryabushinsky House, built between 1900 and 1902 by architect Fyodor Schechtel for the wealthy young industrialist Stepan Ryabushinsky, showcased a meld of traditional Russian forms and modern architectural style (Figure 1). Perhaps the most visible example of this building boom driven by entrepreneurial investment was the 1889–93 construction of the Upper Trading Rows (*Verkhniye torgovïye ryadï*), which transformed Moscow's main trading site directly adjacent to the Kremlin from a "chaotic warren of shops" into a modern space with three parallel arcades whose size dwarfed any other complex in Russia (Figure 2).[12] Eclectic in architectural style and driven by private more than state interests, Moscow's

Figure 2. Moscow, Upper Trading Rows, designed by Vladimir Shukhov, constructed 1889–1893.

transformed city-scape also incorporated new performing spaces for classical music, which marshalled an alternate aesthetic ideology for audiences. Whereas the elegant neoclassical Pillar Hall within the Assembly of Nobility (*Kolonnïy zal*, home of RMO concerts since 1860, shown in Figure 8) continued to emphasize the noble and culturally European heritage of the city, an assertively Pan-Slavic musical vision was visually celebrated in the more intimate concert hall at the hotel-restaurant Slavic Bazaar (*Slavyanskiy Bazar*, 17 Nikolskaya Street), with 450 seats.[13] The artistic centerpiece of the hall was Ilya Repin's 1872 painting *Slavic Composers* (Figure 3), whose imagined unity of Russian, Czech, and Polish composers echoed the Pan-Slavic ideals of its commissioner, Moscow nobleman turned entrepreneur Aleksandr Porokhovshchikov.[14]

In contrast, the dramatically remodeled Moscow Conservatory provided city residents at the turn of the century with a glamorous new concert space that offered an alternate visual framing of Russian music's development (Figures 4, 5, 6, and 7).[15] Funded by state and private donations, the Large Hall of the conservatory celebrated Russian music as inherently European, offering a pictorial narrative of music history rooted in German Classicism and ending in Russian accomplishments (while omitting Italian and French influence). When the glittering new space opened in 1901, it hosted 2,500 seats, electric lights, a Cavaillé-Coll

Figure 3. Ilya Repin, *Slavic Composers* (1872), which was initially displayed in the Slavic Bazaar concert hall.

Figure 4. Old building of the Moscow Conservatory (1894).

Figure 5. Concert hall, old building of the Moscow Conservatory (1890s).

organ, and a visual narrative of Russia's musical development. Portraits of Tchaikovsky, Beethoven, Handel, Schubert, Schumann, Gluck, and Anton Rubinstein adorned the left of the hall, and Glinka, Bach, Mozart, Haydn, Mendelssohn, Wagner, and Borodin were displayed on the right. Pride of place was given to the Conservatory's founder Nikolai Rubinstein in a bas-relief above the stage.[16] This visual linking of German and Russian

Figure 6. Remodeled Moscow Conservatory (early 1900s).

Figure 7. Large Hall of the remodeled Moscow Conservatory, 1901.

musical accomplishments was echoed at the venue's opening by the conservatory's director Vasily Safonov. In his inaugural speech, Safonov declared, "We hope that our hall will serve the glory of our national [*rodnogo*] art, we wish that the great people whose pictures decorate this hall may serve as an example to many generations, inspiring young strength in the service of humanity, and—who knows? Perhaps our beloved homeland is fated to give the world a new Beethoven."[17] The evening's performance similarly expressed this ideal: works by Glinka, Tchaikovsky, Borodin, and Anton Rubinstein were followed by a performance of Beethoven's Ninth Symphony.[18] Russia was thus held up as the natural heir to a European (particularly German) classical music tradition, and Moscow was framed as the newest link in an unending chain of artistic development.

The aesthetics of Orthodox Church spirituality also attracted renewed interest from an entrepreneurial elite with links to Old Believer communities. In addition to supporting contemporary Russian and European painters, businessman Pavel Tretyakov collected medieval Russian icons for his personal use; these were ultimately gifted, along with his art collection, to the city of Moscow and placed on public display.[19] Railroad magnate Savva Mamontov (1841–1918) turned his private estate Abramtsevo into an artistic collective in the 1870s where artists including Konstantin Korovin and Mikhaíl Vrubel developed visual styles inspired by Russian medieval icons and popular prints and woodcuts.[20] Similarly, Moscow stood at the center of state attempts to develop a style of Russian Church music free from European influence. Due to the devoted work of chant scholar Stepan Smolensky (1848–1909), who directed the Moscow Synodal School for Church Singing from 1889 to 1901, the reinvigorated Synodal Choir drew attention from musicians and audiences alike and helped spark the development of a new compositional style that paralleled the neo-national architectural developments transforming Moscow's urban landscape.[21]

As a music student in Moscow, Rachmaninoff benefited from performances of the Synodal Choir, as well as operas at the Bolshoi Theater (where an 1893 performance of his first opera, *Aleko*, launched his professional career), and concerts organized by the RMO and the Moscow Philharmonic Society.[22] Although the newly founded *Russian Musical Gazette* still ranked Moscow's concert life as "provincial" in comparison with St. Petersburg, concert opportunities proliferated over the course of the 1890s as music education expanded. By 1899, Ivan Lipayev, the Moscow correspondent for the *Gazette*, proudly noted that the total number of RMO concerts in Moscow had surpassed those in Petersburg.[23] Of these new organizations, two had particular influence on Rachmaninoff's emerging career, embodying the varied faces of this new society and strengthening a distinctive image of Russian music: the Moscow Private Opera (MPO) and the Circle of Lovers of Russian Music.

Founded in 1885 by Mamontov, the MPO was successfully carving out a niche for itself as the leading presenter of Russian operas when Rachmaninoff joined the company as assistant conductor in 1897.[24] Rachmaninoff only remained in this post for a single year (1897–98), but this experience, which came shortly after the disastrous March 1897 premiere of his First Symphony, had long-lasting implications for his professional and creative development. In addition to providing the composer with his first extensive conducting experience, it was here that Rachmaninoff met singer Fyodor Chaliapin, who would become his lifelong friend, and oversaw Chaliapin's preparation of the role of Boris Godunov for a new production of Musorgsky's opera. The MPO exposed the composer to some of the most innovative artistic trends of the day, including modernist set designs by Vrubel and Korovin that drew inspiration from the two-dimensionality of Russian icon-painting.[25] Rachmaninoff fondly remembered Korovin's "wonderful" melding of tradition and modernity in the stage and costume design of what was arguably the MPO's greatest coup: the premiere of Rimsky-Korsakov's opera *Sadko*. Rejected by the Imperial Theaters, the opera's plot, "a parable of free enterprise, capitalism *avant le mot*," was a fitting symbol of the growing significance of Moscow's entrepreneurs in Russian cultural life.[26] Though impressed with Mamontov's skill in staging and visual art, Rachmaninoff found the MPO lacking from a musical perspective, and later shuddered at the memory of a *Sadko* performance in Rimsky-Korsakov's presence in which singers, unprepared for the performance, struggled to hide musical scores in the large sleeves of their costumes.[27] Finding that the demands of the position impinged on his compositional focus, Rachmaninoff, after a final concert tour with singers from the troupe in Crimea in September 1898, left the company. Nonetheless, the experience gained at the MPO served him well in his later post as conductor of Russian opera at the Bolshoi Theater (1904–6), and the innovative collectivist spirit of the company lingered in his memory even in emigration.[28]

While the MPO enjoyed the financial and artistic support of one of Moscow's wealthy entrepreneurs, the Circle of Lovers of Russian Music, or Kerzin Circle (1896–1912), was the product of activists within educated society committed to the image of music as a public good.[29] Founded by former Rimsky-Korsakov student and music critic Semyon Kruglikov (1851–1910), prominent Moscow lawyer Arkady Kerzin (1856–1914) and his wife, amateur pianist Mariya Kerzina (née Pospelova, 1864–1926), to propagandize Russian chamber music, the Kerzin Circle concerts contained a strong pedagogical intent. In keeping with Kerzin's view of music as "the highest [art form] in its ideal content and strongest in its emotional action," the concert stage re-created the "creative atmosphere" of the featured composer(s), incorporating photographs, busts of the composers, and relevant quotations from articles, letters, notes, and reminiscences of contemporaries.[30] Concert admission was initially free, artists performed

Figure 8. Pillar Hall in the Assembly of the Nobility (*Kolonnïy zal*), home of RMO concerts.

without remuneration, and venue costs, including refreshments, were covered by the Kerzins. The Kerzin Circle quickly expanded beyond its modest beginning in a private apartment where four performers and an audience of twenty-four gathered. By 15 February 1900, performances were held at the hotel-restaurant Slavic Bazaar, with ten performers and 450 audience members, and ultimately moved in December 1902 to the Pillar Hall of the Assembly of the Nobility (Figure 8).[31] Such success was a double-edged sword; though pleased by the enthusiasm their concerts had awakened, Kerzina worried that the increased audience size contained too many members who lacked the "right attitude" toward music, causing the circle to lose its former intimacy.[32]

The Kerzin Circle's exclusive dedication to Russian music was an innovation in Moscow, where music critics often lamented a lack of Russian repertoire in concerts.[33] Earlier aesthetic debates over the proper path for Russian music were secondary to the Kerzin Circle's conception, despite the close personal relationship between Kerzina and former kuchkist César Cui. As one of Moscow's emerging musical stars, Rachmaninoff, like his contemporaries Aleksandr Scriabin and Nikolai Medtner, was featured at concerts alongside music by Tchaikovsky, the *kuchka*, and lesser-known Russian composers.[34] The Kerzin Circle propagandized Russian music among performers as well as audience members. As Kerzina later remembered, one of the greatest initial challenges came from musicians who simply did not know the Russian chamber music repertoire.[35]

Personal interaction between composer, performers, and audience was encouraged; Cui and Rimsky-Korsakov were featured guests at concerts devoted to their music. Rachmaninoff was first invited to a 14 February 1903 performance, where several of his works were presented alongside other composers, and by January 1904 he was featured at a Kerzin Circle concert performing his own works.[36] Impressed with Rachmaninoff's conducting of a 1904 performance of Glinka's *A Life for the Tsar* at the Bolshoi, the Kerzins ignored the reservations expressed by Cui about the young composer's shortcomings and engaged him to conduct the new symphonic concerts added to their offerings in January 1905.[37]

Despite venturing into the realm of symphonic works, the Kerzin Circle continued to grant particular attention to chamber music works in their concerts. In addition to promoting the artistic value of smaller-scale works, the Circle thus offered composers a space to showcase shorter compositions with potentially wide commercial appeal. Ever increasing numbers of piano and vocal students, particularly young women from families eager to demonstrate their place within the ranks of educated society, helped to drive the ubiquitous nature of domestic music making, which had been noted by Shaginyan in her reminiscences, and provided a ready market for such compositions.[38] Rachmaninoff's *Fifteen Romances*, Op. 26 (1906), dedicated to the Kerzins, were thus simultaneously an exploration of new compositional directions and a practical solution to financial need. Composed in little more than a month in summer 1906, the songs show a "philosophical force unusual in the earlier songs," and a compositional style often more declamatory than lyrical.[39] The choice of poetry and its related philosophical tone must be imputed at least in part to Kerzina, who, at the composer's behest, selected potential texts for the cycle. Noting their predominantly dark hue, Rachmaninoff requested additional poems that were "more major" in character.[40] Nonetheless, the choice of "We will rest" ("My otdokhnyom"), the closing monologue from Anton Chekhov's play *Uncle Vanya* that promises peace "after a life of fruit-less labors and disappointed hopes," might well have been Rachmaninoff's own selection.[41] It demonstrates Rachmaninoff's interest in contemporary Russian theater and search for a declamatory vocal style. Premiered on 12 February 1907 before a large audience, many of them drawn by the promise of hearing Rachmaninoff's latest composition, the songs received a cool reception—a result not entirely unexpected by the composer who had previously warned the Kerzins of the challenges several of the pieces posed in performance.[42] Nonetheless, their 1907 publication by Gutheil provided much-needed funds that allowed Rachmaninoff to leave the turmoil of Moscow, still reeling from the effects of the 1905 Revolution, for the relative quiet of Dresden.[43]

The fates of the MPO and the Kerzin Circle underline both the bene-fits and drawbacks of private art patronage. As institutions built upon the artistic visions and financial solvency of an individual (or, in the case of the Kerzins, a couple), disruptions in personal life had an immedi-ate impact on the entire cultural endeavor. After Mamontov's arrest on embezzlement charges in 1901, the MPO limped on briefly as a collec-tive before reforming under a new entrepreneurial benefactor, Sergei Zimin, in 1904. The Kerzin Circle ceased activity in 1912 due to Kerzin's declining health. However, the private patronage model lent itself well to the innovative dreams of an increasingly active educated society. New private initiatives, building on the success of the MPO and Kerzin Circle, emerged. In 1909 Sergei Koussevitzky, inspired by private discussions with Rachmaninoff, founded a new symphonic concert series and pub-lishing house, the latter devoted explicitly to Russian music and financed by his wife's fortune.[44] Inspired by their experiences performing at Kerzin Circle concerts, Mariya Deysha-Sionitskaya's Musical Exhibitions (*Muzykal'niye vïstavki*, 1907–11) and Mariya Olenina d'Alheim's House of Song (*Dom pesni*, 1908–18) followed a similar goal of propagandizing chamber music through education, though they eschewed the exclusively Russian focus of the Kerzin Circle in favor of programming that included a wider range of European composers.[45]

These private initiatives also played an important role in transforming the conception of Russian music. The division of musical life into hostile "nationalist" (associated with St. Petersburg) and "conservatory" (asso-ciated with Moscow) camps was an image preserved in rhetoric by critic Vladimir Stasov long after it stopped reflecting reality. By 1912, however, St. Petersburg-based music critic Vyacheslav Karatygin asserted that formerly sharp divisions between the Moscow and St. Petersburg schools were disap-pearing: both Rimsky-Korsakov and Tchaikovsky's styles offered acceptable compositional models for a more broadly conceived Russian music.[46] By 1910, Moscow music critic Yuly Engel went so far as to assert that Russian music and art had undergone a "revolution [*povorot*] from national-every-day to general human, from real to symbolic-ideal art," a shift echoed in a general lessening of interest in folk music.[47] This "new, third period in the evolution of Russian music," particularly after Rimsky-Korsakov's death in 1908,[48] was viewed as abandoning the "national" distinctiveness of folksong for a more "general human" form of expression, giving rise to a musical style equally Russian and European.[49] In this spirit, Yu. Pomerantsev railed against French critics in 1909 who called Rachmaninoff's Second Piano Concerto more "German" than "Russian" in spirit, fuming, "Why must Russian music be exotic and entirely foreign to the general European spirit for the French to recognize it?"[50] Similarly, in 1914 the Moscow branch of the RMO showcased "all Russian music presented in its historical development," beginning with Glinka and ending with Rachmaninoff, Scriabin, Myaskovsky, and Shteinberg.[51] This synthesis was possible in part through Moscow's social milieu, in which individuals like Mamontov and the Kerzins helped to broaden the range of Russian repertoire and forge an image of Russian music that transcended earlier divisions.

Traversing Moscow's Soundscapes

Rachmaninoff's creative world was shaped not just by elegant concert halls and musical circles, but by the larger urban soundscape. In his 1955 reminiscence, composer and pianist Aleksandr Gyodike provided a vivid glimpse into what Rachmaninoff's Moscow had sounded like. Waking at seven in the morning, Rachmaninoff would take a cab to the Andronikov Monastery where he would stand through an entire liturgy, "listening to ancient strict singing (*starinnïye surovïye pesnopeniya*) from the Oktoechos, performed by monks in parallel fifths," which never failed to evoke a strong impression in him.[52] After a full day of work at home, Rachmaninoff would attend an evening symphony concert in the Catherine-era splendor of Pillar Hall and end the day at the restaurants Yar or Strelna in Petrovsky Park on the outskirts of the city, where he would sit until late at night, listening to the singing of gypsies (Figures 9a and 9b). As Gyodike reflected, "Clearly these sharp contrasts: a half-lit monastery with strict singing from the Oktoechos, a symphony concert, and then the society of gypsies at Yar with their unique song repertoire and even more unique performing manner were necessary for Sergei Vasilyevich, and without these impressions he could not live, as he made these trips quite often."[53]

There can be no question that Gyodike was influenced by secular biases in later Soviet predispositions toward music. His account nonetheless rings true, not least because it corroborates contemporary evidence on how, in this rapidly changing city, aesthetic expressions of tradition and modernity coexisted in complex ways. Movement from one realm to another and the experience of multiple (often contradictory) influences defined the late Imperial soundscape. Yet which sounds and emotions should a composer eternalize in his music? Which should he avoid? What did these sounds and the emotions they roused suggest about the nature of modern Russian society? In answering these questions, contemporary discourse on music granted great importance to the role of the composer,

Figure 9a. Yar restaurant, Moscow, Winter Room.

and ultimately placed Rachmaninoff and his music at the forefront of discussion over the future of Russia itself.

Though absent from Gyodike's account, Moscow's soundscape was also deeply inflected by the sharp social contradictions that had transformed Muscovite society since the end of serfdom in 1861. As peasant migrants poured into the city to find work, Moscow rose from a population of 602,000 in 1871, to 1,043,000 in 1897, and 1,612,000 in 1912.[54] While most cultural institutions, including the Bolshoi Theater, Moscow Conservatory, and Slavic Bazaar, were centrally located, Moscow—in contrast to other European metropoles—did not develop a spatial segregation of urban classes. Rather, the working population resided throughout the city, making their presence a visible part of daily life.[55] The visibility of this working population helped to strengthen a paternalistic sense within educated society of moral responsibility to educate the less privileged.

Musicians in Rachmaninoff's Moscow came from varied social backgrounds, but generally held a shared sense of their professional identity

Figure 9b. Yar restaurant, Moscow, Summer Room.

and moral responsibility within a world in which they were members of a relatively small educated portion of society. The successful careers of Rachmaninoff's contemporaries Chaliapin (born to a peasant family in Kazan) and Koussevitzky (born to a Jewish family in Vishniy Volochyok) demonstrate the possibility of a musical career path even for those from the less privileged strata of society.[56] On the other side of the social spectrum, Rachmaninoff and his elder sister, descendants of an impoverished noble family, had been encouraged by their family to pursue musical careers.[57] Nonetheless, as institutional records from the Moscow Conservatory and Musical-Dramatic School of the Moscow Philharmonic Society demonstrate, the vast majority of music graduates came from "middling groups" within Russian society—children of bureaucrats, merchants, teachers, doctors, and clergy.[58] This opening of music as a possible (if not always lucrative) profession had roots in the founding of the Russian Music Society by Anton Rubinstein in 1859, and the granting of the title of "Free Artist" to graduates of Russia's conservatories. Nonetheless, professional musicians often struggled to earn a sufficient wage to allow them to remain members of educated society, even as their cultural ambitions, sense of social mission, and education placed them firmly within this relatively small group. Alongside edifying discussions of music's transformative power on society, calls for the formation of professional unions and mutual aid societies were common in the music periodical press. At the same time a growing distaste for "dilettantes" involved in governing musical societies and suspicion of the poor taste of audiences highlights a widespread anxiety and policing of boundaries over who had the right to define acceptable music.

Nor did members of educated society agree among themselves over the sort of music that was acceptable in the rapidly transforming modern world. As Rachmaninoff struggled to overcome the anxiety awakened by the failure of his First Symphony, he made a pilgrimage in 1900 to the Moscow residence of famed Russian writer and self-defined elder (*starets*), Lev Tolstoy, where he performed his vocal romance "Sud'ba" (Fate) with Chaliapin.[59] Tolstoy's dismissive query, "Is such music needed by anyone?" was morally weighted toward peasant artistry over the "corrupted" influence of society. Only Chaliapin's performance of the folksong "Nochen'ka" elicited a positive response from Tolstoy, considering it not "polluted" by the degenerate morals of educated society.[60] Moscow educated society did not share Tolstoy's dismissive reaction to Rachmaninoff's music, however. Works like the Second Piano Concerto established him as one of the rising stars of Russian musical life, and his famed piano Prelude in C-sharp Minor quickly became a mainstay for pianists at the Moscow Conservatory.[61] In a general sense, Tolstoy's philosophical rejection of Rachmaninoff's music was representative of the same tendency to grant deep philosophical significance to musical style that Shaginyan later considered a hallmark of the era. One common question posed by educated society was thus: How could music's positive moral impact on society be harnessed while avoiding the potential moral, spiritual, and social chaos that the wrong musical style might elicit? In 1896, Ivan Lipayev lamented the lack of "cultured" entertainment for Moscow's poor, and called for the need to provide "spiritual fodder" for this "quickly demoralized population." Though by 1898 he lauded attempts by "the best literary, artistic and musical figures from Petersburg and Moscow" to answer this need, the sense that there was insufficient access to "cultured" entertainment for workers in Moscow remained widespread.[62]

Just as Tolstoy warned against the corrupting power of modern society on the Russian peasantry, members of educated society, professional musicians included, expressed deep concern that urbanization had a detrimental effect on the lives of workers and peasants, leading to drinking, carousing, and fighting. As Lynn M. Sargeant has shown, by the late nineteenth century, traditional Russian folk music, once celebrated as the "pure spring" that had nurtured Russian art music from Glinka through the kuchkists, was perceived as polluted by urban influences such as the factory song, and "the café-chantant, the movie palace, the operetta, and the dance hall equally threatened to corrupt the tastes of educated society, which itself had only recently, and precariously, been persuaded to appreciate and consume 'good' music."[63] Indeed, emotions such as *toska* (melancholy) were often explicitly linked to the dissipating experience of modern urban life. The expression of such emotions in the "cruel romances" of cabaret or in the emotional performance of "gypsy" singers found a ready audience, both among workers and educated society.[64] Rachmaninoff's trips to restaurants Yar and Strelka thus marked his participation in a sonic space at once popular and threatening for the cultural elite.

As revolution swept across the Russian Empire in 1905, musical society reacted as a microcosm of deeper social concerns. New music periodicals focused renewed attention on the financial plight of professional musicians as well as the potentially uplifting influence music could have on audiences.[65] As earlier calls to offer "cultured" education to the poor took on a more pressing tone, the Moscow People's Conservatory opened its doors on 3 September 1906, with the mission of spreading "musical knowledge to as broad a range of the population of Moscow and Moscow province as possible," through providing music courses, concerts, lectures, affordable books and teaching material as well as libraries, museums, and instrumental equipment to the city's working class. Following a similar logic, Moscow's City Duma joined with private initiatives to provide more musical opportunities for Moscow audiences.[66] Free lectures and general admission (*obshchedostupnïy*) concerts demonstrated a shared belief that music could have a positive impact on the ordinary people (*narod*).[67] By 1912, a music library was opened to the Moscow public that offered access to the latest periodical and scholarly literature on music from across Europe.[68] As music critic Yu. Engel declared in relation to the growth of musical life: "It is clear that the general slogan of our time—'Education, education, education!'—has found expression in the musical realm."[69]

The quest for general accessibility and sense of moral obligation to bring music to the *narod*—a common aspect of educated society's sense of purpose—was sometimes at odds with attempts to protect the professional rights of musicians. Numerous commentators criticized "benefit" concerts in which musicians were expected to perform free of charge. At the same time, increasing conflict over who had authority to make decisions within musical life took on sharply political overtones. Calls for control to be wrested from "dilettantes" and "amateurs" and turned over to trained musicians demonstrated a growing sense of professional self-sufficiency and resentment of the vagaries of the private patronage model, whether from state or private donors. Critiques of the "dictatorial nature" of the advisory boards of the conservatories in Petersburg and

Moscow, and of directors like Vasily Safonov at the Moscow Conservatory and Grigory Krein at the Moscow Philharmonic School echoed broader complaints within society over the dictatorial control of the Russian autocracy—a style of governance increasingly viewed as outdated for modern society.[70] Thus, as society responded to the strains of revolutionary change and calls for democratic reform, musical life similarly sought new models through which to self-define its purpose.

Ideals about music transcended practical images of moral tutelage. As Shaginyan observed, a deeply philosophical attitude to music emerged from a confluence of concerns related to a modernizing society, particularly after 1905. It was fostered by an active music press in which influential critics, together with philosophers, poets, artists, and other members of educated society offered competing interpretations of music's task in contemporary society. Images of unity and social harmony gained greater sway within a society lacking both. Nietzsche's image of music as a Dionysian unifying force able to transcend the divisions of the modern age from *The Birth of Tragedy* melded with Russian philosopher Vladimir Solovyov's vision of art as *theurgy*—the spiritualization of the material world—providing a conceptual framework within which individual composers and their works were assessed, leading to sometimes bitter disputes between supporters of one or another artistic direction. Though some composers, like Scriabin, explicitly placed themselves within this philosophical framing of music, the impact of German idealist philosophy and its melding with Russian religious philosophy was also felt by musicians who were less outspoken about these influences. Indeed, the Russian translation of Nietzsche's *Thus Spake Zarathustra* (1899) was apparently among the few books that Rachmaninoff carried with him on his flight from Russia. It remained a treasured volume, ultimately finding its permanent place in his library at Villa Senar in Switzerland.[71]

Despite their obsession with reaching the "masses," most of the educational possibilities established by Moscow's musical elite found an audience, not among workers but among aspiring members of the middle strata of society. The majority of students at the Moscow People's Conservatory, much to the chagrin of its founders, was drawn from university students and members of the bureaucratic classes rather than genuine workers. Moreover, there was a clear disconnect between the aspirations of the students and those of their instructors. While the People's Conservatory sought to focus on teaching choral song as the most perfect embodiment of unity, students often expressed an interest in music, not as an edifying force through which to reforge society or preserve "true" Russian identity but as a form of personal expression.[72] The "gypsy mania" (*tsiganshchina*) that swept urban society demonstrates that, for many listeners, it was the expression of raw emotion, *toska*, and individuality that appealed to audiences more than the moral calling often espoused in the musical press.[73] Nor was educated society more broadly willing to embrace the mantle of leadership that the cultural elite called on it to perform. Commenting on a fundraising effort by the House of Song to offer a free concert for workers, music critic Grigory Prokofyev lamented how few tickets had been sold, seeing in this a general lack of interest within educated society to support such important pedagogical efforts.[74] It was within this context of hope and anxiety over the emerging modern world that critics and audiences reacted to Rachmaninoff's creative output, employing concepts that were linked to narratives of Russia's changing experience of modernity after 1905.

Listening to Rachmaninoff in Late Imperial Moscow

The conceptual framing within which music was discussed shifted with Russia's lurching and uneven path to modernity, and new categories, intimately connected with the experiences of—and responses to—a rapidly modernizing society supplanted earlier aesthetic categories of analysis. Rachmaninoff's compositional style came to be regularly contrasted with that of fellow Moscow-based pianist-composer Scriabin in the periodical press, particularly following the return of both composers to Moscow after several years abroad.[75] Each came to encapsulate opposing musical—and by extension, philosophical—responses to modernity.

Supporters of Scriabin celebrated his innovative harmonies and sounds, arguing that a new type of music was needed to express the experiences and emotions awakened by modernity. Only a composer like Scriabin, who rejected tradition and embraced a dramatic utopian leap to the future— as the breathtaking speed of development of his compositional language demonstrated—could serve as a model for the emergence of a fundamentally *modern* Russian culture. In contrast, Rachmaninoff's music, firmly rooted in the tonal world of extended harmony, was believed to embody a music of the past rather than one suitable to the challenges of modernity. Music critic K. Stel captured this sense, claiming, "For Rachmaninoff everything is in the past, his ideals are not ahead [of us] but behind."[76] Sabaneyev, one of Scriabin's most vocal supporters, dismissed Rachmaninoff as a "completer of the past rather than bringer of the new."[77]

Such assessments of musical style were commonly linked to broad social commentary. For G. Prokofyev, Rachmaninoff's inability to write in large forms was not so much a sign of the composer's individual failure as a commentary on the "tempo of our spiritual life," which made it impossible to master larger forms.[78] Moreover, Rachmaninoff's popularity among audiences was explained by his attunement to the widespread mood of the modern era. However, these very moods, which Rachmaninoff's music captured so effectively, were themselves suspect. As Sabaneyev concluded in a 1912 assessment:

> The sphere of his emotions was the tragic helplessness of a man, lacking in strong will. His music is the music of a whining intellectual, and perhaps it has found such universal recognition, has so spontaneously subdued the musical masses, because within these masses there are so many individuals akin to Tchaikovsky, whiners like him, subjects who are lacking in willpower and who are submerged in the reflexes of their own helplessness. In general, there are many such people in *Rus'*.[79]

Sabaneyev's condescending view of contemporary Russian society is palpable. He employs the term *Rus'*, the ancient name for the people who inhabited the lands near Novgorod who had, according to the Old East Slavic *Primary Chronicle*, requested that a foreign king (Rurik) come and rule over them. The story had been employed in the narrative of the founding of the Russian state and legitimization of the autocracy by eighteenth-century historian Nikolai Karamzin; its use here was simultaneously a critique of Rachmaninoff's music and of those individuals who, like ancient *Rus'*, lacked individual will and sought an external hand to dictate their future.[80] In contrast, Sabaneyev asserted, though less appreciated by mass audiences, Scriabin awakened listeners to entirely new, modern feelings and emotions. His music was full of Nietzschean "will" and "striving." It was the very essence of modernity.[81]

The "pessimistic" and "melancholic" mood perceived to be infecting urban society was an abiding concern in Russia's growing periodical press. Particularly as hopes for progress toward a more democratic society faded after 1905, discourse focused on the question of "public mood" (*obshchest-vennoye nastroyeniye*), with many commentators expressing concern over a sense of melancholy, uprootedness, and helplessness that seemed to define contemporary urban existence.[82] A spate of 1910 suicides in Moscow were blamed on the effects of urban poverty and social upheaval.[83] The phrases used by critics to describe Rachmaninoff's music often tended toward similar evocations of a dark public mood: gloominess (*mrachnost'*), melancholy (*toska*), pessimism.[84] Though perhaps more explicit in assigning blame, Sabaneyev's assessment affirmed that Rachmaninoff embodied a widespread contemporary mood of helplessness and weakness in the face of modernity.

Shaginyan's fiery defense of Rachmaninoff in 1912 rejected such negative interpretations of his music. Appalled by what she saw as the metaphysical import of Scriabin's music, she attacked the contemporary obsession with "ecstasy," the "cosmic," and "supra-natural" themes, and mourned that modernists had forgotten that music was an art that should be accessible to all. Chaos of harmony, structure, and rhythm, endemic to modern music, threatened to destroy humanity in the modern age. "For us in Russia," she fumed, "it is enough to delve into the creation of the highly talented Scriabin in order to see the dehumanization of contemporary music."[85] His abandonment of harmony and rhythm and embrace of extreme dissonance sounded the disintegration of modern society and the loss of its human, individual element (*lichnost'*). In contrast, she held up Rachmaninoff's music as an example of healthy music that remained within the boundaries of the human. While Scriabin employed dissonance with no regard for its resolution according to the laws of classical harmony, Rachmaninoff used dissonance to "color the human element" but never allowed it to take over his music, which remained within a tonal spectrum. Preservation of the individual was thus directly associated with the preservation of tonality in music. Shaginyan identified a similar philosophical significance in rhythm. "The crisis of our 'transitional' (as they love to call it) time is particularly clearly expressed in the loss of rhythm. . . . We have lost rhythm not only in art (this is particularly noticeable in painting and in music), but also in society, and in daily life [*bit*]."[86] Shaginyan's analysis echoed the concern that urban capitalist modernity threatened the very existence of the individual, and she framed Rachmaninoff's music as a potential solution to this crisis.[87] Similar claims were made by other admirers, though voiced in less turgid philosophical language. For Rachmaninoff's 1911 biographer V. Yakovlev, the composer was "deeply human" in contrast to Scriabin's striving for cosmic significance.[88] Nor was the melancholic hue of his music necessarily a sign of spiritual weakness. Unlike Tchaikovsky, G. Prokofyev concluded, Rachmaninoff was not overcome by pessimism—his music exuded strength rather than defeat by the world.[89]

Such heady debates, while appealing to music's deep metaphysical meaning, were not the only (or even most common) rationale offered by many of Rachmaninoff's admirers, however. Rather, it seems that Rachmaninoff's popularity was due in part to his particular blend of Romantic melody and rich harmonies, which appealed to an audience seeking an affirmation of their own personal experiences amid the flux of modernity. In contrast to Scriabin's increasingly abstract harmonies, Rachmaninoff's music, contemporaries agreed, had immediate, subjective emotional appeal to audiences.[90] According to M. L. Chelishcheva, a contemporary, Rachmaninoff's playing "entered the soul of every person and in response caused those strings to sound which no other musician was able to touch."[91] Emphasis on one's internal emotions and self-fulfillment was finding voice across a wide swathe of the population. Similar to the gypsy songs that Rachmaninoff enjoyed at Yar (or in renditions by his friend Chaliapin), or the operettas and other forms of "popular" entertainment derided by cultural elites, Rachmaninoff's music was perceived to offer an immediate, subjective emotional appeal. The "pessimism," "melancholy," and "gloominess" of his music spoke to a shared sense of living through uncertain times. For a cultural elite that sought to provide moral and spiritual uplift, however, the evocation of such negative emotions, together with the sheer popularity these emotions seemed to enjoy, brought Rachmaninoff's music uncomfortably close to the unsavory forms of entertainment that they sought to combat. The anxieties of this cultural elite demonstrate both an enduring paternalism and a deep skepticism about the actual tastes of the emerging "mass" audience that they intended to guide to a "correct" understanding of music.

Conclusion

Although Rachmaninoff's Moscow career began in a musical world still shaped by the aesthetic battles of the 1850–70s, the unique confluence of wealthy entrepreneurs devoted to articulating their own image of a modern Russian identity, an increasingly assertive educated society, and a rapidly transforming urban landscape redefined the categories through which music was interpreted. The activities of the Moscow Private Opera and the Kerzin Circle both offered an institutional space for the performance of Russian music to enthusiastic audiences within Moscow educated society. As the strains of modernizing culture and social divisions openly clashed with an autocratic state in 1905, the power of music to overcome those divisions was increasingly emphasized. Perhaps former kuchkist César Cui's shifting views on Rachmaninoff best encapsulates how music's conceptual framing changed from the late nineteenth to the early twentieth century. Cui had panned Rachmaninoff's First Symphony in 1897 for its "sickly perverse harmonization" and "complete absence of simplicity and naturalness," likening it to the work of a talented student of a "Conservatory in Hell," but by the 1910s Cui celebrated Rachmaninoff's music as healthy, simple, and classical in contrast to modernists like Scriabin.[92] Ultimately, contemporary debates about musical style were never simply about aesthetic preference. By exploring the urban milieu in which Rachmaninoff worked, debates over his "traditional" composing style and "pessimistic" mood are shown, like Rachmaninoff's music, to be the product of a modernizing society seeking new symbols of identity.

NOTES

1. Marietta Shaginyan, "S. V. Rakhmaninov (muzïkal'no-psikhologicheskiy etyud)," *Trudï i dni* 4–5 (1912): 97–114, at 103.

2. Marietta Shaginyan, "Vospominaniya o S. V. Rakhmaninove," in *Vospominaniya o Rakhmaninove*, Z. Apetyan, ed., 5th ed., 2 vols. (Moscow: Muzïka, 1988), 2:90–258, at 90.

3. Ibid., 94. On the philosophical understanding of music and its impact on music education in late imperial educational institutions, see V. I. Adishchev, *Muzïkal'noye obrazovaniye v zhenskikh institutakh i kadetskikh korpusakh Rossii vtoroy polovinï XIX—nachala XX veka* (Moscow: Muzïka, 2007), esp. 159–61.

4. Glenn Carruthers, "The (Re)appraisal of Rachmaninov's Music: Contradictions and Fallacies," *Musical Times* 147/1896 (2006): 44–50.

5. Richard Taruskin, "Not Modern and Loving It," in *Russian Music at Home and Abroad: New Essays* (Oakland: University of California Press, 2016), 120–33, at 121.

6. Marshall Berman, *All That Is Solid Melts Into Air: The Experience of Modernity* (New York: Penguin, 1988), 15.

7. See for instance Edith W. Clowes, Samuel D. Kassow, and James L. West, eds., *Between Tsar and People: Educated Society and the Quest for Public Identity in Late Imperial Russia* (Princeton: Princeton University Press, 1991); Laura Engelstein, *The Keys to Happiness: Sex and the Search for Modernity in Fin-de-Siècle Russia* (Ithaca, NY: Cornell University Press, 1994); Catriona Kelly and David Shepherd, eds., *Constructing Russian Culture in the Age of Revolution: 1881–1940* (Oxford: Oxford University Press, 1998); Louisa McReynolds, *Russia At Play: Leisure Activities at the End of the Tsarist Era* (Ithaca, NY: Cornell University Press, 2003); Daniel Beer, *Renovating Russia: The Human Sciences and the Fate of Liberal Modernity, 1880–1930* (Ithaca, NY: Cornell University Press, 2008); Mark Steinberg, *Petersburg Fin de Siècle* (New Haven: Yale University Press, 2011).

8. Epigraph: C. Cui to M. Kerzina, 19 December 1904. Quoted in Sergei Bertensson and Jay Leyda, *Sergei Rachmaninoff: A Lifetime in Music* (Bloomington and Indianapolis: Indiana University Press, 2001), 72.

9. Alfred Rieber, *Merchants and Entrepreneurs in Imperial Russia* (Chapel Hill: University of North Carolina Press, 1982), 133–77.

10. John O. Norman, "Pavel Tretiakov and Merchant Art Patronage," in *Between Tsar and People*, 93–107; John E. Bowlt, "The Moscow Art Market," in *Between Tsar and People*, 108–130; James L. West, "Visions of Russia's Entrepreneurial Future: Pavel Riabushinskii's Utopian Capitalism," in *Merchant Moscow: Images of Russia's Vanished Bourgeoisie*, ed. James L. West and Iurii A. Petrov (Princeton: Princeton University Press 2014), 161–72. I use the term "modern" not in reference to a particular artistic style, but to the emergence of a modern society in which capitalist investment and patronage began to replace older models of noble patronage in the arts.

11. For contemporary evaluations of the range of such opportunities in Moscow, see for instance L. Sabaneyev, "V nedrakh muzïkal'nogo mira," *Golos Moskvï* 4 (6 January 1911): 4; n.a.,"Muzïkal'nïy 1907 god v Rossii," *Russkaya muzïkal'naya gazeta* 1 (1908): 1–8. Henceforth *RMG*.

12. William Craft Brumfield, "Aesthetics and Commerce: The Architecture of Merchant Moscow, 1890–1917," in *Merchant Moscow*, 119–31.

13. The Assembly of the Nobility (*Blagorodnoye sobraniye*) was built between 1784 and 1790 as a clubhouse for the nobility in Moscow and designed by neoclassical architect Matvei Kazakov. The Assembly's famed Pillar Hall, originally a ballroom, served as the location for symphony concerts offered by the RMO from 1860. After 1917, it was renamed the House of the Unions (*Dom soyuzov*) and used for state functions. The hotel-restaurant Slavic Bazaar, founded in 1872 by nobleman and entrepreneur Porokhovshchikov, was a favored meeting place for Moscow's business elite.

14. Nikolai Rubinstein chose the specific composers depicted, but the Pan-Slavic theme came from Porokhovshchikov. This painting replaced the stained-glass window depicting Saint Cecilia in the Moscow Conservatory's Large Hall after it was destroyed during the Great Patriotic War (Second World War, 1941–45). In 2011, the stained-glass window was reconstructed, and Repin's *Slavic Composers* was moved to the foyer. On Porokhovshchikov's involvement with Pan-Slavism, see Thomas Owen, *Capitalism and Politics in Russia*, 89–93. For a discussion of Porokhovshchikov's Moscow house, designed in a similarly Pan-Slavic manner, see William Craft Brumfield, *The Origins of Modernism in Russian Architecture* (Berkeley: University of California Press, 1991), 9–10. The twenty-two musicians depicted were: Mikhaíl Glinka (1804–1857), Vladimir Odoyevsky (1804–1869), Nikolai Rimsky-Korsakov (1844–1908), Aleksandr Dargomyzhsky (1813–1869), Ivan Laskovsky (1799–1855), Aleksei Lvov (1798–1870), Aleksei Verstovsky (1799–1862), Anton Rubinstein (1829–1894), Nikolai Rubinstein (1835–1881), Aleksandr Serov (1820–1871), Aleksandr Gurilyov (1803–1858), Dmitry Bortnyansky (1751–1825), Pyotr Turchaninov (1779–1856), Polish composers Stanisław Moniuszko (1819–1872), Frederic Chopin (1810–1849), Michał Kleofas Ogiński (1765–1833), Karol Lipiński (1790–1861), and Czech musicians Eduard Nápravník (1839–1916), Bedřich Smetana (1824–1884), Karel Bendl (1838–1897), Václav Horák (1800–1871).

15. Designed by Vasily Zagorsky, funding for the building came from state funds, benefit concerts, and donations from wealthy Moscow entrepreneurs. See *Otchyot po postroyke i torzhestvennomu otkrïtiyu zdaniya konservatorii* (Moscow: Pechatnya S. P. Yakovleva, 1905); Lipayev, "Moskovskiye pis'ma," *RMG* 45 (1903): 1100–1103.

16. I. Lipayev, "Iz Moskvï: novïy bol'shoy kontsertnïy zal konservatorii," *RMG* 6 (1901): 471. In 1953, the portraits of Mendelssohn, Gluck, Haydn and Handel were replaced with portraits of Rimsky-Korsakov, Chopin, Dargomyzhsky, and Musorgsky.

17. *Otchyot po postroyke i torzhestvennomu otkrïtiyu zdaniya konservatorii*, 16.

18. "Epokha N. G. Rubinshteyna, S. I. Taneyeva, V. I. Safonova, M. M. Ippolitova-Ivanova," in *Moskovskaya konservatoriya: Materialï i dokumentï iz fondov MGK imeni P. I. Chaykovskogo i GTsMMK imeni M.I. Glinki*, ed. E. G. Sorokina, 2 vols. (Moscow: Progress-Traditsiya, 2006), 2:41.

19. Tretyakov gifted his art collection to Moscow in 1892; his private icon collection was first displayed in 1903. V. I. Antonova, *Gosudarstvennaya Tret'yakovskaya galereya* (Moscow: Iskusstvo, 1968), 208.

20. Olga Haldey, *Mamontov's Private Opera* (Bloomington: Indiana University Press, 2010), 68–87.

21. In 1886 the Moscow Synodal School for Church Singing was rechartered by Chief Procurator of the Holy Synod Konstantin Pobedonostsev. On the revival of Russian chant and the emergence of the "New Direction" in church music, see Marina Frolova-Walker, *Russian Music and Nationalism: From Glinka to Stalin* (New Haven: Yale University Press, 2008) and the ongoing multivolume *Russkaya dukhovnaya muzïka v dokumentakh i materialakh* (Moscow: Yazyki slavyanskoi kul'turï, 1998–).

22. [Iv. Lipayev], "Moskovskoye Filarmonicheskoye Obshchestvo (yubileynaya spravka)," *RMG* 44 (1903): 1047–50.

23. Lipayev, "Iz Moskvï," *RMG* 6 (1899): 178–81.

24. Though the MPO performed both foreign and Russian opera, it was the Russian that resonated with audiences, and for which the organization is generally remembered. For a critical assessment of this phenomenon, see Olga Haldey, "The Repertoire Politics of Mamontov's Enterprise: Francophilia, Wagnerism and the Nationalist Crusade," *Revue des études slaves* 84/3–4 (2013): 421–32.

25. S. Rakhmaninov, "Vospominaniya," in *Literaturnoye naslediye*, ed. Z. A. Apetyan, 3 vols. (Moscow: Sovetskiy kompozitor, 1978–80), 1:51–61, esp. 53–57; Maxim Gorky,

Chaliapin: An Autobiography, ed. Nina Froud and James Hanley (New York: Stein and Day, 1967), 128; Lipayev, "Muzïkal'naya zhizn' Moskvï," *RMG* 3 (1898): 311–15. On the modernism inherent in the MPO, see Olga Haldey, "Savva Mamontov, Serge Diaghilev, and a Rocky Path to Modernism," *Journal of Musicology* 22/4 (2005): 559–603.

26. Richard Taruskin, "Sadko," in *Grove Music Online*, https://www.oxfordmusiconline. com/grovemusic.

27. Rakhmaninov, "Vospominaniya," in *Literaturnoye naslediye*, 1:57.

28. The Bolshoi performed both Russian and non-Russian works, but Rachmaninoff was solely in charge of Russian repertoire. See ibid., 1:57– 61.

29. M. S. Kerzina, "Vospominaniya," quoted in A. A. Shteinberg, "Kerzinskiy kruzhok lyubiteley russkoy muzïki (Iz proshlogo russkoi muzïkal'noi kul'turï)," *Voprosï muzikoznaniya* 3 (1960): 598–619, at 599.

30. Ibid., 609–10.

31. For a list of all the concerts from 1896 to 1906, including performers, repertoire, and locations, see *Kruzhok lyubiteley russkoy muzïki* (Moscow: I. I. Pashkova, 1906). As the performance scope expanded, a fee was introduced to help cover costs, though the concerts were still heavily subsidized. Shteinberg, "Kerzinskiy kruzhok," 605.

32. Cui to Kerzina, 5 April 1905, in Ts. Kyui, *Izbrannïye pis'ma* (Leningrad: Gosudarstvennoye muzïkal'noye izdatel'stvo, 1955), 346–48.

33. On the lack of Russian repertoire in Moscow RMO concerts, see for instance Lipayev, "Iz Moskvï," *RMG* 6 (1899): 178–81. The Kerzin Circle had similarities to Mitrofan Belyayev's "Friday" chamber music concerts and "Russian Symphony Concerts," where many new Russian symphonic works were premiered after 1885. However, the Kerzin Circle did not exert the same control over stylistic development as the so-called Belyayev Circle. On the St. Petersburg school and this issue, see Richard Taruskin, *Stravinsky and the Russian Traditions*, 2 vols. (Berkeley: University of California Press, 1996), 1:47–71.

34. The focus of the Kerzin Circle on the nationalist music of the *kuchka*, though evident, has been overstated. In the first ten years of its existence, only eight composers were featured in concerts devoted entirely to their own music: Cui (five concerts), Rimsky-Korsakov (four concerts), and one concert each devoted to Glinka, A. Rubinstein, Arensky, Tchaikovsky, Borodin, and Musorgsky. Nonetheless, many performances featured a wide range of contemporary Russian composers, including Stravinsky, Scriabin, and minor modernist composers like Leonid Sabaneyev. See for instance Gr. P., "Teatr i muzïka," *Russkiye vedomosti* 61 (14 March 1912): 4; *Muzïka* 4–5 (1910): 101.

35. Shteinberg, "Kerzinskii kruzhok," 605–6.

36. Rakhmaninov, *Literaturnoye naslediye*, 1:337–38, 576; and *Kruzhok lyubiteley russkoy muzïki*, 24, 28.

37. Shteinberg, "Kerzinskii kruzhok," 601–2; Cui to Kerzina, 3 March 1904, in Kyui, *Izbrannïye pis'ma*, 319–20. In January 1905, Rachmaninoff conducted the Circle's first symphonic concert, which featured S. Taneyev as soloist in a program of Rimsky-Korsakov, Glinka, and Tchaikovsky. See *Kruzhok lyubiteley russkoy muzïki*, 32.

38. Lynn M. Sargeant, *Harmony and Discord: Music and the Transformation of Russian Cultural Life* (Oxford: Oxford University Press, 2011), 141–54.

39. Richard D. Sylvester, *Rachmaninoff's Complete Songs: A Companion with Texts and Translations* (Bloomington: Indiana University Press, 2014), 141.

40. Rachmaninoff to Kerzina, 2 August 1906, in *Literaturnoye naslediye*, 1:396–97. Nonetheless, only five of the fifteen are in major keys.

41. The personal friendship between the elder playwright and the young composer dated to Rachmaninoff's involvement with the MPO in 1898, and his attendance at the 1904 premiere of Chekhov's final play, *The Cherry Orchard*, at Konstantin Stanislavsky's Moscow Art Theater. Discussions of a possible collaboration on an opera project had

been cut short by the writer's death two years prior to the composition of Opus 26. See Sylvester, *Rachmaninoff's Complete Songs*, 141–43.

42. "Vecher kruzhka lyubiteley russkoy muzïki," *Golos Moskvï* 41 (February 1907): 3–4; Rachmaninoff to Kerzina, 18 February/3 March 1907, *Literaturnoye naslediye*, 1:425–26.

43. Rachmaninoff's publisher, Gutheil, paid 250 rubles for a song. See Sylvester, *Rachmaninoff's Complete Songs*, 94.

44. Nikolay Kashkin, "Moskovskiye muzïkal'nïye dela," *Moskovskiy yezhenedel'nik* 44 (10 November 1907); and "Obshchedostupnïye kontsertï v Moskve," *Moskovskiy yezhenedel'nik* 49 (11 December 1907); Yu.Engel', "Muzïka," *Russkiye vedomosti* 1 (1 January 1910): 14–15; Yu. Engel', "Itogi muzïkal'nogo sezona," *Russkiye vedomosti* 102 (6 May 1909): 2; Nikolay Kashkin "Russkoye muzïkal'noye obshchestvo," *Moskovskiy yezhenedel'nik* (1908–9); Yu. Engel', "Muzïka," *Russkiye vedomosti* 1 (1910): 14–15; "Muzïkal'nïy 1910 god v Rossii," *RMG* 1 (1911): 1–5.

45. On Olenina d'Alheim's House of Song, see Alexander Tumanov, *The Life and Artistry of Maria Olenina-d'Alheim*, trans. Christopher Barnes (Edmonton: University of Alberta Press, 2000), 144–94; Rebecca Mitchell, *Nietzsche's Orphans: Music, Metaphysics, and the Twilight of the Russian Empire* (New Haven: Yale University Press, 2016), 37–38. On Deysha-Sionitskaya's Musical Exhibitions, see Anonymous, "Muzïkal'nïy 1907 god v Rossii," *RMG* 1 (6 January 1908): 5.

46. V. G. Karatïgin, "Skryabin i molodïye moskovskiye kompozitorï," *Apollon* 5 (May 1912): 25–38.

47. Yu. Engel', "Muzïka," *Russkiye vedomosti* 1 (1 January 1910): 14–15. For similar arguments, see Yu. E., "Muzïka N. Metnera," *Russkiye vedomosti* 57 (11 March 1911): 4; P. Blaramberg, "Russkaya narodnaya pesnya i yeyo vliyaniye na muzïku," *Muzïkal'nïy truzhenik* 4 (1909): 1–7; and *Muzïkal'nïy truzhenik* 6 (1909): 7–10.

48. Yu. Engel', "Muzïka," *Russkiye vedomosti* 1 (1 January 1909): 7.

49. Yu. Engel', "Teatr i muzïka," *Russkiye vedomosti* 30 (6 February 1908): 4.

50. Yu. Engel', "Teatr i muzïka," *Russkiye vedomosti* 44 (24 February 1909): 7; Yu. Pomerantsev, "Russkaya muzïka v Parizhe," *Moskovskiy yezhenedel'nik* 26 (4 July 1909): 41–50.

51. A similar framing was offered in a series of 1916 concerts titled "Evenings of Russian Music" performed at the Moscow People's Conservatory. See Anonymous, "Teatr i muzïka," *Russkiye vedomosti* 232 (8 October 1916): 4; Yu. E., "Teatr i muzïka," *Russkiye vedomosti* 245 (23 October 1916): 6; "Teatr i muzïka," *Russkiye vedomosti* 223 (28 September 1914): 6.

52. Andronikov Monastery was the site where famed medieval icon painter Andrei Rublyov spent the final years of his life and was buried. The *oktoechos* is the source for Orthodox Church chant melodies.

53. A. F. Gyodike, "Pamyatnïe vstrechi," in *Vospominaniya o Rakhmaninove*, 2:4–17. Both Yar and Strelna were famous for their gypsy performers. See *Putevoditel' po Moskve ot Slavyanskogo Bazara* (Moscow: Leon Dekroz, 1896), 139. On Yar and Strelna as symbols of emerging urban culture, see McReynolds, *Russia at Play*, 196–210.

54. *Glavneyshiye predvaritel'nïye dannïye perepisi goroda Moskvï 6 marta 1912*, as cited in Anna Mazanik, "The City as a Transient Home: Residential Patterns of Moscow Workers Around the Turn of the Twentieth Century," *Urban History* 40/1 (2013), 51–70, at 54. Of the employed population, there were approximately 3.9 laborers to every member of a professional, civil servant, and white-collar manager (60–61).

55. On the centralized geography of cultural institutions, see Pavel Il'in, "Geografiya kul'turï Moskvï v kontse XIX—nachale XX veka," in *Moskva rubezha XIX i XX stoletiy: vzglyad v proshloye izdaleka*, ed. P. Il'in and B. Ruble (Moscow: Rosspen, 2004): 131–92.

56. Fyodor Shalyapin, *Vospominaniya* (Moscow: Lokid, 2000); Viktor Yuzefovich, *Sergey Kusevitskiy: Russkiye godï* (Moscow: Iazyki slavianskoi kul'tury, 2004).

57. A gifted singer, sixteen-year old Yelena Rakhmaninova accepted a contract with Moscow's Bolshoi Theater in 1885 before her early death from pernicious anemia the same year. Bertensson and Leyda, *Rachmaninoff*, 6–7.

58. This is demonstrated in the records from both institutions. As an example, of thirty-nine graduates of the Philharmonic school in 1904–5, there were seven who did not list their social background; four nobles, three peasants, and the remainder were from "middling groups." At the Moscow Conservatory, of 128 piano students in 1904, there were four peasants, eight nobles, and the rest were from "middling groups." See Rossiyskiy gosudarstvennïy arkhiv literaturï i iskusstva (RGALI) f. 2098, op. 1, d. 10: "Spiski okonchivshikh uchilishche s biograficheskimi dannïmi," ll. 31–34, ll. 35–37, ll. 76–78; RGALI f. 2099, op. 1, d. 239, "Spiski uchashchikhsya konservatorii po klassu fortepiano za 1904 g." On the social demographics of musicians at this time, see Lynn M. Sargeant, *Harmony and Discord*, 121–74.

59. In Russian Orthodox tradition, a *starets* was "an experienced monk who possessed special gifts of spiritual wisdom and acted as a mentor." Famously represented in the character of Father Zosima in Fyodor Dostoyevsky's *Brothers Karamazov*, the tradition of the *starets* was an influential aspect of popular Orthodoxy, though not officially sanctioned by the Church. On Tolstoy's self-fashioning as a *starets*, see Pål Kolstø, "The Elder at Iasnaia Poliana: Lev Tolstoi and the Orthodox *Starets* Tradition," *Kritika* 9/3 (Summer 2008): 533–54.

60. Quoted in Rakhmaninov, *Literaturnoye naslediye*, 1:551.

61. Gyodike, "Pamyatnïye vstrechi," 5.

62. Lipayev, "Muzïkal'naya zhizn' Moskvï," *RMG* 7 (1898): 666–72. See also Iv. Lipayev, "Moskovskiye pis'ma: Doklad g. Sakharova o razvlecheniyakh," *RMG* 45 (1903): 1100–103.

63. Lynn M. Sargeant, "High Anxiety: New Venues, New Audiences, and the Fear of the Popular in Late Imperial Russian Music," *19th-Century Music* 35/2 (2011): 93–114, at 94.

64. On cabarets and other popular entertainment in late Imperial Russia, see McReynolds, *Russia at Play*, 193–252. On emotions like *toska* and their expression in the late Imperial Russian press, see Steinberg, *Petersburg Fin de Siècle*, 234–67.

65. Examples of these new Moscow journals were *Muzïkal'nïy truzhenik* (1906–10), *Muzïka i zhizn'* (1908–12), and *Orkestr* (1910–12).

66. Lipayev, "Moskovskiye pis'ma," *RMG* 2 (1905): 57–60.

67. Concerts in Sokolniki Park, initially ad hoc, were organized from 1892 as a formalized space for cultured entertainment and subsidized by the city from 1910. See Sargeant, "High Anxiety," 110–11. On the Moscow People's Conservatory, see Mitchell, *Nietzsche's Orphans*, 55–59.

68. "Ot obshchestva muzïk.-teoretich. biblioteka v Moskve," *RMG* 4 (1909): 116; "Ot obshchestva muzïk.-teoretich. biblioteka v Moskve," *Muzïkal'nïy truzhenik* 2 (1909): 12–13; Yu. È., "Obshchedostupnaya muzïkal'naya biblioteka v Moskve," *Russkiye vedomosti* 233 (10 October 1910): 4; and *Russkie vedomosti* 48 (28 February 1912): 4.

69. Yu. Engel', "Muzïka," *Russkiye vedomosti* (1 January 1910): 14–15.

70. A. Livin, "Tormazï iskusstva (k voprosu o reforme muzïkal'nogo obshchestva)," *RMG* 41 (1904): 904–9; L. Sabaneyev, "Muzïkal'nïye zametki," *Golos Moskvï* 207 (8 September 1911): 4; A. Livin, "Nazrevshiye voprosï," *RMG* 11 (1905): 297–301; Sargeant, *Harmony and Discord*, 219–60.

71. Fr. Nitshe, *Tak govoril Zaratustra* (Moscow: D. P. Efimov, 1899). See "Rachmaninoff Library Inventory," from the Serge Rachmaninoff Archives at Villa Senar, courtesy of Serge Rachmaninoff Foundation/Rachmaninoff Network. For a closer examination of this philosophical interpretation of music, see Rebecca Mitchell, *Nietzsche's Orphans*, and "Musical Metaphysics in Late Imperial Russia," in *Oxford Handbook of Russian Religious*

Philosophy, Caryl Emerson, George Pattison, and Randall A. Poole, eds., (Oxford: Oxford University Press, 2020), 379–95.

72. Mitchell, *Nietzsche's Orphans*, 57–58.

73. McReynolds, *Russia at Play*, 223–52.

74. G. Prokof'yev, "Moskovskiy muzïkal'nïy sezon 1909-10 gg.," *Moskovskiy yezhenedel'nik* 34 (1910), 57–64.

75. From fall 1906 to spring 1909, Rachmaninoff spent winter seasons abroad and summers on his family estate Ivanovka. Scriabin left Moscow in 1904 and returned permanently in 1910.

76. K. A. Stel', "O Rakhmaninove," *Yuzhnïy muzikal'nïy vestnik* 6 (1915): 1–3. For a similar assessment, see Karatïgin: "Skryabin i molodïye moskovskiye kompozitorï," 27.

77. A. Gorskiy, "Rebikov," *Yuzhnïy muzikal'nïy vestnik* 15–16 (1916): 100–104, at 100.

78. G. Prokof'yev, "Pevets intimnïkh nastroyeniy (S. V. Rakhmaninov): Opït kharakteristiki," *RMG* 38 (19 September 1910): 782–85, at 783. Prokofyev explored all of Rachmaninoff's extant compositions in a recurring article of this title over the course of 1909–10. See G. Prokof'yev, "Pevets intimnïkh nastroyeniy (S.V. Rakhmaninov): Opït kharakteristiki," *RMG* 48 (1909): 1133–37; *RMG* 49 (1909): 1162–67; *RMG* 51–52 (1909): 1230–33; *RMG* 2 (1910): 36–43; *RMG* 6 (1910): 161–65; *RMG* 7 (1910): 193–96; *RMG* 26–27 (1910): 588–93; *RMG* 28–29 (1910): 617–21; *RMG* 30–31 (1910): 639–42; *RMG* 37 (1910): 750–54; *RMG* 38 (1910): 782–85; *RMG* 40 (1910): 841–45.

79. Sabaneyev, "Skryabin i Rakhmaninov," *Muzïka* 75 (5 May 1912): 390–95, at 390–91.

80. Serge Zenkovsky, *Medieval Russia's Epics, Chronicles, and Tales* (New York: Penguin Books, 1963); Nikolay Karamzin, *Istoriya gosudarstva Rossiyskogo* (St. Petersburg: N. Grecha, 1816–29).

81. Sabaneyev, "Skriabin i Rakhmaninov."

82. Steinberg, *Petersburg Fin de Siecle*, 234–67.

83. Statistik, "Samoubiystva v Moskve za 1910 god," *Russkiye vedomosti* 84 (4 April 1911): 4.

84. Viktor Val'ter, "Teatr i muzïka," *Rech'* 44 (14 February 1911): 3.

85. Shaginyan, "S. V. Rakhmaninov," 102.

86. Ibid., 108.

87. Steinberg, *Petersburg Fin de Siecle*, 152.

88. V. Yakovlev, *S. V. Rakhmaninov* (St. Petersburg: Elektro-tipografiya N. Ya. Stoykovoy, 1911), 8. For similar claims, see Iv. Lipayev, *Rakhmaninov* (Saratov: M. F. Tideman, 1913), 1.

89. Prokof'yev, "Pevets intimnïkh nastroyeniy," *RMG* 51–52 (1910): 1230–33. See also D. Arakchiyev, *Muzïka i zhizn'* 3 (1910): 12; Lipayev, *Rakhmaninov*, 1, 12.

90. Prokof'yev, "Pevets intimnïkh nastroyeniy," *RMG* 48 (1909): 1133; Anonymous, "Kontsertï," *RMG* 3–4 (1905): 89.

91. M. L. Chelishcheva, "S. V. Rakhmaninov v Mariyinskom uchilishche," in *Vospominaniya o Rakhmaninove*, 1:402–6, at 405–6.

92. Ts. Kyui, "Tretiy russkiy simfonicheskiy kontsert," *Novosti i birzhevaya gazeta* (17 March 1897): 3; Kyui, *Izbrannïye pis'ma*, 667.

Love Triumphant: Rachmaninoff's Eros, the Silver Age, and the Middlebrow

MARINA FROLOVA-WALKER

Despite his Cinderella status in musicology for many years, Rachmaninoff has enjoyed continuous prestige and popularity with the public, and well beyond the confines of concertgoers. From time to time, sensationalist headlines about his music float to the surface. One that recently caught my attention was "Quand la musique procure des orgasmes,"[1] an article that summarized scientific research investigating our physical reactions to music, presented in a form digestible for the non-specialist.[2] As Psyche Loui, one of the researchers, explained to a journalist: "I was in a friend's dorm room in my third year as an undergraduate. Rachmaninov's Piano Concerto No. 2 came up on the radio and I was instantly captivated. . . . There are these slight melodic and harmonic twists in the second half [movement] that always get me!"[3] Admittedly, the title of the article is clickbait, since the attention-catching word is qualified to "orgasme de la peau," which turns out to mean nothing more than "goosebumps" (normally *chair de poule* in French, or simply *frisson*). But the notion that Rachmaninoff's music is somehow erotic has a long pedigree in popular culture. In 1945, not long after the composer's death, the film *Brief Encounter* made serious use of the Second Piano Concerto to assist its story of illicit passion. A decade later, *The Seven-Year Itch* was able to employ the same music for comedic purposes, in a parody of the earlier film (Marilyn Monroe's character even says that the music gives her goosebumps). The Second Piano Concerto still has its erotic potential, as demonstrated in the 2019 YouTube clip of Lola & Hauser, which is neither earnest nor ironic, but merely cynical.[4]

Despite this, nothing of substance has yet been written on the matter, in contrast to the erotic aspect of Scriabin's music, which is routinely addressed in scholarly writing. Part of the reason lies in the fact that Scriabin openly discussed the issue and left a multitude of suggestive performance directions in his scores, all the time acknowledging that the erotic played an essential role in his aesthetic. Rachmaninoff, by contrast, never broached the subject. The abstract and elevated nature of Scriabin's eroticized later music also makes it more amenable to scholarly discussion. Russian commentators often characterize mainstream Russian culture as "asexual."[5] As Boris Paramonov colorfully put it, "If in the West they say 'sex,' we demand eros; Freud isn't enough for us, we need the divine Plato with his metaphysics of Eros (capitalized, of course)."[6] In this context, it is understandable that Rachmaninoff's more immediate and concrete eroticism should remain unacknowledged, unlike Scriabin's more rarified eroticism.

Taking Rachmaninoff's eroticism as a point of departure, the first part of this essay will explore the cultural context, relevant musical devices, and reception of this music. The most appropriate repertoire for this purpose is Rachmaninoff's song literature (Russian refers to the genre as the "romance"), and these will lead us to a consideration of the poetic texts the composer chose, and outward to the Russian literary scene of the period, known as the "Silver Age." Within this literary scene, however, we will direct our attention toward the emerging middlebrow literature (including literature written by women), rather than to the more ambitious and hermetic high Symbolism that is better known today. As I will argue, it is this middlebrow verse and prose, focused on the everyday rather than the transcendent, and boldly tackling issues of sexuality for the first time, that is the closest literary counterpart to much of Rachmaninoff's music. From there we will move on to the issue of Rachmaninoff's popularity as both a performer and composer, and his self-advertised connections with popular culture. Finally, we will consider whether some of his music actually benefits from being viewed as "middlebrow," so long as we can accept this as a neutral term, shorn of its derogatory associations. With this concept of the middlebrow at our disposal, we are better equipped to tackle common accusations of "bad taste."

Eros, Women, and Mass Literature

Let us begin with a landmark song from 1890, "V molchan'i nochi taynoy" (In the Silence of the Secret Night), Op. 4, No. 3. The infatuated first-person narrator of the poem recalls in the night every tiny detail of an encounter with the object of his love, and as he fantasizes about her, he disturbs the silence by calling out her name. Afanasy Fet's poem (1844) includes the following couplet:

> Дыша порывисто, один, никем не зримый,
> Досады и стыда румянами палимый . . .

> Fitfully breathing, alone, observed by none,
> Hot with the blush of frustration and of shame . . .[7]

Rachmaninoff chose to omit these lines, since his music could cover the same ground with greater eloquence: there is an intense climax, and at the top of the wave, the piano enunciates a two-note motive and keeps repeating it, as the force of the music gradually dissipates. What name did Rachmaninoff have in mind for these repetitions? Looking at the first page, we see that the dedicatee is Vera Skalon.

Let us see if any biographical information might set this putative association on firmer ground. In 1890, the seventeen-year-old Rachmaninoff spent the summer of 1890 on the estate of Ivanovka, flirting with all three of the Skalon sisters, but developing a particularly tender relationship with Vera, who was then fourteen. In Vera's diary, we find a moving account of her feelings of love for Seryozha Rachmaninoff, her first pangs of jealousy (mainly toward her sister Tata/Tatyana, who was twenty-one), her discovery of little seductive gestures (rolling cherries from a plate into her mouth), and her failure to respect certain boundaries (she was scolded for going into his room to wake him).[8] All this eventually led to serious trouble, as recounted in Sergei Bertensson and Jay Leyda's biography:

> All the young people enjoyed sitting on the long bench in the dusk, and Vera and Seryozha used this opportunity to sit close together, holding hands—until Vera Siloti noticed this habit and reported it to the girl's horrified mother. Poor Verochka was scolded, and Seryozha was forbidden to write to her when he returned to Moscow at the end of August for the opening of the conservatory; so that communication had to be maintained through her older sisters.[9]

The relationship never developed any further in real life, but artistically, it became the inspiration for a song, in which Rachmaninoff discovered a vital formula for his music: the dynamic profile of a wave, with a well-defined crest and a lingeringly slow descent from it (Rachmaninoff repeats the last line of the text to fulfill his musical purpose here). It is worth focusing on a couple of other details to show how the climax of the song is realized: on the ascent, the harmonic rhythm speeds up to two chords per measure, but then slows down drastically, with a chord III stretched out over three measures in a kind of pre-climactic plateau. The peak of the wave is a chromatically altered secondary dominant (V of IV), after which the progression of IV–V^6_4–V–I is articulated as a gradual release of tension. Both the V and the

I are complicated yet further, slowing down the final resolution as much as possible. Rachmaninoff's handling of the timing is most impressive in this early song and an important precursor of later characteristics of his music.

A similar dynamic profile occurs in "Eti letniye nochi" (These Summer Nights), Op. 14, No. 5 (text by Daniil Rathaus), although the temperature here is several degrees higher, since the text presents the joy of love consummated. Here the vocal line plays a greater part in the gradual buildup: the first verse, beginning with narrow intervals in the low register, reaches a high G; the second uses wider intervals and reaches an A, the third culminates on a high B, which is held the longest, while the pianist reiterates the melodic motto. The climax here is more conventionally rendered, the long high note falling on the V^6_4, and the post-climax savoring in the piano postlude takes as long as eleven measures.

But what happens when the song begins just before the point of arrival, with the approach to the V^6_4? This occurs in "Utro" (Morning), Op. 4, No. 2 (text by the little-known M. Yanov), which uses erotic imagery allegorically: "I love you, whispered the dawn to the day" is the first line of the poem (in Russian, "dawn" is a feminine noun and "day" masculine). The song begins with the declaration of love, and everything that follows is a reaction to this confession, the motto phrase receiving many reharmonizations. This means that the potential harmonic climax has already been used up, and this determines that "Morning" will have a very different harmonic profile from "Secret Night." The song moves from the main key of F major to the very distant E major, which would allow a climax on the return to F major, but Rachmaninoff forgoes even this and renders the return delicate and mysterious instead. This tells us that Rachmaninoff is not at all wed to his winning "wave" formula, and that he would experiment with the harmonic-cum-dramatic profile in order to serve the text (or his interpretation of it).

The erotic subject matter that appears so prominently in the early songs is also present in the instrumental piece "La nuit . . . l'amour," from the Suite No. 1 for two pianos, Op. 5. The poetic epigraph is taken from the head of Byron's *Parisina* (1816), which sets the scene for a night of passionate incestuous love that leads to a tragic denouement:

> It is the hour when from the boughs
> The nightingale's high note is heard;
> It is the hour when lovers' vows
> Seem sweet in every whisper'd word;
> And gentle winds, and waters near,
> Make music to the lonely ear.

Initially, Rachmaninoff seems content to evoke the sound of the "gentle winds and waters" through swathes of harmonic figuration, punctuated by the repeated notes of the nightingale's song. Eventually an *amoroso* theme appears in the bass, and a buildup commences, with a sigh motive that eventually sounds as if it has been spirited over from the Venusberg.[10] The climax is gigantic, and even on the page, its extravagance is immediately evident; the culmination, marked *fff*, is on an F-sharp-major chord, far from the main key of D major.[11] The location of this climax before the piece is halfway through (measure 59 out of 131) is unusual even for Rachmaninoff, and the descent from the peak is especially protracted, with the figuration moving lower and lower. The rhetoric of the climax and the celebration of erotic love draws from Wagner and Liszt.

The texts of the early songs unfold, implicitly, in the setting of the Russian country estate, those "nests of the gentry," where secret trysts would take place out of doors, on moonlit summer nights (Rachmaninoff effectively repurposed Byron's verses to this end). The biographical connection of "Secret Night" to Rachmaninoff's Ivanovka summer of 1890, noted above, and many other songs suggest a similar environment. We are so familiar with it from Russian literature that the little glimpses into life on a country estate afforded by these songs can be enriched by a multitude of associations. In Pushkin's *Yevgeny Onegin* (1823–31), Tatyana rushes through the garden, with its flowerbeds, lilac trees, and little bridges, to meet Onegin and rejection; in Goncharov's *The Precipice* (*Obrïv*, 1849–69), Vera gives herself to Mark on the edge of a ravine that is at the end of her garden; the lovers of Fet and Turgenev are immersed in the sensory richness of summer nights in the sprawling parks and hidden pavilions.

Fet's "Secret Night" and other lyric works stand out in the Russian poetry of his time for their almost obsessive focus on nights of love and the tender mornings that follow them. Images of nature or surrounding objects are often eroticized on behalf of the characters: it is the breeze that is hot, and it is the strings of a wide-open grand piano that are trembling, and the "perfumed night" that draws lovers together. Fet knows well how to suggest rather than state bluntly. In his most famous lyric, "Whispering and timid breathings, the trilling of a nightingale," not a single verb appears, so that events must be inferred from sounds and shadows.[12] Music, likewise, is called upon to speak the unspoken. Turgenev's novels contain some extraordinary descriptions of music representing love. In *A Nest of the Gentry* (*Dvoryanskoye gnezdo*, 1859), the love affair in the central story comes to a bitter conclusion before it has had a chance to flourish, and in place of its consummation is music: "A sweet, passionate melody gripped the heart from the very first note; it was wholly radiant, achingly inspired in its joy and beauty, and it grew, then melted away; it touched everything that is precious, secret, and sacred on this earth; it breathed with an immortal sadness and went off to die in the heavens."[13]

Rachmaninoff was drawn to several of Turgenev's works for potential opera plots, although nothing ever came of them.[14] One of these was Turgenev's brief tale, *The Song of Triumphant Love* (*Pesn' torzhestvuyushchey lyubvi*, 1881), set in Ceylon. The story featured a fatal passion ignited by music: "A passionate melody began to flow from under the bow, coiling like a snake, enveloping the body of the violin with its skin; the melody glowed and burned with such fire and triumphant joy that terror entered the hearts of Fabio and Valeria, and tears welled up in their eyes."[15] This "song of happy, satisfied love" would have been at the center of any opera based on the story. Several Rachmaninoff melodies could have served this purpose very well, such as the climactic theme in the finale of the Second Piano Concerto, which even includes the requisite touch of exoticism.

Turgenev and Fet, however, belonged to an earlier generation, and Rachmaninoff's career did not take off until after their deaths (in 1883 and 1892 respectively). When Rachmaninoff found a distinctive voice in "Secret Night," a new era in Russian literary eros had been inaugurated by Tolstoy's novella *The Kreutzer Sonata* (*Kreytserova sonata*, published in 1890), which circulated illegally after the manuscript fell foul of the censor.[16] The novella was the author's response to the "woman question": the idea came to him after he received a letter from a woman who felt oppressed by the sexual demands of men.[17] It portrays male sexuality purely in terms of swinish excess and effectively advocates for complete sexual abstinence (even if it means the end of the human race). *The Kreutzer Sonata* caused a great stir and inspired many literary responses rejecting Tolstoy's extreme position—two of the contributions even came from Tolstoy's own family circle, namely from his wife, Sofya, and his son Lev.[18] But although no one adopted Tolstoy's position, many followed him by engaging in a more frank and explicit discussion of sexual relations.

Part of the response came in the form of women's literature, which presented first-person accounts of female sexuality for the first time in Russian literature. The most iconic figure in this respect was the poet Mirra Lokhvitskaya, who achieved great popularity in the second half of the 1890s, while at the same time commanding respect from her male peers and literary critics. Her poetry was erotic and often ecstatic, as suggested by lines such as "You have been caressing me for so long, you coiled snake" and "Together at last, we are happy like gods."[19] She paved the way for many other female poets over the following decade, and by 1909, the poet and critic Innokenty Annensky was able to declare:

> Lyric poetry has become so individual and so remote from the commonplace that it now needs women's musicalities. Perhaps she will even reveal new lyric horizons to us, this woman, who is no longer a mute idol but a comrade in our shared, free, and endlessly variegated work on Russian lyric poetry.[20]

Rachmaninoff was a pioneer among Russian composers in setting the new women's poetry to music, and much of his reputation as a songwriter stems from these lyrics. He began even before Lokhvitskaya's fame, in 1894, taking up a poem by Mariya Davydova, "Ya zhdu tebya" (I'll Wait for You), Op. 14, No. 1.[21] The principal melodic phrase "ya zhdu tebya" is a variation on his phrase for "lyublyu tebya" ("I love you") in his earlier song "Morning," but the harmonic underpinning gives the phrase a very different effect in each case. In "Morning," the poem starts with the declaration of love, which Rachmaninoff underlays with a pre-cadential progression (VII of V–V$^6_4$) and the rest of the song repeatedly brings harmonic closure. In "I'll Wait for You," the melodic phrase is heard over a Rachmaninoff trademark: a modified plagal cadence (II inflected by modal mixture going to I). This may seem more conclusive than its counterpart in "Morning," but Rachmaninoff is using a different harmonic palette here, and relative to the scheme of the song, the modified plagal cadences repeatedly express doubt, until certainty finally comes when the phrase achieves its jubilant consummation in a climactic perfect cadence. The vocal rendering of the climax, which lifts the initial melodic phrase up by an octave (peaking on a high B♭), is already quite extravagant, but where words are no longer necessary, the pianist continues, raising the dynamic level further, from *ff* to *fff*. In this song, Rachmaninoff ends at the crest of the wave because the text demands it. And in contrast to "Secret Night," it is the urgency of a specifically *female* desire that is being presented here with such powerful affirmation.

It was women's poetry that led Rachmaninoff to the discovery of another of his trademark devices: the quiet climax. In "Zdes' khorosho" (Here It's So Fine), Op. 21, No. 7, written to words by Galina Galina,[22] Rachmaninoff subverts the erotic expectations that he himself had set. The title, and the beginning of the poem suggest another tryst, the speaker addressing her companion in search of a pleasant spot where they can sit down together, and the music, gathering momentum, creates a sense of expectation. But the poem takes a surprising turn: "There are no people here, only God, me, the flowers, an old pine tree, and you, my dream!" There was a crescendo, but it is reversed by a diminuendo so that the apex of the vocal line, a high B on the word "you," is sung *pianissimo*. The poignancy of this reversal is acute, and since the physical phenomenon of goosebumps was mentioned earlier in this essay, this turn in the song is a "goosebumps moment" if anything is.[23] Harmonically, it is marked by an interrupted cadence (or fleeting modulation to the key of VI), a change of direction that is rectified in the piano postlude. Here we find ourselves face-to-face with Rachmaninoff's perfect ambiguities, couched between the sensual and the spiritual, between reality and dreams.

Another example of this is "Siren'" (Lilacs), Op. 21, No. 5, a setting of a poem by Yekaterina Beketova.[24] Here, the melody's pentatonic profile lends the music an innocent, pastoral mood, but the climactic point elicits a frisson at the words "my poor happiness," as the arrival of the harmony on an expected V_4^6 is suddenly inflected by a chromatic appoggiatura (a flattened sixth degree of the scale). This moment of pain is fleeting, and the vocal line returns to its pentatonicism, as if the listener has become party to a secret hidden among the lush lilac blooms. Beketova's protagonist seems to relish her secret dream in plain view, and Rachmaninoff lends her his sensitive support.

To round up this survey of "women's musicalities" projected by Rachmaninoff, let us look at one of his later songs, "Dissonans" (The Dissonance), Op. 34, No. 13. Yakov Polonsky's poem is a free translation from Ada Christen, an Austrian poet who was one of the first to explore female sexuality (in the 1870s), bringing her both success and notoriety. This long and elaborate song has a complex erotic plot: the female protagonist fantasizes about her former beloved while in the arms of her current partner, whom she does not love. A powerful climax is reached within that fantasy space (an E-major triad with a high B in the voice), but instead of harmonic resolution, it creates "the dissonance" of the title, because this E major is a $\flat$II chord in the main key of E-flat minor, which is about to return with a vengeance. This song relates a specifically female experience, and a reversal of the sexes would not work here (at any time before the past half-century).

Such attempts to place female desire on a par with male desire had an element of failure built in, and emphasized the chasm between the sexes in Russian society of the time. A case in point is the novel *Sanin* by Mikhaíl Artsybashev (1907), which became a scandal to rival *The Kreutzer Sonata*.[25] Its protagonist Vladimir Sanin, who lives by the sole principle of following his own desire, seems to suffer no ill consequences. His sister Lida tries to do the same, until she finds that she is pregnant, and believes that she must choose between suicide and an unwanted marriage. Anastasiya Verbitskaya created her own Lida-type character in her novel *Keys to Happiness* (*Klyuchi schast'ya*, 1909), featuring the passionate and many-talented protagonist Manya Yeltsova, who declares, "You, men, have taken the keys to happiness. Long ago you found a simple solution to the problem that preoccupies us women. But just you wait... We will get our hands on them too!"[26] Manya boldly goes from one liaison to another, and sometimes back again; she accepts the challenges of single motherhood and seeks financial independence by becoming a dancer in the mold of Isadora Duncan. The story is in a continuous state of agitation, and its length threatens to exhaust the reader (there are six volumes). Finally, as if unable to draw any ending organically from all the foregoing events, Verbitskaya simply shuts down the enterprise by having Manya commit suicide.

Placing Rachmaninoff's work in this literary milieu allows us better to appreciate one of his most unusual songs, "Vchera mï vstretilis'" (When Yesterday We Met), Op. 26, No. 13. Polonsky's poem, although written back in 1844, sounds strikingly modern in its casual, almost conversational verses: "When yesterday we met, she stopped, / and I did too, we looked in each other's eyes. / My God, she is so changed." Rachmaninoff matches this with declamation rather than melody, with piano accompaniment that is sparse rather than flowing. The backstory to this encounter is missing from the poem, and must be supplied by the reader's imagination. The scene could be described along the following lines: the protagonist meets his former love, but the fire in her eyes is gone, and her cheeks are pallid. He bids farewell to this "fallen yet sweet creature," a formulation so potent that it inspired another writer to use the phrase as the title for his own novella.[27] Within what seems to be an urban setting, we sense a young life brought low by sexual adventure, poverty, and disease. There is nothing the woman can now do to extricate herself from the situation, but even so, she rejects the protagonist's pity and his belated apology (as we guess in our attempts to flesh out the scenario). Death haunts the piano postlude through a hint of the Dies irae.

Such a plot brings to mind the neorealist novels of Aleksandr Kuprin and Leonid Andreyev, who went far beyond Tolstoy's *Kreutzer Sonata* in exploring the dark aspects of desire and its grim repercussions. Kuprin's novel *The Pit* (*Yama*; Part 1 came out in 1909) was set in several brothels, and became the first literary work to address in any depth the subject of prostitution in Russia. *The Pit* was received with a wave of indignation and outrage (even Tolstoy thought it had gone too far), but it threw light on the underworld that drew in a far from negligible section of the Russian populace. Its omission from previous treatments of relationships between the sexes gave a skewed picture of the reality. Leonid Andreyev's novella *In the Fog* (*V tumane*, 1902) was already notorious for similar reasons: the plot centers around a student who has contracted syphilis; removed physically and mentally from respectable society, he ends up killing a prostitute.

After the Bolshevik Revolution, this cohort of popular writers—Andreyev, Kuprin, Artsybashev, Verbitskaya, Lokhvitskaya, and others—were written out of the literary canon. Their work was a decadent part of the old society that was to be cut out, not encouraged, in the view of the regime and the new revolutionary writers. More surprisingly, Russian émigré culture was equally hostile to them. As Otto Boele writes in his monograph on *Sanin*: "The myth of the Silver Age, as it was created in memoirs, essays and (auto-)biographies, was purged of names and works that contradicted the perceived essence of that period."[28] All the works were bestsellers and their authors were trendsetters; even when banned, their writings still enjoyed a wide illegal circulation. But after the Revolution, they were remembered, if at all, as a grubby backdrop to the glittering elite culture of the Silver Age: Blok, Bryusov, Balmont, Akhmatova, Tsvetayeva.[29] Those Symbolists, Acmeists, and other -ists were stylistic pioneers who prided themselves on obscurity and abstraction, in contrast to the stylistically conservative prose and poetry of the others. The new licentiousness was, however, common to both strands, as Laura Engelstein puts it: "The prevalence of erotic themes in the writing of both schools tended to obscure their philosophical and aesthetic differences and to create confusion between the domain of high-minded cultural production and the disreputable commercial practices of the boulevard."[30] Erotic preoccupations, then, bound the two cultural strata together, even though we separate them out today as "highbrow" and "middlebrow" literature.

In Defense of the Human

In music, I would claim, these two strata of highbrow and middlebrow were visible too, with their chief representatives in Scriabin and Rachmaninoff. This becomes abundantly clear from one of the richest contemporary treatments of the Russian musical world during this period, namely, Marietta Shaginyan's "musical-psychological etude" of Rachmaninoff.[31] Shaginyan was herself a poet, aligned with the Symbolists, but at the same time, she was an ardent fan of Rachmaninoff's, and even an aspiring muse. This deep personal involvement makes her account biased, but it also endows her with insights available to very few others. In the whole of Shaginyan's lengthy essay, Scriabin is mentioned only twice by name, but he acts as a foil for Rachmaninoff, an opposition essential to the understanding of both.

Shaginyan's angle is that Rachmaninoff's music represents the "ordinary"—it is even "self-consciously ordinary." In her eyes, it resists the bracing novelties of the prevailing trend, which revolves around the "cosmic," "superhuman," and "supernatural": "'No, I am not with you, I want to be human. I don't want to lose the human element'—this is what Rachmaninoff's music stubbornly tells us, again and again, resisting the chaotic world that rages around it."[32] While Scriabin and some dubious unnamed followers (in 1912 there was no band of Scriabinist composers) lead music toward depersonalization, fragmentation, decadence, and degradation, Rachmaninoff (and Medtner, she adds) are faced with a desperate struggle not just for music, but for the preservation of the individual and personal dimensions of art. Shaginyan even speaks presciently about an emerging trend of "dehumanization," using the word that Ortega y Gasset, a decade later, established as a defining characteristic of modernist art (although what Shaginyan condemned, he praised).[33]

Shaginyan argues that Rachmaninoff can even humanize material that seems purely Symbolist, showing how he takes Arnold Böcklin's celebrated canvas, *The Isle of the Dead*, and psychologizes it, passing through grief to gradual acceptance. Then, Shaginyan makes an admission that is of great importance for our discussion of Rachmaninoff's song texts: "Even the most negligible of verses, such as those of by Galina and Rathaus, for example . . . find a thoughtful and subtle response in his music, because they express an unadulterated 'humanity.'"[34] This public statement is particularly surprising because Shaginyan told Rachmaninoff in their private correspondence that she thought his choice of poetry was poor. We know of this through Rachmaninoff's gently teasing reply (Shaginyan, in the early stages of their correspondence, was still using the pseudonym "Re," as in the scale note "D"):

> First, a few words on your lack of fairness, for in your last letter, dear Re, you sometimes do me an injustice. Here are a few examples. After giving the most ruthless account of Galina's "doggerel," you note (with a little malice), that I myself have used this doggerel "willingly." I used it, actually, in just two or three cases out of a total of fifty-one [songs]. . . . And elsewhere, you warn me not to seek after the "tawdry success of the music hall" for my romances! This is still worse! Is there any need to say such things to me, dear Re?[35]

In Shaginyan's letter, she had warned Rachmaninoff that his adoption of middlebrow poetry could give him the public image of a merely middlebrow composer, who could only achieve a "tawdry success" ("middlebrow" is our word, not Shaginyan's). Perhaps, in her published article for the public, she had reconciled herself to Rachmaninoff's use of such poetry, or perhaps she is simply unwilling to say anything negative about the composer, and tries to put the matter in the best possible light.

Whatever the case might be, Shaginyan's misgivings in her letter had been voiced more stridently by Vyacheslav Karatygin a year earlier:

> It is that extraordinary openness in his musical personality, his tendency to bare his artistic soul completely before his audience (I almost said "his shamelessness"), the high temperature of his musical emotionalism—together, these explain the fondness of the widest musical circles for Rachmaninoff's music. . . .
>
> He has undoubtedly mastered the art of rapidly winning over human hearts *en masse*: this overt "passion," the crude "cordiality" of his music, the perpetual "heart on sleeve" manner, the composer's constant and self-assured presumptuousness in offering us a rich collection of the most obvious musical truisms under the cover of pianistic or orchestral ornamentation (delightfully assembled, but highly superficial); all the bombastic heat and ardor of Rachmaninoff's "buildups" in the manner of a diluted Tchaikovsky— the more "sincerity" and "soul" we sense at every turn of Rachmaninoff's musical thinking, the more fake, trite, and cheap it appears to me.[36]

Karatygin, it should be said, was *parti pris*: he was pursuing a modernist agenda, and in his zeal, he presented Scriabin's (later) music as genuinely "sincere and unaffected" in contrast to Rachmaninoff's, presumably because novelty, to his mind, guaranteed authenticity.

Karatygin was only the tip of the iceberg. Hostility toward Rachmaninoff was rife in several influential circles, including the leading composers of St. Petersburg, although the nature and strength of their complaints must be gleaned from private remarks. At the Rimsky-Korsakovs' soirées, at which Rachmaninoff's songs or piano pieces were occasionally programmed, they generally agreed that he was "seriously overrated."[37] Once, after listening to some songs by Maximilian Steinberg (his pupil and son-in-law), Rimsky-Korsakov described them as "subtle, graceful, and at the same time, novel," and then added, "Yes, this is not Rachmaninoff," with the implication that Rachmaninoff's songs were quite the opposite.[38] Anatoly Lyadov agreed that Rachmaninoff lacked "grace," which this circle regarded as an important quality for Russian music. He went further, claiming that Rachmaninoff was worth "almost nothing," that he was an "enfeebled Tchaikovsky," and that his fame as a composer stemmed from his talents as a conductor and pianist, helped by Siloti's promotional work.[39] Alexandre Benois, another St. Petersburg artist (and associate of Diaghilev), tried to shame Fyodor Chaliapin simply for taking a role in *Aleko*, Rachmaninoff's early opera. Benois considered that opera to be "an unacceptable vulgarity."[40] Against this very negative judgment, there were sporadic exceptions, such as Rimsky-Korsakov's admiration for the final page of "Lilacs" (singled out above for its quiet climax).

Shaginyan noted in her article that Rachmaninoff's music seemed to trigger a physiological dislike among some listeners: "as if someone had stepped on their toe, or something had hit a nerve," or even as if they had been "dealt a personal insult."[41] The same circles expressed a similarly visceral hostility toward middlebrow literature. Rimsky-Korsakov was nauseated by a novella by Andreyev that consisted of "stink, dirt, and nothing else,"[42] and Tolstoy resented Andreyev's "manipulations," which routinely overstepped the mark.[43] One female member of the public was reported as feeling as if she had ingested some "disgusting and bitter poison" after reading Artsybashev's *Sanin*, although tellingly, she acknowledged that it expressed a "horrible truth" that she did not want to confront.[44] Karatygin, as late as 1923, still insisted that Tchaikovsky's and Rachmaninoff's songs made him "seasick, to put it mildly."[45]

Pierre Bourdieu has commented on such "physiological" expressions of taste: "Tastes . . . are perhaps first and foremost distastes, disgust provoked by horror or visceral intolerance ('sick-making') of the tastes of others."[46] While the dismissals of Rimsky-Korsakov and Lyadov used milder terms than Karatygin, all three spoke as cultural gatekeepers. Bourdieu again: "The most intolerable thing for those who regard themselves as the possessors of legitimate culture is the sacrilegious reuniting of tastes which taste dictates shall be separated."[47] Rachmaninoff's critics rejected his music because it threatened to import middlebrow tastes into the citadels of high culture.

Shaginyan, of course, could not discuss Rachmaninoff's middlebrow tendencies with complete frankness, not least because she herself felt ambivalent. So when she posed the question "What is it that they hate in Rachmaninoff?" she preferred to answer in more elevated terms. She suggests that because Rachmaninoff resists the trend toward depersonalization and dehumanization, he does not offer any escape route into a kind of cosmic chaos that makes no human demands. This refusal to be escapist, she says, makes some listeners uncomfortable, and they express this in terms of disgust. Through either intimacy or tragedy, his music brings listeners back to the human level and makes them face their own human limitations. Shaginyan is, of course, volunteering herself as a public relations agent for Rachmaninoff, and her argument is tendentious, but it is still possible to find some substance to her contention. So, often in his music a climax is reached, but instead of closure, the phrase continues at length, as in life, where after some startling moment that allows us to soar above routine, we still have to live on at a more mundane level. In Scriabin, by contrast, the great climax is some moment of ultimate transcendence beyond which there is nothing: the *Poem of Ecstasy* and *Prometheus* both end at that moment, while the Seventh Sonata, after the great dissonant chord of the climax, continues for another half-minute, but only in exhausted whimpers. Rachmaninoff, indeed, pours much of his ingenuity into fashioning the descent from the climax so that it convinces and even has its own kind of lingering nostalgic beauty.

Popularity, Stylistic and Personal

Three decades later, Sergei Prokofiev had occasion to reflect on the contest between popularity and prestige in a letter to his friend Vladimir Dukelsky, who had emigrated to the United States and found fame as a composer of popular songs under the name Vernon Duke. Dukelsky had composed art music while he was still in Russia, and Prokofiev disapproved of his new career in popular music, warning his friend that he might eventually be unable to cross back from the popular to the serious.

Dukelsky's only recent concert music was a meager harvest of piano pieces that Prokofiev found "rather dry":

> Russian music already offers a precedent, oddly enough, in the case of Rachmaninoff. He, too, was three times more talented than those around him, but although he never debased himself by writing cancans, he *did* loosen up, and allowed some over-the-top songs to spill out. When musical circles registered their disapproval, he tried to adopt a serious expression, and started to produce works of such aridity that he quickly lost his reputation in this area [i.e., in serious music] and instead retains his reputation as a composer of "songs for the wider public."[48]

Prokofiev's views on this subject are intriguing. In the 1910s, he was the only young modernist to admire Rachmaninoff (or who would admit to it), and he even came under the older composer's influence, particularly in *Five Poems of Anna Akhmatova*, Op. 27, inspired by Rachmaninoff's Opus 38.[49] In the wake of the Revolution, he and Rachmaninoff were both in the United States, competing for limited public attention as Russian émigré pianists, and it was only in the midst of this rivalry that Prokofiev's former enthusiasm waned. The letter to Dukelsky demonstrates that Prokofiev had added himself to the elite consensus that Rachmaninoff was a middlebrow composer. Although the term "middlebrow" was not yet in circulation, Prokofiev meant precisely this: he rules out the possibility that Rachmaninoff is lowbrow when he writes "although he did not debase himself by writing cancans." Elsewhere in the same letter, Prokofiev tells Dukelsky that he is a "prostitute" for writing popular songs (which are actually well crafted and distinctive), so the implication is that Dukelsky had sunk much further than Rachmaninoff—to the level of "cancans."

Here, Prokofiev is rehearsing the myth that Rachmaninoff had found himself the victim of his own popularity, and tried in vain to swim against the current. He suffered (allegedly) under the burden of fame and resented the pressures his adoring fans imposed on him. I would like to correct this image, with clear evidence that he embraced various popular styles throughout his career, and that he actually drew sustenance and inspiration from his fans.

We may begin with his passion for Gypsy songs,[50] and his period of immersion into the culture of Roma performance in the early 1890s, when he struck up a friendship with the famous Gypsy singer Nadezhda Aleksandrova. During these years, he also had an affair with this singer's sister, Anna Lodyzhenskaya, who was married to Pyotr Lodyzhensky, a leading composer in the "cruel romance" genre (where betrayal in love always led to a sorry end). This genre was the backbone of the Gypsy repertoire, and Rachmaninoff decided to contribute a song of his own to the repertoire. The result was "O net, molyu, ne ukhodi" (Oh No, I Beg You, Do Not Leave), Op. 4, No. 1, dedicated to Lodyzhenskaya, with a text by Dmitry Merezhkovsky that has a classic "cruel" ring and some rather routine rhyming (*blednïy*/pale – *bednïy*/wretched): "I've come to you again, I am sick, exhausted and pale, look at how weak and wretched I am, how I need your love."[51] Although elements of the "cruel romance" can easily be detected by anyone familiar with the genre, Rachmaninoff's setting contains clear signs of a more accomplished artistry, which disturbs the regular phrasing and introduces more unusual modulations.

From the same period comes Rachmaninoff's *Capriccio on Gypsy Themes*, Op. 12, which at first seems to be another of those exquisitely crafted Russian pieces designed to elevate folk themes into the realm of art music through their ingenious harmonies, orchestral development, and other sophisticated devices. Now, it is one thing for a Russian composer to write, say, a piece evoking a distant and exotic Spain, and quite another to write a piece evoking the all-too familiar sounds of drunken revelries at local brothels. Rachmaninoff's choice of Gypsy themes threatened to drag the piece down into the lowbrow category, and as if he decided to make the best of this, the composer gives full vent to the spirit of abandon typical of cruel romances (take, for example, the characteristic interrupted cadence at six measures after rehearsal number 11, marked *ffff*). The piece prompted one critic to grumble that Rachmaninoff had allowed a certain "licentiousness" to creep into his music.[52]

Karatygin, as we saw above, complained that Rachmaninoff's emotional world was "crude," "trite," and "fake." In the light of the *Capriccio*, we can understand better when, in a 1923 article, Karatygin takes particular offense at Rachmaninoff's "almost Gypsy phrases . . . the syncopations, rests, and dynamics that damage the smooth contours of the melody in favor of Gypsy affectation and hysteria."[53] If the popular Gypsy style was confined to the *Capriccio*, we could say that Karatygin's criticisms were unjustly selective, but the style also seeps into the songs, and it did not stop there, either. Rachmaninoff acknowledged Gypsy song as an inalienable part of the Russian urban soundscape, adopted it as material and entered, to some extent, into its aesthetic. Scriabin, by contrast, cultivated a language that was ever more abstract and demanding. Karatygin believed that these two aesthetics could not coexist, and as a partisan of Scriabin, he had to reject Rachmaninoff.

Jumping ahead three decades, we find that Rachmaninoff, in exile, maintained his enthusiasm for the popular music of his homeland. In 1926, while living in the United States, Rachmaninoff made a recording of the song "Belilitsï, rumyanitsï" (Powder and Paint) with Nadezhda Plevitskaya (1884–1940). He composed a piano accompaniment especially for the occasion. Plevitskaya was ethnically Russian, but before the Revolution she had associated with the Roma singers Rachmaninoff so admired, and this particular song featured prominently in her repertoire. She first came to public attention as a resident singer at the celebrated Yar restaurant in Moscow, and later rose to international fame. When Rachmaninoff heard that she was on tour in the United States, he sought her out, and they made their recording of Plevitskaya's "Belilitsï" simply for their own pleasure (although it later came into the public domain). The lyrics present a dark tale: a woman whose husband believes that she is having an affair awaits his homecoming with trepidation. It is once again a powerful statement of female erotic agency, and it also harks back to Zemfira's song from Rachmaninoff's Gypsy opera *Aleko*, where a woman asserts her choice to love whomever she wishes even in the face of death. The story in "Belilitsï" is rather elliptical: we are not told whether the narrator is guilty or innocent, nor how severely she will be punished, but much can be inferred from Plevitskaya's rich inflections. The little frissons in her voice, the off-pitch whoops and off-beat stresses all received a sympathetic response in Rachmaninoff's playing. The liveliness of the voice is mixed with darkness (again, the clash that is ideal for producing goosebumps), while Rachmaninoff's accompaniment hints at the heroine's fears by incorporating the Dies irae.

Let's say, though, that Plevitskaya is not your cup of tea, as was the case with Vladimir Nabokov, who heard her and placed this description in his short story, "The Assistant Producer":

> Style: one-tenth *tzigane*, one-seventh Russian peasant girl (she had been that herself originally), and five-ninths popular —and by popular I mean a hodgepodge of artificial folklore, military melodrama, and official patriotism. The fraction left unfilled seems sufficient to represent the physical splendor of her prodigious voice.[54]

This is penetrating, and although not friendly, it concedes that Plevitskaya has a fine voice. But Nabokov was only warming to the task, and he continues in a withering vein:

> Her artistic taste was nowhere, her technique haphazard, her general style atrocious; but the kind of people for whom music and sentiment are one, or who like songs to be mediums for the spirits of circumstances under which they had been first apprehended in an individual past, gratefully found in the tremendous sonorities of her voice both a nostalgic solace and a patriotic kick. She was considered especially effective when a strain of wild recklessness rang through her song. Had this abandon been less blatantly shammed it might still have saved her from utter vulgarity. The small, hard thing that was her soul stuck out of her song, and the most her temperament could attain was but an eddy, not a free torrent. When nowadays in some Russian household the gramophone is put on, and I hear her canned contralto, it is with something of a shudder that I recall the meretricious imitation she gave of reaching her vocal climax, the anatomy of her mouth fully displayed in a last passionate cry.[55]

It is worth considering, though, that Nabokov had other reasons to despise Plevitskaya beyond those of performance aesthetics, since he knew that she had been recruited (in 1930) as an agent by Soviet intelli-gence, and he incorporates this into her portrayal in the story. Even so, his disdain for this popular style is stated with sufficient conviction that we have no grounds for doubting his sincerity. Nabokov is also precise in assigning her to what is, in his mind, the correct artistic level: "She was a celebrated singer. Not opera, not even *Cavalleria Rusticana*, not anything like that." Opera in general, for Nabokov, is highbrow, but can descend to middlebrow in "*Cavalleria Rusticana* [or] anything like that."[56] Plevitskaya, however, is a further level down—she is lowbrow.

Rachmaninoff's meeting with Plevitskaya inspired him, that same year, to compose his *Three Russian Songs* for choir and orchestra, in which "Belilitsï" serves as the grim finale. Many deft touches in the orchestra-tion seem designed to evoke Plevitskaya's "wild" inflections, to make up for the fact that no choir can be expected to reproduce her unique, grat-ing voice. Compared to the voice-and-piano prototype, the later version for choir and orchestra pushes the song up toward the highbrow level, but for all that it gains, it also loses some of its former power.

Many other episodes in Rachmaninoff's career tell of his genuine affin-ity for more popular art. Take the *Italian Polka* (ca. 1906). It was based on a tune he heard on the mechanical pianos carted around by street musicians in Italy, and in itself, is not dissimilar to Tchaikovsky's "Pimpinella," based on a song he had transcribed during his sojourn in Florence. But when his nephew Sergei Siloti (the dedicatee) asked Rachmaninoff to give his per-mission for a military band arrangement, Rachmaninoff not only assented, but entered fully into the spirit of the enterprise, and spiced up the band-leader's (perhaps over-respectful) arrangement with extra fanfare figures in the trumpets.[57] On another occasion, the bandleader Paul Whiteman made an arrangement of the C-sharp Minor Prelude for his jazz orchestra; Rachmaninoff was an enthusiast of Whiteman's work and took no offense at this tribute. He called it "authentic American music" and bought each new Whiteman recording to send to his daughter in Europe.[58]

He showed a similar attitude with a more solidly highbrow work, namely his own *Rhapsody on a Theme of Paganini*. Although it was an ostensibly non-programmatic concert piece, he pressed Fokine to turn it into a ballet, even offering a detailed scenario of his own devising.[59] This is in stark contrast to events two decades earlier, when Rimsky-Korsakov's widow went to court in order to protect the artistic integrity of *Scheherazade*, because Diaghilev, in her opinion, had distorted and vulgar-ized the piece in his ballet production. Yet Rachmaninoff acted as his own Diaghilev in pursuing the project of turning his own, more demanding concert piece into just such a "distorted and vulgar" ballet.

Rachmaninoff, of course, had his own cachet as a much-admired performer with a commanding stage presence, both as a pianist and conductor. He had an advantage over most composers: his stage presence could impart an extra sheen to his own compositions, and he was able to promote his music until it equaled and even overtook his popularity as a performer. Rachmaninoff's respectable reception history consists of all the positive reviews by highbrow critics, but there were also the legions of adoring female fans, screaming for an encore (the C-sharp Minor Prelude, of course), and mobbing the pianist outside the concert hall. His music duly absorbed all these erotic projections, in addition to the erotic elements already present (the American fans were generally unaware of his earlier songs).

On stage, Rachmaninoff, "the six-and-a-half-foot scowl" looked forbidding, but this belied his readiness to please his public.[60] "Rachmaninoff ingratiates himself with the crowd," grumbled Prokofiev, referring to the programming, where lollipops were doled out after serious fare (although Prokofiev himself, looking for a slice of Rachmaninoff's success, programmed his ever-popular G-minor Prelude). Whatever misgivings Rachmaninoff had over the popularity of his early C-sharp Minor Prelude, he was always ready to indulge his audience when the piece was demanded as an encore. As a composer, too, he was nourished by praise and adoration, and sometimes profited artistically from the feedback loop with his admirers. When the mysterious "Re" began writing to him (she revealed herself only later as Shaginyan), she elicited confidences from him, both artistic and human, and once he knew who she was, he drew upon her poetic expertise to procure texts for his Opus 38. (He remained politely silent, however, about her psychological portrait of him.) It is no secret that the idea for *The Bells* came from another female admirer.[61]

I have built up this picture, much of it familiar, to show that Rachmaninoff was not merely content to accept his popularity, but indulged it and benefited from it. This was quite the opposite of Scriabin's cultivation of his hermetic and mysterious image, which eventually became a kind of messianism. Rachmaninoff, instead, found himself at the center of an emerging middle-class fan culture that sought emotional fulfillment from celebrity artists.[62] The communicative power of his music was supported by his genuine immersion in middlebrow literary culture, and this enabled him to win over swathes of the (largely female) readership of such novels and poetry.

In the period considered here, the terms "lowbrow" and "highbrow" had not yet appeared, and "middlebrow" was a still later arrival. But even in the absence of the labels, the behavioral patterns were already established. A mass audience for culture had only recently emerged in Russia (some decades after that happened in Western and Central Europe), but it was already treated with disdain by the gatekeepers of high art. Boris Asafyev commented critically on this elite behavior as early as 1917, long before it could earn him credibility with the Bolshevik regime: "The trouble is, of course, that Rachmaninoff is loved by the public. But isn't it time to abandon this hypocrisy, i.e. that the public is nothing but an empty space and that composers don't need it?"[63] After the Revolution, when Rachmaninoff moved to the United States, his new audience was an order of magnitude larger than his following in Russia, and this was made possible through the highly developed entertainment industry. Theodor Adorno, of course, was not to be found in Rachmaninoff's fan base, but he commented on the composer as a product of the entertainment industry that he condemned. Adorno gives an account of the Prelude in C-sharp Minor as an example of "commodity music."[64] The piece, he says, is a "colossal bagatelle," that is, musically negligible for all its grand gestures, and he explains its success through its ability to fire up delusions of grandeur among amateur performers, since the piece can create a great impression even though its technical demands are quite modest. Both performers and listeners are, accordingly, "infantilized" by the experience.

Adorno was contributing here to the "battle of the brows" that first thrived in the Anglophone press during the 1920s and '30s. Rachmaninoff actually received the most scathing verdicts from American and British critics. The Fourth Piano Concerto was described as a variety of "super-salon music," which "Mme. Cécile Chaminade might safely have perpetrated . . . on her third glass of vodka."[65] The *Rhapsody on a Theme of Paganini* "isn't philosophical, significant, or even artistic. It's something for audiences," wrote the *New Yorker*, before condescending to a pat on the back: "More music for audiences means more audiences for music," implying that listeners attracted by some Rachmaninoff in the program will also have the chance to hear some "real music."[66] John Culshaw, a British classical record producer who worked for Decca and the BBC, noted in 1946 that "it proved highly undesirable even to mention the name of Rachmaninov in London musical circles . . . impossible to suggest that such works might contain a grain of musical merit."[67] The year 1946 is significant, since audiences of the time had just seen *Brief Encounter* and heard the young Frank Sinatra sing "Full Moon and Empty Arms" (based on the Second Piano Concerto).

It seemed at that time that Rachmaninoff would forever belong to popular culture. This led to the notorious prediction, in the 1954 edition of *Grove's Dictionary of Music and Musicians*, that Rachmaninoff's popular success would surely turn out to be a mere passing fad (the writer of the Rachmaninoff entry was Eric Blom). From a highbrow perspective, the popular is by nature ephemeral, and it follows from this that popular art cannot possibly pass the test of time, since this is a characteristic of high art alone, or so the argument goes. As Peter Franklin states, Western musicology "subsumed [Rachmaninoff] within the officially marginalized and critically repressed Other of twentieth-century European music," that is, "film music."[68]

In the Soviet Union, during the 1930s, Rachmaninoff was not fully accepted, and for a short time, his music was even banned. In the 1940s, once Soviet musicologists were finally allowed to embrace him and add him to the Pantheon of great Russian composers, they treated him with full seriousness, and showed none of the condescension or disdain of their Western counterparts. Even then, the middlebrow problem reemerged: though the music was worthy of high praise, the poetry of the songs was not; the excellence of the songs was a result of the music overcoming the lyrics, whereas we have seen that Rachmaninoff ingeniously shaped even the grammar of his music to the texts.[69] This is the consensus when it comes to the middlebrow female poets, but even the more highly regarded Fet, the poet of "Secret Night," was thought to have benefited from Rachmaninoff's treatment, which enhances the emotional contrasts of the poem.[70] When Soviet scholars looked for writers who were worthy counterparts of Rachmaninoff, they usually mentioned Chekhov and Bunin (who had also become part of the Soviet canon). On one occasion, musicologist Yury Keldysh drew an unusual and fascinating parallel between Rachmaninoff and Andreyev, comparing Rachmaninoff's song "Vesenniye vodï" (Spring Waters), Op. 14, No. 11 (1896) and his cantata *Spring* (1902) to Andreyev's novellas *Spring* and *Spring Promises* (written in 1902 and 1903).

The discussion of Rachmaninoff's erotic settings within the prudish culture of high Stalinism resulted in descriptions most notable for their effortful euphemisms. Old-fashioned poetic words like *istoma* (languor) and *upoyeniye* (rapture) stand next to vague references to *polnokroviye* (full-bloodedness) and *radost' zhizni* (joy of life).[71] Vital fluids course through the metaphors in Keldysh's effusive description of the central climax in the slow movement of the Second Piano Concerto.[72] In the description of the E-flat Major Prelude, Op. 23, No. 6, Vera Bryantseva finds that the "shade of sweet oriental bliss" (*nega*) is mitigated by a "chaste purity and tenderness."[73] These authors often associate Rachmaninoff's sensuality with Borodin's Orientalism, and there is some justification for this, but the link is often overstated in an attempt to keep this sensuality at arm's length, so that Russian culture proper can be kept pure and innocent. Sometimes they suppose that the songs' narrators are taking delight in the Russian landscape, and by this means, they explain away the suspicious ubiquity of rapturous emotions. This habit has continued into the post-Soviet period. Thus, Olga Chebotarenko in 2013: "Rachmaninoff's music is dominated by a sensual element, but it is an idealized sentiment, a kind of spiritual phenomenon attained in moments of ecstasy."[74]

It is my contention that studies of the middlebrow, which have been a lively strain of literary studies in the past decade (and most recently in musicology), can shift our perspective on Rachmaninoff so that we need no longer blind ourselves to the "taint" of his popularity, his "bad taste," or his frequent assimilation into popular culture. The mass literature of the Russian Silver Age, all those "novels suffused with sex and suicide" and risqué female verses, provides new and pertinent contexts for considering Rachmaninoff's music and its first audiences.[75] A neutral application of middlebrow allows scholarly discourse to pass beyond the old dichotomy of either condemning or denying the "embarrassing" characteristics of Rachmaninoff's music: non-modernist, feminized, accessible, entertaining, enjoyable, visceral, emotional.[76] All these qualities are now available to become new focal points of study. This is not to say that all of Rachmaninoff's music is middlebrow; some works, like the First Symphony or the Piano Sonatas, are resolutely highbrow. But much of his oeuvre would undoubtedly benefit from being viewed through the lens of the middlebrow. We can then appreciate more readily the aptness of popular adaptations such as the score of *Brief Encounter*, in which the Second Concerto gives voice to a socially constrained female protagonist.[77] In the pivotal scene, the Rachmaninoff extract is positioned so that the climactic point of the music coincides exactly with the moment of the kiss. And, no less important, we can accord Rachmaninoff's audiences of the past and present the respect they deserve and finally agree that their persistent love for this music is not cause for sneering.

NOTES

1. *France musique*, 28 July 2015, https://www.francemusique.fr/musique-classique/quand-la-musique-procure-des-orgasmes-1416.

2. Luke Harrison and Psyche Loui, "Thrills, Chills, Frissons, and Skin Orgasms: Toward an Integrative Model of Transcendent Psychophysiological Experiences in Music," *Frontiers of Psychology* 5/790 (2014).

3. Loui quote, https://www.bbc.com/future/article/20150721-when-was-the-last-time-music-gave-you-a-skin-orgasm.

4. Clip of Lola & Hauser: https://www.youtube.com/watch?v=HtioazvOoRk.

5. Galina Binová, "K probleme 'erotika i literatura' v svete russkoy klassicheskoy traditsii," *Sborník prací filozofické fakulty Brněnské Univerzity, D, Řada literárněvědná* 45 (1996): 99–106.

6. B. Paramonov, "Zapad i Rossiya: analiz protiv sinteza," *Zvezda* 10 (1994), quoted in Galina Binová, *Russkaya literaturnaya erotika: Istoricheskiye i esteticheskiye metamorfozï* (Brno: Masarykova univerzita, 2007), 48.

7. This and further translations are by Jonathan Walker unless otherwise indicated.

8. V. D. Skalon, "Dnevnik (1890 god)," in Z. Apetyan, ed., *Vospominaniya o Rakhmaninove*, 5th ed., 2 vols (Moscow: Muzïka, 1988), 2:431–67.

9. Sergei Bertensson and Jay Leyda, *Sergei Rachmaninoff: A Lifetime in Music* (Bloomington: Indiana University Press, 2001), 26.

10. The Venusberg scene from Wagner's *Tannhäuser* had already become the touchstone of musical eroticism, see Lawrence Dreyfus, *Wagner and the Erotic Impulse* (Cambridge, MA, and London: Harvard University Press, 2010), 88–92.

11. The C-sharp major climax in the slow movement of the Second Piano Concerto seems to be a direct descendant.

12. I am referring to several Fet poems here: "Yeshchyo akatsiya odna" (Yet One More Acacia); "Siyala noch'" (The Night Was Shining); "Blagovonnaya noch'" (Fragrant Night); and "Shyopot, robkoye dïkhan'ye" (Whispering and Timid Breathings).

13. Ivan Turgenev, "Dvoryanskoye gnezdo," in *Polnoye sobraniye sochineniy i pisem*, 2nd ed., 30 vols. (Moscow: Nauka, 1978–), vol. 6 (1981), 5–156, at 106.

14. Bertensson and Leyda, *Sergei Rachmaninoff*, 141.

15. Ivan Turgenev, "Pesn' torzhestvuyushchey lyubvi," in *Polnoye sobraniye sochineniy i pisem*, vol. 10 (1982), 47–66, at 53.

16. The ban was lifted after Tolstoy's wife, Sofya, interceded for the work in an audience with Alexander III.

17. Michael R. Katz, *The Kreutzer Sonata Variations: Lev Tolstoy's Novella and Counterstories by Sofiya Tolstaya and Lev Lvovich Tolstoy* (New Haven and London: Yale University Press, 2014), 319.

18. Ibid. Both were published in this English translation.

19. Lines from "Kol'chatïy zmey" (A Coiled Snake) and "Pesn' torzhestvuyushchey lyubvi" (Song of Triumphant Love).

20. Innokentiy Annenskiy, "O sovremennom lirizme," first published in *Apollon* (1909), reprinted in N. A. Bogomolov, *Kritika russkogo simvolizma*, 2 vols. (Moscow: AST, 2002), 2:333–59, at 336.

21. Mariya Davydova (1863–1943) was also a music critic and the author of several biographies of composers.

22. This was one of several pen names adopted by Glafira Rinks (1870?–1942), née Glafira Nikolayevna Mamoshina. In addition to this song, Rachmaninoff also set her "Kak mne bol'no" (Sorrow in Springtime) and "U moyego okna" (Before My Window) in his set of songs, Opp. 21 and 26.

23. Jerrold Levinson noticed that such physiological reactions occur most frequently when the listener detects a mixture of negative and positive emotions in the music. "Musical Frissons," *Revue française d'études américaines* 86 (2000): 64–76.

24. Yekaterina Krasnova (née Beketova, 1855–92) was a widely published poet, author of children's stories, and translator. Incidentally, she was an aunt to the much better-known Russian poet Aleksandr Blok.

25. *Sanin* was banned several months after its initial serialized publication in the journal *Sovremennïy mir*, and did not resurface until the 1990s. By today's standards, the charge of "pornography" seems overwrought.

26. Anastasiya Verbitskaya, *Klyuchi schast'ya*, 2 vols. (St. Petersburg: Severo-zapad, 1993), 2:20.

27. The novella, by Aleksandr Levitov (1835–1877), *Pogibsheye, no miloye sozdaniye*, is an elaborately realistic filling-out of Polonsky's poem, in which the narrator/protagonist meets a lively and witty woman from his youth who has succumbed to alcoholism and debauchery.

28. Otto Boele, *Erotic Nihilism in Late Imperial Russia: The Case of Mikhail Artsybashev's "Sanin"* (Madison: University of Wisconsin Press, 2009), 7–8.

29. This canonization was first established within Russian émigré culture, but it was later upheld in the Soviet culture of the 1960s "Thaw" and afterward.

30. Laura Engelstein, *The Keys to Happiness: Sex and the Search for Modernity in Fin-de-Siècle Russia* (Ithaca, NY: Cornell University Press, 2018), 12.

31. Marietta Shaginyan, "S. V. Rakhmaninov (muzïkal'no-psikhologicheskiy etyud)," *Trudï i dni* 4–5 (1912): 97–114.

32. Ibid., 104.

33. José Ortega y Gasset, *La deshumanización del arte: Ideas sobre la novela* (1925), translated by Helene Wehl as *Dehumanization of Art and Others Essays on Art, Literature and Culture* (Princeton: Princeton University Press, 1968).

34. Shaginyan, "S. V. Rakhmaninov," 106.

35. Rachmaninoff to Shaginyan, 29 March 1912, in S. Rakhmaninov, *Literaturnoye naslediye*, ed. Z. A. Apetyan, 3 vols. (Moscow: Sovetskiy kompozitor, 1978–80), 2:44.

36. V. Karatïgin, "Kontsertï Kusevitskogo i Ziloti," *Russkaya khudozhestvennaya letopis'* 5 (1911), quoted in A. D. Alekseyev, *Rakhmaninov* (Moscow and Leningrad: Muzgïz, 1954), 140–41.

37. V. V. Yastrebtsev, *Nikolay Andreyevich Rimskiy-Korsakov: Vospominaniya*, 2 vols. (Leningrad: Gosudarstvennoye muzïkal'noye izdatel'stvo, 1960), 2:417, entry for 11 March 1907.

38. Ibid., 2:441, entry for 31 October 1907.

39. Ibid., 2: 497–98, entry for 20 November/3 December 1913.

40. A. N. Benua, *Dnevnik, 1908–1916* (Moscow: Zakharov, 2016), 188, entry for 20 November/3 December 1913.

41. Shaginyan, "S. V. Rakhmaninov," 99.

42. Yastrebtsev, *Nikolay Andreyevich Rimskiy-Korsakov*, entry of 2/15 January 1908, 2:460.

43. As recorded by Tolstoy's secretary Nikolai Gusev on 6 February 1908. N. N. Gusev, *Dva goda s L. N. Tolstïm* (Moscow: Khudozhestvennaya literatura, 1973), 94. Further, Tolstoy's revulsion upon reading Andreyev's *The Abyss* (*Bezdna*) was recorded by Aleksandr Goldenweiser in 1902; A. B. Gol'denveyzer, *Vblizi Tolstogo, Zapisi za 15 let* (Moscow: Zakharov, 2002), 79, entry for 25 July/7 August 1902.

44. Lyudmila Dayanova, diary entry from 1907, at https://prozhito.org/person/1037.

45. V. Karatïgin, "Chaykovskiy i Rakhmaninov," *Zhizn' iskusstva* 40 (9 October 1923) and 41 (16 October 1923).

46. Pierre Bourdieu, *Distinction: A Social Critique of the Judgement of Taste*, trans. Richard Nice (Cambridge, MA: Harvard University Press, 1979), 56

47. Ibid.

48. Prokofiev to Dukelsky, 9 November 1930. See "Sergey i Lina Prokof'evy i Vladimir Dukel'skiy, Perepiska, 1924–1946," ed. I. Vishnevetskiy, in *Sergey Prokof'ev: Pis'ma, Vospominaniya, Stat'i*, ed. M. P. Rakhmanova (Moscow: Deka-VS, GTsMMK im. Glinki, 2007), 7–74, at 24.

49. Prokofiev's diary entry of 3/16 November 1916, in Sergei Prokof'yev, *Dnevnik*, 2 vols. (Paris: sprkfv, 2002), 2:623. It might be added that the performer—and dedicatee— of Rachmaninoff's Opus 38, Nina Koshetz, was a love interest to both composers.

50. I use this phrase to refer to a particular genre that was developed by Russian Roma singers and choirs, but was also popular among singers of other ethnicities who imitated the "Gypsy style."

51. Merezhkovsky (1865–1941) may be better known today as one of the leading figures of Russian Symbolism, but he clearly had a connection with Gypsy song: his translation of Baudelaire's "L'invitation au voyage" became one of the most popular romances, "Golubka moya" (My Dove), and was even released on record.

52. Quoted in Yuriy Keldïsh, *Rakhmaninov i yego vremya* (Moscow: Muzïka, 1973), 97.

53. V. Karatïgin, "Chaykovskiy i Rakhmaninov."

54. Vladimir Nabokov, "The Assistant Producer," *The Atlantic* 171/5 (1943): 68–74, at 68. The "physical splendor of her prodigious voice" is, then, just over one-fifth of the total Plevitskaya package.

55. Ibid., 71.

56. Ibid., 68.

57. Bertensson and Leyda, *Sergei Rachmaninoff*, 166.

58. Ibid., letter of 1924, 237. Several other popular arrangements appeared, including the "Russian Rag" by George L. Cobb (1918), and an arrangement by Chappie Willet written for Duke Ellington's band (1938).

59. Bertensson and Leyda, *Sergei Rachmaninoff*, 333.

60. Igor Stravinsky, in Robert Craft, *Conversations with Igor Stravinsky* (New York: Doubleday, 1959), 42.

61. For more on this episode and on Rachmaninoff's fan base in general, see Rebecca Mitchell, *Nietzsche's Orphans: Music, Metaphysics, and the Twilight of the Russian Empire* (New Haven and London: Yale University Press, 2015), 150–52.

62. More on this in Mitchell, *Nietzsche's Orphans*; and Anna Fishzon, *Fandom, Authenticity, and Opera: Mad Acts and Letter Scenes in Fin-de-Siècle Russia* (Basingstoke: Palgrave Macmillan, 2013).

63. Igor' Glebov, "Vpechatleniya i mïsli," in *Melos*, Book 1 (St. Petersburg: Gosudarstvennaya tipografiya, 1917). Quoted in Alekseyev, *Rakhmaninov*, 114.

64. Theodor Adorno, "Commodity Music Analyzed," in *Quasi una Fantasia: Essays on Modern Music*, trans. Rodney Livingstone (New York: Verso, 1998), 37–52. See also Karen M. Bottge, "Reading Adorno's Reading of the Rachmaninov Prelude in C-sharp Minor: Metaphors of Destruction, Gestures of Power," *Music Theory Online* 17/4 (2011).

65. New York critic Pitts Sanborn in the *New York Telegram* (1927), quoted in Bertensson and Leyda, *Sergei Rachmaninoff*, 250.

66. Robert A. Simon in *The New Yorker* (1934), quoted in Bertensson and Leyda, *Sergei Rachmaninoff*, 309.

67. John Culshaw, "Rachmaninov Revisited," *Soundings* 3 (1973): 2, quoted in Peter Franklin, *Seeing Through Music: Gender and Modernism in Classic Hollywood Film Scores* (Oxford: Oxford University Press, 2011), 29.

68. Franklin, *Seeing Through Music*, 36. Interestingly, on the release of *Brief Encounter*, the film critic John Huntley found the Second Piano Concerto too highbrow for a soundtrack, since he had to visit the cinema "once to see Noel Coward's film and once to listen to the Rachmaninoff concerto" (34).

69. See, for example, Keldïsh, *Rakhmaninov i yego vremya*, 238; or Alekseyev, *Rakhmaninov*, 122.

70. Keldïsh, *Rakhmaninov i yego vremya*, 121.

71. Alekseyev, *Rakhmaninov*, 69; and Keldïsh, *Rakhmaninov i yego vremya*, 121.

72. Keldïsh, *Rakhmaninov i yego vremya*, 188.

73. V. N. Bryantseva, *Fortepiannïye p'yesï Rakhmaninova* (Moscow: Muzïka, 1966), 114–15.

74. O. Chebotarenko, "S. V. Rakhmaninov, Sonata Op. 28, No. 1: K probleme ispolni-tel'skogo ponimaniya," *Muzychne mistetstvo i kul'tura* 17 (2013): 340–47.

75. Boele, *Erotic Nihilism in Imperial Russia*, 6.

76. More on features of the middlebrow in Beth Driscoll, *The New Literary Middlebrow: Tastemakers and Reading in the Twenty-First Century* (London: Palgrave Macmillan, 2014). I have engaged with this text in "Music History with Love? The Hits, the Cults, and the Snobs," *Muzikologija* 27 (2019): 71–91. See also Isobel Madison, "The Middlebrow and Popular," *The Cambridge Companion to British Literature in the 1930s*, ed. James Smith (Cambridge: Cambridge University Press, 2019), 81–96.

77. See more on this in Richard Dyer, *Brief Encounter* (London: Bloomsbury Publishing, 2015).

Rachmaninoff and the "Vocalise":
Word and Music in the Russian Silver Age

PHILIP ROSS BULLOCK

Like the slow movement of the Second Symphony, the opening themes of the Second and Third Piano Concertos, or the eighteenth variation of the *Rhapsody on a Theme of Paganini*, the "Vocalise" stands as one of the most well-known instances of Sergei Rachmaninoff's distinctive lyricism.[1] Emerging as if from nothing, tracing a series of gently pulsing arabesques, supported by a chain of modally inflected minor harmonies, and creating a haunting sense of suspended time, it articulates a bittersweet mood of melancholy and nostalgia. In Russian, this mood is called *toska*, whose various meanings are best glossed by Vladimir Nabokov:

> No single word in English renders all the shades of *toska*. At its deepest and most painful, it is a sensation of great spiritual anguish, often without any specific cause. At less morbid levels it is a dull ache of the soul, a longing with nothing to long for, a sick pining, a vague restlessness, mental throes, yearning. In particular cases it may be the desire for somebody or something specific, nostalgia, love-sickness. At the lowest level it grades into ennui, boredom, *skuka*.[2]

Whether or not emotions are universal, analogues in other languages might include other such supposedly "untranslatable" terms as French *ennui*, German *Weltschmerz*, and Portuguese *saudade*.[3]

The elegiac longing conveyed by the "Vocalise" was seemingly central to Rachmaninoff's musical aesthetics, as suggested by the following poetic précis, penned in late 1932 in response to an enthusiastic fan who had asked for his definition of music:

> Что такое музыка?!
> Это тихая лунная ночь;

Это шелест живых листьев;
Это отдаленный вечерний звон;
Это то, что родится от сердца и идет к сердцу;
Это любовь!
Сестра музыки это поэзия, а мать ее—грусть![4]

What is music?!
It is a quiet moonlit night;
It is the rustling of living leaves;
It is the distant sound of evening bells;
It is what is born from the heart and goes to the heart;
It is love!
The sister of music is poetry, but her mother is sorrow![5]

Moreover, Rachmaninoff linked the melancholy of his music to his identity as a Russian composer, as evinced by an interview he gave shortly
after his arrival in the United States in late 1918:

> "What, in a word, is Russian music?"
> "Sad," Mr. Rachmaninoff answered with mirthful readi-
> ness. "The Russian is the greatest musical school to-day. I
> marvel that you Americans do not know more of it, for it has
> the universal emotional appeal which none can resist. But
> as time goes on, you will doubtless hear Russian music more
> and more and—"
> "Just a moment!" the interviewer implored. "Do you say
> we will hear more Russian music because it is sad and every-
> body is sad nowadays?"
> "No; you will hear more of it because it is beautiful."
> "But you said it is sad. What is it to be called if you discard
> that adjective?"
> "I meant to say that it was predominantly melancholy
> in character at present. As to what it will be in future, how
> should I know?"[6]

Accounts of Rachmaninoff's music in terms of its emotional impact are
hardly original; indeed, they are so common as to be conventional and
even misleading, playing into national stereotypes about Russian music
more generally.[7] This essay proposes a rather different approach to the
"Vocalise." To borrow Rachmaninoff's own metaphor, it deals less with
the "maternal" genealogy of sorrowful emotion, than with song's "sibling"

relationship with poetry, focusing on Rachmaninoff's engagement with the world of Russian literature and examining the potential significance of the placement of the "Vocalise" as the last of his *Fourteen Romances*, Op. 34.

Why, though, has the "Vocalise" become so detached from its original context to become as iconic (and misunderstood) as the once ubiquitous Prelude in C-sharp Minor? The basic outline of its composition occurs in a short memoir of Rachmaninoff written by its dedicatee, the soprano Antonina Nezhdanova:

> Rachmaninoff would bring his "Vocalise" to me before it appeared in print and played it through many times. Together, we deliberated over nuances and inserted breath marks in the middle of phrases to make it more convenient to perform. As we rehearsed together, he would suddenly stop and change various passages, each time finding some alternative harmony, new modulation, or other nuance. Then, after the "Vocalise" was orchestrated, I performed it for the first time with orchestra under the direction of the conductor Serge Koussevitzky in the Main Hall of the Assembly of the Nobility. As a great composer, Rachmaninoff's success was colossal. I was infinitely glad that part of the well-deserved success also belonged to me as performer. I have kept the manuscript of the "Vocalise," which he presented to me before the concert, as a precious memory of the great composer.[8]

Rachmaninoff and Nezhdanova worked on the song in the spring of 1915; her copy (now in the possession of the Russian National Museum of Music, Moscow) is dated 1 April 1915. Rachmaninoff revised it that summer; his fair copy is dated 21 September 1915, and the song was published by Gutheil later that year.[9] Performances followed quickly: Nezhdanova's performance of the song (in Rachmaninoff's own orchestration) took place in Moscow on 24 January 1916, although this was preceded the month before by an arrangement for double bass and orchestra, with Koussevitzky taking the solo part.[10]

Arrangements for other instruments soon proliferated, effectively effacing the origins of the "Vocalise" in song. Mikhaíl Press published a transcription for violin and piano in 1916, and this was followed by versions for clarinet and piano by Sergei Rozanov in 1917, and for cello and piano by Anatoly Brandukov in 1922.[11] Rachmaninoff himself conspired in this process, publishing an orchestral version of the "Vocalise" in 1919, yet a comment in a letter dating from December 1918 suggests that he never entirely lost sight of its unspoken relationship with poetry. Writing to émigré conductor Modest Altschuler, Rachmaninoff proposed what he saw as an ideal performance of the "Vocalise":

> Most of all, I liked your idea of performing the "Vocalise" in the style of a Bach aria. That's true, and I thought as much myself. The melody should be played by several violins in unison. Do you remember how Hřimalý once did it? I don't remember in which city I heard the "Vocalise" performed like this by ten violins in unison (in Press's arrangement). It sounded marvelous, and I was very satisfied. Try to do this yourself, only transpose it into E minor.[12]

The comparison between the "Vocalise" and a Bach aria is a telling one, as the affective connotations of Bach's melodies are always intimately linked to the rhetorical impact of their Lutheran texts.[13] Strikingly, Rachmaninoff never made a solo piano arrangement of the "Vocalise," as he had done in the case of two other romances, "Lilacs," Op. 21, No. 5, and "Daisies," Op. 38, No. 3, not to mention his ravishing final work—an exquisitely wrought paraphrase of Tchaikovsky's "Lullaby," Op. 16, No. 1 (1943)—all of which were designed to showcase his ability to make the piano sing. Wordless the "Vocalise" may be, yet it is still characterized by a powerful, if unspoken relationship to the world of literature.

So what, then, is the relationship between the "Vocalise" and the art of poetry? It is an important question, since Rachmaninoff's taste in poetry has long been the object of criticism. However, a careful examination of the relationship between the "Vocalise" and the preceding songs in the Opus 34 collection reveals a discerning, if diffident literary sensibility. Admittedly, Rachmaninoff enjoyed few close friendships with contemporary writers and avoided Moscow's literary salons and intellectual circles. His reading was dictated more by what was at hand in the family library than by an awareness of the latest artistic trends. His friend and former student, Yelena Zhukovskaya, recalls how she and Rachmaninoff's cousin (and wife-to-be), Natalya Satina, would comb books and periodicals for suitable poems:

> She and I were always busy looking for texts for Sergei Vasilyevich. I had already become accustomed to apprais-ing every poem I read to see whether it would make a good romance. We assembled a "store cupboard," which Sergei Vasilyevich would use when necessary. We had read and reread all the classics and famous poets. For this reason, we

began to turn to the thick journals, where one could occasionally encounter good poems by little-known and even
totally unknown authors.[14]

In Zhukovskaya's account, song emerges from the long-standing cultural
practices of the Russian gentry, rather than from a firsthand engagement
with the world of contemporary literature. Where new authors do materialize, it is by serendipity rather than design.

On other occasions, Rachmaninoff sought out the advice of trusted
friends and advisers. In the summer of 1891, he wrote to his friend the
singer Mikhaíl Slonov with the following request:

I don't have any verses here and I'd like to write another
song. Try to get hold of A. Tolstoy if you can. Find a few
poems suitable for setting as songs there, no more than three
stanzas, ideally two: write them out and include them in a
letter, that is, of course, if you feel like writing to me. When
my song to the words you have sent me is ready, I'll send it to
you, and you can easily insult me behind my back.[15]

Aleksey Tolstoy (a distant cousin of the novelist Leo Tolstoy) had been a
mainstay of the song repertoire for several decades, so Rachmaninoff's
preference for his verses suggests that his relationship to poetry at this
point was mediated primarily through music.[16] The texts for his *Fifteen
Romances*, Op. 26 (1906), were suggested by Mariya Kerzina. Thanking
her for an initial selection, Rachmaninoff asked her for some further texts:

Might you be so kind as to send me a few more poems for my
songs? Only don't be cross with me, for heaven's sake, for
making such a request. I have the booklet that you wrote out
for me before, but it's not entirely satisfactory. I have taken
what I could from it, but it's not quite enough. Moreover, all
of the words in this booklet demand minor keys. How about
a few more poems in a more major key?[17]

Rachmaninoff's literary conservatism was certainly dictated by a feeling
for what would work in song and can be traced to the nineteenth-century
romance tradition. He showed a particular affinity with the poets that
Tchaikovsky had favored before him: Aleksey Pleshcheyev and A. K. Tolstoy
(six settings of each poet), Afanasy Fet, Daniíl Rathaus, and Fyodor Tyutchev
(five settings of each poet).[18] He was also drawn to Tchaikovsky's friend and

contemporary, Aleksey Apukhtin, whom he set on three occasions.[19] Musically, too, Tchaikovsky's influence was paramount, especially when it came to Rachmaninoff's earliest vocal works—the *Six Romances*, Op. 4 (1890–93), the *Six Romances*, Op. 8 (1893), and the *Twelve Romances*, Op. 14 (1896)—all of which cultivate the older composer's lyric style.

By contrast, the *Twelve Romances*, Op. 21, mark a more confident assimilation of Tchaikovsky's influence. Written between 1899 and 1902, they date from a period of considerable turmoil in Rachmaninoff's life. The poor performance and hostile reception of his First Symphony in March 1897 had plunged him into creative despair. A contract to conduct a series of operas at Savva Mamontov's Private Opera in Moscow offered a way out. Here, Rachmaninoff not only discovered a new vocation to add to those of pianist and composer, but also encountered some of the most exciting voices in turn-of-the-century Russia, most famously, Fyodor Chaliapin. At the Private Opera, and later the Bolshoi Theater, he would also be exposed to a vast range of the Russian and European operatic repertoire, and in particular, to Modest Musorgsky's *Boris Godunov*. The impact of *Boris Godunov* (even in Nikolai Rimsky-Korsakov's sanitized edition), and of Chaliapin's interpretation of the title role, can be felt in the Opus 21 songs, where the declamatory heritage of the Russian song tradition takes precedence over the lyric one. Many of the songs are closer to miniature dramatic scenes than conventional romances and attest to the influence of Musorgsky's musical reworking of human speech. These developments were taken yet further in the *Fifteen Romances*, Op. 26. Composed for Arkady and Mariya Kerzin (and setting, as we have seen, texts selected by Kerzina herself), these songs formed part of the Kerzins' Moscow concert series, which was noted for its prominent inclusion of songs and chamber music, as well as for its espousal of the composers of the *moguchaya kuchka* (Mighty Handful), especially César Cui and Musorgsky. In both their musical style and handling of poetic texts, Rachmaninoff's Opus 26 songs illustrate how his assimilation of the more declamatory influence of Musorgsky, alongside his earlier debt to Tchaikovsky's lyricism, established the foundations for his mature vocal style.

The songs that Rachmaninoff wrote between 1890 and 1907 emerge organically from the Russian song tradition as it had developed in the second half of the nineteenth century. To be sure, there is no sense that these songs are blandly derivative or lacking originality, and they soon came to enjoy enormous popularity with audiences and performers alike. To a younger, more belligerent generation of critics, however, Rachmaninoff's music was not merely conservative, but devoid of artistic integrity altogether. Writing in 1913, for instance, the critic Vyacheslav

Karatygin situated Rachmaninoff at the very heart of petty-bourgeois culture, rather like elite critics in Europe and the United States would later denigrate him as the embodiment of the middlebrow. Karatygin writes:

> Should one lament or rejoice that we have yet further confirmation of the ardent sympathy in which Rachmaninoff is held by the general public? In essence, there is no justification for indulging in either feeling. One can lament when the public is delighted by gypsy trash [*tiganshchina*]. One can rejoice when you observe that people are becoming increasingly interested in Bach, Beethoven, Reger, Debussy, Scriabin, and Stravinsky. But in applauding Rachmaninoff, the public is exploring neither the extreme depths nor the elevated heights of taste to which its individual elements are capable of either falling or rising. Rachmaninoff's music responds, so to speak, to the arithmetically average aesthetic standard of the general public. The public bows down before him because in his music, Rachmaninoff has somehow managed to hit the very center of everyday, philistine musical taste.[20]

Karatygin's association with avant-garde artistic circles in pre-revolutionary St. Petersburg meant that he was never likely to be sympathetic toward Rachmaninoff's late Romantic muse. Yet such anxieties about Rachmaninoff's aesthetic allegiances were shared more widely in literary and musical circles, even by those more sympathetic to his music.

In early 1912, for instance, Rachmaninoff received a letter from a young music lover who signed herself simply as "Re" (the note D in solfeggio). "Re" was in fact the poet Marietta Shaginyan, who was shortly to publish a substantial "musical-psychological study" in a leading Symbolist journal. It is a complex, diffuse article, larded with references to German Romantic philosophy that were characteristic of certain strands of Russian Symbolism: "Music is, in and of itself, the precious internal cement which, as it were, binds together all the 'ranks' of the universe. It was present at the act of creation from the first day to the last, and was, perhaps, that 'blessing' which the Creator pronounced at the end of each day."[21] Its main aims were to dispute the very comparisons between Rachmaninoff and Tchaikovsky that had been so central to the young composer's early reception, to downplay the fascination held by Scriabin's heady mysticism, and to promote instead Rachmaninoff's humane and well-ordered music as a more effective means of bringing unity to a fractured world.[22] Shaginyan's principal focus is on the Second Piano Concerto, and she has correspondingly little to say about his songs. What is significant, however, is that her criticisms of Rachmaninoff's vocal works focus on his allegedly poor taste in poetry, whereas she exempts his music from similar charges: "Even the most negligible of verses, such as those of Galina and Rathaus, for example . . . find a thoughtful and subtle response in his music."[23]

In private, Shaginyan voiced similar concerns, gently trying to persuade Rachmaninoff to realize his gifts more thoroughly through a combination of flattery and artless remonstration (as her side of the correspondence has not survived, her views have to be reconstructed on the basis of his replies to her). As in the case of Slonov and Kerzina, Rachmaninoff quickly recognized that Shaginyan could be a useful source of literary inspiration. In his second surviving letter to her, dated 15 March 1912, he made the following request:

> I need texts for my romances. Could you not suggest something suitable? It seems to me that "Re" knows a lot about this subject, almost everything, and perhaps even everything. I don't care whether it's by a modern author or a dead one, as long as it's an original work and not a translation, and no longer than 8–12 lines, 16 at most. And one more thing, the mood should be sad rather than jolly. Bright tones don't come easily to me![24]

His reply to her initial suggestions was polite, if cautious, and he appears to have taken on board a few of her ideas.[25] At the same time, Shaginyan took the opportunity to criticize his literary and even musical taste, as his affronted reaction suggests:

> In your last letter, dear Re, you sometimes do me an injustice. Here are a few examples. After giving the most ruthless account of Galina's "doggerel," you note (with a little malice), that I myself have used this doggerel "willingly." I used it, actually, in just two or three cases out of a total of fifty-one. . . . And elsewhere, you warn me not to seek after the "tawdry success of the music hall" for my romances! This is still worse! Is there any need to say such things to me, dear Re?[26]

Such misunderstandings notwithstanding, their correspondence soon became more candid, intimate, and affectionate. Rachmaninoff's fifteen surviving letters to her have been extensively cited in the biographical and critical literature precisely because they employ a rather different tone from the business-like manner of much of the rest of his correspondence (in this sense, they might be seen as analogous to Tchaikovsky's correspondence with his patron, Nadezhda von Meck, although far less extensive or expansive).[27] Shaginyan not only suggested texts for him to set to music, but even provided detailed commentaries on their rhythmic prosody, so that he could capture their "musicality" more faithfully in his melodies.[28]

By June 1912, Rachmaninoff had completed thirteen new songs, of which around half were based on poems proposed by Shaginyan.[29] Yet her attempts at cultivating his literary taste still met with a certain resistance, and her gift of a copy of a recently published collection of contemporary verse produced the following reaction: "I have received the copy of the *Anthology* that you sent me. I like some of it, but I am horrified by most of the poems. I would often chance upon one of Re's markings: 'This is good' or 'This is all good.' And I would spend a long time trying to understand what good Re could have found there?!"[30] Rachmaninoff continued to solicit her advice when it came to contemporary Russian literature, and Shaginyan's ideas may have had an indirect influence on other works, too. Although she had no hand in it, the work that followed the Opus 34 songs was his cantata *The Bells* (*Kolokola*), Op. 35, to verses by Edgar Allen Poe in euphonious Russian translations by the Symbolist poet Konstantin Balmont.[31] When it came to song, Shaginyan's influence proved fundamental to the conception of the *Six Poems*, Op. 38, composed in 1916. She initially provided Rachmaninoff with a selection of texts, including fifteen poems by Mikhaíl Lermontov, and twenty-six by contemporary poets.[32] Of these, he selected six verses by Balmont, Andrey Bely, Aleksandr Blok (a Russian translation of an Armenian text by Avetik Isahakyan), Valery Bryusov, Igor Severyanin, and Fyodor Sologub. This was the first and only time that Rachmaninoff embraced modern poetry without equivocation, and in describing them as "poems" rather than "romances," he appears to have accepted the primacy of Shaginyan's guidance rather than his own intuition as a composer. Their dedication was not, however, to Shaginyan (who was offended by what she perceived as a deliberate slight), but to the soprano Nina Koshetz, who premiered them, accompanied by the composer, in a series of concerts in Moscow, Petrograd, Kharkiv, and Kyiv in the winter of 1916–17.[33]

The *Six Poems*, Op. 38, have attracted rather more commentary than the *Fourteen Romances*, Op. 34, but before exploring the literary and musical contexts of the latter, it is necessary to survey the broader cultural context to see how Shaginyan's views were in keeping with debates within Symbolist circles.[34] Much Russian poetry of the turn-of-the-century was beholden to the ideal of music and musicality, whether in terms of its aspirations to a transcendent realm beyond material reality, or in its extensive use of euphony, assonance, increasingly resourceful rhyme, and innovations in meter and prosody.[35] Bely's writings give a good sense of the central role played by music in Symbolist aesthetics. In "The Forms of Art" ("Formï iskusstva," 1902), for instance, he explored how music's lack of referentiality makes it the ideal vehicle by which to challenge the representational strategies of realism (a key aim of Symbolist aesthetics):

> In all religions, there exists an opposition between our world and some other, better one.
>
> In the arts, we have just such an opposition between spatial and temporal forms. Architecture, sculpture, and painting deal with images of reality; music—with the internal aspect of these images, that is, the movement that governs them. As Hanslick says: "The beauty of a piece of music is specifically a musical beauty, that is, it is present in the way that the notes are combined, without any consideration of any extra-musical set of ideas that is alien to them." . . . "The kingdom of music is not, in fact, of this world."
>
> Beginning with the lowest forms of art and finishing with music, we are in the presence of a slow but sure deterioration of the images of reality. In architecture, sculpture, and painting, these images play an important role. In music, they are absent. As it approaches music, a work of art becomes both deeper and wider.
>
> I consider it necessary to repeat the words I expressed earlier: any form of art has its origin in reality and its endpoint in music, as pure movement. Or, expressing myself in the language of Kant, all art penetrates the "noumenal." Or, in the words of Schopenhauer, all art leads us to a pure appreciation of the world will. Or, to use the language of Nietzsche, all forms of art can be characterized by the extent to which they are manifestations of the spirit of music. Or, in the words of Spenser, all art is a striving for the future. "The kingdom of music is not, in fact, of this world" (Hanslick).[36]

The characteristic elements of Russian Symbolism are all present here: a metaphysical distinction between the real and the ideal; a preference for the beauty of form over the reality of representation; a vision of creativity that bordered on the priestly; and a brooding sense of impending apocalypse.

It was not just in his theoretical writings that Bely advanced the notion that poetry and music were intimately, even organically, related. His musical ambitions shaped his four "symphonies"—experimental and impressionistic prose poems written between 1899 and 1907 that were modeled on an eclectic range of courses, including Richard Wagner's music dramas.[37] However, by the time he wrote *After the Separation: A Berlin Songbook* (*Posle razluki: Berlinskiy pesennik*, 1922), Bely had moved away from some of the abstraction of his earlier Symbolist writings to embrace techniques and ideas that were closer to song. In particular, its preface—significantly titled "Let Us Seek Out Melodies" ("Budem iskat' melodii")—illustrates his interest in songfulness as a manifestation of modern poetry:

1. The lyric poem is a song.
2. The poet carries melodies within himself: he is a composer.
3. In pure lyric poetry, *melody* is more important than image.
4. When it comes to *melody*, the excessive use of conventional elements of verse (image and sound harmony) transforms the very riches of these elements into a veritable means of killing verse.
5. Enough of metaphorical surfeit—let us have a little less imagism, and a little more song, a few more simple words, and a less sonic prattle (fewer horns). Great composers are great not on account of their instruments, but on account of their *melodies*. Beethoven's orchestration is simpler than that of Strauss.
   In the future, Russian verse can expect a wealth of inexhaustible melodic worlds.
   All hail "melodism"![38]

Bely took a lively interest in contemporary musical life as well. He was an ardent admirer of the music of Nikolai Medtner, for instance, describing him as "perhaps the only composer to affirm rather than destroy life," and arguing that his music brought about "something positive, something that affirms the values of existence."[39] Referring to Medtner's settings of the poetry of Goethe, Bely argued: "One is involuntarily struck by the fact that the music to Goethe's songs is not composed, but is, as it were, extracted from the songs themselves."[40] Bely's enthusiasm for Medtner was only heightened by hearing them in performance. He wrote ecstatically, for instance, of the singer Maria Olenina-d'Alheim, whose artistry served to convey the mystical essence of the work of art:

When she stands before us—this portrayer of the depths of the soul—when she sings her songs to us, we dare not say

that her voice is beyond reproach, that first and foremost, it
is not large.

We forget about the qualities of her voice because she is
something greater than a singer.

Music's relationship to poetic symbols deepens these
symbols. Olenina-d'Alheim conveys these deepened symbols
with remarkable expressivity. She emphasizes her attitude
to the symbols, which she conveys with incomparable facial
expressions. The poetic symbol, rendered more complex by
music's treatment of it, transformed by the voice and emphasized by the singer's gestures, is expanded beyond measure.[41]

He overhears a fellow concertgoer describe her as "a talented singer,"
but dismisses this limited understanding of her seemingly meager gifts in
favor of a more radical vision of her art:

A tall woman dressed in black walks out, rather gauchely,
onto the stage. In her silhouette, there is something oppressive, something too large for a person. One should listen to
her among the abysses; one should hear her in the breaks
between the clouds. In the sharp contours of her face, simplicity is combined with the utmost distinction. She is entirely
too simple, entirely too strange. Her uncertain eyes burn us
with their extravagant brilliance, as if she were approaching
the stars through flights of a hazy life.[42]

For Bely, Olenina-d'Alheim was not so much a singer as a priest who was
capable of revealing the hidden essence of art and even the world itself.[43]

Temperamentally, Rachmaninoff was always rather skeptical of such
extravagant claims, understanding that Symbolism's interest in music was
above all metaphorical, not practical. Bely's worldview is so saturated
with its own eccentric ideas about music that it leaves little room for any
kind of creative collaboration with actual musicians; so confident is he of
his own musicality that an actual composer is always likely to constitute a
rival, rather than an equal. Yet the *Fourteen Romances*, Op. 34, can nonetheless be interpreted as a contribution to contemporary debates about
the relationship between words and music in Russian modernist culture.
Emerging as they do from Rachmaninoff's friendship with Shaginyan,
they illustrate his sensitivity to poetry's aspirations to a particular form of
musicality, while also constituting a very particular riposte to the coher-
ence of such claims.

At this point, we should exclude the "Vocalise" from consideration, as it postdates the rest of the collection. All but one of the remaining songs were composed at great speed in the early summer of 1912 on Rachmaninoff's estate at Ivanovka:

1. "The Muse" ("Muza")—Pushkin (6 June 1912)
2. "In the Soul of Each of Us" ("V dushe u kazhdogo iz nas")—Apollon Korinfsky (5 June 1912)
3. "The Storm" ("Burya")—Pushkin (7 June 1912)
4. "The Vagrant Wind" ("Veter perelyotnïy")—Balmont (9 June 1912)
5. "Arion" ("Arion")—Pushkin (8 June 1912)
6. "The Raising of Lazarus" ("Voskresheniye Lazarya")—Aleksey Khomyakov (4 June 1912)
7. "It Cannot Be!" ("Ne mozhet bït'!")—Apollon Maykov (7 March 1910)
8. "Music" ("Muzïka")—Yakov Polonsky (12 June 1912)
9. "You Knew Him" ("Tï znal ego")—Tyutchev (12 June 1912)
10. "I Remember That Day" ("Sey den' ya pomnyu")—Tyutchev (10 June 1912)
11. "The True Servant" ("Obrochnik")—Fet (11 June 1912)
12. "What Happiness" ("Kakoye schast'ye")—Fet (19 June 1912)
13. "Dissonance" ("Dissonans")—Polonsky (17 June 1912)[44]

At first glance, Shaginyan's impact on Rachmaninoff's literary preferences seems to have been minimal; for a work written in 1912, these poets look decidedly traditional and even old-fashioned. Only Balmont and the little-known Korinfsky were active in the early twentieth century. Yet Russian Symbolism was not merely a contemporary movement; it was also a self-consciously syncretic attempt to restore aspects of earlier periods of literary history to modern consciousness. Writing about modernist periodicals, for instance, Bely observed:

> On the one hand they support talented young authors, and on the other, they resurrect the forgotten past: they stir interest in the monuments of eighteenth-century Russian art, restore the cult of the German romantics, Goethe, Dante, and the Latin poets, and they bring Pushkin and Baratïnsky closer to us once again, and write marvelous studies of Gogol, Tolstoy,

and Dostoyevsky; and stir interest in Sophocles, study productions of Euripides, and renew ancient theater.[45]

For the symbolists, nineteenth-century poets such as Fet, Khomyakov,
Maykov, Polonsky, Pushkin, and Tyutchev were important precursors and
here represent not so much the literary past, as a form of ongoing dialogue with tradition. Tyutchev, in particular, was regarded as a symbolist
avant la lettre, so Rachmaninoff's inclusion of two of his verses points to an
unsuspected modernity at work in the songs. Equally striking are the three
Pushkin settings, which appear as the first, third, and fifth of the songs
respectively, embracing the two modern poets Korinfsky and Balmont.
The resulting cluster of five songs is divided temporally, yet thematically
coherent. Moreover, the three Pushkin settings embody a prophetic and
metapoetic strain in his verse that was highly valued by the Symbolists,
yet seldom explored in the song repertoire.[46] This is most obviously the
case in "The Muse," but also in "Arion," which deals with the fate of a poet
whose singing saves him from a storm in which his captors perish. Songs
to texts by other poets also explore themes of the artist, the artistic vocation, and the artist's relationship to society, often against a background of
natural imagery. Tyutchev's "You Knew Him" depicts the poet as a figure
disdained by society, but who shines with divine radiance by night. Fet's
"The True Servant" is not one of the poet's charming love lyrics or amia-
ble depictions of nature (the kind of poems that had been extensively set
to music from the 1850s onward), but instead constitutes a stern defense
of the poetic vocation and the potency of Russia's lyric tradition.

Although they still largely shun contemporary poetry, the Opus 34 songs
nonetheless explore themes that were widespread in Russian Symbolism.
The transformative influence of Shaginyan is clear throughout, if not
in the choice of individual poets, then certainly in the type of verse now
favored by Rachmaninoff. Yet songs in no way represent a "capitulation"
of music to poetry, and the set does not simply reiterate Shaginyan's representation of poetry in terms of prophecy, vocation, and inspiration.
Rather, it interrogates such ideas from the point of view of Rachmaninoff's
own calling as a composer, staging an argument that moves from an interest in literary creativity toward a more specifically musical form of lyric
address. As far as the musical language of the set is concerned, it is notable how many of the songs in the first half employ a terse and etiolated
form of expressivity, evidence perhaps of Rachmaninoff's refusal to seek
the kind of "tawdry success of the music hall" that Shaginyan had criticized in his earlier songs. His setting of Polonsky's "Music," for instance,
is pared down, eschewing surface glitter in favor of chaste interiority. In

many ways, "Music" constitutes a significant turning point in the set and ushers in a new type of sensibility in the songs that follow. Having worked through the explicitly literary conceits of the early poems, Rachmaninoff employs a freer and far more expansive form of musical dramaturgy in the final songs in the set, something that is only heard when all thirteen numbers are given in a single sitting.

This macro-structure is replicated at the level of individual songs, too. The pairing of two poems by Fet, for instance, establishes a crucial juxtaposition between the exploration of the poet's art in "The True Servant" and the unfeigned lyric élan of "What Happiness," in which two lovers are reunited by night. This pair of songs (11 and 12) is then followed by "Dissonance," a long dramatic monologue in which Rachmaninoff traces the emotional development of Polonsky's fifteen rhymed couplets with extraordinary vividness. If these songs show Rachmaninoff yielding to an ever greater sense of musical eloquence (and notice how the titles of songs 8 and 13 explicitly invoke music), then this development is taken to its logical extreme in what would eventually become the concluding song of the collection, the "Vocalise." As this number was added to the existing thirteen songs only in 1915, it cannot be argued that it articulates the composer's initial conception of the set as a whole. Yet his decision to return to the Opus 34 songs suggests he felt that there was something unfinished about them in their original form. The temporal distance between the first thirteen songs and the newly composed "Vocalise" lends it the status of a commentary, standing apart from what has come before and reflecting on it from the vantage point of creative distance.

By dint of its very form, the "Vocalise" expresses Rachmaninoff's intuitive belief in the supremacy of music, a belief reinforced by its dedication to the soprano Antonina Nezhdanova. With the exception of individual songs written in memory of the actress Vera Komissarzhevskaya ("It Cannot Be!," composed after her death in February 1910 and therefore predating the other songs by more than two years), and of Tchaikovsky (a setting of Polonsky's "Music"), all but one of the remaining songs are dedicated to three living singers: Chaliapin (nos. 2, 6, 9, and 11); the dramatic soprano Feliya Litvinne (no. 13); and the tenor Leonid Sobinov (nos. 3, 4, 5, 10, and 12). Only the first song, a setting of Pushkin's "The Muse," eschews this pattern; its dedication to Shaginyan aptly acknowledges her decisive influence on the literary conception of the cycle, yet situates this debt within a realm more closely associated with music.[47] There is a certain poetic justice about this, inasmuch as the notion that poetry was a form of transcendent verbal expression bordering on the musical was widespread in literary circles around the turn of the century. In the "Vocalise," Rachmaninoff literalizes that conceit by doing without words altogether and translating song into the realm of pure, almost instrumental sound. It may be tempting to adduce parallels here with other wordless vocal works of the early twentieth century, such as Igor Stravinsky's early *Pastorale* (1907), Sergei Prokofiev's *Five Songs without Words*, Op. 35 (1920), Medtner's *Sonata-vocalise*, Op. 42, No. 1 (1922) and *Suite-vocalise*, Op. 42, No. 2 (1926), or even Reinhold Glière's extravagant Concerto for Coloratura Soprano (1943), yet that would be to overlook the intellectual context out of which the "Vocalise" emerged. It may be an exaggeration to suggest it, but possibly no other vocal work of the Silver Age offers such a multifaceted imbrication in the literary culture of the time. No mere reflection of a single artistic or philosophical point of view, the "Vocalise" is the culmination of a series of interlocking dialogues, whether between the individual songs that make up the *Fourteen Romances*, Op. 34, or between the composer and his various collaborators.

It is for this reason that the "Vocalise" potentially suffers when transcribed for solo instrument. It suffers equally when heard outside the context of the Opus 34 songs, or simply appended to a concert program as a satisfyingly familiar encore. Separated from its original context, the "Vocalise" loses its status as a commentary on the art of song, or as an intervention in early twentieth-century debates about lyric poetry, the relationship between poetry and music, and the vocation of the artist. Although it has no words, the "Vocalise" nonetheless conveys some kind of expressive meaning, at least when it features as the final number in what may, after all, be a coherent cycle. The narrative of the *Fourteen Romances*, Op. 34, is not, admittedly, that of the classical song cycle, such as Schubert's *Winterreise* or *Die schöne Müllerin*, or Schumann's *Frauenliebe und -leben*, in which a lyric hero relates details of his or her life and emotional experience. Yet if the Opus 34 songs do not constitute a conventional song cycle as such, they nonetheless stage a series of debates—between classical and modern poetry, between literature and music, between sense and sensibility, between the denotive and conative, between the concrete and the abstract—that reveal them to be a kind of modernist *paragone*, a philosophical and aesthetic exploration of the relationship between the arts at a crucial moment in Russian cultural history. In Rachmaninoff's world, then, music must always have the last word.

NOTES

This essay is based on a lecture first delivered as the keynote address at the conference *Rethinking the Impact of the Liberal Arts—Music*, held at the University of Cologne, 11–12 December 2018. I am especially grateful to Dr. Jan Czarnecki for his kind invitation to give this address, as well as for many stimulating conversations thereafter. My thanks also go to Sung-Won Yang for an invitation to talk about Rachmaninoff in Seoul in October 2019 and for a memorable series of performances of the Cello Sonata and the instrumental "Vocalise."

1. There have been as many attempts to explain Rachmaninoff's melodic style as there are critics and commentators. Richard Sylvester, for instance, draws parallels between the "Vocalise" and the melodic contours of the *All-Night Vigil*, which was composed in the preceding months. See *Rachmaninoff's Complete Songs: A Companion with Texts and Translations* (Bloomington: Indiana University Press, 2014), 220–21. Similarly, Joseph Yasser claims that the opening melody of the Third Piano Concerto was derived from a specific Orthodox liturgical chant. See "The Opening Theme of Rachmaninoff's Third Piano Concerto and its Liturgical Prototype," *The Musical Quarterly* 55/3 (1969): 313–28. When, more than three decades earlier, Yasser had put this supposition to the composer, Rachmaninoff objected: "The first theme of my Third Concerto is borrowed neither from folksong forms, nor from ecclesiastical sources. It just 'wrote itself' like that. You will probably interpret this as an instance of the 'unconscious.' But if I had any intentions when composing this theme, they were purely to do with sound. I wanted to 'sing' this melody on the piano, just as singers do—and to find a suitable orchestral accompaniment, or rather, one that would not drown out the song. That's all!" See letter of 30 April 1935, in S. Rakhmaninov, *Literaturnoye naslediye*, ed. Z. A. Apetyan, 3 vols. (Moscow: Sovetskiy kompozitor, 1978–80), 3:49. Such ethnographic claims were likewise rejected by Nikolai Medtner, whose description of the main theme of the first movement of the Second Piano Concerto explicitly rejects local color: "Here, there is not a single ethnographic artifact, no peasant's smock [*sarafan*], no country fair, no turn-of-phrase taken from folksong, yet each time, from its very first bell-like blow, one feels Russia rising up to her full height." See untitled article by N. K. Medtner, in M. V. Dobuzhinskiy, *Pamyati Rakhmaninova* (New York: Izdaniye S. A. Satinoy, 1946), 140–44, at 143.

2. Aleksandr Pushkin, *Eugene Onegin: A Novel in Verse*, trans. Vladimir Nabokov, rev. ed., 4 vols. (Princeton: Princeton University Press, 1975), 2:141.

3. Disappointingly, *toska* receives no mention in Barbara Cassin, ed., *Dictionary of Untranslatables: A Philosophical Lexicon*, trans. Steven Rendell (Princeton: Princeton University Press, 2014).

4. Undated letter (after 13 December 1932), in Rakhmaninov, *Literaturnoye naslediye*, 2:343.

5. For a freer English translation, see Sergei Bertensson and Jay Leyda, *Sergei Rachmaninoff: A Lifetime in Music* (Bloomington: Indiana University Press, 2001), 291.

6. "Rachmaninoff Champions Music of Native Land," *Musical America* 29 (7 December 1918): 3–4, at 3.

7. Marina Frolova-Walker, "Music of the Soul," in *National Identity in Russian Culture: An Introduction*, ed. Simon Franklin and Emma Widdis (Cambridge: Cambridge University Press, 2004), 116–31, esp. 124–29.

8. A. V. Nezhdanova, "O Rakhmaninove," in *Vospominaniya o Rakhmaninove*, ed. Z. Apetyan, 5th ed., 2 vols. (Moscow: Gosudarstvennoye muzïkal'noye izdatel'stvo, 1988), 27–32, at 31.

9. For a modern Urtext edition of the song, with an authoritative textual commentary on the sources for the "Vocalise," see Sergei Rachmaninow, *Vocalise, für Singstimme und Klavier, Opus 34, Nr. 14*, ed. Dominik Rahmer (Munich: Henle, 2014).

10. Sylvester, *Rachmaninoff's Complete Songs*, 227–28.

11. For a long list of arrangements and performers, see ibid., 228–31.

12. Letter of 26 March 1918, in Rakhmaninov, *Literaturnoye naslediye*, 2:105.

13. For more on Bach, see Daniel R. Melamed, *Hearing Bach's Passions* (Oxford: Oxford University Press, 2005); Eric Chafe, *Tonal Allegory in the Vocal Music of J. S. Bach* (Berkeley and Oxford: California University Press, 1991); and Jaroslav Pelikan, *Bach Among the Theologians* (Philadelphia: Fortress Press, 1986).

14. E. Ye. Zhukovskaya, "Vospominaniya o moyom uchitele i druge S. V. Rakhmaninove," in *Vospominaniya o Rakhmaninove*, 1:251–342, at 294.

15. Letter of 18 June 1891, in Rakhmaninov, *Literaturnoye naslediye*, 1:173.

16. For details of the very many songs to texts by Tolstoy up to 1917, see G. K. Ivanov, *Russkaya poeziya v otechestvennoy muzïke (do 1917 goda): Spravochnik*, 2 vols. (Moscow: Muzïka, 1966–69), 1:338–49. Numerically, only Balmont, Pushkin, Fet, and Lermontov were more popular with composers.

17. Letter of 2 August 1906, in Rakhmaninov, *Literaturnoye naslediye*, 1:397.

18. A short memoir by Ivan Bunin corroborates this view of Rachmaninoff's taste in poetry and lists Fet, Lermontov, Maykov, Pushkin, and Tyutchev as poets they both admired. Bunin also recalls an occasion where both men lamented "the decline in prose and poetry that had then taken place in Russian literature." See I. A. Bunin, "S. V. Rakhmaninov," in *Vospominaniya o Rakhmaninove*, 2:25–26.

19. Richard Sylvester, *Tchaikovsky's Complete Songs: A Companion with Texts and Translations* (Bloomington: Indiana University Press, 2002).

20. V. Karatïgin, "Rakhmaninov," in *Zhizn', deyatel'nost', stat'i, materialï* (Leningrad: Academia, 1927), 204–5, at 204. Karatygin's article originally appeared in the newspaper *Rech'* in 1913.

21. Marietta Shaginyan, "S. V. Rakhmaninov (muzïkal'no-psikhologicheskiy etyud)," *Trudï i dni* 4–5 (1912): 97–114, at 102. Her later memoir not only gives a detailed account of the circumstances surrounding their friendship, but also vividly evokes musical and intellectual life in early twentieth-century Moscow. See Marietta Shaginyan, "Vospominaniya o Sergeye Rakhmaninove," in *Vospominaniya o Rakhmaninove*, 2:90–158. For further discussion of Shaginyan's writings on Rachmaninoff and her place in the musical life of early twentieth-century Moscow, see Rebecca Mitchell's essay in this volume.

22. On music as a means of effecting social reconciliation, and the polemics surrounding the music of Scriabin, Rachmaninoff, and Medtner in early twentieth-century Russia, see Rebecca Mitchell, *Nietzsche's Orphans: Music, Metaphysics, and the Twilight of the Russian Empire* (New Haven and London: Yale University Press, 2015), which includes a discussion of Shaginyan's article (141–49).

23. Shaginyan, "S. V. Rakhmaninov," 106.

24. Letter of 15 March 1912, in Rakhmaninov, *Literaturnoye naslediye*, 2:43.

25. Letter of 29 March 1912, in ibid., 2:44.

26. Letter of 29 March 1912, in ibid., 2:44. Galina was the pseudonym of Glarifa Mamoshina, a turn-of-the-century poet who enjoyed considerable popularity with general readers. Rachmaninoff set her poetry on three occasions. For other settings, see Ivanov, *Russkaya poeziya v otechestvennoy muzïke*, 1:91–93.

27. The letters were first published in the Soviet Union in 1943, shortly after Rachmaninoff's death. See "Pis'ma S. V. Rakhmaninova k Re," *Novïy mir* 4 (1943): 105–13. They were translated into English in Victor I. Seroff, *Rachmaninoff* (New York: Simon & Schuster, 1950), although Shaginyan objected to the romantic light in which Seroff painted their relationship. The letters have formed a central element of biographical works ever since, including Bertensson and Leyda, *Sergei Rachmaninoff*.

28. Shaginyan, "Vospominaniya o Sergeye Rakhmaninove," 2:120.

29. Letter of 19 June 1912, in Rakhmaninov, *Literaturnoye naslediye*, 2:50.

30. Ibid. The anthology referred to here is a collection of contemporary verse by poets such as Andrey Bely, Valery Bryusov, Sergei Gorodetsky, Vladimir Solovyov, Yury Verkhovsky, Maksimilian Voloshin, Nikolai Gumilyov, Mikhaïl Kuzmin, and others, published by the Moscow publisher Musaget in 1911. See commentary in Rakhmaninov, *Literaturnoye naslediye*, 2:392.

31. The suggestion that Rachmaninoff should set Poe's poetry came from a young woman who sent him a copy of Balmont's translations. See A. F. Gyodike, "Pamyatnïye vstrechi," in *Vospominaniya o Rakhmaninove*, 2:4–17, at 15. The cellist Mikhaíl Bukinik gives a rather more vivid description of Rachmaninoff's mysterious muse in his memoir of the composer, in which he identifies her as "a certain Danilova from Sevastopol." According to Bukinik, Danilova "would wear short skirts, half-masculine jackets, and a tie, and would cut her hair in a boyish fashion." She became obsessed both with Poe's poetry and the idea of hearing it set to music, so sent a copy of *The Bells*—anonymously and without a return address—to Rachmaninoff. See M. E. Bukinik, in *Vospominaniya o Rakhmaninove*, 1:213–26, at 225–26.

32. Shaginyan, "Vospominaniya o Sergeye Rakhmaninove," 2:152.

33. Ibid., 170.

34. On the *Six Poems* see, for instance, Anna Simpson, "Dear Re: A Glimpse into the Six Songs of Rachmaninoff's Opus 38," *College Music Symposium* 24/1 (1984): 97–106.

35. For more on the "musicality" of Russian poetry, see L. L. Gerver, *Muzïka i muzïkal'naya mifologiya v tvorchestve russkikh poetov (pervïye desyatiletiya XX veka)* (Moscow: Indrik, 2001); B. Kats, *Muzïkal'nïye klyuchi k russkoy poezii* (St. Petersburg: Kompozitor, 1997); and Paul Friedrich, *Music in Russian Poetry* (New York: Peter Lang, 1997).

36. Boris Bugaev [Andrey Belïy], "Formï iskusstva," *Mir iskusstva* 8/12 (1902): 343–61, at 356. Bely's essays are crucial documents when it comes to tracing the importance of music in Russian intellectual culture of the Silver Age. For a comparative study of his fiction from the same perspective, see Ada Steinberg, *Word and Music in the Novels of Andrey Bely* (Cambridge: Cambridge University Press, 1982).

37. Vladimir E. Alexandrov, "The Symphonies," in *Andrei Bely: The Major Symbolist Fiction* (Cambridge, MA: Harvard University Press, 1985), 5–67.

38. Andrey Belïy, *Posle razluki: Berlinskiy pesennik* (St. Petersburg and Berlin: Epokha, 1922), 16.

39. Andrey Belïy, "Nikolay Metner," in *Arabeski: Kniga statey* (Moscow: Musaget, 1911), 369–75, at 373.

40. Ibid., 375.

41. Andrey Belïy, "Okno v budushcheye," in *Arabeski*, 138–46, at 142–43.

42. Ibid., 145.

43. Maria Razumovskaya, "Nikolai Medtner: Championing the German Lied and the Russian Spirit," in *German Song Onstage: Lieder Performance in the Nineteenth and Early Twentieth Centuries*, ed. Natasha Loges and Laura Tunbridge (Bloomington: Indiana University Press, 2020), 154–78.

44. The dates in this list indicate when the songs were completed, rather than necessarily composed. Rachmaninoff arrived at Ivanovka in late April, so work on them must have taken place no earlier than May 1912. On April 28, en route from Moscow, he had written to Shaginyan to thank her for the poems she had copied out for him "so patiently and heroically." See *Literaturnoye naslediye*, 2:46.

45. Andrey Belïy, "Simvolizm i sovremennoye russkoye iskusstvo," in *Lug zelyonïy: Kniga statey* (Moscow: Al'tsiona, 1910), 29–50, at 30.

46. Boris Gasparov, Robert P. Hughes, and Irina Paperno, eds., *Cultural Mythologies of Russian Modernism: From the Golden Age to the Silver Age* (Berkeley and Oxford: California University Press, 1992).

47. In return, Shaginyan dedicated her volume of poetry, *Orientaliya* (1913), to Rachmaninoff, although he never set any of her verses to music. Shaginyan was rather underwhelmed by Rachmaninoff's setting of Pushkin's "The Muse," which she felt was "dry." Instead, she much preferred Medtner's version (1913), also dedicated to her, although in later life she claimed to have come to understand much better the subtleties of Rachmaninoff's song. Shaginyan, "Vospominaniya o Sergeye Rakhmaninove," 2:121.

Three Operas

Tchaikovsky's Echoes, Chaliapin's Sobs: *Aleko*, Rachmaninoff, and the Contemporary

EMILY FREY

In January 2020, social media—at least, the corner of it inhabited by musicologists—was atwitter with news from the data science world. An algorithm had finally settled a debate we music lovers had been waging for centuries: who was the most innovative composer of the Common Practice Period?[1] The winner, who earned the highest marks for novelty relative to both his own oeuvre and those of his historical predecessors, was unexpected, though perhaps not for readers of this book: Sergei Rachmaninoff.

Chuckles abounded. "Hilarious!" wrote one of the kinder comment-ers on *Slipped Disc*.[2] Some took to criticizing the study's methodology; the researchers, after all, had studied only piano music, and they had defined their innovation index in terms of melody and harmony, neglect-ing to consider as criteria such nonessentials as rhythm, meter, and form. The verdict of the classical music commentariat was that this study had resulted in vindication, though not for Rachmaninoff, that most beloved and least respected of "serious" twentieth-century composers. It was vin-dication, instead, for musicians—who, it turned out, still knew a thing or two that the computers did not.

For if there is one thing everybody knows about Rachmaninoff, it is that he was behind his times, not ahead of them. In twentieth-century textbooks, Rachmaninoff stands as the six-and-a-half-foot poster boy for epigonism, an imitator of Tchaikovsky and Chopin (composers whose own avant-garde credentials are hardly unimpeachable), who remained stubbornly—and worse, lucratively—resistant to the demands of musi-cal "progress." Rachmaninoff's entry in the fifth edition of the *Grove Dictionary of Music and Musicians* (1954) pronounced him an anachro-nism: "As a composer he can hardly be said to have belonged to his time at all."[3] And Rachmaninoff himself made several well-publicized state-ments to that effect in the 1930s and 1940s, describing "modern music" as antipathetic, incomprehensible, and heartless. "I feel like a ghost wandering in a world grown alien," he wrote to Leonard Liebling in 1939. "I cannot cast out the old way of writing, and I cannot acquire the new. I have made intense effort to feel the musical manner of today, but it will not come to me."[4] Since that time, musicologists of a contrarian bent have occasionally attempted to demonstrate that Rachmaninoff comes up not so short on the modernist yardstick as the composer's late-in-life statements would indicate. In a Rachmaninoff-themed issue of *Tempo* from the early 1950s, Joseph Yasser wrote that Rachmaninoff's harmonic language "represents evidently a significant even if not necessarily a 'spectacular' contribution to musical progress. In view of this fact, one will be justified perhaps in the conclusion that . . . Rachmaninoff should be placed somewhere among the moderately progressive composers, and in no wise among those who are frankly conservative."[5] But this is notably timid and couching language for a rescue effort, and Richard Taruskin has treated such attempts to make Rachmaninoff modern to a characteristic debunking in an article titled "Not Modern and Loving It."[6] And still, the scholarly spotlight remains fixed on Rachmaninoff's relationship to Euro-American modernism—a relationship so vexed, so mutually and so deliciously antagonistic, as to draw the preponderance of attention dedicated to the composer.

Any comparison between Rachmaninoff the composer and interwar modernism is bound to be an uneven one, for though he lived until 1943, Rachmaninoff wrote only a handful of new pieces after his emigration from Russia in 1917. The vast, vast majority of his own compositions that he performed and recorded after his emigration really were backward-looking, for they had been written years before, in an empire that no longer existed. Even from the standpoint of pre-revolutionary Russia, however, the famously scowling Rachmaninoff did not always appear in step with the times. According to the Marxist philosopher and revolutionary Georgy Plekhanov (1856–1918), it was Scriabin's transcendent ecstasy, not Rachmaninoff's intensely personal gloom, that represented "the era transposed into sound."[7] But when Rachmaninoff and Scriabin graduated from the Moscow Conservatory in 1892, critical opinion had been reversed. Scriabin was by all accounts a successful music student, winning a Small Gold Medal from the Conservatory, but Rachmaninoff received a far more glittering sendoff. Rachmaninoff's graduation exercise, the one-act opera *Aleko*, earned the Conservatory's highest honors, the outspoken admiration of Tchaikovsky, and the patronage of Aleksandr Gutheil, a music publisher who offered Rachmaninoff a contract to make any budding composer boil with envy. It is easy to see what Moscow's musical elite liked about *Aleko*, which is an extraordinarily proficient and self-assured work even notwithstanding the precocious age of the composer, who turned nineteen while composing the opera, and the frankly scorching speed at which he wrote it—eighteen days, including the orchestration. "It was no student essay, but a real work of art," remembered the cellist and composer Mikhaíl Bukinik (1872–1947), one of Rachmaninoff's classmates at the Conservatory. He continued: "I was in the orchestration class, and while rehearsing it, we not only marveled at [Rachmaninoff], but took pride and delight in his daring harmonies, and we were ready to see in him a reformer."[8] Later commentators, however, have been less struck by *Aleko*'s novelties than by its more or less overt borrowings from Tchaikovsky, from Glinka and Borodin, and (improbably enough) from Mascagni. In sum, then, *Aleko*—the work that launched Rachmaninoff's career—has often seemed to exemplify the very criticisms that dogged him until the end of it.

This essay takes on *Aleko* from two angles. First, I consider Rachmaninoff in relation to the musical past of which he was supposedly an epigone, exploring the ways in which his youthful opera deals with the methods and conventions of operatic realism, which reigned in Russia from the 1860s through the 1880s. I argue that the relationship between *Aleko* and realism is not entirely uncritical: though *Aleko*, the work of an attentive conservatory student, clearly references and synthesizes realist models, it also undermines them in ways that would resonate throughout Rachmaninoff's subsequent career as a vocal composer. Then, complicating the idea of Rachmaninoff as an artist out of touch with his times, I will examine the ways in which Rachmaninoff's attempts to move beyond realism mapped onto the efforts of a group of contemporaries with whom he had close personal and creative ties. They were not composers or mystic poets but, like Rachmaninoff himself, pathbreaking Muscovite performers: the singer Fyodor Chaliapin and the theater director Konstantin Stanislavsky, both of whom played significant roles in *Aleko*'s performance history before and after the Revolution.

Realizing "The Gypsies"

Rachmaninoff's musical education was nothing if not intensive. From his arrival in Moscow at the age of twelve, Rachmaninoff attended a never-ending circuit of operas, concerts, and plays at the behest and largesse of his piano teacher, Nikolai Zverev. At Zverev's house, too, Rachmaninoff participated in weekly gatherings with a rotating cast of Moscow's leading artistic figures, including Tchaikovsky, Taneyev, and Arensky. By the time he graduated from the Conservatory, Rachmaninoff had a catholic command of the operatic, symphonic, and theatrical repertoire performed in Moscow during the 1880s and early 1890s.

The composers whose works dominated those stages and concert halls, including Tchaikovsky and the members of the now-defunct *moguchaya kuchka* (Mighty Handful), had come of age in a time when a peculiar vision of realism held sway over the Russian arts. They were all affected by it, though they manifested that influence in diverse ways. Indeed, it changes the usual narrative about nineteenth-century Russian music quite dramatically when we remember that composers as dissimilar as Musorgsky and Tchaikovsky—typically opposed as progressive vs. conservative, nationalist vs. cosmopolitan—both saw themselves as realists.[9] At this late date it is a cliché to complain of the perils in attempting to define nineteenth-century realism, especially in the area of music, traditionally assumed to be the most romantic of the arts.[10] But to speak in the broadest terms, what the heterogeneous works of Musorgsky, Tchaikovsky, Rimsky-Korsakov, and their contemporaries often share is a combination of precise, "objective" social description and penetrating, "subjective" psychological representation. While the detailed examination of social reality is a key ingredient in any nineteenth-century European realism, the elevated status of subjectivity, in both the target and the means of representation, has often distinguished the Russian version. The eminent Tolstoy scholar Donna Tussing Orwin writes:

> Contemporary European naturalist realism with its links to science tended . . . to be reductive and therefore to undercut or distort the inner life it was describing. In Russian realism, objective distance is suspended to an unprecedented degree by the author; as a result the subject retains its original "subjective" appearance and complexity. . . . The defense of subjectivity posed a unique challenge. . . . The works of Russian realism had to be objectively true and yet remain sympathetic to subjectivity.[11]

This "unique challenge"—of depicting both the outward, objective life of society and the inner, subjective life of the individual, and capturing both at high resolution—was faced by Russian opera composers no less eagerly than it was by Russian writers. Like their literary colleagues, Russian composers of the time also shared the crucial (if tacit) conviction that the two elements of this great juxtaposition, private emotion and social environment, were indissolubly related to each other. That, after all, had been Glinka's great realization in *A Life for the Tsar*: that musically speaking,

Ivan Susanin could retain his peasant's accent even while behaving like a tragic hero. By and large, Susanin's successors likewise do not adopt "unmarked" musical styles as soon as they begin to feel. Inner life, for many operatic characters in the age of realism, is neither hermetic nor universal. It always bears the imprint of the social.

For an example of how Russian operatic realism worked in practice, let us take a glimpse at the libretto to *Aleko*, which was written on commission by the playwright Vladimir Nemirovich-Danchenko (1858–1943) as a graduation exercise for the fledgling composers of the Moscow Conservatory in 1892. The text is an adaptation of an 1824 narrative poem called "The Gypsies" (*Tsyganï*), written by that most-musicalized of all Russian writers, Aleksandr Pushkin. While Pushkin's works present legendary problems for those who adapt them to the dramatic stage, "The Gypsies" is surprisingly forgiving. It is a relatively direct, plot-forward work containing little of the poet's characteristic meta-literary dazzle; almost unusually for Pushkin, the tale matters as much as the telling. It also offers highly sympathetic material for a Russian artist of realist inclination, for at its base, "The Gypsies" is a story about the ways in which upbringing and social environment define and constrain personal feeling. The plot describes how Aleko, a Russian cosmopolite sulking about in Bessarabian exile, meets the young Zemfira and takes up with her nomadic tribe. Aleko immediately embraces the tribe's carefree lifestyle, though Zemfira's father warns him that the group's moral code, which precludes personal possession in the name of universal freedom, is not always tolerable to those of "tender breed."[12] Aleko's psychological incompatibility with the tribe becomes violently clear two years later, when he discovers that Zemfira, who has recently borne his child, no longer loves him. Zemfira's father tells Aleko the story of his own abandonment by Zemfira's mother years before, and Aleko is incredulous at the old man's decision not to seek revenge. "Who would vainly try / To hold young love, free as a bird?" replies the old man, in words presaging those of Carmen's Habanera.[13] Aleko swears that he would not be able to leave such a romantic betrayal unavenged, and he proves it shortly thereafter by murdering Zemfira and her new lover after discovering them together. The tribe parts ways with Aleko, with the old man noting that Aleko's idea of freedom was only ever a selfish one—"This heathen freedom you have known / You claim it for yourself alone"—declaring that while their society has no laws, they will not live with murderers.[14] Though he valorizes the nomads' wild existence as superior to the rigid mores of the city, Aleko's own psychology has been molded, indelibly, by the very city he has shunned; his mind has evidently not followed his body into exile. Inner experience and outer environment remain inextricable from each other.

Nemirovich-Danchenko's methods in forging a libretto from this source were entirely typical of Russian operatic adaptations during the later nineteenth century, when textual preservation was held to be a cardinal virtue. Fortuitously, "The Gypsies" already contained a relatively large amount of dialogue that could be imported straight into the libretto, as well as aria-friendly set pieces for Zemfira and her father. Where Nemirovich-Danchenko could incorporate Pushkin's text directly, he did so, often truncating lines to manageable operatic proportions. Where he could not, Nemirovich-Danchenko repurposed Pushkin's words by a number of well-tested means, such as putting the narrator's comments about a character into that character's own mouth (as in the introduction to the old man's tale) and stitching together lines taken verbatim, or nearly so, from disparate parts of the poem (as in the nomads' chorus at the beginning of the opera). Otherwise, apart from a few quick insertions to motivate the set pieces and Aleko's Oneginish cry of despair at the end of the opera, Nemirovich-Danchenko included only two sustained interpolations of his own text.[15] One is at the denouement, in order to pump up the drama—for Pushkin deals with the murders in an economical thirteen lines—and to bring the chorus onstage as the curtain falls. The other is in the emotionally wrought monologue he created for Aleko, the text of which might serve to exemplify Nemirovich-Danchenko's procedures throughout the opera (Table 1).

The words to this monologue are cobbled together from four different extracts from Pushkin's poem, some of which comprise Aleko's direct speech and some the narrator's comments about Aleko. Pronouns, verbs, and time markers are adjusted as required, with the midday sun becoming the midnight moon; Nemirovich-Danchenko also makes a few minor alterations to the text for the sake of rhythm and length. As for the twelve-line interpolation near the end of the cavatina, it is easy enough to surmise why Nemirovich-Danchenko might have found it necessary. While Pushkin's poem takes place over a span of two years, encompassing all of Zemfira and Aleko's relationship, Nemirovich-Danchenko compresses the opera's time frame down to an Aristotelian single night. And so, while Pushkin's aggrieved Aleko had not needed to recount his romantic history at length, Nemirovich-Danchenko was compelled to invent a happy past for the operatic couple, much as Arrigo Boito had done a few years before in his libretto for Verdi's *Otello*. The impact of this "recollection of happiness from a time of misfortune" (to quote from the

Table 1. Aleko's Cavatina. Minor adjustments to Pushkin's text are underlined; wholesale additions are italicized.

Libretto text	English translation	Original source
Весь табор спит. Луна над ним полночной красотою блещет. Что ж сердце бедное трепещет? Какою грустью я томим?	*The whole camp sleeps.* The moon above Shines in midnight beauty. Why does my poor heart race? What sorrow weighs upon me?	Lines 100–103; time changed from midday to midnight; words made to be spoken by Aleko instead of about him.
Я без забот, *без сожаленья* веду кочующие дни.	I am without cares, without regrets, My days are spent wandering.	Lines 231–32; pronouns and verbs shifted from third to first person.
Презрев оковы просвещенья, я волен так же, как они.	Scorning the enlightened world's chains, I am just as free as the nomads are.	Lines 229–30; pronouns adjusted.
Я жил, не признавая власти судьбы коварной и слепой. Но, боже, как играют страсти моей послушною душой!..	I have lived, not recognizing the power Of blind, insidious destiny. But, God, how the passions play Upon my willing soul!	Lines 138–41; pronouns adjusted; verb tense ("how the passions play") shifted from past to present.
Земфира! Как она любила! Как нежно преклонясь ко мне, в пустынной тишине часы ночные проводила! Как часто милым лепетаньем, упоительным лобзаньем задумчивость мою в минуту разогнать умела!	*Zemfira!* How she loved me! How tenderly she bent to me, In the silence of the wilderness The nocturnal hours sped by! How often, with sweet words, With passionate kisses, My gloomy pensiveness Could she dispel in a moment!	Lines 359–67; line 363 omitted, lines 361, 365, and 366 slightly truncated. (In Pushkin, this is now Aleko's direct speech, not the narrator's.)
Я помню: с негой, полной страсти, шептала мне она тогда: «Люблю тебя! В твоей я власти! Твоя, Алеко, навсегда!» И всё тогда я забывал, когда речам ее внимал и как безумный целовал её чарующие очи, кос чудных прядь, темнее ночи, уста Земфиры. . . А она, вся негой, страстью полна, прильнув ко мне, в глаза глядела. . .	*I remember: with bliss, full of passion, She whispered to me then: "I love you! I am in your power! I am yours, Aleko, forever!" And I forgot all else then, When I listened to her speeches, And like a madman I kissed Her spellbinding eyes, Her wondrous braids, darker than night, Zemfira's lips... And she, Full of ecstasy and passion, Nestled against me, looked in my eyes...*	Nemirovich-Danchenko's interpolation.
И что ж? Земфира неверна! Моя Земфира охладела!	And what now? Zemfira is unfaithful! My Zemfira is cold!	Lines 368–69.

libretto of another Rachmaninoff opera) is to intensify—drastically—the hero's psychological predicament at the climax of the drama.

This kind of emphasis on and heightening of the psychological elements of Pushkin's story was another way in which Nemirovich-Danchenko's libretto approached the norms and methods of Russian realist opera. Geoffrey Norris complains of the libretto that "the whole action is far too slow," and that apart from "only two significant events which advance the drama . . . the rest of the text comprises static, reflective arias," though *Aleko* is hardly unique in this regard.[16] A too-ponderous tempo and a lack of external action are the very hoariest of criticisms hurled at Russian operas (and Russian novels, for that matter) by those who seek their "drama" in the wrong place. As Boris Gasparov writes in his classic study *Five Operas and a Symphony*:

> A typical Russian opera evolves as a series of loosely con-
> nected tableaux, now picturesquely static, now jumping
> into a new situation over a number of presumed events. . . .
> Although often lacking in external dramatic movement, [the
> operas] foreground the introspective, implicit, psychological
> underpinnings of their actions. . . . The listeners' attention
> is focused not so much on the events . . . as on shifts in the
> characters' state of mind and on overall changes in their per-
> sonality caused by those events—the inner changes.[17]

Those inner changes, depicted at length in such "static, reflective" solo passages as Aleko's cavatina, are indeed the main source of "action" in *Aleko*.

Meanwhile, this sustained airing of subjectivity is nestled within a depiction of the life of the tribe: compared with Pushkin's original poem, Nemirovich-Danchenko's libretto amplifies the role of the chorus and calls for social entertainment in the form of dancing. Exotic dances of this sort may be an operatic commonplace, but Nemirovich-Danchenko's placement of them at an emotional apex—right after Aleko's ominously impassioned response to the old man's tale—is quintessentially realist.[18] As in Tchaikovsky's most famous operas, the protagonist is here forced to watch the spectacle in a state of inner turmoil. The plot machine may stop, but Aleko still seethes; the psychological drama continues to unfold in time as the crowd enacts its public ritual. Here, at the meeting point of private feeling and social activity, Aleko's emotional distance from his adopted tribe—the very conflict that drives the opera's denouement—is made dreadfully plain. The "uncomfortable [wrench] of mood" that Norris identifies at this moment is deliberate: it is a realist feature, not a bug.

Aleko's much-derided libretto is no masterpiece, but a masterpiece could hardly be expected from a playwright hired to adapt Pushkin for student composers. Choose just about any other nineteenth-century Russian libretto and you will find the same faults: too disjointed, not dramatically effective, a "hotch-potch of . . . Pushkin."[19] This is because, in discharging his commission, Nemirovich-Danchenko had relied on the same methods as those earlier librettists (who were very often not professional writers, but the composers themselves), and like them he had constructed his text to highlight and juxtapose emotional expression and social experience. We need not wonder, then, that as sensitive a critic as Nikolai Kashkin (1839–1920) could call Nemirovich's libretto "stageworthy (*stsenichniy*)."[20] Kashkin, an old friend and colleague of Tchaikovsky's, had after all seen many similar librettos succeed on the Russian stage.

Pro and Contra Realism

Whatever the brilliant reception *Aleko* received in 1892, Rachmaninoff eventually came to regard his student work the way most of us do our own. A singer with the Moscow Art Theater recalled Rachmaninoff's curt refusal to attend the company's 1925 performance of *Aleko* in New York: "I am ashamed to have written such nonsense."[21] He elaborated on his disdain for the work elsewhere: "[*Aleko*] is written on the old-fashioned Italian model, which Russian composers, in most cases, have been accustomed to follow."[22]

The Italianism of *Aleko* deserves a closer look, for Taruskin has called the opera "the very last instance of a Russian composer of any stature adopting an Italian model for opera,"[23] and Geoffrey Norris has claimed that "the main influence on the opera's overall structure came not from Russian music but from Italian."[24] These remarks are based on certain similarities between *Aleko* and *Cavalleria rusticana*, which was playing in Moscow to great acclaim as Rachmaninoff started work on *Aleko*. But this could not have been what Rachmaninoff had in mind when he described *Aleko* as having been "written on the old-fashioned Italian model," for in 1892 Mascagni's juggernaut would have been the *new*-fashioned Italian model, and considering the more continuous, Wagnerian structure of Rachmaninoff's later operas, it seems more likely that he meant simply that *Aleko* had numbers. In any case, beyond the transparently referential intermezzo that Rachmaninoff inserted before the denouement of his opera, *Aleko*'s debt to *Cavalleria rusticana* is not so very great. Norris claims that "the formation of [*Aleko*'s] libretto was almost certainly influenced" by *Cavalleria rusticana*,[25] but as we have seen, most of *Aleko*'s words come straight out of "The Gypsies," which predated the *Cavalleria*s of Verga and Mascagni by over half a century and had long

Example 1. Rachmaninoff, *Aleko*, nomads' chorus: "Our camp is as joyful as freedom itself, and we sleep peacefully beneath the heavens."

been a well-known work in its own right. And as the broad plot themes shared by *Aleko* and *Cavalleria*—exoticism, romantic jealousy, violent death—are convention itself in opera, it is hard to imagine Nemirovich-Danchenko's libretto would have had anyone in the audience thinking of Sicily.[26] As Rachmaninoff himself intimated in the quotation above—"the old-fashioned Italian model, which Russian composers . . . have been accustomed to follow"—the Italianism of *Aleko* is of a more indirect sort, filtered through a long history of Russian tradition.

Example 2. Anton Rubinstein, *The Demon*, Act 2, melisma in Georgian girls' chorus.

That Russian tradition had left very clear precedents regarding the ways in which the cultural conflict at the center of *Aleko*—ethnic Russians vs. Asiatic Others—should be conveyed in music, and Rachmaninoff's depiction of Zemfira's tribe hewed closely to type. The nomads' chorus that opens the opera offers up a smorgasbord of Orientalist conventions, beginning with the prominent timpani in the introduction. At the choral entrance in Example 1, the low strings drone away on F while the bassoons slither reedily among the natural sixth, flat sixth, and fifth scale degrees, briefly reaching up to touch the flat seventh. Rachmaninoff's sopranos, meanwhile, end their phrase with the kind of mid-range melismatic noodling that has been a cherished pastime of Russian exotics from Glinka's Ratmir onward; compare with Example 2, the Georgian chorus in Anton Rubinstein's *The Demon* (1871), whose accompaniment also incorporates the inevitable "chromatic pass" from ♮6–♭6–5 in the last two bars. These and other well-worn devices litter the ensemble numbers, including the women's dance, set in the conspicuously alien key of A-flat minor, and the succeeding men's dance, whose opening bars provide a sort of missing link between Musorgsky's *Night on Bald Mountain* and Khachaturian's *Sabre Dance*.[27]

Example 3. Rachmaninoff, *Aleko*, old man's motive.

Quite "realistically," however, Rachmaninoff does not confine the Orientalisms to local color from the chorus. After an introduction whose text and orchestration recall the bard Bayan from *Ruslan and Lyudmila*, Zemfira's father begins his sad ballad to the tune of an evocative motive that will shadow him throughout the number. This motive is "exotic" in both its melody, where an augmented second precedes a tritone leap, and its harmony, which is decorated by a chromatically altered subdominant chord with a half-diminished sonority (Example 3). This particular altered chord would become something of a signature in Rachmaninoff's music, such that Russian theorists now know it as the "Rachmaninoff subdominant" (*rakhmaninovskaya subdominanta*), and its precedent is often found in the introduction to Tchaikovsky's *Romeo and Juliet* (Example 4).[28] The old man's leitmotif, however, references not just Tchaikovsky's harmony but his melody as well, for the top voice in his Fantasy-Overture

Example 4. Pyotr Tchaikovsky, *Romeo and Juliet*, mm. 30–37.

Example 5. Rachmaninoff, *Aleko*, Zemfira's cradle song: "Old husband, terrible husband, stab me, burn me."

had executed that very same tritone leap after an augmented second. What Rachmaninoff creates here, then, is not a thoughtless echo of Tchaikovsky's *Romeo and Juliet* but an allusion—and an eminently appropriate one given that the old man is recounting his own romantic tragedy in this moment. Equally apt is the fact that, as Taruskin has shown, *Romeo and Juliet* also fits into the tradition of Russian musical Orientalism; Balakirev, who was no novice on the subject, chided Tchaikovsky for making Shakespeare's lovers sound Eastern rather than European.[29] The allusion thus telegraphs, and fuses, the old man's sad emotional history and his "exotic" social type—and shows off the student Rachmaninoff's mastery of both the Russian repertoire and the semiotics of musical style.

Zemfira's cradle song presents another instance of Rachmaninoff's skillful interweaving of the personal and the social. In this number Zemfira needles Aleko with an old lullaby whose shockingly unmaternal words—"Old husband, terrible husband, stab me! Burn me!"—fit the couple's personal situation a little too well (Example 5). The musical markers of Zemfira's tribe are in place, notably the constant alternation of F♮ and F♯, the flat and natural sixth scale degrees within the context of A minor. Musically, however, this is no mere genre piece unconnected with the rest of the opera, as the song's opening theme comes to function as

Example 6. Rachmaninoff, *Aleko*, Introduction.

a leitmotif of sorts. We hear this theme first in the overture, in a lyrical, major-mode variant quite remote in character from the strident cradle song, perhaps referring to Aleko and Zemfira's happier past (Example 6). We also hear it—now in the minor mode, nostalgic and *espressivo*—in Aleko's cavatina, right after he sings "Zemfira! How she loved me!" and in a truncated, harmonically unstable form as Zemfira dies (Examples 7 and 8). This is the very same device that Tchaikovsky used to such great effect in *Evgeny Onegin*: the use of a motive extracted from the heroine's diegetic song to characterize the heroine herself. The old lullaby—which Zemfira presumably heard first at her own cradle, sung by the mother whose example she imitates—becomes an indelible part of Zemfira's musical self. It is a clever illustration of a quintessentially realist idea: that inner

Example 7. Rachmaninoff, *Aleko*, Aleko's cavatina: "Zemfira! How she loved me!"

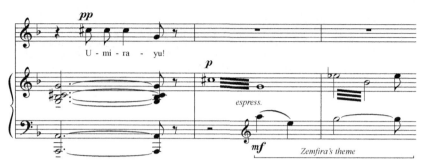

Example 8. Rachmaninoff, *Aleko*, Zemfira's death: "I'm dying!"

experience is conditioned by outer experience, that people recapitu-
late in their personal lives what they see and hear in their environment.

Aleko, meanwhile, is painted largely from Tchaikovsky's harmonic
palette. This was not an inevitable choice on Rachmaninoff's part, for
a folkishly modal idiom was more often the favored costume of Russian
characters who come into contact with emissaries from exotic or supernatural realms. The precedent for this diatonic ("Russian") vs. chromatic
("foreign") conflict was set, inevitably, by Glinka in *Ruslan and Lyudmila*,
and followed by Borodin in *Prince Igor*, Rimsky-Korsakov in *Sadko*, and
Rachmaninoff himself in his first series of songs, Opus 4, written within a
year of *Aleko*. Number 4 from that collection, the famous "Sing Not to Me,
O Beauty" ("Ne poy, krasavitsa, pri mne"), slings the Orientalisms even
more lustily than *Aleko* does, while Number 5, "The Harvest of Sorrow"
("Uzh ti niva moya") is written in a folk-Russian style with Aeolian coloring, "drawn-out" melisma, and frequent detours into $\frac{7}{4}$ time. Aleko
is no folk hero, however, but an urban sophisticate who has read a bit
too much Byron, and his musical garb recalls that of Evgeny Onegin,
another Pushkin hero who fits that description.[30] Aleko's semitone-based
leitmotif (Example 9) is even suspiciously reminiscent of a little musical
tag that introduces Onegin (Example 10), and accompanies him in various guises and at various points in Tchaikovsky's opera (see Example 11,
from the end of Act 1, and Example 12, from the beginning of Act 3).
Once again, Rachmaninoff deploys his musical references judiciously—
and what he loses in musical contrast by granting his hero access to the
full range of chromatic possibilities, he undeniably gains in psychological richness. The monologue Nemirovich-Danchenko created for Aleko
would become the centerpiece of Rachmaninoff's opera, and in its
through-composed structure, its harmonic range, and its interspersion
of speechlike passages with lyrical ones, Aleko's cavatina is a descendant

Example 9. Rachmaninoff, *Aleko*, Aleko's leitmotif in an unharmonized form.

Example 10. Tchaikovsky, *Evgeny Onegin*, Act 1, scene 1: "I'm very pleased to meet you!"

Example 11. Tchaikovsky, *Evgeny Onegin*, Act 1, scene 3: "But I don't want to praise you; I will repay you with an equally artless confession."

Example 12. Tchaikovsky, *Evgeny Onegin*, Act 3, scene 1: "I'm bored here too!"

of the big, psychologically complex monologues for low male voice in such operas as Musorgsky's *Boris Godunov* and Rimsky-Korsakov's *The Maid of Pskov*. Like those pieces, Aleko's cavatina has become a showpiece for singing actors from Chaliapin onward.

So far, so realist. But, having demonstrated his command of Russian operatic tradition, Rachmaninoff then demonstrated his willingness to disregard it. At the end of *Aleko*, the tribe takes its leave of the hero with an abandonment of the musical idiom that has defined it throughout the opera. "We are wild, we have no laws," sings the old man, and the chorus follows with an extended passage in whole tones (Example 13). In and of themselves, whole tones were common enough in Russian opera; this passage was probably not what Rachmaninoff's cellist classmate had in mind when he spoke of *Aleko*'s "daring harmonies." The inevitable Glinka had set the precedent in *Ruslan*, using whole-tone harmonies to represent the magical mischief of the dwarf wizard Chernomor. A host of Russian supernatural villains followed in Chernomor's hexatonic wake, from the statue in Dargomyzhsky's *The Stone Guest* to the countess's ghost in Tchaikovsky's *Queen of Spades*. Tchaikovsky stretched the convention

Example 13. Rachmaninoff, *Aleko*, Finale, beginning of whole-tone passage: "We are wild, we have no laws, we demand nothing."

Example 14. Rachmaninoff, *Aleko*, Finale, Chorale, second statement of theme: "We are timid and good-hearted; you are vicious and bold. Leave us, leave us."

Example 14, continued.

a little in his last opera, *Iolanta* (a close contemporary of *Aleko*), apply-
ing a whole-tone shimmer to the moment when the heroine recovers
her eyesight—but here again, the whole tones still indicate the presence
of the miraculous and the unexplainable even if they do not adhere to
a particular character.[31] And so, though whole tones may have been an
effective way to convey Aleko's alienation from the tribe, Rachmaninoff's
use of them also flew in the face of fifty years' worth of operatic tradition that had linked this sonority with a very specific, and very different,
association. Immediately after their whole-tone excursion, this group of
Bessarabian nomads launches into a churchy chorale. In this 23-measure
section, chromaticism is restricted to distinctly unexotic secondary domi-
nants, which the tribe has categorically shunned until this point. Also,
unlike the rest of the tribe's music, the passage is marked by fluctua-
tion not between the natural and flat sixth scale degree, but between
the natural and raised seventh—a conflict, as Marina Frolova-Walker has
noted, that also characterizes Rachmaninoff's later religious music, such
as the *All-Night Vigil*.[32] Like the whole-tone passage that precedes it, this
Requiem-like moment is appropriate to the "inner" circumstances of the
drama, for it is sung as two bodies are carried offstage. And certainly,
neither of the two styles sung by the tribe at the end is unusual on its

Example 15. Rachmaninoff, *Aleko*, No. 8: "One more, one more kiss! One more, one more kiss!"

own (*The Queen of Spades* also ends with a chorale, after all). Putting those two idioms in the mouths of *this* chorus, however—and thus having a Bessarabian tribe sing like a Russian Orthodox choir staffed with sorcerers—really was a departure (Example 14).

Rachmaninoff's musical treatment of Zemfira's lover departed further. As with the ensemble at the end of the opera, Rachmaninoff assigns this character a musical idiom that is both instantly recognizable (to a Russian audience, anyway) and "wrong" given his social type. This "Young Gypsy" is no musical exotic; his role is largely free of the Orientalist stereotypes that characterize his tribe. Rather, the tenor's vocal line is shot through with what Russian music scholars have termed *sekstovost'* (sixthiness) and identified as a hallmark of the nineteenth-century Russian romance. Example 15, from the Young Gypsy's duettino with Zemfira, is a case in point: the first phrase ends with a descending major sixth, and the second encompasses a minor sixth in its melodic span. Such sixthiness is a prominent feature of the Young Gypsy's style from the very beginning, and his first solo utterance even paraphrases the sixthiest tenor role in

Example 16. Rachmaninoff, *Aleko*, No. 4: "He is jealous, but I am not afraid."

Example 17. Tchaikovsky, *Evgeny Onegin*, Act 2, scene 2, Lensky's aria: "If I fall, pierced through by an arrow."

Example 18 a–c. Rachmaninoff, *Aleko*, unresolved ninths in the "Romance of the Young Gypsy," No. 12.

all Russian opera—compare Example 16 with Example 17, Lensky's aria from *Evgeny Onegin*. Yet again, this reference makes a great deal of sense from a characterological standpoint. In their respective operas, Lensky and the Young Gypsy are both impassioned and idealistic tenors sent to early graves by baritonal ne'er-do-wells. The trouble, from a realist point of view, is that the Young Gypsy's indefatigable sixthiness was by convention a *Russian* trait.[33] While the romance's sixthy style had perfectly suited Lensky—who in Pushkin is regularly assailed with Russian songs caterwauled by marriage-minded local girls—it was a curiously unrealistic choice for a character who had never even seen the inside of a nineteenth-century Russian salon.

Or a fin-de-siècle French one, for that matter. The pinnacle of the Young Gypsy's salon style comes in his solo number, explicitly labeled a romance in the score. The sixthy opening phrase, encompassing a melodic span from B♭ to high G, and the light harp accompaniment are emblematic of the Russian romance. The harmony is not, for the ends of important phrases are decorated with major ninth chords—see Examples 18a and b, the latter in the fourth inversion. Built on the subdominant (the local tonic is F in Example 18b) these chords simply alternate with the tonic, leaving their dissonances to hang in the air. At the end of the romance, Rachmaninoff swaps in a dominant ninth on E♭—which, again, does not "resolve" to A♭ but simply rocks back to the B♭ tonic as if conventional tonal resolution were unnecessary (Example 18c). This seemingly slight little number thus contains the most "daring" of all harmonic feats in *Aleko*, and they had no precedent in Tchaikovsky. The sparse, waltzing accompaniment and dangling dissonances much more closely resemble the first *Gymnopédie*, which had been published four years earlier and which the pianist Rachmaninoff must have known—but even Satie had not asked his listeners to accept a *dominant* ninth as a "stable dissonance."[34]

The imagery called up by the Young Gypsy's stylistic mishmash is rather delightful: Lensky in a modish beret? Well, why not: had Lensky lived at the end of the nineteenth century instead of the beginning of it, Pushkin surely would have sent him off to study in Paris rather than Göttingen. As social description, the Young Gypsy's cosmopolitan salon style is completely nonsensical. But his insouciant Gallicisms do serve a critical dramatic purpose, for they characterize him much more acutely than the expected cocktail of augmented seconds and chromatic descents might have done. This Young Gypsy is the furthest thing from a Byronic brooder—to borrow Turgenev's famous typology, he is a Don Quixote, not a Hamlet—and the difference between his lightweight, fashionable idiom and the tortured chromaticism of Aleko makes that distinction immediately audible. Indeed, it is tempting to conclude that psychological contrast was Rachmaninoff's primary concern in his adaptation of the *Aleko* story, for he delineates it much more carefully than he does the social conflict between Russian and Roma. A realist, of course, would not have acknowledged a difference, seeing individual feeling and social experience as inextricably connected. Abounding in allusions to the works of Tchaikovsky, Borodin, Glinka, and others, *Aleko* very often sounds like a nineteenth-century Russian opera. But in suggesting—as with the Young Gypsy—that psychological type could be cleaved from social type, and in privileging the former over the latter as a subject of representation, Rachmaninoff parted ways with the Russian operatic past and undermined realism's most fundamental principles.

Drama Kings

Rachmaninoff's creative biography after his spectacular launch is familiar: the deaths of two mentors, Zverev and Tchaikovsky, in quick succession; the stunning failure of his First Symphony; the years of depression, the foray into hypnosis, the long-impassable writer's block. Rachmaninoff had written *Aleko* in under three weeks, but it would be thirteen years before he finished another opera.

Yet Rachmaninoff's most trying years, between the failure of the First Symphony (1897) and the success of the Second Piano Concerto (1901), were only barren from a compositional point of view. During this time he wore other musical hats—that of pianist, that of (generally begrudging) teacher, and that of opera conductor, with Savva Mamontov's Private Opera Company in Moscow.[35] It was this last position that brought Rachmaninoff into closer connection with some of Moscow's leading dramatic performers: Fyodor Chaliapin, newly engaged with Mamontov's Company, and through him the actor-directors Konstantin Stanislavsky and Vladimir Nemirovich-Danchenko—yes, the very same Nemirovich-Danchenko who had written the libretto to *Aleko* in the previous decade—who were at that time hatching a theatrical enterprise of their own, the Moscow Art Theater (Moskovskiy khudozhestvennïy teatr, or MXT). Rachmaninoff's relations with these artists would remain warm even after his emigration. He counted Chaliapin, six-and-a-half weeks his senior and his rare equal in height, among his closest friends and most frequent collaborators until the singer's death in 1938. Figures 1 and 2 show photographs of Rachmaninoff and Chaliapin at around the time they met and then nearly twenty years later; their intimacy is as apparent as their antipodal personalities. As for Stanislavsky and MXT, Rachmaninoff recalled to Oskar von Riesemann: "From the very beginning I took the greatest interest in

Figure 1. Rachmaninoff and Chaliapin when they first met, ca. 1898.

Stanislavsky's venture and its development, for personal as well as artistic reasons. I had the greatest respect for Stanislavsky and his artistic aims."[36] He demonstrated that respect in more than words, composing a musical "Letter to Stanislavsky" to congratulate the director on MXT's tenth anniversary and sending gifts and aid to the indigent students at MXT after the October Revolution.[37] Stanislavsky and Nemirovich-Danchenko

Figure 2. Rachmaninoff and Chaliapin, 1916.

returned Rachmaninoff's esteem, bringing *Aleko* to New York with MXT's American tour in 1925–26.

Like Rachmaninoff, these artists spent the 1890s grappling with the legacy of the nineteenth century. Chaliapin's autobiography, *Man and Mask*, contains a number of diatribes against the conventionality of late nineteenth-century operatic performance. While such criticisms of the operatic status quo—spectacle over substance, technical brilliance over emotional potency—were the typical ones lodged by operatic reformers in any time or place, Chaliapin's method of overcoming these maladies would not be a musical one. "I turn[ed] to the dramatic theatre for enlightenment," reads the subheading of a chapter covering the mid-1890s.[38] He credits his conversations with actors such as Mamont Dalsky (1865–1918) and Olga Sadovskaya (1849–1919) with his realization of the importance of words and his rejection of bel canto ideals. When applied without consideration of individual words, Chaliapin wrote, abstract ideals of vocal beauty led to a kind of emotional uniformity:

> Now I understood why *bel canto* nearly always gives rise to boredom. I thought of singers I knew . . . who nearly all sang notes to which the words were merely of secondary importance. Singers in this category sing in an agreeable manner . . . but should they have to sing several times in an evening, no one song would sound very different from any other.[39]

Chaliapin may paint himself as an iconoclast here, but he is engaging in a very old polemic. Undergraduate music majors will likely recognize the Artusi-Monteverdi controversy—should music be the servant or the mistress of words?—here applied to vocal style rather than harmony.

More immediately, it is striking how much Chaliapin's word-based, "expressive" rather than beautiful aesthetic resonates with the realist proclamations made by Dargomyzhsky and Musorgsky some thirty years earlier. Other elements of Chaliapin's practice, from his sometimes *parlando* delivery to his meticulous attention to his costumes and makeup, recall the realist performance style associated with the operas of Aleksandr Serov (1820–1871). (It was no accident, perhaps, that Chaliapin's most celebrated Russian roles were in operas written by precisely those three composers.) Taruskin quotes from the reminiscences of A. Abarinova, who sang Spiridonova at the premiere of Serov's *The Power of the Fiend* in 1872:

> After the *bel canto italiano* . . . you can imagine my feelings when Napravnik, after my attempt to sing, closed the score and said, "That's all wrong; you are singing an Italian recitative. Here you don't need a voice; do it as if speaking, trivially." I burst into tears and did not know what to do. . . . Suddenly Vasiliev had a brilliant idea: "Make her up, put a peasant blouse on her, get her some cheap boots, tie her in a headdress—then she'll know what to do." Jacoby, the

> makeup man, was called. He did me up as requested, and
> no sooner had I seen myself in the mirror, than all the right
> gestures and phrasing came to me.[40]

This sounds perfectly Chaliapinesque, but for one critical distinction. Chaliapin always described the creation of a character as proceeding from the inside out, rather than the outside in. The cheap boots and the headdress did not determine the character, for the process worked in reverse: "If we are aware of a man's inner nature," wrote Chaliapin, "we can almost accurately guess his physical aspect."[41] Moreover, Chaliapin continued, the portrayal of a character's external appearance and internal feelings did *not* require the same level of detail. "Individuality is a very precious possession, but in spirit only, not in flesh. . . . No makeup will help an actor to create a lifelike personality unless he can combine it with the inspirations that spring from his own mind—in other words, with *psychological* makeup."[42] While realism had sought to capture the mutual interaction of the social and the psychological, the general and the individual, Chaliapin speaks of this relationship as unidirectional. It is the inner world's manifestation in the outer one that concerns him, far more than the opposite. The characters he hoped to create onstage were less "types" than highly individuated psychological entities, whose variegated pronunciations and carefully calibrated "intonations" revealed more about the hidden crevices of their minds than they did about the influence of their social backgrounds.

This kind of granular, inside-out performance style is also associated—almost synonymously—with the teachings of Stanislavsky, for whom Chaliapin was an important muse. Stanislavsky's ever-evolving System was intended, in fact, to give lesser talents (like himself, in his own estimation) the tools to achieve onstage what actors like Chaliapin did instinctually. Stanislavsky too had spent the 1890s renovating Russian realism. MXT's early productions were almost hyper-realistic in the unprecedented (and expensive) detail of their sets and costumes and their infamous inclusion of live farm animals, real-life peasants who could not refrain from swearing onstage, and other "authentic" but intractable non-actors. As with Chaliapin's performances, these ostensibly realistic devices in fact undermined realism's careful balance between the general and the particular. The theater scholar Anna Muza writes: "The sophistication and unprecedented material culture of the Art Theatre's sets was a result not only of [Stanislavsky and Nemirovich-Danchenko's] fascination with the Real, but also of their unwavering—and costly—rejection of the generic in favor of the specific and individual."[43] Over the next decade Stanislavsky would begin to manifest that interest in the specific and individual in less visible ways, moving the details, in effect, from the porch into the cellar. In his most "inward" phase between 1906 and 1912, Stanislavsky stripped MXT's sets and costumes down to a proto-black-box aesthetic. Physical gestures and other such externalizations were likewise restricted to a minimum; Stanislavsky's aim during this period was to have his actors "radiate" their characters' inmost feelings rather than communicate them outwardly.[44]

Rachmaninoff's approach to musical drama was developing at the same time, and in largely the same direction. The most obvious difference between *Aleko* and the two operas Rachmaninoff completed in 1905, *Francesca da Rimini* and *The Miserly Knight*, lies in the expanded role of the orchestra. Whereas *Aleko* had followed Russian realist practice in concentrating the dramatic interest in the vocal line, *Francesca* and *The Miserly Knight* transfer much of the expressive burden to the orchestra, which constantly communicates—radiates, even—nonverbal emotional subtexts that may not be consciously understood by the characters. Social description, already attenuated in *Aleko*, all but disappears in the later works: it matters not a bit that Francesca and Paolo are fourteenth-century Italians, nor that Albert and the Baron are medieval Englishmen. Psychological portraiture, the main attraction in *Aleko*, becomes almost the sole one in the later operas—particularly *The Miserly Knight*, which in Taruskin's estimation "achieves near-expressionistic intensity at climaxes."[45] If *Aleko* may be faulted for its preponderance of "static, reflective arias," in *The Miserly Knight* this problem becomes a pathology: the opera devotes nearly half of its running time to the monologue of one character, the avaricious Baron, whose individual psychological grotesqueries Rachmaninoff renders in painstaking, and utterly riveting, detail. Where Russian psychological realism had taken as its aim the narration of consciousness, Rachmaninoff's *The Miserly Knight* traffics in the revelation of the *un*conscious, in all its aberrant particularity. (Appropriately enough, the Baron's scene is set in a cellar.) The Baron is not a social type, he is a musical case study.

This change in Rachmaninoff's operatic thinking has traditionally been understood as the exchange of one nineteenth-century model for another: Tchaikovsky giving way to Wagner. What I want to suggest here, however, is that Rachmaninoff's operatic trajectory, from the unsettled realism of 1892's *Aleko* to the highly interiorized world of 1905's *The Miserly Knight*, also paralleled the evolving performance styles of Chaliapin and the Moscow Art Theatre circle. Some level of artistic cross-pollination was probably inevitable given how often and how closely Rachmaninoff and Chaliapin worked together, beginning with their joint tenure at Mamontov's Private Opera in 1897–98. Later in their lives, both artists left a wealth of statements portraying their working relationship as one of immense sympathy and symbiosis. Chaliapin recalled one of their earliest collaborations, on Rimsky-Korsakov's *Mozart and Salieri* (1898):

> The more I studied Boris Godunov, Ivan the Terrible, Dositheus . . . the more convinced I became that acting equated with singing, and had to be so. In opera we must sing as we speak. . . . It never became more clear to me than when the occasion arrived for me to sing and play the part of Salieri, a task I found more difficult than all the previous ones. . . . Here was a new task, bristling with potential as well as difficulties, and I knew at once that all that was worth solving could be done by one man only, Rachmaninov. To him I went. Wonderful, magnificent Rachmaninov.[46]

Rachmaninoff, meanwhile, often affirmed both Chaliapin's lifelong friendship and the influence the singer had had on his own musical activities. For his debut as Principal Conductor of the Bolshoi, Rachmaninoff chose Dargomyzhsky's *Rusalka* as a star vehicle for the bass; the role of the mad Miller elicited a predictable tour de force from Chaliapin.[47] More than once, too, did Rachmaninoff describe his compositions as having been influenced by his friend's dramatic gifts. One of those compositions was, of course, *The Miserly Knight*. "It was Chaliapin who inspired me to write it," Rachmaninoff recalled to Oskar von Riesemann, "One can easily understand how the character of the old Baron . . . would appeal to Chaliapin's dramatic instinct. I composed the opera for him."[48]

That much might be obvious even without Rachmaninoff's explicit acknowledgment, for the Baron's monologue is practically a sonic portrait of Chaliapin. Inspired by a singing actor fervent in his belief that "in opera we must sing as we speak," and who was well on his way to becoming the most celebrated Boris Godunov of all time, Rachmaninoff wrote vocal lines that are notably "speechy"—far more so than those in *Aleko*. The Baron's role contains a horde of angular, unsingerly intervals and

Ne - mno - go,   ka - zhet - sya,   no   po - ne - mno - gu

Example 19. Rachmaninoff, *The Miserly Knight*, Scene 2: "Little by little, it seems, [my treasure grows]."

rhythmic features that all but scream "Musorgsky," such as the evaded downbeats and end-of-the-bar triplets in Example 19. Where Aleko's cavatina had been conventionally constructed—an opening scena and then an ABA form with continuous, romance-like accompaniment— the Baron's formally *sui generis* monologue proceeds by fits and starts, with kaleidoscopic shifts of mood and musical setting. It seems justifiable to speak of this stop-and-go, text-forward idiom as Rachmaninoff's "Chaliapin style," as it also characterizes the five romances Rachmaninoff dedicated to the singer, such as "Sud'ba" (Fate), Op. 21, No. 1, which the nervous pair performed *chez* Tolstoy in 1900; as opposed to the long phrases, continuous lyricism, and vocal radiance of so many other Rachmaninoff songs, such as "Muza" (The Muse), Op. 34, No. 1; "Zdes' khorosho" (Here It's So Fine), Op. 21, No. 7; or the Vocalise, Op. 34, No. 14.[49] Vocally, *The Miserly Knight* was written in a way that appeared calculated to show off Chaliapin's peculiar gifts for expressive declamation and psychological nuance, and Rachmaninoff's Wagnerian orchestra effectively musicalized Stanislavsky's contemporary interest in unconscious, nonverbal emotional revelation.

The irony is that Chaliapin declined to sing the Baron, for reasons that were never clear to Rachmaninoff. Rather, it was Aleko that became one of his signature roles, and it was in no small part his influence that helped to give *Aleko*, of all Rachmaninoff's operas, the longest life on the Russian stage. Aleko's cavatina was a staple of Chaliapin's concert repertoire, and his two marvelously different recordings of it (in Hayes, June 1923, and London, November 1929) display so many of the vocal devices now regarded as Chaliapin trademarks. His hyper-expressive singing violates all the rules of bel canto technique: at times his voice breaks into a shout, as at the end of his second statement of "Zemfira ne verna!" (Zemfira is unfaithful!); in other places he applies a speechlike tone, as in "Sheptala mne ona togda" (She whispered to me then). In the louder passages Chaliapin often disrupts his legato flow with emphatic consonants, and at other points still he distorts vowels—such as the deliberately ugly, widened first "*a*" vowel in "Moya Zemfira okhladela" (My Zemfira has grown cold). Most notable of all are his non-lexical additions to almost every line of Aleko's cavatina: the growls, the sighs, the breaks, the sobs. These, along with a propensity for long dramatic pauses, were the elements of Chaliapin's performance style that Rachmaninoff commented upon most frequently and most approvingly. "I can still hear how he sobbed at the end of the opera," he remarked after *Aleko*'s St. Petersburg premiere in 1899. "Such sobbing can only come from a great theatrical artist, or a man who has in his own life suffered as deeply as Aleko."[50]

Bertensson and Leyda also quote Ivan Ostromyslensky, who recalled a party at Rachmaninoff's house in 1923: "With Sergei Vasilyevich at the piano Chaliapin pranked and charmed us all night. . . . Next day at lunch I saw Rachmaninoff again. . . . 'Tell me, Ivan Ivanovich, what made the greatest impression on you last night?' Without waiting for my answer, he went on, 'I'm sure it was "Dark Eyes"—I don't doubt it. How he [Chaliapin] sighed, that villain, how he sobbed "You have ruined me!"—I couldn't sleep, for thinking, "How God endowed you beyond other men!" . . . Oh, that sigh!'"[51]

Those sighs, sobs, pauses, and other such performerly emendations are possible when the singer is allowed to take the lead, especially when that singer has an accompanist as supportive and sympathetic as Chaliapin found Rachmaninoff to be. "When he is at the piano," Chaliapin often remarked, "I am not singing alone—we are *both* singing."[52] Russian realist opera, particularly those works by Musorgsky and Dargomyzhsky that had made Chaliapin a star, had been tolerant of such expressive accessorizing. Once again, those operas—the ancestors to Rachmaninoff's own "Chaliapin style" of vocal writing—had placed the center of dramatic gravity in the word-carrying vocal line. In *The Miserly Knight*, however, Rachmaninoff had supplemented a *kuchkist*-sounding vocal line with a much heftier and more independent orchestral apparatus. This beefed-up, intensely expressive orchestration was designed, I have argued, to accomplish just what Chaliapin did with his sighs and sobs, to reveal emotional nuances that the words alone could not convey. Perhaps, however, this was precisely the problem: the orchestration of *The Miserly Knight* rendered Chaliapin-like vocal insertions and pauses both less feasible—because the orchestra was no longer "accompaniment," dependent on the voice and thus able to accommodate its expressive whims—and less necessary, as the orchestra would be doing much of a Stanislavskian actor's job for him. By attempting to incorporate contemporary dramatic performance practice into the composition of his opera, perhaps Rachmaninoff had obviated the need for it in the theater; by writing Chaliapin into the score, Rachmaninoff may well have crowded him off the stage. Thus *Aleko*, ostensibly so beholden to nineteenth-century norms of operatic composition, would become—of all Rachmaninoff's operas—the most contemporary in its twentieth-century performance.

Rachmaninoff and His Worlds

In its way, *Aleko* is emblematic of the state of Russian art in the 1890s, when composers, writers, and painters alike sought ways of moving beyond the realist craze that had dominated Russian art for the previous half-century. Consider, for example, Rimsky-Korsakov's classicizing revision to 1860s realism in *Mozart and Salieri* (1897), or the ways in which Tchaikovsky's *Queen of Spades* (1890) upends and destabilizes the arch-realistic sound-world of his earlier Pushkin opera, *Evgeny Onegin* (1878), which had been so consistently, so painstakingly specific as to the time and place of its setting. Rachmaninoff's own realist revisions in *Aleko* were subtler but just as profound, involving a privileging of psychological drama over social description and a rejection of the realist assumption that those two things had to be intimately related. In his precocious student opera, Rachmaninoff had demonstrated not only mastery of a rapidly stagnating realist status quo, but also a willingness to break from the status quo in fairly provocative ways.

All that teenaged chutzpah came to naught, runs the traditional narrative about Rachmaninoff. The new century progressed; Rachmaninoff stayed put. But, as I have argued here, Rachmaninoff's compositional style *did* change, in ways that—when it came to opera, at least—closely paralleled contemporary trends in drama, the evolving performance practices of Chaliapin and Stanislavsky. Of course, the creative symbiosis among this troika of early twentieth-century artists was not the only interaction between musical and spoken theater in Imperial Russia. That relationship was rich and longstanding, though as yet all but unexplored. For example, one consequence of Russia's belated establishment of specialized conservatories was that actors and singers trained at the same institutions until the later nineteenth century; as employees of the crown, too, opera singers in imperial Russia were often compelled to pinch-hit in the spoken theater, in case of a dramatic actor's illness or a role that required singing. Osip Petrov (1806–1878), who created nearly every major bass role in Russian opera from Ivan Susanin in *A Life for the Tsar* (1836) to Varlaam in *Boris Godunov* (1874), was a friend and collaborator of the great serf actor Mikhaíl Shchepkin (1788–1863); Stanislavsky himself trained as an opera singer with Fyodor Komissarzhevsky (1832–1905), the Mariyinsky's leading tenor of the 1870s and a model for the figure of the director in Stanislavsky's books on acting. On the other side of the performer-author divide, playwrights such as Aleksandr Ostrovsky (1823–1886) often served as librettists when Russian composers adapted contemporary dramatic works to the opera stage—a situation that occurred far more frequently in Russia than in any other nation in the nineteenth century. Clearly, this is a history in need of telling.

What Rachmaninoff's operatic evolution demonstrates so beautifully, however, was that the performer-author divide was not, or not always, absolute—the relationship between opera and theater in Russia was not

simply a matter of performers influencing performers and writers inter-
acting with composers. Those influences and interactions could flow in all
directions. This point is especially important in the case of Rachmaninoff,
who—as a composer, performer, and conductor—moved among and participated in diverse artistic worlds. Those worlds did not always harmonize
with one another, as *The Miserly Knight* perhaps demonstrates: attempting
to profile Chaliapin too closely, Rachmaninoff may have stepped on his
toes. But Rachmaninoff's artistic outlook was defined by that mixing of
worlds: the performer with the composer, the musician with the actor
and the dancer. "What a great sorrow!" remarked Rachmaninoff on the
death of Mikhaíl Fokine (1880–1942), less than a year before the end of
his own life. "Chaliapin, Stanislavsky, Fokine—this was an epoch in art."[53]

It was Rachmaninoff's epoch, too. What he shared with Chaliapin,
Stanislavsky, and Fokine was a profound concern for the emotions and
experiences of individuals, who could not be typified (*pace* realists), diminished and automatized (*pace* Stravinsky), or transcended (*pace* Scriabin
and Meyerhold). This concern was already manifest in *Aleko*, and it would
abide throughout Rachmaninoff's subsequent career. Humanists in an
era of constantly looming dehumanization, Rachmaninoff, Chaliapin,
Stanislavsky, and Fokine all struggled against certain twentieth-century
tides. Performers all, they could not countenance seeing the performer's
role debased, reduced from creator to executor of some other author's
uncompromising vision. And like Rachmaninoff, none of the other
epoch-defining artists would be "modern" in the paradigmatic sense of
the term. By focusing so much of our attention on all the ways in which
Rachmaninoff was not modern, however, we risk losing sight of all the
rich and varied ways in which he was contemporary.

NOTES

1. For the original paper, see Doheum Park, Juhan Nam, and Juyong Park, "Novelty and Influence of Creative Works, and Quantifying Patterns of Advances Based on Probabilistic References Networks," *EPJ Data Science* 9/2 (30 January 2020), https://doi.org/10.1140/epjds/s13688-019-0214-8. For a sampling of press coverage, see Rhys Blakely, "Rachmaninov Shines as the Most Inventive Composer in 200 Years," London *Times*, 30 January 2020, https://www.thetimes.co.uk/article/rachmaninov-shines-as-the-most-inventive-composer-in-200-years-c3xnrd5j6; and Henry Bodkin, "Rachmaninoff the Most Innovative Composer Ever . . . Says Computer," *Telegraph*, 30 January 2020, https://www.telegraph.co.uk/science/2020/01/30/rachmaninoff-innovative-composer-eversays-computer/.

2. See M. McAlpine's comment on Norman Lebrecht, "Computer Says: Rachmaninov Was More Original than Beethoven," *Slipped Disc* (blog), 30 January 2020, https://slippedisc.com/2020/01/computer-says-rachmaninov-was-more-original-than-beethoven/.

3. "Rakhmaninov, Sergey Vassilievich," in *Grove Dictionary of Music and Musicians*, ed. Eric Blom, 5th ed., 10 vols. (London: Macmillan, 1954), 7:27–29, at 27. The author of this article is given as Rosa Newmarch, who died in 1940, leaving Eric Blom, as editor of the dictionary, to update the entry after her death.

4. Leonard Liebling, "Variations," *The Musical Courier*, 5 April 1943, 16–17, at 17.

5. Joseph Yasser, "Progressive Tendencies in Rachmaninoff's Music," *Tempo* 22 (1951–52): 11–25, at 25. See also Garry Ziegler, "Rachmaninoff's Early Voice," *Studies in Music from the University of Western Ontario* 15 (1995): 39–47; and Charles Fisk, "Nineteenth-Century Music? The Case of Rachmaninov," *19th-Century Music* 31/3 (2008): 245–65.

6. Richard Taruskin, "Not Modern and Loving It," in *Russian Music at Home and Abroad* (Oakland: University of California Press, 2016), 120–33.

7. G. V. Plekhanov, *Literatura i estetika*, 2 vols. (Moscow: Gosudarstvennoye izdatel'stvo khudozhestvennoy literaturï, 1958), 2:495, quoted in Ralph E. Matlaw, "Scriabin and Russian Symbolism," *Comparative Literature* 31/1 (1979): 1–23, at 1.

8. M. E. Bukinik, untitled essay in *Pamyati Rakhmaninova*, ed. M. V. Dobuzhinskiy (New York: Izdaniye S. A. Satinoy, 1946), 20–35, at 24.

9. Musorgsky's claim to the title of opera's quintessential realist probably needs no gloss, but Tchaikovsky also described himself in realist terms. "It seems to me," he wrote to an official of the Imperial Theatres, "that I am truly gifted with the ability to express *truthfully, sincerely, and simply* the feelings, moods, and images suggested by a text. In this sense I am a *realist* and fundamentally a Russian." V. N. Pogozhev, "Vospominaniya o P. I. Chaykovskom," in *P. I. Chaykovskiy: Vospominaniya i pis'ma*, ed. I. Glebov (Petrograd: Gosudarstvennaya akademicheskaya filarmoniya, 1924), 77. This translation is Taruskin's, from *Defining Russia Musically: Historical and Hermeneutical Essays* (Princeton: Princeton University Press, 1997), 54. On the diverse manifestations of Russian realism in literature and visual art, see Molly Brunson, *Russian Realisms: Literature and Painting, 1840–1890* (DeKalb, IL: Northern Illinois Press, 2016).

10. The classic overview of this problem may be found in Carl Dahlhaus's influential but idiosyncratic *Realism in Nineteenth-Century Music* (Cambridge and New York: Cambridge University Press, 1985), 1–11.

11. Donna Tussing Orwin, *Consequences of Consciousness: Turgenev, Dostoevsky, and Tolstoy* (Stanford, CA: Stanford University Press, 2007), 10–11.

12. Aleksandr Pushkin, "The Gypsies," trans. Walter W. Arndt, *Slavic Review* 24/2 (1965): 273–90, at 277.

13. Ibid., 284. In the opera these Carmen-like lines are assigned to Zemfira.

14. Ibid., 288–89.

15. Aleko closes his namesake opera with the lines "O, woe! O, grief! Again alone, alone!" (O, gore! O, toska! Opyat' odin, odin!), words that are suspiciously reminiscent of Onegin's "Shame! Grief! O, my miserable fate!" (Pozor! Toska! O zhalkiy zhrebiy moy!).

16. Geoffrey Norris, "Rakhmaninov's Student Opera," *The Musical Quarterly* 59/3 (1973): 441–48, at 443.

17. Boris Gasparov, *Five Operas and a Symphony: Word and Music in Russian Culture* (New Haven: Yale University Press, 2005), 16.

18. Gasparov describes the function of these ostensibly action-stopping performances within nineteenth-century Russian opera: "The embedded songs, dances, and theatrical and concertlike performances that litter Russian operas, to the chagrin of those who would like to see them be more dramatically effective, contribute to the general trend of reducing the weight of the outward actions and shifting the emphasis to the introspective element. To understand the inner logic of those seeming discontinuities, one has to focus attention on what is silently implied—on the psychological drama triggered by a concertlike presentation. It is not only the audience of the opera that listens to the interpolated concert; the characters onstage are listening to it, too." (Ibid., 17.)

19. Norris, "Rakhmaninov's Student Opera," 443.

20. Kashkin also noted (correctly) that the libretto "contains many of [Pushkin's] verses, which stand out sharply from the supplementary, inserted ones." Quoted in Sergey Denisenko, *Pushkinskiye tekstï na teatral'noy stsene v XIX veke* (St. Petersburg: Nestor-Istoriya, 2010), 115.

21. Julia Fatova, quoted in Sergei Bertensson and Jay Leyda, *Sergei Rachmaninoff: A Lifetime in Music* (Bloomington: Indiana University Press, 2001), 242.

22. Quoted in ibid., 55.

23. Taruskin, *Defining Russia Musically*, 234.

24. Norris, "Rakhmaninov's Student Opera," 447.

25. Ibid., 447. Norris does note that "the distribution of the vocal pieces is rather different" in *Aleko* vs. *Cavalleria*.

26. Seville would have been a more likely mental destination, for as David Lowe has shown, the libretto of *Carmen* also quotes from "The Gypsies," incorporating a few passages from Prosper Mérimée's 1852 translation of Pushkin's poem. As a result, Bizet's Carmen and Rachmaninoff's Zemfira actually sing the same words, though not in the same language, at several different moments in their respective operas. To cite only one example, Mérimée translated a line from Zemfira's cradle song, "Rezh' menia, zhgi menia," as "Coupe-moi, brûle-moi"—words that Carmen famously sings to Zuniga. David A. Lowe argues that it is uncertain whether (or how much) Mérimée knew of "The Gypsies" when he wrote his novella *Carmen* in 1844, but he translated Pushkin's poem into French, as "Les Bohémiens," eight years later. When preparing the libretto for the operatic *Carmen*, Meilhac and Halévy incorporated some text from "Les Bohémiens"; they also emphasized the theme of personal freedom, which is much more prominent in Pushkin's story than it is in Mérimée's. See "Pushkin and 'Carmen,'" *19th-Century Music* 20/1 (1996): 72–76. For an elaboration on, and extension of, this argument, see A. D. P. Briggs, "Did *Carmen* Really Come from Russia (with a Little Help from Turgenev)?," in

Turgenev and Russian Culture: Essays to Honour Richard Peace, ed. Joe Andrew, Derek Offord, and Robert Reid (Amsterdam and New York: Rodopi, 2008), 83–102. The Soviet musicologist Abram Gozenpud suggested that Rachmaninoff may have de-emphasized the relationship between Zemfira and her new lover to downplay the parallel with *Carmen*. See *Russkiy operniy teatr na rubezhe XIX–XX vekov i F. I. Shalyapin, 1890–1904* (Leningrad: Muzïka, 1974), 74–75.

27. Richard Taruskin's chapter "Entoiling the Falconet" from *Defining Russia Musically*, 159–85, lays out these and other Orientalist devices in detail.

28. See, in particular, Viktor Berkov, "Rakhmaninovskaya garmoniya," *Sovetskaya muzïka* 8 (1960): 104–9. See also S. A. Petukhova, "'Rakhmaninovskiy akkord': Istoki vozniknoveniya," *Iskusstvo muzïki: Teoriya i istoriya* 17 (2017): 143–70.

29. See Taruskin, *Defining Russia Musically*, 185.

30. In an unpublished canto from *Evgeny Onegin*, the hero spends some time wandering around Russia's south in Aleko-like voluntary exile. These parallels are perhaps unsurprising, given that Pushkin wrote "The Gypsies" while at work on chapter 3 of *Evgeny Onegin*. For a comparison of the two works, see Leslie O'Bell, "*Evgenii Onegin* as Pushkin's Central Novel of Development," in *The Pushkin Handbook*, ed. David M. Bethea (Madison: University of Wisconsin Press, 2005), 179–81.

31. During rehearsals for the Bolshoi's production of *Aleko* in 1893, Tchaikovsky asked Rachmaninoff if he would consent to produce the opera in a double bill with *Iolanta* in the next season. The younger composer found this offer incredibly flattering, but plans were scuttled after Tchaikovsky's death in the fall.

32. See Marina Frolova-Walker, *Russian Music and Nationalism from Glinka to Stalin* (New Haven: Yale University Press, 2007), 297–98.

33. Rutger Helmers has demonstrated that *sekstovost'* was heard as a national marker by nineteenth-century Russian audiences; see "French Theatricality and Inadvertent Russianisms," in *Not Russian Enough? Nationalism and Cosmopolitanism in Nineteenth-Century Russian Opera* (Rochester, NY: University of Rochester Press, 2014), 82–112.

34. I borrow this term from Taruskin's discussion of the *Gymnopédies* in *The Oxford History of Western Music*, vol. 4, *Music in the Early Twentieth Century* (Oxford and New York: Oxford University Press, 2005), 68.

35. For a history of this enterprise and an exploration of Mamontov's artistic philosophies, see Olga Haldey, *Mamontov's Private Opera: The Search for Modernism in Russian Theater* (Bloomington and Indianapolis: Indiana University Press, 2010).

36. Oskar von Riesemann, *Rachmaninoff's Recollections Told to Oskar von Riesemann* (New York: Macmillan, 1934), 150. Sergei Bertensson, Rachmaninoff's biographer and the General Manager of MXT after the Revolution, wrote that "Sergei Vasilyevich had always been a devoted worshiper of the Art Theater; his attitude toward Stanislavsky was based on extraordinary admiration—I may even say tenderness." Bertensson and Leyda, *Sergei Rachmaninoff*, 229.

37. Bertensson and Leyda quote Stanislavsky's letter of thanks for Rachmaninoff's gifts: "You cannot know how your attention and memories touch our hearts. It is a very fine thing that you are doing, for the artists are really starving." *Sergei Rachmaninoff*, 228.

38. Feodor Chaliapin, *Man and Mask: Forty Years in the Life of a Singer*, trans. Phyllis Mégroz (New York: Alfred A. Knopf, 1933), 59.

39. Ibid., 60.

40. Quoted in Richard Taruskin, *Opera and Drama in Russia as Preached and Practiced in the 1860s* (Ann Arbor: UMI Research Press, 1981), 234.

41. Chaliapin, *Man and Mask*, 93.

42. Ibid., 98.

43. Anna Muza, "The Organic and the Political: Stanislavsky's Dilemma (Ibsen, Tolstoy, Gorky)," in *The Routledge Companion to Stanislavsky*, ed. R. Andrew White (London and New York: Routledge, 2014), 37–51, at 39.

44. Stanislavsky eventually came to see this approach as misguided, and his later productions and writings would emphasize the importance of such externalizations as physical movement and voice. For an accessible history of Stanislavsky's creative evolution, see Jean Benedetti, *Stanislavski: An Introduction* (New York: Routledge, 1982).

45. Richard Taruskin, *Miserly Knight, The* (Oxford and New York: Oxford University Press, 2002), https://www.oxfordmusiconline.com/grovemusic/view/10.1093/gmo/978156 159 2630.001.0001/omo-9781561592630-e-5000008322.

46. Fyodor Chaliapin and Maksim Gorkii, *Chaliapin: An Autobiography as Told to Maxim Gorky*, ed. and trans. Nina Froud and James Hanley (New York: Stein and Day, 1969), 131.

47. This role had been created by Chaliapin's greatest nineteenth-century predecessor, Osip Petrov (1806–1878), another bass known as much for his acting as for his vocal technique. Like Chaliapin, Petrov was highly receptive to performance trends within the Russian dramatic theater.

48. Von Riesemann, *Rachmaninoff's Recollections*, 130.

49. Apart from "Fate," the other Chaliapin dedications among Rachmaninoff's songs come from Opus 34: "In the Soul of Each of Us" (V dushe u kazhdogo iz nas, No. 2), "The Raising of Lazarus" (Voskresheniye Lazarya, No. 6), "You Knew Him" (Ty znal yego, No. 9), and "The True Servant" (Obrochnik, No. 11). The "Letter to Stanislavsky," which Rachmaninoff wrote for Chaliapin to perform at MXT's tenth anniversary celebration, might also be counted as an honorary "Chaliapin song."

50. Bertensson and Leyda, *Sergei Rachmaninoff*, 87.

51. Ibid., 233.

52. Chaliapin, *Man and Mask*, 145.

53. Quoted in Bertensson and Leyda, *Sergei Rachmaninoff*, 376.

Rachmaninoff's *Miserly Knight*
(On Money, Honor, and the Means to Create)

CARYL EMERSON

In the fall of 1830, on his remote ancestral estate of Boldino, Aleksandr Pushkin, age thirty-one, composed four *Little Tragedies* over a period of fourteen days. These are exquisite dramatic miniatures in blank verse, each highlighting a human vice or vulnerability: miserliness, envy, lust, and frivolity or lack of awe in the face of mass unnatural death.[1] So compact in events and spare of words are these tiny playlets—they have been called no more than the denouement, or "fifth act," of a tragedy—that they present themselves to composers as ready-made libretti.[2] By the turn of the century, three had been musicalized as "little operas," chamber works set almost word-for-word. Aleksandr Dargomyzhsky had finished his *Stone Guest* (*Kamennyi gost'*, Pushkin's variant on the Don Juan legend) in 1869; Nikolai Rimsky-Korsakov his *Mozart and Salieri* in 1897; and César Cui his *Feast in Time of Plague* (*Pir vo vremya chumï*) in 1900. Sergei Prokofiev, as a teenager, had also tried his hand at setting the plague playlet. When, in 1903, Rachmaninoff (also age thirty-one) took on the last of Pushkin's *Little Tragedies*, *The Miserly Knight* (*Skupoy ritsar'*), there were unsettling biographical parallels between the Romantic-era poet and neo-Romantic musician.

These similarities were not "Romantic" in the scandalous, charismatic sense that E. T. A. Hoffmann had lent to the word with reference to Beethoven: heroic rebel, avatar of the shocking and the new, indifferent to the performer's comfort and the audience's pleasure.[3] Rachmaninoff was sooner a knight defending an aging canon. He performed, composed, conducted: the ideal model of a complete and integrated creator of music.[4] Beginning in the late 1820s, Pushkin had tried to be just such an integrated master creator, the poet-chronicler-historian of Nicholas I's Russia. But this ideal comes with a cost.

To begin with the costs for the poet. In Pushkin's time, the fine arts— literature and history as well as music—were gentlemanly pursuits, not professions at which one earned a living. Born into an impoverished but aristocratic family, Pushkin fought hard to be paid what his work was worth. But in pre-Reform Russia, it was unclear what that meant. Russia in the 1820s was not a bourgeois culture. Poets wrote for one another in salons and heard their poems sung at private gatherings; commercial book culture and public concert life were undeveloped. For the propertied classes, wealth was either won (say, at cards) or inherited in the form of land and enserfed peasants—but it did not have to be *earned*.[5] During that first "Boldino Autumn" in 1830, Pushkin was at a crossroads. He was hoping to marry a very beautiful seventeen-year-old girl, also not rich, whose mother considered the famous poet a cultural trophy but financially an unpromising match. To make his son more competitive in the marriage market, Pushkin's father (himself a wastrel, and stingy as well) gave him the family's Boldino property, with its two hundred serfs. The anxious fiancé set off to that distant village, hoping to write some lucrative works. Then an unexpected cholera quarantine prolonged his retreat. Pushkin was miraculously creative in that isolated spot, finishing, among other masterpieces, *Yevgeny Onegin*. But would he earn enough?

Pushkin won the hand of his beloved and immediately mortgaged Boldino as dowry for the nagging mother-in-law. Four children were born to Pushkin and his wife in five years, and she did her best at household management, but life near the Imperial Court was expensive. Pushkin started a fine literary journal, but it ran a deficit. The absence of money was a constant humiliation to him, as testified by the gentle banter of his spousal correspondence. "Do not be angry, wife," he wrote in June 1834, "I've never thought of reproaching you for my dependent state. . . . The dependence of family life makes a man more moral." The following month, while mortgaging another paternal estate and dreaming of quitting St. Petersburg altogether for a less extravagant rural life, he confided to his wife: "Let me make some money, not for myself, for you. I have little love for money—but I respect in it the sole means of dignified independence."[6] When, in 1837, the poet died in a duel defending his wife's honor, a total of seventy-five rubles cash were found in their apartment—with personal debts approaching 140,000 rubles.[7] Upon hearing of Pushkin's death, Nicholas I agreed to pay all the poet's debts and settle money on the children. Honor, pride, financial autonomy, and forced subservience to the caprices of power defined the poet's final years. They also resonated in twentieth-century images of the poet, as in the Soviet playwright Leonid Zorin's 1970 play about Pushkin in 1834, which focuses not on poetry but on debts, loans, and loss of self-respect.[8] In 2009, after two post-Soviet decades of robber-baron capitalism among a population naive about economic issues, the Russian State Pushkin Museum in Moscow mounted an exhibit on Pushkin, money, and the "freedom of creativity."[9]

Now fast-forward nearly seventy years from 1837 to the late summer of 1903, from poet to musician. At his family estate Ivanovka, Sergei Rachmaninoff began work on a musical setting of Pushkin's *The Miserly Knight*, acting as his own librettist. He had married the year before (also stressfully; Natalya Satina was his first cousin and such marriages required dispensation from the tsar). Like Pushkin, Rachmaninoff had a wastrel father who had squandered several estates; also like the poet, he had received a small manor house as a wedding gift. But now, with serfdom abolished, capitalism on the rise, and the status of "Free Artist" conferred along with a conservatory degree, a musical professional was expected to earn a living. Teaching piano was one reliable means, but Rachmaninoff was bad at the job and hated it.[10] His problem was too many talents, not too few. None guaranteed an adequate income. To concertize across Europe was exhausting. Rachmaninoff's two seasons in 1904–1905 as conductor of the Bolshoi Theater were musical triumphs—but they took their toll. Under contract for five operas a season, he answered for very long runs. As he later admitted: "When I am concertizing I cannot compose . . . when I feel like writing music, I have to concentrate on that—I cannot touch the piano. When I am conducting I can neither compose nor play concerts."[11] Throughout the 1890s, his letters, like Pushkin's, had been full of worry. "I have nothing to live on," he wrote to a friend in 1894, "nor do I have anything for sprees. And I cannot live counting every kopek, considering and calculating every kopek."[12] But it was one thing to be a bachelor chafing at his lack of ready cash or absence of privacy, reduced to using a mediocre piano in rented rooms. It was another matter, as Pushkin well understood, to become a family man, a type of dependence that "makes a man more moral." Having money was a matter of honor as well as livelihood. Writers of Pushkin's enlightened generation whose fathers went bankrupt were enamored of Adam Smith.[13] Hard work, competition, and rational self-interest would guarantee economic prosperity. But what if the pursuit of money compromised both honor and creativity? This painfully personal situation, a staple on the European comic stage but uncongenial for serious opera, had the makings of tragedy for both artists.

Pushkin's Little Play Becomes Rachmaninoff's Libretto

Pushkin, raised bilingually in Russian and French, was wholly at home in French neoclassical culture. As early as 1826 he had been considering a drama on miserliness. But it would not resemble Molière's 1668 comedy *L'avare* (*The Miser*). Comedies of character, or type, were simplistic and predictable. Pushkin's inspiration would be pan-European and include Roman comedy (Plautus), Goldoni, Walter Scott, and of course Shakespeare. "Molière's Miser is miserly—and that is all," Pushkin noted many years later, but "Shakespeare's Shylock is miserly, resourceful, vindictive, a fond father, sharp-witted."[14] By the time of his 1830 *Miserly Knight,* Pushkin was one year into a renewed interest in Dante—especially in the usurers, lodged deep among violent sinners in the seventh circle of the Inferno.[15] Of the five characters (all male) in Pushkin's play, one of them is by profession a "shylock," that is, a Jewish usurer in a predominantly Christian culture. Pushkin's title applies not to him, however, but to the central character, more complex than Molière's miser, more bred to honor, and more contradictory than the embittered, justice-seeking Shylock of Shakespeare's Venice.[16] Pushkin gives us a miserly, hoarding, moneylending *knight*. As in the other *Little Tragedies*—indeed, this is what makes them tragedies—the hero's fate is fully compatible with his free will. This personal will can be maniacal, but it can also denote self-discipline, hard work, risk, and lofty vision. The fact that Pushkin in 1829 was freshly alert to Dante and the complexities of venial or deadly sin, and that Rachmaninoff paired his *Miserly Knight* with his *Francesca da Rimini* for their joint premiere in 1906, is a creative and psychological overlap, that we will revisit throughout this essay.

Pushkin's plot (and Rachmaninoff's setting of it) unfolds in abstractly European medieval space, a world and value system in irreversible decay. Pushkin reflects this anxiety by opening on a victory of arms that has backfired and turned bitter. To mimic this aura of nervous deterioration, Rachmaninoff will rely on archaic modal sounds, in particular the Phrygian mode, and dotted rhythmic values that approximate, if only stutteringly, the rhythmic modes of Renaissance polyphony. The plot is as follows: In the first scene young Albert, son of our miserly knight the Baron, complains of his poverty to his valet, Ivan. Albert had been spectacularly brave in a tournament the day before, unseating and injuring his foe, but he is now ashamed: his valor had been less the result of bravery than of fury at his opponent, whose well-aimed blow had ruined his helmet. Albert has no money to replace it—nor his lame horse. Kept a pauper in his father's castle, he cannot purchase decent court raiment or equipment. When the Jewish moneylender Solomon turns up, Albert partly begs, partly demands, another loan. Quite reasonably, Solomon demurs; none of the knights repay him. When Albert reminds the moneylender that his father is very rich and that he, an only son, will inherit, Solomon reminds Albert that the Baron is still hearty and may well live another thirty years—at which point the son falls into despair. Solomon then ventures that the Baron's death might be speeded up with discreetly administered poison. Albert is horrified (or makes a show of horror) and kicks the usurer out.[17] But first the two men exchange several words on the topic of the Baron and money. Solomon remarks that it is the habit of young men to spend wealth, whereas old men guard it as a trusty friend. Albert objects: his father neither puts money to pleasurable use nor befriends it, but serves it abjectly, as its slave. Like a dog on a chain, the Baron enjoys neither freedom nor leisure. Only his gold knows any leisure. In the modal uncertainty of Rachmaninoff's orchestration, even precious metal, that heavy sinking matter that moves by semitones, trembles and sways.

Scene 2 is one huge monologue. The Baron descends to the vault to feed his daily handful of gold to his chests. The steady growth of these glittering piles of wealth is his power; he is convinced that mere possession of it bestows on him infinite freedom from any want, need, desire, or subservience to any other will. Tenderly he recalls the history behind certain ducats, extracted from grieving widows and desperate thieves. "I know my power [*moshch'*]," he declaims, "and that awareness is enough." Then the Baron remembers his son. Albert will strip the keys from his corpse and squander what he, the son, had not the patience, discipline, or self-control to accumulate himself. Although the miserly father, in defiance of knightly tradition, has settled nothing on his heir, he nevertheless feels insulted by Albert. He is certain that his son refuses to grant him any pangs of conscience, any complexity of spirit. Let him accumulate his own wealth before passing judgment, the distraught father cries. At all costs the Baron must repudiate what the son intuits: that power is paralysis (and thus impotence) when the wealth out of which it is built does not circulate.

Here is the venial side of the vice of greed, its awful paradox: to be "above all desire" is not to be free, but to be disabled and trapped. Pushkin's concern in these *Little Tragedies* was to investigate the psychological effects of the essential passions, each vital in its own way but with dark aspects that triumphed irreversibly when the passion passes a certain threshold. In this he follows Aristotle as well as Dante: every natural virtue is flanked by negative vices at its two extremes. On either side of the normal need to eat lie gluttony and crippling anorexia; of the normal need to love, lust at one pole and prideful asceticism as its opposite; of the prudent need to allocate resources, the greed of hoarding at one extreme and profligate wastefulness at the other. Pushkin, who was always keenly aware of sexual energy and its creative potential, is clear here about the Baron's tragic error. The Miserly Knight creates nothing, enables nothing, lusts after no living thing. He compares the pleasure of turning a key in the lock of his money chests not with what we might expect—sexual consummation—but with the "pleasant and terrible" sensation flooding a murderer when a knife penetrates its victim. Those are the options now open to him: solitary wealth or solitary murder. In Pushkin's value system, erotic fantasies involving other desiring bodies might be selfish, but they are always creative (as they are for his poet, the irresistible Don Juan). Whatever is joy-bearing and potentially fertile is always in principle redeemable. But in the Baron's underground vault, desire has become utterly, lethally perverse. Every possible pleasure has been squeezed out and dried up by dead gold. By the turn of the century, buried wealth had become a popular operatized theme—the dragon Fafner guarding the Rheingold in *Siegfried*, for example. Indeed, mention is often made of Rachmaninoff's honeymoon trip to Bayreuth in 1902 and traces of Wagner in the orchestration of his subsequent two chamber operas.[18] But no mythological plot can match the barren perversity of the Baron's nightly descent to his money chests.

The brief Scene 3 takes place at the Duke's court. The Duke, of a generation midway between Albert and the Baron, is the ideal Renaissance ruler. (He too is a Shakespearean type, like the Duke of Vienna in *Measure for Measure*, a play that Pushkin would adapt into his dramatic poem *Angelo* in 1833.) The Duke has summoned the Baron in an attempt to reconcile father and son. Albert is concealed offstage. The Baron, who is as respectful of ruling authority in its presence as he is dismissive of it while gloating alone over his gold, is cornered into telling lies to protect his wealth from his heir. When the Baron accuses his son of attempting to murder and then to rob him, Albert bursts out of hiding, calls his father a liar, and when the infuriated Baron throws down the gauntlet, accepts the challenge. The Duke, appalled by this spectacle, reprimands them both. Suddenly the Baron clutches at his heart, calls out for his keys, and falls. The Duke cries out: "On umer. Bozhe! / Uzhasnïy vek, uzhasnïye serdtsa!" (He's dead. Oh God! / A dreadful age, dreadful hearts!) This closing cry echoes Albert's opening lament to Ivan, his valet: "O, bednost', bednost'! / Kak unizhayet serdtse nam ona!" (Oh, poverty, poverty! / How it humiliates our heart!)[19] *Skupost'* (miserliness) gives rise to *bednost'* (poverty), and poverty in turn leads to callously ungenerous behavior. From here, the son fears, it is but a small step to his father's senseless and insensate cruelty. All are sins against knightly honor, that is, all are deformations of the heart.

For his own *Miserly Knight*, Op. 24, Rachmaninoff fastidiously respected Pushkin's text, as had the other composers who musicalized the *Little*

Tragedies. Only minor deletions were made, some forty lines out of a total of almost four hundred, with the verse-line preserved intact on either side of the incision.[20] The textual cuts were most certainly the work of the Dramatic Censor, an office of the Imperial Theaters, in accordance with guidelines provided by the ecclesiastical and state censorship in the nervous atmosphere around the 1905 Revolution. We cannot know how much Rachmaninoff chafed at these deleted lines, or whether he preemptively proposed to delete them himself, since censorship often entailed bargaining between creative artist and pragmatic bureaucrat. In any event, censoring a musical adaptation of an absolute classic—and Pushkin's verse is absolute for a Russian audience—is perilous. Since Pushkin is widely known by heart, the omission of a single word or line can create an unexpected gap in the listener's inner ear that actually draws attention to what has been left out. In the libretto's central scene (the Baron's monologue), deletions are relatively minor. In the final scene, the confrontation of ruler, father, and son, a larger number of lines are deleted, including a pair of affectionate backstories that humanize both the Duke and the Baron. But it is the first scene, which omits twenty of Pushkin's lines, that holds the most interest when the libretto is considered as an artistic and psychological whole. The valet Ivan no longer boasts of his master's success at wounding his jousting opponent. No mention is made of Albert's lame horse. Albert does not threaten to have the Jew Solomon frisked. At scene's end, an exchange was cut in which Pushkin's Albert asks for wine but must make do with water, since he had gifted his last bottle to an ill blacksmith. After these deletions, Albert's librettistic profile is less impetuous but also less generous, especially with the reference to the miracle of water-into-wine removed. Albert now resonates less with the exemplary Christian knight. But to close readers of Pushkin and his evocation of medieval knighthood, the deletion of a single word in Scene 1, and of four words that echo it at the very end of Scene 3, might have mattered more.

Albert's signature lament in the first scene is "Poverty! How it humiliates our heart." In the libretto, the line loses the word *heart*, becoming simply: "Poverty! How it humiliates us" (Bednost', kak unizhayet nas ona). And the play's final, very famous judgment, pronounced by the Duke over the Baron's dead body—"What a dreadful age, what dreadful hearts!"—is deleted from the libretto altogether, thus bringing the opera to an end on Pushkin's penultimate line: "He's dead. Oh God!" The refrain of an injured, humiliated heart has thus been removed from the frame of the opera. The detail is small, but the image huge. Medieval culture and its scriptural authority were organized around the heart. Before a modern reliance on calculation and reason caused our vital center to migrate upward to the head and expressive speaking face, the heart was "the *literal* site of memory, understanding, and imagination."[21] Thus to grasp one's place in time (both one's own time, and God's) meant to reckon first of all with the heart, to make its moves articulate. In his Little Tragedy of calculation and accumulation, Pushkin, an Enlightened poet in what was still largely a medieval country, would surely have been alert to this pre-modern symbolism when he showcased its key word. For his musicalized staged version, however, Rachmaninoff (or some censor above him with scissors in hand) sheared this symbol off. Only the sinful carnal envelope—the dead body—remains, reinforced by a finale of chordal thunderbolts. Pushkin's inflammatory words about a "dreadful age" could not be sung as requiem in the aftermath of a tumultuous revolutionary year. But in this instance, every Russian ear in the audience would have instantly supplied the phrase. The damaged, deleted heart resounded louder than ever.

Leitmotifs, Leit-timbres, Leit-images
(First Reviews and More Recent Defenses)

Were the changes to Pushkin's verse a factor in the reception of the opera by the musicians Rachmaninoff most wanted to please? *The Miserly Knight* premiered at Moscow's Bolshoi Theater on 11 January 1906, under the baton of Rachmaninoff himself, in a double bill with his *Francesca da Rimini*. Reviews were mixed. The hall was not full and the stage far too large for a chamber work, especially one whose theme—miserliness—required cramped and secretive space. The composer had written the part of the Baron and of the elder Malatesta for his good friend Chaliapin. When the great bass declined to perform in the premieres, Rachmaninoff was keenly disappointed. According to the singer's daughter Irina, the falling-out over *The Miserly Knight* was the single instance of discord between them. "For some reason, my father did not like the music," she wrote in 1957. "He expressed his opinion frankly to Sergei Vasilyevich. 'Pushkin's words here are stronger than what you've written,' he said. Rachmaninoff took offense."[22] Pushkin's centenary was celebrated in 1899 with cult-like devotion and mass reprintings of the poet's works. It had become canonical not to obscure the poetry of a Little Tragedy by too lush or autonomous an orchestration. Rimsky-Korsakov, an orchestrator of genius, had kept himself in check with his *Mozart and Salieri*—so perhaps felt entitled to complain about Rachmaninoff. "Certainly, the music in this opera is very talented," he reportedly said, continuing:

> There are some strong, brilliantly dramatic moments. The scene of the baron gloating over his stockpiled gold is

Figure 1. Rachmaninoff with the first performers of *The Miserly Knight* (Georgy Baklanov, Ivan Gryzunov, and Anton Bonachich).

remarkable. But overall, the all but uninterrupted flow of a dense orchestral texture suppresses the voice. A ratio is achieved that is the opposite of *The Stone Guest*. There, the role of the orchestra is reduced to a minimum, to simple harmonic support of the vocal part. Dargomyzhsky's orchestra, without the voice part, is devoid of value. With Rachmaninoff it's the other way around: the orchestra swallows up almost all the musical interest, and the vocal part, deprived of the orchestra, is unpersuasive; in the end, the ear longs for a melody that simply isn't there.[23]

On balance, the published reviews were more positive than the comments of personal friends.[24] "Mr. Rachmaninoff, as composer and conductor, was a success," reported the "Theater and Music" column of *Russkiy listok* for 13 January 1906. "After *The Miserly Knight*, he was presented with three wreaths."[25]

But every review contained a reservation. No female role meant no lyrical relief. And what about the desperately non-operatic vice of *skupost'* (miserliness)? As one review noted, as a theme it "was not the most appropriate for the fine arts"—and all the more so because an entire scene is given over to a "musical portrait of this repulsively miserly baron."[26] The young operatic baritone Georgy Baklanov (in emigration Georges Baklanoff) sang the Baron; for all his gifts as an actor-singer, however, he could not compete with Chaliapin as the ideal theatrical interpreter of Pushkin's words. And then, the poet's words and concepts are so subtle and supple, how could an orchestra possibly follow them?[27] A review by the Germanophile Emil Medtner in the Symbolist journal *Zolotoye runo* (The Golden Fleece) for January 1906 added yet another unanswerable, anachronistic twist to these complaints. Rachmaninoff had failed to respect the "internal music" of Pushkin's play, especially its pauses—which Pushkin, "as if listening with his inner ear to some invisible orchestra, had placed in his second scene in a wholly Wagnerian manner."[28] Only rarely did a reviewer suggest that Rachmaninoff might have had his own plan with Pushkin, one that entailed choosing "a channel between two currents, which flowed neither into Dargomyzhsky, nor into Wagner."[29] Between 1903 and 1908 (the twentieth and twenty-fifth anniversary of Wagner's death), a growing cult of Wagner on the Russian stage greatly increased audience literacy in the operas and gave rise to a more refined and diversified music criticism about him.[30] Even Chaliapin sang an occasional Dutchman. In 1910, the critic Grigory Prokofyev, a friend of Rachmaninoff's, contributed an essay on the composer to the solidly pro-Wagner *Russkaya muzïkal'naya gazeta* with the title "A Singer of Intimate Moods."[31] In it he notes that Rachmaninoff, for all that he might have learned about orchestras from Bayreuth, had not adopted the underlying Wagnerian principle of "endless melody out of polyphonic orchestral texture." His motifs were still built off uttered words, after the manner of the more minimalist *kuchkist* nationalist composers. Since Rachmaninoff was not especially strong in recitative, however, his vocal declamation fell short of his orchestration. But this criticism did not imply failure; it was mere growing pains. "Were someone to ask me: in general, should we have Russian musical drama? I would say yes! Of course! But precisely in the form that Rachmaninoff gives us, not slavishly imitating Wagner's operas."

By the time the two Rachmaninoff operas were revived at the Bolshoi Theater in 1912, more perspective had been gained on the vexed question of Wagner versus the Russian national tradition. There were still complaints that chamber works were poorly served on the big stage, that the words could not be heard, and that the orchestra overwhelmed the singers.[32] But a new tone was struck soon after the revival by the lawyer, composer, and music critic Evgeny Gunst, which at last cut across the old pro- and anti-Wagnerian lines.[33] Gunst was no friend of the Bolshoi Theater's sluggish conservative repertory. He was appalled that Rachmaninoff's two operas had been dropped from the stage in 1906, presumably so that the theater could return to its familiar diet of Verdi's *La Traviata* and Gounod's *Faust*. But finally the Bolshoi was waking up and mounting works of real innovative genius: Wagner, Rimsky-Korsakov, and now a revival of these two miniatures. "Rachmaninoff is not entirely at home in opera," Gunst admitted. "The language of his operatic music remains by its very nature absolute language—which loses its simplicity and sincerity when forcibly attached to an operatic text."[34] If compared with Scriabin, Gunst wrote, Rachmaninoff's music is quite conservative harmonically. Both *Francesca* and *Miserly Knight* lack any "sound of the epoch," any sense of the scene or spirit of the time; the two works could even be the first and second acts of the same opera, so closely did the elder Malatesta resemble the Baron musically. Motifs are not attached to plot events or even to specific acting persons as much as to habits, attitudes, and psychological impulses. And here Rachmaninoff is being completely himself, Gunst insists, creating a type of music drama wholly distinct from any *Siegfried*, *Sadko*, or *Mozart and Salieri*. In fact, "the aspects that seem most strongly under the influence of Wagner or Tchaikovsky are the least successful, they leave a negative impression."[35] Rachmaninoff's operas must not be "ostracized" for their departures from convention, but assessed on their own terms.

Unfortunately, those terms were not met in the Bolshoi double-bill production, which was full of errors and cuts and indifferent to the composer's stage directions. With new works, Gunst insisted, such liberties are impermissible. Lacking a developed performance history, a given production quickly becomes too authoritative. Gunst was especially annoyed at the use of electric lights on the huge Bolshoi stage. The theater had been fully electrified around 1890 (with energy generated by means of various noisy devices), but here electric light seemed utterly false. The Baron's monologue down in the vault is fastidiously paced according to degrees of darkness, and to the progressive introduction of flickering, deceptive points of light. The chests of gold should be illuminated by "one tallow candle at a time, with its feeble sickly light"—for only then "would the spectator be grabbed by the truth, only by the truth, and by an unconcealed, wholly undistorted realism."[36]

Gunst's wording here is remarkable, given the heated debates around theatrical realism in the prewar period. Stanislavsky had founded the Moscow Art Theater in 1898 on the revolutionary call for psychological realism and mimetic "illusionism" on stage (the illusion of real life). Vsevolod Meyerhold, backed by theater theorists such as the Symbolist poet Valery Bryusov, had countered with the demand for heightened stylization, for a return to theater's natural home in commedia dell'arte and self-conscious convention. Gunst, discussing opera (that most stylized of all staged musical-dramatic genres), appears to argue that Pushkin's Little Tragedy—unlike, say, the *Ring* Cycle or *Parsifal*—is "real," not allegorical or mythopoetic, and that the truth of this realism must be communicated by a certain modesty of theatrical means. Since unified music-drama combines many art forms—literary, musical, actorly, visual, scenic—it can be realistic and abstract simultaneously, on different planes. Rachmaninoff is a master of "absolute music." Thus he tailors his score not to concrete historical times or bodies, and not to concrete national myth, but to universally panhuman symbols of miserliness, hypocrisy, power-lust. In Pushkin's poetry if not in Dante's, such psychological symbols are always embedded in everyday objects and details: a ducat, a helmet, a tallow candle, actual stage darkness. We might conclude from Gunst's review that this Pushkinian concreteness was the truth Rachmaninoff strove toward in his *Miserly Knight*, an operatic experiment pitched beyond the already haggard opposition between the Russian nationalists and Bayreuth.

Of course, Wagner remained a background reckoning point, and some referencing of him was inevitable. The *Ring* is about the pursuit of a piece of gold jewelry that can end the world; in *The Miserly Knight*, gold is privatized, internalized, and ends the life of the man who would hoard it. Both Wagner and Rachmaninoff rely on disconnected minor triads to signal foreboding and dread. But Rachmaninoff avoids anything like the waves of majestic major chords that open the *Ring*. For him there is no triumphant mythical envelope. Musical triumph, such as the orchestra expresses in the second scene, serves delusion. As in Pushkin, everything real is palpable and perishable and must answer for its actions. In the quiet opening signature motif of *The Miserly Knight* prelude, dominated by an ostinato descending chromatic line, we can literally hear pitches a semitone apart rub up against one another like falling coins, only to find a shifting, modally uncertain resting point in the Baron's chests (as the coins settle, the bottom pitches of these sinking melodic lines are shifted down by a half-step). The Soviet music historian Tamara Livanova, alert to the evocative role played in the score by tangible objects and mimetic musical gestures, asks us to think beyond musical leitmotifs to more three-dimensional concepts such as "leit-images" (*leyt-obrazï*) and "leit-texture" (*leyt-faktura*), relieved only occasionally by "arioso-like oases."[37]

A good discussion of this realistic-symbolic matrix was provided in 1973 by the Soviet musicologist Yury Keldysh.[38] The Wagnerian footprint should not be overstated, Keldysh insists. *The Miserly Knight* is not symphonic in the sense of a strict unfolding of musically autonomous structure. There are no closed musical numbers, no set pieces or rounded ensembles. The score is still recognizably a variant on Dargomyzhsky's melodic recitative, sensitive to the mood and intonation of the uttered word. But Rachmaninoff does practice a distinctive "symphonization of operatic form" that governs his distribution of motifs.[39] Importantly, it does not matter to him (as it did to Musorgsky and Dargomyzhsky) whether each personage has a musical tag that sounds whenever that person moves, thinks, or speaks. Identities occur at another, higher level, and in this opera there are fewer identities than we think. Of the five acting parts in *The Miserly Knight*, the Servant is wholly episodic (his theme is heard only in the scene where he appears—glued, as it were, to his physical body). The Moneylender too, for all his insinuating sinuous chromaticisms, is only of transitory and local significance.[40] The Duke at the end is crucial for the denouement of the plot, but his musical profile is vertical, static, timeless, justice-bearing; he represents stable authority in the form of benign and stately chords. "In essence the entire action is based on the collision of two persons, the old Baron and his son Albert, a conflict that is irreconcilable and must lead to the death of one of them," Keldysh writes. Although a "fatal dependence on gold binds the two together," the father's dependency is far more developed.[41] Albert's motif is simpler. In Scene 1 it is all "military ardor, courage and impetuous impulse," the punctuated rhythm of a horse's gallop, full of youthful "upward flights of melody."[42] But these leaps are joyless and frantic, more like leaps of disbelief. He had won the tournament—but in terms of his honor and knightly future, he had lost it. For all the frenzied movement, the key (E-flat major) remains stable. When the Moneylender enters, Albert modulates hopefully out of that tonality for the duration of their bargaining—but returns to it at the end, for he is trapped in it.

The Baron in Scene 2 is also trapped, but because he is more willing to be deceived, his resources are weightier and more lethal. He has three motifs, all prefigured in the Prelude. The first is Gold, a "slippery chromatic figure" featuring diminished fourths that suggests a "ghostly shimmering."[43] A second theme Keldysh calls "the leitmotif of Gloomy Obsession": a lyrical line that rises, hesitates at its highest point, and then chromatically sinks. The third motif, human "Grief and Tears," is built off Gold. Both Tears and Gold are ostinato-like themes that tremble and glisten and even appear to flow—although one is alive, the other dead. Obsession and human Tears together give rise to a theme that Keldysh identifies as Conscience.[44] But conscience is an unwelcome mental state for the Baron, one that he would like to banish or keep at bay. The conclusion he must resist at all cost is the "perishability of his wealth and the futility of all his efforts to pile it up."[45] When the Gold motif darkens and goes minor, passing through oboes, English horns, and bassoons, it begins to lose its flicker and glitter. As greed becomes less mesmerizing and charismatic, moral responsibility finds other ways to make itself felt. Although Keldysh does not discuss this aspect of the opera, we are struck by the rich dialogue of Russian sources and performance history that Rachmaninoff codes into his score. Midpoint in the Baron's fantastical vision of universal power, at a moment when Pushkin, in his Little Tragedy, is slyly self-referencing his own earlier play *Boris Godunov*, Rachmaninoff reinforces the cue by musically quoting from Musorgsky's operatic setting of that play.[46] In both *Boris Godunov* and *The Miserly Knight*, a doomed and deluded "false ruler" insists that he is still reigning, still in control, but in fact he is trapped impotently inside his own head. This textual moment is Pushkin at his multidimensional best, and it prompts Rachmaninoff to stitch together two of the poet's dramas within the tradition of Russian national music. Had these double-voiced lines of the miserly Baron's been sung (as the composer had hoped) by Chaliapin, already the world's signature Tsar Boris, the effect would have been tremendous.

Scene 3 is the shortest and most laconic—overly short, as Rachmaninoff himself came to feel, and constructed largely out of earlier themes. Keldysh closes his menu of motifs on this observation, that the Baron's monologue "rises so high above everything else, that the two scenes bordering it seem to some extent non-obligatory side-curtains."[47] But a case could be made for the brevity of the final confrontation. The second scene, in Rachmaninoff as in Pushkin, is almost unbearably lonely and long. The third scene must be a contrast to it. Before the opera closes down with merciless finality, on several measures of a repeating fortissimo chord, we are treated to the opera's first and only embryonic three-way "ensemble": Baron, Duke, and Albert in active interrelation. Their overlap of voices is a shouting match. Within a minute or two the father has thrown down his glove ("Let the sword decide!"), the son has picked it up ("I thank you: my father's first gift!"), and the Duke responds furiously ("What do I see happening here?").[48] It is the closest to a communication among all parties that we have in the entire work—though that condition cannot be sustained for very long. After a solitary life spent dropping coins into his chests, the Baron at last comes above ground. But he cannot endure the pressure of actual circulation in anything like the real world. In the final minutes of that life, he receives a jaggedly rising melodic line as he challenges his son—and then again another leaping line as he clutches at his failing heart.

Rachmaninoff's highly refined, detailed, and flexible use of the leitmotif, without strict or mechanical ostinato, might be perceived as lacking sustained or rounded melody. This was Rimsky-Korsakov's complaint. These textured "leit-images" do constitute a story, but unlike the stories told musically in the other *Little Tragedies*, there is no contrast with a positive energy, and no lyrical principle.[49] Counter to those earlier three operas, no one sings or plays music diegetically, that is, inside the story space; there are no inserted songs or dances performed and heard as such by the characters on stage. The themes of *The Miserly Knight* grow unrelievedly more tense, heavy, anti-lyrical, suspicious, "ever more subjugated to the passion for gold, gloomy and ill–omened."[50] Although Albert is young, passionate, energetic, he cannot relax or spend—and the lyric, in keeping with its erotic core, must be able to spend. Likewise the Duke, introduced by slow-moving chords, is a stabilizing and disciplining presence, but his part has little forward momentum and does not "sing." The only fully lyrical moments—the Baron's expansive fantasies, with lush orchestral support—are delusional.

In 1985, with the Silver Age a distant, distinct historical period and *glasnost* almost on the horizon, the Soviet musicologist Anatoly Tsuker offered a broader cultural view of *The Miserly Knight*.[51] Like Chekhov's fin-de-siècle plays, Tsuker argues, Rachmaninoff's opera opposes the Symbolist-era image of ideal "knightliness" (*rïtsarstvo*)—impulsive generosity and poetry—to the new commercial ethos of "miserliness" (*skupost'*), which was destroying Russia's gentry estate culture. In the post-Communist period, the focus of Rachmaninoff criticism shifted again, from the creeping evils of capitalism under the old regime to émigré (and native Russian) nostalgia for an idealized Old Russia.

As coda to the present essay, I suggest a more cosmopolitan approach to the composer's legacy appropriate to the two operas that premiered at the Bolshoi Theater in 1906. In their own time, Pushkin's *Little Tragedies* were pointedly pan-European. Francesca and Paolo's story from the Inferno's Third Circle had long belonged to the world, both as legend and as music. The universalism of both Pushkin and Dante does not render Rachmaninoff's settings of them any less Russian. The larger lens that I propose is also supra-national and panhuman: sin.

A Coda on the Deadly Sins (*The Miserly Knight* and *Francesca*)

In his book on Rachmaninoff, Max Harrison describes Pushkin's four *Little Tragedies* as dramatic texts that "deal vividly, concisely, in non-moralizing fashion, with a selection of the seven deadly sins."[52] Rosters of sin and virtue go back to pagan antiquity. A mortal sin is one that, if unrepented, separates the sinner eternally from God. A venial sin, by contrast, only wounds the Divine connection, it does not sever it forever; sins are venial if they are not "grave matter," or if they are committed without full knowledge or free consent. The gradations between mortal and venial have been richly annotated, but for our cast of characters in these two operas, the following distinctions are key.

The three lustful appetites—gluttony, fornication, avarice—are usually distinguished from corruptions of the mind or heart: pride, ambition, envy, despair, various forms of apathy or sloth. The sins that Rachmaninoff showcased in 1906 were both of appetite: Francesca and Paolo fall to Lust (and the elder Malatesta to Wrath), the Miser falls to Greed. But these are failings of different degree. For all the popularity of carnal lust as an artistic theme, it is considered the least serious of the deadly (that is, venial) sins. As the disordered love of individuals (Dante's definition), lechery or lust is an error of the flesh shared with animals and less damning than errors of the spirit. Usury and miserliness, however, are sins of the most severe gravity. Usury is a sin of violence, punished deep in the Inferno's seventh circle together with murderers, suicides, blasphemers, and sodomites as an act against nature. (As Thomas Aquinas explains, following Aristotle, "Charging for the loan of money is unjust as such, for you are selling something that does not exist"; profit can be made virtuously only off human effort or natural goods.)[53] It should be noted that the Russian Orthodox Church slightly reconfigured the mortal and venial sins. Envy was classified under the greater sin of *sre-brolyubiye* (love of silver, or money-lust), which was separate from other types of desire or greed. Culturally, Russia nurtured a special suspicion against wealth, and especially against hoarded wealth.

As Vladimir Golstein remarks in his discussion of Dante as guide to *The Miserly Knight*, by the end of the 1820s Pushkin was surely familiar with medieval views of usury. Usury is based on growth in time (the Russian word for usurer, *rostovshchik*, is built off the root "to grow"), and yet, Golstein points out, "This is not an organic growth, like the growth that occurs in nature."[54] A complementary vice in this Little Tragedy, therefore, is the milder and more neoclassical one of disobedience to the natural temporal order. The timing of an action is its virtue. To the mature Pushkin, the proper sequencing of events and passions was a matter of abiding concern. Fathers had to give way to children, the old must prudently provide for the young. The old Baron has no right under God to lasciviously compare, as he does, nightly visits to his chests of gold with visits to a harlot he might have once seduced. That frolicking time, appropriate to the appetites of youth, is past; such energy now belongs to his son and the Baron cannot buy it back. And we might speculate that Rachmaninoff, too, in setting this old Baron to music as he was also setting the elder Malatesta, looked with compassion at the careless, illicit lovers who were frozen forever in time for succumbing to a sin that was natural to their age, place, and bodies.

Consider again the double bill. Simon Morrison opens his essay on *Francesca da Rimini* for this volume by noting that special challenges come with dramatizing a romantic heroine and hero who are already and eternally dead. No grand love duet, no moment of exquisite passion or violence. And thus, Morrison writes, "Of all the musical treatments of Dante, Rachmaninoff's may come the closest to capturing his conception of love as a spiritual force that does not funnel toward death but rather spirals away to the divine." *The Miserly Knight*, experienced in the Bolshoi on the same evening with *Francesca*, reverses this dynamic in the most awful way. Love, from Plato onward, has always had a selfishly posses-sive and carnally satisfying function as well as an ennobling, illuminating one. Money-lust, or greed, knows only the possessive appetite. And thus Rachmaninoff, moving from the second circle of Hell to the seventh, cap-tures the concept of money-lust as a force that cannot "spiral away to the divine" but rather funnels everyone in the opera toward death. A dread-ful age, dreadful hearts.

NOTES

1. Blank verse is unrhymed, but with meter; Pushkin's *Little Tragedies*, like Shakespeare's plays, are in unrhymed iambic pentameter without caesura. The plays were never published together during Pushkin's lifetime, and the poet left a list of other potential topics, including Romulus and Remus, Tsar Paul I, Prince Kurbsky (intimate friend and then political opponent of Ivan the Terrible), and the devil in love.

2. The "fifth act" designation is from Nancy K. Anderson, introduction to her translation of Aleksandr Pushkin, *The Little Tragedies* (New Haven: Yale University Press, 2000), 6.

3. This image of the musical Romantic began with E. T. A. Hoffmann, "Beethoven's Instrumental Music" (1813): "Beethoven's music moves the levers of fear, shuddering, horror, pain, and thus awakens that infinite longing that is the essence of Romanticism."

4. See Richard Taruskin: "Rachmaninoff, composer and performer in equal measure . . . was a rare survivor, or atavism, from the pre-romantic era when a complete musician united the roles that late romanticism put asunder." "Not Modern and Loving It," in *Russian Music at Home and Abroad: New Essays* (Oakland: University of California Press, 2016), 120–33, at 128–29.

5. Given the almost mythical role that gold plays in *The Miserly Knight*, it should be noted that in Pushkin's era gold was rare; both silver and gold coins had disappeared from circulation after the Napoleonic Wars. The government urged the population to use paper money (*assignats*), and coins were hoarded. Most Russian subjects (the peasantry) had little contact with paper currency; they traded or bartered, and paid for things in labor or kind. I thank Ekaterina Pravilova, Russian historian at Princeton University, for sharing her work-in-progress on the history of the ruble.

6. A. S. Pushkin, letters of 8 June and 14 July 1834, in *Pis'ma k zhene*, ed. Ya. L. Levkovich (Leningrad: Nauka, 1986), 60 and 67.

7. For Pushkin's unsustainable indebtedness, see T. J. Binyon, *Pushkin, A Biography* (New York: HarperCollins, 2002), 643: "The sum total of Pushkin's obligations at the moment of his death was thus 138,988.33 roubles. He would have had absolutely no hope of paying off even a fraction of this, especially since the sum would have grown larger with each successive month."

8. Leonid Zorin, "Mednaya babushka," in *Pokrovskiye vorota: P'esï* (Moscow: Sovetskiy pisatel', 1979), 213-70. The title of Zorin's play ("The Bronze Grandmother") refers to the equestrian statue of Peter the Great, the "Bronze Horseman" / "Mednyi vsadnik," on the Neva River embankment in St. Petersburg (and subject of Pushkin's famous narrative poem), as well as to a part of Pushkin's wife's dowry, a statue of Empress Catherine II, that the poet was desperate to sell. When, at the end of section 11 of Zorin's play, Vasily Zhukovsky, courtier and fellow poet, calls his friend Pushkin "Russia's genius," the poet responds bitterly: "Genius? No. Genius is proud. Independent. Genius does not take bribes from a monarch" (262).

9. Natal'ya Mikhaylova, "Den'gi veshch' vazhnaya . . ." (Money is an important thing . . .) in *Den'gi—Pushkin—Den'gi* (Moscow: Russkiy put', 2010), 6–7, at 6.

10. "At this time [1902] Sergei Vasilyevich was living very modestly," the pianist Aleksandr Goldenweiser wrote in his memoirs of Rachmaninoff. He was paid fifty rubles a month as musical director at the Girls' institutes and obliged to give private lessons (one a day) for ten rubles a lesson, "despite his sharply expressed dislike of pedagogical activity." A. B. Gol'denveyzer, "Iz lichnïkh vospominaniy o S. V. Rakhmaninove," in *Vospominaniya o Rakhmaninove*, ed. Z. Apetyan, 5th ed., 2 vols (Moscow: Muzïka, 1988), 1:405–26, at 412.

11. Cited in Sergei Bertensson and Jay Leyda, *Sergei Rachmaninoff: A Lifetime in Music* (Bloomington: Indiana University Press, 2001), 110.

12. Letter to Mikhaíl Slonov, 3 September 1984, cited in ibid., 65.

13. See Alexander N. Tumanov, "Merchant, Entrepreneur and Profit in Russian Literature: The Russian Artistic Intelligentsia and Money," in *Literature and Money*, ed. Anthony Purdy (Amsterdam: Rodopi, 1993), 15–43, 26–28 on Pushkin.

14. Entry XVIII in Pushkin, "Table-Talk" (title originally in English,) published posthumously (1837) in Pushkin's journal *Sovremennik* 8, and republished in A. S. Pushkin, *Polnoye sobraniye sochineniy*, 12 vols in 17 (Moscow: Akademiya Nauk SSSR, 1937–59), 12:159–60.

15. For a summary of Dante in the moral subtexts of *The Miserly Knight*, see Vladimir Golstein, "Time or Money: The Paradoxes of Aging in *The Covetous Knight*," in *Alexander Pushkin's Little Tragedies: The Poetics of Brevity*, ed. Svetlana Evdokimova (Madison: University of Wisconsin Press, 2003) 147–71, esp. the subsection "Dante as a Guide to Pushkin's Play," 149–54.

16. Perhaps to cover his autobiographical tracks, the poet titled his tragedy "scenes from Chenstone's tragicomedy *The Covetous Knight*." No dramatist by the name of Chenstone (Ченстон) has been found, and among the works of William Shenstone, an eighteenth-century English poet, no such play exists. For a close discussion of the Shakespearean subtexts, as well as differences between covetous, miserly, stingy, and avaricious in Russian and English, see J. Thomas Shaw, *Pushkin's Poetics of the Unexpected* (Columbus, OH: Slavica Publishers, 1994), 239–55.

17. Solomon as the moneylending, poison-peddling Jew is an uncomfortable image. It should be noted that although Pushkin shared the aristocratic prejudices of his time, anti-Semitism in the European sense was a later development in Russia. For Pushkin, Jews—like gypsies and Georgian singers—were exotic figures (pawnbrokers in the Russian Empire were more often Poles). Since Pushkin presents this Little Tragedy as an imitation of an English original and needs a moneylender in it, he most likely models the usurer he needs on Shakespeare's Shylock and (closer to medieval knightly lore) on Isaac of York in Walter Scott's *Ivanhoe*. It is also possible that Albert is projecting his own parricidal fantasies on Solomon, whom he then threatens furiously to punish. See Oleg Proskurin, "Chem pakhnut chervontsï? Ob odnom tyomnom meste v 'Skupom Rïtsare,' ili intertekstual'nost' i tekstologiya," in *Poeziya Pushkina, ili podvizhnïy palimpsest* (Moscow: Novoye literaturnoye obozreniye, 1999), 348–75.

18. This Wagnerian trace is suggested by Max Harrison in *Rachmaninoff: Life, Works, Recordings* (London: Continuum, 2005), 119.

19. Pushkin, "Skupoy rïtsar'," in *Polnoye sobraniye sochineniy*, 7:120 and 102.

20. The text consulted is the bilingual Russian-German Gutheil piano-vocal score of 1905: *Skupoy Rïtsar': Opera v tryokh kartinakh, Muzïka S. Rakhmaninova, Soch. 24 / Der geizige Ritter. Oper in 3 Bildern, Dichtung von A. S. Puschkin, Deutsche Umdichtung von Friedrich Fiedler, in Musik gesetzt von S. Rachmaninow* (Moscow: Gutheil, 1905). The full libretto (iii–xiv) appears as text before the score.

21. For more on this medieval "pectoral psychology," see Eric Jager, "The Book of the Heart: Reading and Writing the Medieval Subject," *Speculum* 71/1 (1996): 1–26, at 2. The very word *record* (from the Latin *cor*) suggests that the "medieval documentary record was a written extension of the inner, remembering subject" (2) and not a product of mental reckoning.

22. I. F. Shalyapina, "Pamyati S. V. Rakhmaninova," in *Vospominaniya o Rakhmaninove*, 2:190–95, at 191. Rachmaninoff's close friend, the pianist Aleksandr Goldenweiser, was of another opinion. "Chaliapin was an extraordinarily fine sight-reader," the pianist recalls. "But this superb artist was lazy and didn't like to learn new roles or new things from the chamber repertory. . . . When Rachmaninoff showed him his two new operas, Chaliapin sang the part of the Miser and of Gianciotto Malatesta and it made an enormous impression, even though he was sight-reading them. But he was simply too lazy to

learn the Miser, somehow the part didn't appeal to him, and he refused to appear in these operas." "Iz lichnïkh vospominaniy o S. V. Rakhmaninove," 454.

23. Rimsky's summary statement was reported by Rachmaninoff's friend and classmate A. V. Ossovsky in his memorial essay "S. V. Rakhmaninov," in *Vospominaniya o Rakhmaninove*, 1:343–85, at 359.

24. For a survey of reviews 1906–12, see V. V. Yakovlev, "Rakhmaninov i opernïy teatr," in *S. V. Rakhmaninov i russkaya opera,* ed. I. F. Belza (Moscow: Vserossiyskoye teatral'noye obshchestvo, 1947), 144–90.

25. "Teatr i muzyka," *Russkiï listok* 12 (13 January 1906): 3.

26. A. Livin, "Novïye operï na stsene Moskovskogo Bol'shogo teatra," *Russkaya muzïkal'naia gazeta* 4–5 (1906): 124.

27. As Yakovlev, in "Rakhmaninov i opernïy teatr," sums up this objection: "The psychological burden and interpretive demands [of Pushkin] are too great [to be resolved] within the framework of a refined and powerfully developed orchestral accompaniment" (146).

28. Vol'fing [Emiliy Metner], "*Skupoy rïtsar'* i *Francheska da Rimini*," *Zolotoye runo* 1 (1906): 122–23.

29. This rare voice is Semyon Kruglikov, *Russkoye slovo*, 16 January 1906, cited in Yakovlev, "Rakhmaninov i opernïy teatr," 157.

30. Rosamund Bartlett, *Wagner and Russia* (Cambridge: Cambridge University Press, 1995), 81–94.

31. G. Prokof'yev, "Pevets intimnïkh nastroeniy," *Russkaya muzïkal'naya gazeta* 37 (1910): 751–54, at 752.

32. The "orchestral principle" was simply too loud—"and can we even speak about the plot, about the drama (for Rachmaninoff's operas are, after all, music dramas), when even in *The Miserly Knight*, known by heart by absolutely everyone, the text's words only rarely reached the listener, since two-thirds of the time in both operas the singers helplessly floundered in the triumphant thundering of Mr. Kuper's [conductor] orchestral accompaniment. Without a doubt, the hero of the production is Mr. Kuper, but only because the others weren't heard." Unsigned review of a performance at the Bolshoi Theater on 29 September 1912, in *Muzïka* 98 (6 October 1912): 855.

33. Evgenii Gunst, "'Francheska da Rimini' i 'Skupoy rïtsar'" S. V. Rakhmaninova," *Maski* 1 (1912): 60–66.

34. Ibid., 61.

35. Ibid., 62–63.

36. Ibid., 65–66.

37. T. N. Livanova, "Tri operï Rakhmaninova," in Belza, *S. V. Rakhmaninov i russkaya opera*, 39–100, at 81 and 83.

38. Yuriy Keldïsh, "Skupoy rïtsar' i Francheska da Rimini," in *Rakhmaninov i yego vremya* (Moscow: Muzïka, 1973), 254–64. For an introduction in English to the motifs that overlap with Keldysh, see Barrie Martyn, *Rachmaninoff: Composer, Pianist, Conductor* (Aldershot: Scolar Press, 1990), 152–60.

39. Keldïsh, "Skupoy rïtsar' i Francheska da Rimini," 256.

40. Ibid., 257.

41. Ibid., 258.

42. Ibid., 258–59.

43. Ibid., 259-60.

44. Ibid., 262.

45. Ibid., 259.

46. Pushkin's Little Tragedy and the opera's Scene 2 (in the 1905 Gutheil edition, x), in which the Baron compares the power of his glittering gold to a tsardom, contain direct textual allusions to the play *Boris Godunov*, written by Pushkin five years earlier.

The theme is the strength of a tsar's power. But Pushkin distributes the theme between tsar and courtier, burdening it with irony and hypocrisy. In Scene 10 of *Boris Godunov*, before announcing the appearance of Dmitry the Pretender in Poland, the treacherous boyar Prince Shuysky assures Tsar Boris that "your power is great" ("Сильна твоя держава"). In Scene 2 of *The Miserly Knight*, the Baron, imagining himself a tsar, likewise assures himself : "I reign supreme! . . .My power is great!" ("Я царствую! . . . Сильна моя держава!" Rachmaninoff, writing his opera on the far side of Musorgsky's *Boris Godunov* (1869–74), quotes the line Pushkin gives to Shuysky as well as Musorgsky's musicalization of Boris's role, putting the whole in the mouth of the Baron: sole heir to this intricate fabric of self-delusion.

47. Keldïsh, "Skupoy rïtsar' i Francheska da Rimini," 263.

48. Rachmaninoff would seem to have Mozart's *Don Giovanni* in mind here; the ensemble structure resembles that of the death of the Commendatore at the beginning of Mozart's score.

49. Lyrical compositions punctuate the other "Little Operas." Don Juan in *The Stone Guest* is reckless and full of appetite (whatever his ultimate fate), and Dargomyzhsky wrote two songs into his opera, one a Spanish dance piece (with guitar) for Don Juan's paramour Laura. Mozart is playfully buoyant in contrast with the brooding Salieri, and Rimsky-Korsakov saturates his opera with Mozart's music: a blind fiddler plays eight bars of Zerlina's aria from *Don Giovanni*, Mozart performs for Salieri a stylization (composed by Rimsky) of a Mozartian piano sonata, and in his final moments Mozart plays the opening sixteen measures of his own Requiem. Even *Feast During the Plague* has two songs, written by Cui in the late 1880s long before he embedded them in his opera: "Walsingham's Hymn" and "Mary's Song."

50. On this growing gloom without positive or lyrical contrast, see L. Mikheyeva, "Opera Rakhmaninova 'Skupoy rïtsar'," at http://www.belcanto.ru/skupoy.html.

51. A. Tsuker, "K kontseptsii 'Skupogo rïtsarya,'" *Sovetskaya muzïka* 7 (1985): 92–97.

52. Harrison, *Rachmaninoff*, 117.

53. St. Thomas Aquinas, *Summa Theologiae: A Concise Translation*, ed. Timothy McDermott (Notre Dame, IN: Christian Classics, 1989), 396, in the section "Justice," subsection "Unjust sales and loans." Aquinas continues: "Now Aristotle tells us that money was invented for purposes of exchange, and that its prime and proper use is in its consumption and disbursement by being spent in transactions. . . . Silver coin is primarily meant for spending, and one cannot licitly charge for its use and then expect it to be restored" (397).

54. Golstein, "Time or Money," 153.

Burning for You: Rachmaninoff's
Francesca da Rimini

SIMON MORRISON

Rachmaninoff's *Francesca da Rimini* has not been performed much, nor should it be—at least not as a traditional Romantic opera. Truth be told, it is less an opera than an anti-opera: a drama of "concentrated uneventfulness."[1] The most ambitious productions have embellished the stasis with hellish visual effects like iridescent clouds rising from the orchestra pit; candles and lighting have been used to evoke a liturgical "service of the furnace."[2] But even the most stunning stagecraft cannot compensate for a crucial absence. Our heroine and hero are dead, the tale of their love told in a flashback. The score lacks a grand love duet for the principal characters, so never captures in sound the passion that prompts their murder and damnation.[3]

My aim here is to reconsider this supposed absence as instead a sign of something present and prescient. By returning to the source text, Dante's *Divina commedia* (1320), while also exploring the opera's compositional and reception history, we can appreciate anew Rachmaninoff's "quiet culmination,"[4] the arioso he composed for Francesca before what should have been her grand love duet with Paolo. Of all the musical treatments of Dante, Rachmaninoff's may come the closest to capturing his conception of love as a spiritual force that does not funnel toward death but rather spirals away to the divine.[5]

Let me explain. If the *Divina commedia* can be said to have a plot, it features, in traditional summaries, a comforting, idealized maternal figure in heaven looking down on a poor soul lost in the woods. She sends a father figure to guide the Pilgrim on a spiritual journey into Inferno, up through Purgatorio, and into Paradiso. The Pilgrim is a fictional version of Dante himself; the benevolent spirit above is his true love Beatrice, the real-life Beatrice Portinari, the daughter of a Florentine banker. He met her at the age of nine and encountered her again nine years later. She died at the age of twenty-five, long before Dante, and he tended to his image of her as one would a saint. The father figure is the ancient Roman poet Virgil, whom Dante greatly admired.[6]

People and places in Dante's own life populate the flaming circles, through Limbo, Lust, Gluttony, Greed, Anger, Heresy, Violence, Fraud, and Treachery. He witnesses corrupt popes stuffed into a hole, Florentine politicians cast into a burning pit, and the endless reenactment of suicide in the seventh circle. Descending ever deeper, the Pilgrim worries he might never escape, because demons seem determined to keep him there. (He is not explicitly threatened by the damned but is subject to their verbal outrage.) The Pilgrim finally escapes to Purgatorio, where souls have hope yet must trudge through fire.

In his poetry, Dante contrasts emotion with reason and reason with the divine (which was also the project of Thomas Aquinas's *Summa theologica*). Medieval and Renaissance readers privileged Dante's metaphysical musings, his abandonment of the grotesque physicality of hell. Romantic and post-Romantic readers, in contrast, found the spiritual less compelling (and certainly less titillating) than the sin. In the *Divina commedia*, Paradiso is, in terms of stories, considered a letdown: light-filled, luxuriant, and speedily described. Neither Purgatorio nor Paradiso is as interesting as the Inferno to composers, filmmakers, or novelists. Consider the relentlessly unseemly 1995 film *Seven* or Dan Brown's 2013 mystery thriller *Inferno*, which features "screams," "excrement," "disgusting liquid," and "rivers of blood clogged with corpses."[7] Dante's depiction of hell is their source.

Dante was devoted to the number 3, the triad, the whole that contains a beginning middle, and an end. The three sections, or canticas, of the poem comprise 33 cantos each. The metric format devised by Dante is also trinitarian: ABA, BCB, CDC, and so forth, until the end of the canto. The idea is that the middle line of each tercet provides the leading rhyme for the first and third lines of the following tercet. The magic of Dante's *terza rima* lies in its impetus. The metric design pulls the reader along, propelling the Pilgrim through the slithering slime of the caverns of the Inferno and past the grasping hands of condemned souls.

We don't know what Rachmaninoff thought about Dante's arithmomania in 1906, when, at the age of thirty-three, he completed his third opera, *Francesca da Rimini*, which turns a single canto from the *Divina commedia* into 105 minutes of music. The opera explores the sin of lust with Francesca da Rimini as its protagonist. Dante doesn't provide details, but later commentators such as Giovanni Boccaccio did. Like Beatrice, Francesca was also a real person, the beautiful young daughter of an Italian nobleman, Guido I, Lord of Ravenna. He married her off, but she fell in love with her husband's brother, the fetching Paolo.

The rejected husband, Gianciotto Malatesta, takes his revenge by stabbing them both, condemning himself (along with the unfaithful lovers) to Inferno. Malatesta, whose name means "treacherous," presumably lands in the ninth circle, with his wife and her lover in the second, or so Francesca vindictively predicts. The Pilgrim encounters Francesca and Paolo trapped in the vortex of an eternal tornado, tortured forever for their illicit desire: *eros* is sickness and suffering. Francesca describes the circumstances of her and Paolo's mutual seduction so movingly that the Pilgrim faints.

Clearly, the ambiguous tale lends itself to competing interpretations. Is Francesca more or less sympathetic than her husband? Is Paolo in any way at fault? Canto V of Inferno suggests that Francesca and Paolo might have exercised forbearance were it not for the influence of literature, namely the romance of Lancelot and Guinevere, which the lovers recite to each other before embracing. Crucial here is how the lovers read the text and then they decide to read no further. The key passage is offered as a cautionary tale, describing a kiss that brings down a civilization, but Francesca and Paolo don't heed the warning. Instead, they find justification for their passion, then pause, without reading the moral of the story.

Robert Hollander, who translated and annotated the *Divina commedia*, cautions that Francesca is an unreliable narrator. Her "chief rhetorical strategy is to remove as much blame from herself as she is able, finding other forces at fault wherever possible (e.g., Paolo's physical beauty, her despicable husband, the allure of a French romance)."[8] But Dante could be (and indeed was) read as suggesting that Francesca strove for sexual fulfillment in defiance of oppression. She pursued pleasure by reading a romance and then enacting it; she thus became an agent, not an object. But Dante himself saw in her case a perversion of the divine spiritual aspects of love. Hers is a cautionary tale about someone who ignores a cautionary tale.

Like Dante, Rachmaninoff adopted pilgrim's garb and roamed the wood, exploring the nature of love as sinful and spiritual. In 1899, he and his first cousin Natalya Satina became engaged, despite opposition from the official Church. Marriages between relatives also required permission from the tsar. Finding a priest willing to perform the service and securing the blessing of the sovereign took three years and required the intercession of a well-connected aunt.[9] Consider too the cultural context: the mystical, spiritual Silver Age, whose poets wrote of transcendence through erotic experience. The composer's ruminations might be likened to those of the Russian "mystic" Symbolist poet Vyacheslav Ivanov, who wrote about "intense love," the "suffering" caused by the loss of the beloved, "and the attempt to overcome this suffering through a new, more spiritual form of love."[10] Then there is Rachmaninoff's *Affektenlehre*, the sounds he privileged and their associations: liturgical chants, including the Dies Irae; Bachian counterpoint, and Wagnerian chromaticism; ascending sequential patterns in the strings, and thickly interwoven polyphonic lines at high points. He didn't approach Scriabin's decadence, nor did he want to, for he had a magic touch as a melodist. *Francesca da Rimini* has some of the magic, but as operas go, it lacks catharsis, except for a passage, in Scene 2, when purified emotion is afforded expression.

Rachmaninoff had originally planned to base his third opera on Shakespeare's *Richard II* as translated by Modest Tchaikovsky, brother of the deceased composer. Modest, meantime, had immersed himself in Dante's hallowed text, so instead of *Richard II*, Rachmaninoff in 1898 received the scenario for *Francesca da Rimini* (this happened after another composer, Anatoly Lyadov, passed on it). Rachmaninoff began sketching music in 1900, mapping out Francesca and Paolo's Scene 2 declarations of love. Completion of the piano-vocal score waited until the summer of 1904. The orchestration followed a year after that. Both the slow start and fast finish suggest other projects—Rachmaninoff was overcommitted as a conductor and performer—but travel and persistent writer's block might also be factors. The composer famously consulted a hypnotist to spur creativity after the disastrous 1897 premiere of his First Symphony under the baton of an intoxicated Aleksandr Glazunov. Rachmaninoff sank into depression after the fiasco, unable to get out of bed. Memories of this two-year period of creative paralysis haunted him to the end of his days and have become a commonplace of most biographies.

Those who consider Rachmaninoff's opera a failure point less to the work itself than its context, blaming everything from the personal problems to the hypnotist to the 1905 Revolution, which threw cultural life into disarray. Some adopt Francesca's strategy and blame someone and something else—in this case Modest Tchaikovsky's "clumsily crafted libretto."[11] Rachmaninoff's twelve letters to Modest do indeed suggest an ambivalence about the opera and how best to adapt Dante for the stage. These have been published and reproduced online, and the setting of the text has been chronicled by Tatyana Chernova.[12] The original plan involved a prologue, four scenes, and an epilogue that would have described the real-life Francesca's family background, marriage, and relationship with Paolo. Rachmaninoff knew that Dante's tale provided little background detail and was surprised that Modest had researched the subject. He presumably read Boccaccio's *Esposizioni sopra la "Commedia" di Dante*, the notes to the lectures Boccaccio gave on the Inferno at the end of his life (he made it through 17 of the 99 cantos before his death in 1375). Modest also fleshed out the details about *Lancelot du Lac*, the romance that brought Francesco and Paolo together.[13]

Composer and librettist engaged in several epistolary squabbles. The first dispute concerned the chorus in the prologue: Rachmaninoff asked Modest for "thirty lines for the invisible choir in the prologue. Well, maybe not thirty, but a sizable number of words that I'll distribute and have different groups sing." To date, he had but one line for the prologue and a lot of moaning. "For the love of God, provide these words, Modest Ilyich!"[14] Modest dithered, and Rachmaninoff reconsidered, leaving the choir moaning but for a single utterance: "There is no greater sorrow than to recall our time of joy in wretchedness." He called Modest's melodramatic contributions to the second scene "vulgar" in a letter to his friend Nikita Morozov, a music theorist.[15] Rachmaninoff needed more text and a rewrite of what he had in hand, but Modest, perhaps because he felt underpaid, failed to provide it, leaving the opera with a void, what Rachmaninoff called "a lead-in to a duet, the conclusion of a duet, but not the duet itself."[16] Other traditional operatic elements disappeared, including an aria for Paolo.

Chernova insists, however, that Rachmaninoff remained committed to a traditional operatic treatment until 1904. He imagined the great basso Fyodor Chaliapin singing the role of Malatesta or perhaps Paolo, although his became a tenor role. Chernova further insists that in 1903 Rachmaninoff attended rehearsals of a theatrical adaptation of *Francesca da Rimini* by Gabriele D'Annunzio; the composer, she maintains, found himself deeply affected by the acting of Vera Komissarzhevskaya as Francesca.[17] However, D'Annunzio's 1901 play was not performed in Russia until 1908 in a translation by the Symbolist writers Vyacheslav Ivanov and Valery Bryusov. In 1903, Rachmaninoff saw Komissarzhevskaya rehearsing a different play, *Monna Vanna*.

Written by the French Symbolist Maurice Maeterlinck, *Monna Vanna* is another tale of a woman denied who then claims agency. It is set in fifteenth-century Italy, much later than Dante's *Divina commedia*, with Pisa besieged by Florence. The leader of the Pisan soldiers informs his father that the fighting will finally end if he sends his wife to the Florentine commander's tent alone that night. He refuses, but his wife, Monna, agrees; she meets not a blood-soaked barbarian but a kind, sage man seeking peace. She leaves his lair having received but a kiss on the brow and is greeted as the savior of Pisa, despite her husband's denial of her heroism. His loss.

None of this would matter to our account of *Francesca da Rimini* had Rachmaninoff not become so smitten with Komissarzhevskaya's interpretation of Monna and the ethereal intonation of her speaking voice that he decided to write an opera based on Maeterlinck's drama. On stage, it was said, she spoke with a "depersonalized" sound, "the pure sound of an unknown musical instrument."[18] Rachmaninoff worked on a setting of *Monna Vanna* in 1906 and 1907 but finished only one scene. Yet the experience made a mark on the work he would finish. By the time he completed *Francesca da Rimini*, which had been simmering on the back burner for years, it was no longer an opera in the traditional sense. The uncanniness of Francesca's final arioso, the "quiet culmination" of the opera, proves homage to Komissarshevskaya. With her "pure sound" in his head, Rachmaninoff reconceived *Francesca da Rimini*. It would have hell, but it would also have heaven—in the form of a passage invoking the radiance of love. He discarded two scenes that Modest had written in his own words, leaving the prologue, epilogue, and two episodes in between.

The prologue and epilogue represent, in the strings, the second circle's flames, and for the listeners as well as the performers, Sisyphean torment: these largo sections of the score are built in wave formations, with the musical drama pushed up a hill only to fall back down. Rachmaninoff seized on Dante's conception of the Inferno as less musical than noisy. Syncopated octaves in the basses represent Dante and Virgil groping along rocky ledges amid chromatic gooeyness. Certain Rachmaninoff habits can be detected, and what Blair Johnston writes about the composer's first opera *Aleko* as well as his Third Symphony roughly applies to *Francesca da Rimini*: "Instrumental polyphony replaces monophonic quasi-chant. Metric uncertainly becomes syncopation. Phrygian modalism begets Phrygian-derived chromaticism."[19] Rather than a Phrygian b2 and b7 "revolving axially around the tonic," Rachmaninoff relies on chromatic neighbor-note motion, monotonously moving up a half step, down a half step, up two half steps, down two half steps. The prologue opens and closes in D minor, but the pedal E with G♯ suggest the dominant of A minor, and there is a tension in the music between that dominant pull and the E Phrygian mire. When the basses drop out, the texture is less grounded than suspended, as though Rachmaninoff had decided to take the central conceit of the "Tristan" chord—its non-resolution—and expand it to the length of a tone poem.

The harmonic palette is nonfunctionally unadventurous: minor and major 5/3, 6/4, and 7/5 chords, diminished and half-diminished sevenths, augmented sixths, with the basses sometimes asserting non-harmonic tones, rendering certain sonorities spectral, iridescent. The meandering chromatic lines of the opening assemble into a five-voice fugue (rehearsal number 2), so the sliding back and forth of Wagnerian chromaticism cedes into Bachian chromaticism, which places the dissonance under tonal control. There are several pieces in Bach's *Well-Tempered Clavier* (the F-minor and B-minor fugues, the A-minor Prelude) thick with chromaticism that return to points of tonal stability more frequently than Rachmaninoff's fugue. For Bach, the fugue mirrored divine perfection. For Rachmaninoff, the fugue was a kind of anti-music, static and inert.

The subject of the fugue is sequential, privileging, like Dante's text, groups of three: the middle pitch of the first three-note group of the fugue subject becomes the first and third pitch of the second group, whose middle pitch becomes the first and third pitch of the third group, and so on. This moment of contrapuntal delimitation is short-lived; the exposition disintegrates as the texture thickens and chordal complexes expand and contract (rehearsal number 3), the semitone prevalent. Rehearsal number 4 introduces a counter-subject to mark the moment the Pilgrim meets Virgil. The curtain goes up, and shades of these two figures, then of Francesca and Paolo, appear.

At the climaxes of the three waves in the prelude (before the curtain rises, after the Pilgrim and Virgil speak, and after Francesca and Paolo mourn their lot), Rachmaninoff strives for maximal semitonal saturation to depict the Inferno. The music is entropic; order decays into disorder before reassembling in pointlessly circular fashion. The chorus sighs in longer rhythmic values in the distance; the woodwinds and strings slither and writhe. The serpentine tangle is a metaphor, perhaps, of the body tied up with the spirit, or the knot that Francesca, Paolo, and Malatesta find themselves in.

The closed-mouth chorus enters nine measures before rehearsal number 9. Dante's second circle is cacophonous and profane, full of cornets and lutes, groans, moans, and flatulence. Rachmaninoff avoids grotesquerie; his prelude is lachrymal. Before the Pilgrim encounters Francesca, the source text alludes to the lyric of a love song; however, the song itself is never heard—not in the numerous Italian madrigal settings of Canto V, not in later adaptations by Liszt, Tchaikovsky, Thomas Ambroise, Eduard Nápravník, and Riccardo Zandonai, and not here in Rachmaninoff's opera. Shades of the Pilgrim and Virgil appear as swirling sextuplet, sixteenth-note groupings that suggest thick clouds amassing. The Pilgrim glimpses the shades of Francesca and Paolo. His question—Who are you?—is anticipated in the cellos. It's rhetorical: the Pilgrim already knows them.

As vapor fills the stage, D minor, "where spleen and the humors brood," moves via an F-minor triad to D-flat major, the key of "grief and rapture."[20] The 3/2 passage heard after rehearsal number 26 introduces Francesca's *popevka*, or tunelet. The opera is not leitmotific, but

Rachmaninoff assigns sequentially extendable and expandable melodic phrases to the characters—in Francesca's case a line that sinks by seconds and thirds through an octave in the cellos and bass clarinet. It recurs throughout the opera, increasing in length in the first scene and ascending heavenward in the second. Two measures before rehearsal number 31, she and Paolo speak of their misfortune, the sorrow of joy recalled in wretchedness, in an arching semitonal phrase trapped within the range of a diminished fourth. A blasphemed chant atop an E-major seventh chord (joy) cedes to D minor (wretchedness). The chorus will repeat their words at the end of the opera (rehearsal number 91) on the wretched tonic pitch of D. Malatesta's militarism is represented at the start of the first scene by an aggressive march theme in C-sharp minor (rehearsal number 31). His troops head for battle after a cardinal blesses them. The cardinal isn't heard; the lines Modest planned to assign him were replaced by a brief chorale-like passage. Malatesta softens in a one-sided conversation with Francesca, but not before we hear a second theme in E minor (rehearsal number 41). It suggests menace as the tonic seems to stalk the dominant, the horns creeping upward in shorter and shorter rhythmic values and narrower intervals. The troops are gone, but we still hear their music—or at least a distorted version of it. The offstage trumpet fanfares conclude, painfully, with an impossible-to-keep-in-tune *fp* minor ninth.

The words Modest assigns to Malatesta reveal his fragility. He wants love but doesn't know how to get it and admits, pleading with Francesca, that he's "powerless." Rachmaninoff is explicit on this point, changing the scoring from harsh horns and trombones to soft strings. She is silent, at once accepting and resisting his (and our) perception of her as good and evil. He tells Francesca to "come down" from her "starry heights" in a passage of music thought to be derived from an unpublished piano prelude. But he knows she's cheated on him; the Madonna is also a whore. Herein lies the *secretum*, the irresolvable dichotomy, realized as a semitonal split that cannot find a unison. "Damn it all," Malatesta declares. The scene concludes with murderous resolution; once confined to the middle register, the stalking theme blasts throughout the orchestra. Yet Malatesta's power has sapped: whereas the music begins in C-sharp minor, it ends in C.

This first scene has its patterns of three: each of the three vignettes contains a three-part arioso. But what do the numbers matter? How does one get from the self-imposed strictures of trinitarian arithmomania to mysticism? Chernova provides the beginning of an answer, proposing that the absence of a love duet in the second scene is purposeful, and that, musically and verbally, Francesca becomes Beatrice, her analogue in

Paradiso.[21] The tonal scheme of the second scene, featuring the lovers, includes A-flat major, E major, D-flat major, with occasional D-minor jolts as premonitions. The difference between heaven and hell in Rachmaninoff's conception is the difference between the first and last of these keys: a tritone. The *popevka* associated with Francesca is luxuriously elaborated in the second scene, becoming, in Francesca's final arioso, one of Rachmaninoff's most affecting melodies (and this was a composer who produced more affecting melodies than any other in the Russian canon). Broad, breathed through, this sequence of sequences covers two octaves in seconds and thirds, slowing down as the intervals between the pitches widen. It occupies a consonantly light and transparent orchestral texture dominated by the upper strings and woodwinds. *Tutti* is avoided, likewise the brass instruments. For the basses, Rachmaninoff prefers *pizzicato*.

In the second scene, too, there are three parts: Francesca and Paolo reading their book and falling in love, followed by the arioso representing her spiritual departure—the Beatrice moment—and then the crash through the earth in the form of the murder. Francesca's theme, hinted at in the prologue and first scene, is here almost constantly subject to exposition, development, and recapitulation. Chernova dwells on its elaboration in the arioso, writing that Francesca's "spiritual departure . . . binds her to feminine icons of different contexts, some real, some taken from literature"—and, if we take Boris Asafyev's word for it, northern Italian fresco cycles.[22] Chernova recalls Rachmaninoff drawing inspiration from Komissarshevskaya, forcing a parallel with Dante drawing inspiration from the "young sister of angels" Beatrice. Art of this sort encourages contradictory interpretations, Chernova concedes, and she is struck by the fact that the movement in the arioso is as much downward as upward and, quoting the Boccaccio expert Ruf Klodovsky, proposes a tragic lining to it all, a reversal of the "dematerialization" that characterized representations of heaven in "proto-Renaissance" art.[23]

Musically, it is more a case of Francesca directing Paolo's gaze to the dance of light, to her analogue in Paradiso, but he prefers groping, and so there's no hope for them. Chernova's boldest assertion, however, is the notion that Rachmaninoff—and his librettist—sought to approximate the form and meter of a canzona in the arioso.[24] This is a hard sell. A canzona can take all sorts of complicated forms, and Dante turned it into the highest of arts, doubling the length from five or six lines to twelve, with a shorter line, or envoi, for the end. The magic resides in the eleven-syllable organization of the lines, and either the repeated or rhymed words at the terminus. Dante's pre-*Divina commedia* paean to Beatrice, *La vita nuova*, includes four canzoni, amid passages of prose and other poetic forms.

Modest hardly aspired to Dante's poetic complexities. He played it safe with Francesca's arioso. The text is three quatrains of iambic tetrameter with alternating rhymes, one of the most common forms of Russian nineteenth-century poetry. The triple repetition of *zemnoy* (earthly) in lines 3, 4, and 5 feel more like poor versification. There is nothing especially Italian about it, and to argue there is would be like Schumann exclaiming that Mendelssohn's "Italian" Symphony beautifully evoked that country after having heard the "Scottish" one.

Пусть не дано нам знать лобзаний,
Пускай мы здесь разлучены. . . .
Недолог срок земных скитаний,
Мелькнут, как миг, земные сны.
Не плачь, ценой земных мучений
Нас ждет с тобой блаженство там,
Где нет теней, где́ке нет лишений,
Где у любви нетленный храм.
Там в высоте за гранью мира
В твоих объятиях паря,
В лазури светлого эфира
Я буду в вечности твоя!

A kiss may not be in our stars—no matter.
We may be torn asunder now—no matter.
The time we're given to wander the earth is finite,
Our earthly slumbers will flash by.
Weep not, for our earthly torments
Have earned us bliss in the realm
Where no ghosts tread, where no privations abide,
Where the temple of love shall never perish.
There, up above, beyond the edge of this universe,
Soaring as you embrace me,
I will be yours for ever and ever
In the azure glow of radiant ether.

More plausible, and not to discredit Chernova's argument entirely, is that Modest tried to give the arioso an aura of a medieval sung poem. The texture Rachmaninoff chooses for rehearsal number 69, the start of the arioso, is that of a madrigal: the string lines could be sung. Ancient in this context means simpler. As in his romances, Rachmaninoff at once "refines and dematerializes" the harmonic structure.[25] Francesca's arioso uses the most transparent harmonies in the score: I, ii, IV, and vi in E major, most of the chords in root position. At rehearsal number 70, however, the strings slide down by half step, moving to the dominant and tonic of E-flat major. The vocal line, meanwhile, remains in E, and the E♭ drop is better perceived as D♯, the sharps spelled with their flat enharmonic equivalents for practical reasons.

Consider, though, the affect. The strings quietly (*pp*) emphasize B♭ and E♭. The singer, in contrast, reaches love's spiritual realm by ascending from D♯ to A♯, also quietly. Modest's text for the arioso obsessively repeats "earth" three times but references the stars and space beyond the edge of the universe. Here Rachmaninoff matches Dante's conception of love as a spiritual force reaching away from or even beyond death. Rachmaninoff and his librettist tap into the deepest mystical layer of canto V. How? It is a sad and beautiful fact that Francesca's justification for her unfaithfulness is based on a threefold repetition of the word *amor*. She begins her narrative exactly on line 100 of canto V, a number associated for Dante with the other kind of love, a love that moves the sun and the other stars, as the last line of the *Divina commedia*, the 100th canto, reads.

And what of Beatrice? Dante used his unrequited encounters with his beloved to explain (according to Allegra Goodman) "how to become a great poet. The secret was to fall in love with a perfect girl but never speak to her. You should weep instead. You should pretend that you love someone else. You should write sonnets in three parts. Your perfect girl should die."[26] After that happened, Dante was left to write of a desire that could never be fulfilled, of the body failing to conjoin with spirit. Rachmaninoff captured this idea in music, transforming Francesca at a crucial moment into Beatrice. He stresses sound over sense in Francesca's arioso, and has her sing in a "depersonalized" manner. Her voice becomes "an unknown musical instrument" as she reaches for the divine, ascending into her own private hyperspace. The conception defied grand love duets and coloratura exultations—defied, in fact, all that was expected on a grand stage. He assigned his soprano a high note at a quiet volume, maintaining the slight tug upward of sharps over flats. The arioso does not last long, but for twenty-nine measures *agape* supplants *eros*. Paolo abruptly ends the spiritual ruminations with a plea for physical contact, thus sealing their fate. "I'd rather be burning for you," he essentially tells his lover, and burn he does.

The epilogue of *Francesca da Rimini* returns us to the second circle, but in compact, accelerated fashion, as though the composer recognized the audience's limited patience for timelessness. Or perhaps Rachmaninoff wanted to suggest that the hovering souls of the condemned lovers were somehow freed, leaving just their mantra of joy and wretchedness behind.

Rachmaninoff's fondness in the Prologue for upward moving lines capped by pitches hanging in the ether is, at the end, roughly antimeric. The gooeyness has a new destination, downward, the Pilgrim's (Dante's) empathetic faint happening over and over again, the music pointing to even lower depths, the ninth circle to which Malatesta is dispatched.

When it came time to stage the opera, everything, predictably or not, went to hell. Embellishing the role of the Pilgrim, or for that matter Virgil, never seemed to have crossed Rachmaninoff's mind, even though he had secured the great tenor Dmitry Smirnov to sing the part of Dante's stand-in. Chaliapin turned down the role of Malatesta owing to other obligations, and another Russian operatic eminence, Antonina Nezhdanova, passed on Francesca because the part was too low. Another singer, Natalia Yermolenko-Yuzhina, claimed it was too high. Desperate, Rachmaninoff offered the part to Nadezhda Salina, who demurred, claiming that, at a stately forty-three, she could not do Francesca justice. Rachmaninoff brought her onto the stage of the Bolshoi Theater after a ballet rehearsal, put the score on a stand, and begged her to reconsider: "I've written the devil knows what, Nadezhda Vasilyevna. No one can sing it: for one it's too low, for another too high. I'll give you all the phrasing, anything you want, please just try singing it."[27] She accepted the challenge, but the part did not come easily to her and she remembers tossing the score on the floor in frustration. But she persevered, and the opera was premiered. Anton Bonachich clung to her onstage as Paolo, and the baritone Georgy Baklanov, as Malatesta, stuck a blade into their backs. Rachmaninoff conducted the premiere on 11 January 1906, cueing his singers from an unusual place in the Bolshoi. As Wagner had done at Bayreuth, Rachmaninoff moved himself back from "his time-honored seated position immediately behind the prompt box (situated, so to speak, at the singer's feet, with the orchestra players straggling around him)," to a "standing position with the whole performance under his direct surveillance."[28]

Reviews were mixed to poor. Those in favor lauded Rachmaninoff's manipulation of timbre and texture; those against derided *Francesca da Rimini* in detail, complaining that it was either too much or too little like Tchaikovsky's 1876 tone poem on the subject.[29] The audience at the Bolshoi witnessed a confrontation between Francesca and her cuckolded husband, the reading of *Lancelot du Lac*, a kiss lasting fifty measures, and the lovers' murder. *Francesca da Rimini* ended as it began, with a tall, thin Rachmaninoff perspiring over the pit of hell. The kiss provoked laughter.

Writing in the Symbolist journal *Zolotoye runo* (The Golden Fleece), Emil Medtner damned *Francesca da Rimini* and its composer for failing to reach the immense, expressive heights of Richard Wagner. Medtner

Figure 1. Rachmaninoff with Anton Bonachich and Nadezhda Salina, the first Paolo and Francesca in *Francesca da Rimini*.

was a devotee of Wagner's art and anti-Semitism alike, and considered Rachmaninoff old-fashioned, a young fogey, despite Rachmaninoff's reliance on Wagnerian chromaticism in the prelude of his opera. "His *Francesca da Rimini* hasn't the slightest in common with Dante, nor even with Pyotr Tchaikovsky's orchestral fantasy of the same name," Medtner fibbed. "True, Tchaikovsky's horrors are closer to Dostoyevsky than Dante, but at least these are authentic horrors, and not the clichéd spooki-ness Rachmaninoff gives us in his prologue and epilogue, framed by two pale and boring typical operatic scenes." Medtner also lied about Rachmaninoff's "static harmonies" and the lack of balance between "musical declamation, musical representation, and the flow of pure musi-cal elements." He also abused the Bolshoi: the "dull, bland" repertoire, the "old, passive" opening-night patrons, and the "over-plump prima donnas." Newcomers to the Moscow Imperial Temple of Art will rouse from their slumber not knowing what century they're in.[30]

Medtner obviously disliked Rachmaninoff (even though Rachmaninoff tried to help Medtner's composer brother Nikolai in emigration), and it shows. Rachmaninoff and his librettist took on a headier subject than Wagner ever did, a section of "a fourteenth-century allegorical poem on sin and redemption, written in a medieval Italian vernacular and in accord with the Scholastic theology of that period," and did something simple and profound with it, as simple and profound as a poet's tears.[31] Most if not all spiritual practices are premised on connectedness, in the form of symbols and metaphors and allegories. Here, simply and profoundly, is the explanation for Rachmaninoff's emphasis on the semitone, which relates everything in the score to everything else: keys, chords, melodies.

Other reviewers were fairer-minded, especially those like the Moscow correspondent for *Russkaya muzïkal'naya gazeta* (RMG) Grigory Prokofyev, who believed that Russian composers should not be "slaves" to Wagner. The tyrannical Teuton's instrumental combinations might merit imitating, as Rimsky-Korsakov did, but not the leitmotif technique and orgiastic prolon-gations of the dominant. Prokofyev praised Rachmaninoff for "embodying the spiritual drama" of Francesca and Paolo "in beautiful sounds" but thought the prologue overlong, too much like the *Tristan und Isolde* pre-lude.[32] His comments counter those of another RMG reviewer, who felt the prologue and epilogue existed in isolation from the internal scenes, but nonetheless wanted them longer. "The horrors and torments of hell which elicit Dante's suffering tears and profound empathy are inadequately illumi-nated by Rachmaninoff's music." He preferred Tchaikovsky's tone poem.[33]

Another critic imagined *Francesca da Rimini* might have been a stunning *coup de théâtre*, had the décor matched the music and the performance instructions been followed. Yevgeny Gunst documented the opera's problems in the monthly theater journal *Masks*. Sympathetic to Rachmaninoff, he chafed at the "ostracizing" of the opera "owing to the inscrutable and mysterious overconsiderations of the Bolshoi Theater management!" Gunst had a copy of the score, so could point out all of the places where Rachmaninoff's staging instructions had not been followed: For example, in *Francesca*'s prologue, after the introduction, as the curtain rises, we encounter this instruction: "Everything is illuminated by the crimson reflection of clouds quickly passing by." Unfortunately, neither quickly passing, nor slowing moving clouds were visible. On page 16 (in the piano score), there's also this annotation: "Black clouds cover everything," followed, just eight measures later, by "Complete gloom reigns." Evidently the clouds were to cover the stage slowly over the eight measures, with complete gloom reigning from the ninth. But because the backcloth came down so abruptly and the light went out so fast, gloom reigned almost immediately, at the place of the first instruction cited above. Similar things were missed, unacceptably. *Francesca* is not typical of the operas the Bolshoi Theater stages with love—one in which, for example, the murdered hero continues to sing because he needs to complete his aria, after which he can peacefully die. It's not like those of past composers who saw no need for a close relationship between the music and visual action. If Rachmaninoff places a direction here, and not there, it's not because he's doing so unconsciously or pointlessly, without concern, just to get the opera staged, but because the music needs to be organically connected to the text, logically flowing from the musical representation of the visual action.[34]

Francesca da Rimini did not last at the Bolshoi because Rachmaninoff did not last at the Bolshoi. He refused to renew his contract as the Bolshoi's "conductor of Russian opera" in late July 1906, having indirectly complained to the Intendant of the Imperial Theaters in St. Petersburg, Vladimir Telyakovsky, about the theater's bureaucratic Purgatorio. Telyakovsky's subordinate, Nikolai von Bohl, who had risen through the theatrical ranks to become director of the office of the Imperial Theaters in Moscow, had become the artists' bête noire. Bohl, Telyakovsky conceded, was a "real bureaucrat," a bespectacled, mustachioed, buttoned-up lover of order who cared more about his hobby, painting, than opera and ballet.[35]

Telyakovsky learned the specific reasons for Rachmaninoff's resignation from the set designer Konstantin Korovin, who likewise felt hamstrung by Bohl. "New ideas, requests from the artists—these meet so much resistance and interference that you just give up," Telyakovsky recalled in his journal about the conversation. "Bohl is quite arrogant and often decides artistic matters himself for fear of actually having to consult with anyone. Moscow's theaters are falling apart again."[36] Tethered to the podium night after night, conducting more than his contract required, Rachmaninoff had little time to compose, and feared that serving at the helm of an orchestra increasingly unfocused and distracted would damage his reputation. Under another conductor-in-chief of the Bolshoi, Ippolit Altani, the sound of the orchestra had improved. Tuning, balance, and precision had all been refined. The musicians dismissed accused Altani of bias and bribe-taking, and he resigned after twenty-four years of distinguished service. Following his departure standards swiftly declined, further convincing Rachmaninoff that it was time to go. Telyakovsky asked Rachmaninoff to remain with the Bolshoi, if only part-time with the opera, but Rachmaninoff had had enough. *Francesca da Rimini* was revived just once in the original version, on 27 September 1912, under the baton not of Rachmaninoff but of Emil Kuper, who was chiefly an orchestral conductor and pumped up the volume of his troops in the pit to the point of drowning out the singers. Amid the din, Bonachich, trying to project the part of Paolo, instead "buzzed like a fly in a decanter."[37]

Rachmaninoff left the Bolshoi, Moscow, and Russia, traveling with his family to Italy, Germany, and the United States, with periodic returns home. He did not leave, as is fantasized in Anglophone scholarship, as part of the flight of intelligentsia out of Russia following the 1905 Revolution.[38] He left because he was burned out.

NOTES

For help and advice, I am grateful to Caryl Emerson, Denis Feeney, Grigoriy Konson, Hannah McLaughlin, Anastasia Shmytova, Dmitri Tymoczko, Michael Wachtel, Boris Wolfson, and especially Julia Khait and Simone Marchesi.

1. Daniel Albright, *Untwisting the Serpent: Modernism in Music, Literature, and Other Arts* (Chicago: University of Chicago Press, 2000), 81.

2. Reference is to the Byzantine rite called the *Akolouthia tes kaminou* (Service of the Furnace) of the fourteenth century, which inspired the sixteenth-century Russian Orthodox *Peschnoye Deystvo* (Play of the Furnace).

3. Such is the consensus. Boris Asafyev, however, typically an astute music critic, proposed in a program booklet article for a 1921 orchestral concert marking the 600th anniversary of Dante's death that the entire opera is a love duet, introduced and concluded by "decorative" representations of hell. Yet the duet is in truth a trio: Francesca, her husband, and her lover. Asafyev notes the darkness in the score—it's "one step removed from [Rachmaninoff's] *Isle of the Dead* [1908] and the rumbling horrors of the bells in *The Bells* [1913]"—but he hears nothing tragic. He considers it decadent, the "pale" undulations in Francesca and Paolo's vocal lines suggesting the first blush of romance, "the gaze into the sweetheart's eyes and her self-conscious look to the side." B. V. Asaf'yev, "Poeziya Dante v muzïke," 14 September 1921, http://dante.rhga.ru.

4. To quote the title of an essay by T. Yu. Chernova, "S. V. Rakhmaninov v rabote nad 'Francheskoy da Rimini': 'Tikhaya kul'minatsiya' operï'," in *Rakhmaninov i XXI vek: Proshloye i nastoyashcheye: sbornik statey*, ed. I. Skvortsova (Moscow: RIO MGK, 2016), 74–82.

5. For an excellent discussion of early-modern Dante settings, see Aliyah M. Shanti, "Musical Descents: Creating and Re-Creating Hell in Italian Opera, 1600–1680" (PhD diss., Princeton University, 2017), 174–214. Franz Liszt's *Dante Symphony* (1857) includes choral interludes extracted from Dante, but the bulk of the score is wordless. Pyotr Tchaikovsky's 1877 tone poem is, by definition, entirely so. Ambroise Thomas's 1882 Francesca da Rimini opera is based on a melodramatic text by Michel Carré and Jules Barbier. Eduard Nápravník's 1902 opera, for the Mariyinsky Theater, adapts a play by Stephen Phillips; it is not a point of reference for Rachmaninoff's opera, despite the closeness of the dates of the two works. Riccardo Zandonai's 1914 opera derives from D'Annunzio and includes a "silent duet": Francesca and Paolo fall in love without saying a word. The orchestra provides the sensation, the chorus the emotion. There are numerous other operatic treatments, none a repertory staple.

6. Dante's gendering of characters is much more nuanced than this overview suggests. Virgil is referred to as a mother in more than one passage of the Inferno, and Beatrice is gendered male in Purgatorio, described there as a stern admiral and hailed with a masculine grammatical marker on the word *benedictus*. She is not comforting when judging the protagonist. I am indebted for these points to eminent Dante expert Simone Marchesi.

7. Joan Acocella, "What the Hell: Dante in Translation and in Dan Brown's New Novel," *The New Yorker*, 20 May 2013, https://www.newyorker.com/magazine/2013/05/27/what-the-hell.

8. Princeton Dante Project, Commentary Inf V 107, http://etcweb.princeton.edu/dante/pdp/.

9. Sergei Bertensson and Jay Leyda, *Sergei Rachmaninoff: A Lifetime in Music* (Bloomington: Indiana University Press, 2001), 97. The composer's personal life is the subject of strange gossip. The composer's grandson Aleksandr Konyus claimed without evidence that Rachmaninoff fell in love with the daughter of his therapist, despite being engaged to his cousin, adding that their love lasted his

lifetime. This nugget of fake news was disseminated, then annihilated, online: kul'tsh-pargalka, "Kto avtor feyka pro lyubovnïy treugolnik Rakhmaninova?," zen.yandex. ru, 15 October 2019, https://zen.yandex.ru/media/kultshpargalka/kto-avtor-feika-pro-liubovnyi-treugolnik-rahmaninova-5d9a2fb9e4f39f00b14b9266.

10. Pamela Davidson, *The Poetic Imagination of Vyacheslav Ivanov: A Russian Symbolist's Perception of Dante* (Cambridge: Cambridge University Press, 1989), 192.

11. Richard Taruskin, "Francesca da Rimini (i)," *Grove Music Online*, 2002, https://www-oxfordmusiconline-com.

12. For these letters, see S. Rakhmaninov, *Literaturnoye naslediye*, 3 vols., ed. Z. A. Apetyan (Moscow: Sovetskiy kompozitor, 1978–80), I:277–80, 283, 296–98, 340–41, 343, 346–50; "Pis'ma Rakhmaninova," https://senar.ru/letters.

13. Chernova, "S. V. Rakhmaninov v rabote nad 'Francheskoy da Rimini'," 75–76.

14. Rachmaninoff to Modest Tchaikovsky, 28 August 1898, quoted in ibid., 77.

15. Rachmaninoff to Nikita Morozov, 4 August 1904, in Rakhmaninov, *Literaturnoye naslediye*, I:347.

16. Chernova, "S. V. Rakhmaninov v rabote nad 'Francheskoy da Rimini'," 78; Rachmaninoff to Modest Tchaikovsky, 3 August 1904. He repeated this comment to Morozov. Modest asked for 1,500 rubles at the start of the project, but received much less; he and Rachmaninoff also haggled about the fee from the publisher. Rakhmaninov, *Literaturnoye naslediye*, 544–45, 348.

17. Ibid., 77.

18. Robert Leach, *Makers of Modern Theatre: An Introduction* (London and New York: Routledge, 2004), 80.

19. This and the next quotation is from Blair Johnston, "Modal Idioms and Their Rhetorical Associations in Rachmaninoff's Works," *Music Theory Online* 20/4 (2014), https://mtosmt.org/issues/mto.14.20.4/mto.14.20.4.johnston.html.

20. Christian Schubart, *Ideen zu einer Aesthetik der Tonkunst*, 1806, https://www.wmich.edu/mus-theo/courses/keys.html.

21. Chernova, "S. V. Rakhmaninov v rabote nad 'Francheskoy da Rimini'," 80.

22. Ibid.; Asaf'yev, "Poeziya Dante v muzïke."

23. Chernova, "S. V. Rakhmaninov v rabote nad 'Francheskoy da Rimini'," 80–81, quoting R. I. Khlodovskiy, *Dekameron: Poetika i stil'* (Moscow: Nauka, 1982), 12–13.

24. Chernova, "S. V. Rakhmaninov v rabote nad 'Francheskoy da Rimini'," 81.

25. Ibid., 82.

26. Allegra Goodman, "La Vita Nuova," *The New Yorker*, 26 April 2010, https://www.newyorker.com/magazine/2010/05/03/la-vita-nuova.

27. N. V. Salina, "Iz vospominaniy 'Zhizn' i stsena'," in *Vospominaniya o Rakhmaninove*, ed. Z. Apetyan, 5th ed., 2 vols. (Moscow: Gosudarstvennoye muzïkal'noye izdatel'stvo, 1988), 2:33–36, at 35.

28. Michael Scott, *Rachmaninoff* (Stroud, UK: History Press, 2008), 64. See also Lyudmila Kovalyova-Ogorodnova, *Sergey Rakhmaninov: Biografiya*, 2 vols. (St. Petersburg: Vita Nova, 2015), 1:185–86.

29. Tamara Livanova notes the basic connection in a 1947 article on Rachmaninoff's operas: "The essential thematic material of the prologue is 'whistling' chromaticism in different transformations and broad dynamic, registral, and timbral development, leading to several large phrases of growth. Much of it suggests Rachmaninoff turning to Tchaikovsky's score." T. N. Livanova, "Tri operï Rakhmaninova," in *S. V. Rakhmaninov i russkaya opera: sbornik statey*, ed. I. F. Belza (Moscow: Vserossiyskoye teatral'noye obshchestvo, 1947), 39–100, at 67.

30. Vol'fing [Emil Medtner], "'Skupoy rïtsar' i 'Francheska da Rimini'," *Zolotoye runo* 1 (1906): 123.

31. The quotation is from Acocella, "What the Hell."

32. G. Prokof'yev, "Pevets intimnïy nastroyeniy," *Russkaya muzïkal'naya gazeta* 37 (1910): 751–4, at 753.

33. A. Livin, "Novïye operï na stsene Moskovskogo Bol'shogo teatra," *Russkaya muzïkal'naya gazeta* 4–5 (1906): 126.

34. Yevgeniy Gunst, "'Francheska da Rimini' i 'Skupoy rïtsar'" S. V. Rakhmaninova (K vozobnovleniyu na stsene Moskovskogo Bol'shogo teatra)," *Maski* 1 (1912): 63–64.

35. V. A. Telyakovskiy, *Vospominaniya*, ed. D. Zolotnitskiy (Leningrad: Iskusstvo, 1965), 203.

36. V. A. Telyakovskiy, *Dnevniki Direktora Imperatorskikh Teatrov: 1906–1909: Sankt-Peterburg*, ed. M. G. Tsvetayeva (St. Petersburg: Artist. Rezhisser. Teatr, 2011), 26, entry of 7 September 1906.

37. "Kritika, Bol'shoy teatr. 29, IX: 'Francheska da Rimini' i Skupoy rïtsar'"," *Muzïka* 98 (6 October 1912): 855

38. "Political events of 1905 make conducting impossible." Scott, *Rachmaninoff*, 61.

New Worlds

Rachmaninoff and the Celebrity Interview: A Selection of Documents from the American Press

SELECTED AND EDITED BY PHILIP ROSS BULLOCK

When, on 10 November 1918, Rachmaninoff sailed into New York on the SS *Bergensfjord*, it was not, of course, the first time he had visited the United States. He had earlier toured the country in 1909–10, premiering his newly composed Third Piano Concerto in New York on 28 November under the baton of Walter Damrosch (Gustav Mahler would famously conduct its second performance on 16 January). Although there was much about his trip that he disliked, Rachmaninoff came away with a number of more positive impressions. He had been struck by the quality of the American orchestras he heard, particularly in Boston, noted the high regard in which Tchaikovsky's music was held, and—perhaps most crucially—appreciated the material rewards available to a successful virtuoso. As he confessed in an interview he gave to a musical journal on his return to Russia:

> America bored me. Just think: I concertized very nearly every day for three months, playing nothing but my own works. My success was great, and I was obliged to give up to seven encores, which is a lot for local audiences. Audiences are remarkably cold, having been spoiled by tours by first-rate performers, and are always seeking something unusual, unlike what they have heard before. The local newspapers invariably mention how many times one is called back on to the stage, and for the general public, this is a measure of one's talent.[1]

When, in 1917, Rachmaninoff was forced to abandon property and possessions in Soviet Russia and found himself providing for himself, his family, and many of his friends and colleagues, he rationally calculated that it was America, rather than Europe, that would provide for his extensive material needs.

A notable aspect of his life in the United States was the frequency with which he gave interviews to the press. It was not, admittedly, a genre in which he felt entirely comfortable. In January 1910, when he was still in America, the Russian critic Emil Medtner proposed a short study of his music. Rachmaninoff tactfully declined:

> Dear Emil Karlovich,
>
> I sincerely thank the editors of *Musaget* for their desire to publish a small book about my compositions.
>
> Only, however flattering and pleasant the appearance of such a book would be to me, I must refrain from suggesting a critic who "knows" and "values" my works and who might write an article about me.
>
> I must also refrain from suggesting "an extract from a letter of mine," setting forth my *profession de foi*.
>
> The only thing with which I can help the editors is the question of my portrait. Not only shall I indicate a fine portrait to the editors, but I shall even give them a portrait in my own possession, as soon as I return to Russia (in approximately five weeks).
>
> So, please do not be offended by my refusals, but believe me once again when I say that while the appearance of such a book would be extremely pleasant to me, I simply would not wish to take an active part in its publication.
>
> Yours sincerely,
S. Rachmaninoff.[2]

If Rachmaninoff had reservations about collaborating with a potentially sympathetic critic such as Medtner (whose brother, Nikolai, was a close friend and much admired fellow composer and pianist), he was yet more reticent about dealings with the press.

Later that year, however, Rachmaninoff found himself obliged to speak out. Writing from Berlin to the newspaper *Russkiye vedomosti*, he objected to an interview that had appeared in another paper, *Utro Rossii*, on 2 November. As he explained in his letter to *Russkiye vedomosti*:

> Having read the article, I initially decided that I would not reply. Not because I found it in order and in accordance with the truth, but because it seems to me that few people pay attention to such interviews, and most important, few people believe them, and even if they do, then only

Figure 1. Front cover of *The Etude*, October 1919.

one-tenth of what is contained in them. That, at least, is how I always treat them: I divide everything by ten and take into account the result. After all, even when your spoken words are treated entirely properly, there is a distinction between *what* you express in conversation and *how* this is expressed and published. After all, you speak in simple, conversational language, yet what you say cannot, of course, be recalled literally. This means that you can allow a degree of imagination on the part of the interviewer, who is guided by your main ideas or by the main contents of your conversation, yet conveys all of this *in his*, rather than *your* language. This is why sometimes, when one reads certain interviews, one never tires of being surprised: on the one hand, it is as if one really did say these things, on the other hand, it is as if one is hearing them for the first time.[3]

Yet the number of misrepresentations contained in the interview in *Utro Rossii*, as well as the fact that it had been published, forced Rachmaninoff to respond in print and to distance himself from the critical remarks about the Bolshoi Theater that he was alleged to have made to the newspaper's correspondent.

If this incident confirmed Rachmaninoff's often cautious attitude toward publicity, at least during his career in Russia,[4] then his first American tour revealed to him the potential benefits of using the interview format to cultivate his celebrity, while still guarding his deeply felt sense of privacy. He gave at least four interviews during the three months he spent in America in 1909–10, and when he returned in 1918, he willingly responded to American interest in his music by giving regular interviews to a wide range of publications. He spoke to correspondents from musical periodicals, such as *Musical America*, *Musical Courier*, *Musical Observer*, *Musical Opinion*, *The Musician*, and especially *The Etude*, which published a special "Rachmaninoff Number" in October 1919 (Figure 1). As his fame spread through American cultural life, he appeared in *Vanity Fair*, *Good Housekeeping*, *The New Yorker*, and—posthumously—*Vogue*. His artistic views—as well as his regular comings-and-goings between Europe and North America—were reported in the *New York Times*, and in January 1931, the paper published one of his rare forays into politics. This was a letter—co-signed by Ivan Ostromyslensky and Ilya Tolstoy—attacking the Indian poet Rabindranath Tagore for "his evasive attitude to the Communist grave-diggers of Russia" and lending "strong and unjust support to a group of professional murderers."[5]

Unlike those notable tracts by other Russian émigré composers—Nikolai Medtner's *The Muse and Fashion* (*Muza i moda*, 1935) and Igor Stravinsky's *The Poetics of Music* (*Poétique musicale sous forme de six leçons*, 1942)—Rachmaninoff's interviews cannot be interpreted as a coherent, categorical, or consistent *profession de foi*. Neither can his so-called *Recollections* (1934), the result of a series of conversations with Oskar von

Riesemann. Rachmaninoff was aghast at the book's initial draft, even paying for the proofs to be reset and insisting that the manuscript be revised so that "the entire responsibility for words that are supposedly mine should be borne by him instead."[6]

Nonetheless, a number of common themes emerge in Rachmaninoff's interviews. He is emphatic about his sense of Russianness and his place in the Russian musical tradition, something only heightened by his experience of emigration. He is enthusiastic about the level of musicianship to be found in the United States, while noting that many of its orchestras largely consist of European performers and tactfully avoiding commenting on American composers.[7] His distaste for musical modernism is frankly expressed, although a rather more reflective attitude begins to emerge from 1926 onward, when he returned to composition and proved to be more receptive to contemporary influences than is sometimes appreciated. He repeatedly emphasizes the primacy of emotion, and the idea of music as an expression of a composer's biography. He uses his reputation as a leading virtuoso pianist to comment on the importance of a strong technique and rigorous professional training (and offers a gracious and detailed commentary on how to approach the ubiquitous C-sharp Minor Prelude).

There is no doubting the sincerity of many of Rachmaninoff's published statements, yet they should be treated with a degree of caution, too. When Basil Maine interviewed him for *Musical Opinion* in 1936, he observed that "his look was always that of a world-weary man. But I suspected that this was part of the façade that every public artist must devise for self-protection."[8] Rachmaninoff's interviews were part of that façade too. Just as he embraced the new technologies of the piano-roll and acoustic recording (he rejected the radio, though) and signed to an exclusive relationship with Steinway pianos, he intuited that the celebrity interview could help him to court and cultivate the popular audiences on whom he depended financially, thereby bypassing those critics who dismissed his music as an indulgent hangover of late Romanticism. Rachmaninoff adroitly appealed to interest in a seemingly vanished age of great piano playing, as well as to a vision of a lost world of Russian gentry culture (comparisons with Chekhov and Bunin were routine at the time). This was a dialogue carried out with émigré Russian audiences too, so that it is instructive to compare the content and style of his American interviews with his reception in the publications that circulated in what was known as "Russia Abroad." It is fascinating to see how Rachmaninoff represented his American life to his rather different European audiences; after all, he regularly returned to the "Old World" throughout the 1920s and 1930s, performing extensively across Western Europe, enjoying the company of close friends and family members, and eventually settling in the villa that he had built on the banks of Lake Lucerne.

Out of more than forty known interviews that Rachmaninoff gave throughout his life, eight are given here, all taken from American periodicals and publications.[9] They are presented exactly as originally published and without further annotation or correction of errors of spelling or fact. Although individual phrases and sentences have often been cited in the critical and biographical literature, this is likely the first time that these interviews have been reproduced in full in English.[10]

"Modernism Is Rachmaninoff's Bane," *Musical America* 11/2 (20 November 1909): 23

Famous Russian Composer and Pianist No Friend to Methods of Strauss and Reger—Deplores Latter-Day Musical Sensationalism—Arduous Labors of a Disciple of Tschaikowsky

Sergei Rachmaninoff, the eminent Russian musician, has no ambition to be known as an ultra-modern composer. Emphatically the contrary.

"I have scant sympathy," said he to a MUSICAL AMERICA interviewer, "with those who have allowed themselves to succumb to the wanton eccentricities of latter-day musical sensationalism. Unfortunately I cannot express myself as optimistic regarding the ultimate results of contemporaneous tendencies for I do not believe that future composers will manifest any desire to rid themselves of many obnoxious influences which have found their way into our art. The methods of Strauss and Reger have come to stay. But I, for one, shall steer clear of them."

Americans will have an opportunity of judging Mr. Rachmaninoff's compositions for themselves during his stay in this country.

"I shall remain in America until January 23," said he, "playing with the Boston Symphony Orchestra, the Russian Symphony, and possibly with some others. Among the most important of my works to be heard during my stay will be my new third piano concerto, and a symphonic poem 'L'Isle des Morts,' which was inspired by Böcklein's well known picture of that name. At some of the recitals the 'Preludes' will be given."

A report recently circulated that Mr. Rachmaninoff had studied under Tschaikowsky was declared by the composer to be untrue.

"If I am a pupil of that master it can be only figuratively speaking," he observed; "true, I was acquainted with him for a number of years, during which time he displayed an interest in my compositions, which very frequently received the benefit of his criticism. But at the time of his death, I was only twenty-one. Inasmuch as, in my own works, I have followed his methods rather than those which are affected by most of my countrymen at present it may perhaps, however, be permissible for me to regard myself as a disciple of his. My regular teachers were Siloti, with whom I studied piano, and Arenski and Taniev, who instructed me in composition."

According to his own confession Mr. Rachmaninoff is a hard worker, and the hours he devotes to composition are appallingly long. Most of his time is spent in Dresden, where he can work steadily, uninterrupted by his numerous acquaintances in Russia.

"During the progress of a new composition I can without exaggeration call myself a perfect slave," he remarked. "Beginning at nine in the morning I allow myself no respite until after eleven in the evening. Just what such Herculean labor means to one of a nervous temperament may well be imagined. But something seems to drive me on until my task is completed.

"It may seem strange that though I am a pianist I truly abhor writing for that instrument, and experience far more trouble in this way than when composing for the orchestra or the voice. I consider the piano to be lacking in those varieties of tone color in which I delight."

At the mention of Chopin in attempted refutation of this remark the Russian composer smiled. "Of course, of course," he said, "but Chopin as well as Schumann, and Liszt, are the noteworthy exceptions. They are to my mind by far the greatest composers for the piano, and their wonderful treatment of it has never been surpassed. My opinions of Liszt in particular are of the most exalted. What beauty, what depth in his splendid orchestral conceptions! What a masterpiece in his 'Faust' symphony!"

Mr. Rachmaninoff considers a programmatic idea as essential in facilitating his creative labors. "A poem, a picture, something of a concrete nature at any rate, helps me immensely. There must be something before my mind to convey definite impressions, or the ideas refuse to appear. For this reason I take much pleasure in writing songs. I have also written operas, though the fact is not generally known. There are three in all, each of them short, and the first written on the old-fashioned Italian model, which Russian dramatic composers have mostly been accustomed to follow. The third, written in the style of the modern music drama, is based on the story of 'Francesca da Rimini.' It has been produced at the Théâtre Impériale in Moscow under my own direction.

"Great pianists in Russia are few," declares Mr. Rachmaninoff. "They leave us and go to Germany to live. There is Godowsky, for instance, who, though born in Russia, has adopted Germany as his home and wishes to be known as a German. Gabrilowitsch and Lhévinne are also but infrequently heard in their own country. For the playing of these artists, however, and that of Josef Hofmann, I can speak only in terms of the highest admiration." The composer admits freely that he also absents himself from his country at times in order to appear elsewhere as conductor, and as pianist. "On such occasions I play only my own piano works," he explained, "though I take great pleasure in conducting other music."

Rachmaninoff's antipathy to certain contemporaneous composers has already been hinted at. Indeed, he finds it hard to express himself with sufficient emphasis in the matter. Of Strauss he likes only the earlier works such as "Don Juan," "Tod und Verklärung," "Till Eulenspiegel." "The later ones," as he puts it, "are beneath contempt as music. 'Ein Heldenleben' I find intolerable, and the same is true of 'Salomé.' But even these fade into insignificance when compared with the stupendous ugliness of 'Elektra,' of which I understood not a note. To what end all this polyphonic wilderness when the result is incomprehensible? And when Strauss is not complex he is merely banal. As a young Russian colleague of mine wittily expressed it: 'Strauss is a man who walks most of the time on his head, but who, when he walks on his feet, becomes uninteresting and commonplace.' As for Max Reger, he is an intellectual prodigy, a skillful mathematician, but nothing more."

An ardent admirer of Wagner, Mr. Rachmaninoff considers that master's "Meistersinger" the greatest of his music dramas. "How infinitely more effective," he exclaimed, "is the counterpoint at the close of the second act than all that of 'Salome' and 'Elektra,' for in this case musical beauty is not recklessly cast to the winds!"

With American music the Russian composer declared himself to be but poorly acquainted. Of MacDowell's works he says he knows comparatively little and, in fact, was not even aware of that composer's death.

"I do not even know the names of any other of your composers," he said, "but I trust I shall soon find them out. In my country little is known of them."

Serge Rachmaninoff, "My Prelude in C-sharp Minor," *The Delineator* 75 (1910): 127

Russia to-day is making an interesting effort for supremacy in musical art on both the creative and interpretative sides, and the foremost figure in her musical life is the composer-pianist, Serge Vassilievitch Rachmaninoff. Born at Nijni-Novgorod in 1873, he was educated at Moscow. He entered the great conservatory there and graduated in 1891 with the gold medal for composition. He studied composition under Arensky, and piano with his cousin, the virtuoso Siloti.

For a time Rachmaninoff was conductor of the Imperial Opera at Moscow, and is the Imperial Commissioner for Musical Art for the Russian Empire. This position gives him supervision of the great governmental conservatories, the imperial operas, the governmental bands and orchestras, and all the varied musical activities throughout the vast Russian Empire.

Rachmaninoff has written three operas, a symphony, three piano concertos, and many songs and works for the piano. His C Sharp Minor Prelude was introduced here over a decade ago by Siloti, and has attained a vogue second only to the Paderewski Minuet.

One thing which I hope to achieve by my visit to this country will be the disclosure that I have other claims for my standing in the musical world beyond the fact that I once wrote a Prelude in the key of C Sharp Minor. In my own country I have quite lived down this particular composition. In fact, it had grown to be a far-off memory of my youth, until I went to England a few years ago. There I learned, to my surprise, that all young pianists played it. Shortly afterward I received an invitation to visit the United States. I wrote to inquire if I were well enough known here to be assured of engaging public interest. I was promptly informed that every musician knew me as the composer of the C Sharp Minor Prelude.

Under the circumstances I should be thankful, I suppose, that I wrote the composition. But I am undecided whether my oversight in neglecting to secure international copyright for it was altogether fortunate for me. Had I copyrighted it, I might have had wealth as well as fame from it. And again, I might have achieved neither. For when I learned of the wide success of this little work I wrote a series of ten Preludes, my Opus 23, and took the precaution to have them copyrighted by a German publisher. I think them far better music than my first Prelude, but the public has shown no disposition to share my belief. I can not tell whether my judgment is at fault or whether the existence of that copyright has acted as a blight on their popularity. Consequently it will always be an open question with me whether intrinsic merit or absence of copyright is responsible for the success of my earlier work.

In asking me to discuss my own composition for its interpretation series, THE DELINEATOR has forced me into the position of becoming an iconoclast. Since my arrival in this country I have discovered some peculiar notions current regarding this Prelude and the circumstances of its creation. I may as well take this opportunity to tell the exact truth about it.

When I graduated from the Moscow Conservatory I was a boy of eighteen. Music is not a lucrative profession, even for those who have achieved fame, and for the beginner it is usually desperate. After a year I found myself out of pocket. I needed money, and I wrote this Prelude and sold it to a publisher for what he would give. I realized, all told, forty rubles out of it—that is, about twenty dollars in your money—very little compensation, you will admit, considering the sums the piece has earned for publishers. But in this case the law of compensation has worked out nicely, and I have no reason to complain.

Since my arrival I have been asked frequently what picture I had in my mind when I wrote this music; in other words, what was the source of my inspiration. My only inspiration, aside from the pressing necessity to make some money, was the desire to create something beautiful and artistic.

A prelude, in its very nature, is absolute music, and can not with propriety be twisted into a tone-poem or a piece of musical impressionism. Commentators have read all sorts of fanciful meanings into the Preludes of Chopin. One of them has even been called the Raindrop Prelude. But we may recall how angry he was, as George Sand tells it, when she brought his attention to this alleged imitative harmony.

Absolute music can suggest or induce a mood in the listener; but its primal function is to give intellectual pleasure by the beauty and variety of its form. This was the end sought by Bach in his wonderful series of Preludes, which are a source of unending delight to the educated musical listener. Their salient beauty will be missed if we try to discover in them the mood of the composer. If we must have the psychology of the Prelude, let it be understood that its function is not to express a mood, but to induce it.

The prelude, as I conceive it, is a form of absolute music intended, as its name signifies, to be played before a more important piece of music or as an introduction to some function. The form has grown to be used for music of an independent value. But so long as the name is given to a piece of music, the work should in some measure carry out the significance of the title.

For example, in the work under consideration, I endeavor to arrest attention by the opening theme. These three notes, proclaimed in unison in treble and bass, should boom solemnly and portentously. After this introduction the three-note melody runs through the first section of twelve bars, and counter to it, in both clefs, runs a contrasted melody in chords. Here we have two distinct melodic movements working against each other, and the effect is to arrest the attention of the listener. The nature of the principal theme is that of a massive foundation against which the melody in the chords furnishes a contrast to lighten up the gloom. If worked out too long the effect would be one of monotony, so a middle movement intervenes quickly. The change of mood is abrupt, and for twenty-nine bars the music sweeps along like a rising storm, gaining in intensity as the melody mounts upward. The movement is carried out in single notes instead of chords, and at the climax the original movement reenters with everything doubled in both the right and left hand. After this outburst has spent itself, the music grows gradually more quiet and a coda of seven bars brings the work to a close. The listener has been aroused, stimulated, and then quieted. His mind is alert and open for what follows. The Prelude has fulfilled its office.

If the pupil must have his mental status fixed, let him keep in mind what I have just said. Then let him study carefully the anatomy of the composition. The divisions of the work are simple. After the proclamation of the introductory theme, there are twelve bars consisting of a repetition of this theme with an intervening melody in chords for both hands. Then follows the middle section of twenty-nine bars. The third section is the same as the first with everything doubled, and the coda of seven bars brings the work to a close.

The first technical caution is to strike just the right pace in the proclamation of the opening theme and then maintain that pace strictly throughout the first section. One common mistake is to play this opening theme too loudly. I admit there is great temptation to pound it; but the climax does not come at the outset. I have marked these notes "ff." You will find several "fff" marks later on. So save your strength. The chords of the intervening melody should be pressed out lightly and caressingly, and the player should be careful to make the top note in the right-hand chords sing. The mistakes to avoid are the tendency to strike these chords unevenly or with an arpeggio effect and to lose the evenness of pace. The difficulty in the first section will be to maintain this evenness through the third and fourth beat in each bar. The three notes of the first theme are not to be struck too loudly, but with sufficient force to make the tones carry through.

In the agitated section the melody in the right hand is carried by the first note in each group. But for this I might have marked the passage "Allegro con fuoco." The player must accommodate his pace to his technical ability. He must not hurry the passage beyond his capacity to make the melody stand out.

The repetition of the first movement in doubled octaves calls for all the force the player is capable of. The pupil must be cautioned against mistaking fury for breadth and majesty. It will be safer to take this passage even a trifle more slowly than at the opening, and above all have regard for the evenness of the decrescendo. I begin to let this effect become apparent after the sixth bar of this movement.

Notice particularly that the melody in the coda is carried by the middle notes of the chord in both the right and left hands. These notes must be accentuated slightly. Beware of the temptation to arpeggiate the final chords.

"Rachmaninoff Arrives in America,"
Musical Courier, 14 November 1918, 8

Tells of His European Life Since the War Began—His Victory Day Adventures—Has Completed a New Symphony and Is Revising His First Piano Concerto

Entirely unannounced and unexpected, Sergei Rachmaninoff came into New York last Sunday on a ship from Copenhagen. Rachmaninoff, it is unnecessary to tell MUSICAL COURIER readers, is one of the most prominent figures in Russian musical life. His fame as composer, pianist and conductor is spread throughout the entire musical world.

He was seen soon after his arrival by a MUSICAL COURIER representative in his apartment at the Hotel Netherlands, New York. It is not his first visit to America, incidentally, for he was here nine years ago appearing both as pianist and as guest conductor of the Boston Symphony Orchestra. He seemed to be in the best of health and is a charming, modest gentleman of the world. He was accompanied to this country by Mme. Rachmaninoff and their little daughter. Rachmaninoff is not yet fluently conversant with the English language. Speaking in French, he told of his life since the outbreak of the Russian revolution.

"Conditions in Moscow," said he, "where I had been making my headquarters since the outbreak of the war, leaving only for various concert trips in Russia, became very unpleasant under the Bolshevik regime and I decided to leave there last December. Though I have absolutely no sympathy with the Bolsheviks, I must admit that their officials were entirely courteous to me. When I expressed my desire to leave the country they at once made my way easy and even expressed the best wishes for my success in other lands. I went first to Stockholm, traveling by the way of Finland, and from there on to Copenhagen, arriving there in January of this year and making it my home until I left for America. While staying there I made numerous concert appearances, not only in Denmark, but also in Norway and Sweden."

"What are the conditions there?"

"Quite normal as far as musical life goes; in fact there are rather more concerts than ever before owing to the presence of various artists, who, like myself, would not ordinarily be in Scandinavia. In Denmark and Sweden, although the prices are very high, there is plenty of good food but somewhat of a scarcity in Norway."

"Is it true that you received an offer to conduct the Boston Symphony Orchestra?"

"Indeed, yes; and the report printed by the MUSICAL COURIER, that I declined to accept it on account of the impossibility of properly preparing the necessary programs in the length of time at my disposal was also true. I had not done any conducting in the last five years and I felt that I could do neither myself nor the orchestra justice. I may say that I regard the Boston organization as the finest orchestra in the world without exception and I should be very proud to conduct it at some future time if circumstances permit. There were a number of other offers from America, too, but conditions were so uncertain that I did not find it possible definitely to accept any of them."

"May I ask what brought you to America?"

"Why it was those very offers. It seemed to me that there must be something for me to do here, but even if no regular engagement opens for me in the near future I am very happy to be here. I shall just live quietly and be happy to devote myself once more to composition, which was necessarily interrupted by the disturbed conditions and worries abroad."

"What would you like to do professionally here?"

"Oh, I have come to look upon myself as a pianist in these last few years and have not considered conducting, so it is as a pianist I hope to appear here first, if anybody wishes me to."

"I think we may have little doubt about that," remarked the MUSICAL COURIER representative. "America would be glad indeed again to welcome so distinguished a figure in the musical world as yourself."

The famous Russian artist smiled modestly. "Thank you," said he. "I hope so. At least, I am very glad to be here where it is so quiet and normal—though one can hardly say that after seeing the great demonstration of yesterday. A more spontaneous outburst of joy I have never seen, even in the supposedly more excitable European countries."

"Have you brought any new compositions with you?"

"Unfortunately, it was impossible for me to bring any manuscripts. I was permitted to take nothing from Russia except the necessary traveling equipment. My third symphony has been completed over four years now—but it practically doesn't exist. Just one week before the outbreak of the war I had sent the final revision of the proofs to Leipzig, where, as you know, practically all Russian music was printed and that is the last I have ever seen of that third symphony. I hope now that peace seems to be at hand to be able to obtain it. The only thing I have with me is the manuscript of a revision of my first piano concerto which I was happily able to obtain in Copenhagen through the kindness of the Swedish minister to Petrograd. The Bolsheviki officials allowed him to bring that out with him at my request."

"You say that you are revising your first piano concerto."

"Yes, it is one of my early works and I became quite dissatisfied with its orchestration, so I am revising that and some of the piano part as well."

"And what do you think of the political conditions in Russia today?"

"Frankly, I did not expect the Bolshevik regime to last as long as it has. Contrary to expectations, it seemed to gain in strength. I am hopeful now, however, that with Russia freed from the Germans, who were really the power behind the Bolsheviki, my poor country will soon come upon better times with the help of the Allies and the United States, which so nobly came to the rescue of world democracy. We can none of us ever be sufficiently grateful to your nation and its magnificent President."

"And—to put the inevitable question—what are your first impressions of America?"

"Well, I must admit that my first impressions, at least of New York, were most remarkable ones. Monday morning I went out soon after ten for a walk of half an hour. You know what a crowd we had here that morning! Unfamiliar with the English language, your methods of transportation, and of course, with the exuberance of such a vast throng as was celebrating the greatest day in the world's history, my little walk stretched into an excursion which lasted against my wishes until 4 o'clock in the afternoon, when at last I was able to rediscover the hotel and to have some luncheon and a nap that I sorely needed after my unprecedented adventures of Victory Day."

Dorothy J. Teall, "Rachmaninoff Champions Music of Native Land," *Musical America* 29/6 (7 December 1918): 3–4

Greatest of Living Russian Composers, on Eve of American Concert Tour, Discusses the Tenets of His Musical Creed—Says It Is Too Soon to Tell About War's Effect on Art—Is Sure Culture Will Remain National in Character—German Classics Too Great to Be Shelved—Russia the Source of the Best in Modern Music

Asks Why American Public Knows so Little of Russia's Music—Ten of Rimsky-Korsakoff's Fourteen Operas Were Masterpieces, but America Has Heard Only One—Thinks Music of Future Will Follow Lines of Accepted Forms—"Le Coeur" and Folk-Song Must Eventually Lead to Production of Great Art in Any People

The Russian school of music is today admittedly by far the most important and original, and Sergei Rachmaninoff, the latest and greatest Russian composer to arrive in this country, has exercised the greatest influence in the building up of that mighty structure. You will say that in view of his American appearances in 1909 there should have been no wonderings but only knowledge about his appearance and himself. But 1909 was an antediluvian era. A new generation of music-lovers has grown up since then, and they have been fed not on facts but on the C Sharp Minor Prelude, a piece which only a Titan or a romanticist could have composed.

Mr. Rachmaninoff is not a Titan. He is very tall, it is true, and quite broad of shoulder, but his scholarly stoop conceals much of his breadth and even some of his height. He is clean-shaven and pale of face, and his hair must be recorded as of the all-embracing category brown. Some imaginative persons have traced in his face the marks of his own and his country's sufferings, but though the downward droop of the muscles makes it a rather sad face when it is in repose, it brightens with smiles and good spirits as the great musician talks; one fancies that if this face were caught off guard it would display a constant gaiety, not to say cheerfulness, which would finally and forever prove its possessor a being more human than Russian, as the word has come to be misunderstood among us.

These details of physiognomy are important, because if Mr. Rachmaninoff is not a Titan, he must be—a romanticist!

Mr. Rachmaninoff does not yet speak English, fluently at least; few Americans speak Russian at all. If the exchange of question and answer about to be recorded seems stiff and in the manner of a judicial examination, the blame should be laid on the difficulties of conducting the conversation. Unconsciously, perhaps, Mr. Rachmaninoff revealed himself as a nationalist, a patriot, a democrat, a conservative and a romanticist. There is critical ammunition for the concert-goers who will hear him in the coming months!

In the present war-induced dearth of creative music everyone necessarily wonders how the art will come to its own again; and how, when it does reappear, it will show itself to have been affected by the war. Composers are men like other men; any great tide in human affairs must sweep them along as it does others, toss them about and give them at least some of the same hard knocks. If, as statesmen have constantly maintained, the war's outstanding social consequence is to be an era of unparalleled internationalism, surely this all-pervasive internationalism must set its impress on music. Hence the first question which was put to Mr. Rachmaninoff.

"Do you think culture—and, in particular, of course, music—will be cosmopolitan in nature in the *postbellum* period, or must it always remain nationalistic? Must there always be distinct and separate musical literatures for Russia, France, Germany?"

A Bas **Musical Internationalism!**

"Musical internationalism? Never! Indeed, there must always be separate national styles. Artistic differences between nations will continue because of the immutable differences in climate, if for no other reason."

"Ah, you are an evolutionist!"

"My music is scarcely revolutionary, so I suppose I must be called an evolutionist." Mr. Rachmaninoff's face wore a puzzled expression which invited explanations.

"Yes, it is obvious that you are more evolutionist than revolutionist in music. But if that exclamation had been properly put as a question, it would have specified rather your sociological than your artistic views. The meaning was that you are a determinist, since you believe music to be the product of climate and similarly impersonal forces. Well, then, if nationalism is the eternal, unchangeable law in music, it may be profitable to characterize the various national styles. What, in a word, is Russian music?"

"Sad," Mr. Rachmaninoff answered with mirthful readiness. "The Russian is the greatest musical school to-day. I marvel that you Americans do not know more of it, for it has the universal emotional appeal which none can resist. But as time goes on, you will doubtless hear Russian music more and more and—"

"Just a moment!" the interviewer implored. "Do you say we will hear more Russian music because it is sad and everybody is sad nowadays?"

"No; you will hear more of it because it is beautiful."

"But you said it is sad. What is it to be called if you discard that adjective?"

"I meant to say that it was predominantly melancholy in character at present. As to what it will be in future, how should I know? Everything depends on what great musicians happen to arise. It is all a matter of the individual. We have Medtner, who is doing very great work; his six piano sonatas are epoch-making, and his songs are the rich, full-voiced expression of a master-spirit. Stravinsky composed some excellent things for the Ballet Russe; as for the others—there may be many great men writing at this very moment, but while we may pick out the individual genius, or madman, and characterize his work, we cannot yet tell what is the lowest common denominator of all their work. Perhaps—but no, it is impossible to say."

"Well, then, German music."

"There is not much to say about that, either. Strauss had written himself out by the time the war began."

"But on German music of the past the war is having a very obvious and clear-cut effect. We hear less of the German classics, and the spell of their prestige seems broken. How does that condition impress you?"

"Oh, it is sheer folly to shelve Bach, Beethoven, Mozart! A boycott of great masters like those can be injurious only to the boycotters. Nothing can alter the just reputation of those masters as the sublimest figures in music."

"Before the war there was a feeling, here in America at least, that because they were the most sublime, no others could be sublime in even a minor degree. Is it not well that such a despotism should be overthrown? For now that only the terms of peace remain to be settled, the works of the German masters are bound to be heard again, and thus no lasting harm has been done."

"Yes, if you put it that way, that the German classics were crowding all else out of the field in this country, that they were exercising a veritable tyranny, then certainly one might say that the war-time reaction against them was a rather good thing."

A turn in the conversation brought up the subject of opera, and rather amusingly in view of the fact that he himself has written in the operatic form, Mr. Rachmaninoff was asked whether he liked it.

"Of course I like it! Some of the greatest Russian musical works have been of that sort. But I forget; you do not know our operas here. It is very regrettable, for they are as rich and marvelous as anything in modern music. I said regrettable, but it is perhaps also reprehensible of you not to know them. Fourteen of Rimsky-Korsakoff's compositions were cast in that form; ten out of the fourteen were great. 'Le Coq d'Or' you know; of the rest you do not hear one note; nine of these tremendous works are closed books to you! Yet nowhere in the world are there fuller opportunities for producing great new works than here in your country. Why do you restrict yourselves to a diet of old Italian operas (which, however pretty they may be, are worn quite threadbare), and a few French works? Especially now that the Wagnerian and other German operas are banished, I should think you would feel the need of new works."

"Not the least count in the indictment against us is our inability to name a reason for our neglect of the operas which you have mentioned, Mr. Rachmaninoff. It is a condition which the modest music-lover must accept as he does heat or cold; it is simply one of the things that are there, independently of his will or choice. At any rate, it is evident that you like opera. Perhaps you would be willing to make some statement as to the effect the war will have on other accepted musical forms."

A smile and a shrug. "I cannot tell. I dare not attempt prediction."

Evolution Rather Than Revolution

"Do you not think it likely that the germs of revolution which are afloat in the European atmosphere may establish themselves in the musical organism? Perhaps old musical forms will become obsolete along with old political forms."

"I hope not. I hope not. Still, hopes are vague affairs; if they could be counted on, with their force I would long since have checked the spread of political Bolshevism. It seems to me, however, that there really is ground for expecting music to adhere to the same general lines of form in the future as in the past."

"How about program music? Has not that revolutionary movement already set its standard awave over the musical field?"

"Yes, the use of a program, the introduction of an element of poetic interest, has come to stay; not programmism as Strauss, for instance, has sometimes employed it, an attempt to translate into musical terms what are essentially visual perceptions; but programmism as practiced, though of course not under that name, by the early nineteenth-century romanticists, Schumann and Chopin, for example. What I am saying amounts to this: that the composer not only *may* but to some extent even *ought* to have a program in mind, a thread of interest on which to string the emotions which he seeks to express in his work; whereas to put the program ahead of the emotions to be expressed is to follow a method illegitimate insofar as its results are bound to have a primarily unmusical interest."

"What about Debussy, Ravel and the other so-called futurists of France? Is there a new generative element in them?"

"Scarcely. They themselves acknowledge their indebtedness to the Russians and the influence of Russian composers."

"If we were to attempt to sum up what has been said, Mr. Rachmaninoff, would you agree to this way of putting it, that the heart should be the composer's guide through the labyrinths of accepted forms?"

"Yes, *le cœur* above all. Of course, *la tête* must aid in the building of great musical structures, but by itself *la tête* is impotent. If a composer is devoid of heart or hasn't his heart in the right place, it is impossible for him to conceal his deficiency. This explains why Russian music is so superlatively great; it speaks so directly to the heart. That is what gives it its vital beauty, its universality of appeal. You see now what I meant when I said that you in America would hear constantly more of our music because of its beauty instead of because of its sadness! Probably our music does carry the accent of sadness before all else; but if it spoke of sadness alone or of any one emotion to the exclusion of all others, it would be bad, and could not have attained the great popularity it enjoys. Everyone's heart knows and responds to all emotions; that is the basis of similarity which binds human beings together. What individualizes men is the varying importance of a single emotion or group of emotions in different personalities. Thus all great art is universal and national in character—it were better to say local instead of national—at one and the same moment."

American Musical Possibilities

"It would be interesting, if possible, to apply those remarks of yours to American music, or to the American lack of music. Do you know the works of any American composers?"

"Only of MacDowell."

"And what would you say was distinctive about him?"

"If you mean distinctively American, I must remain silent because ignorant. I know, as yet, so little about Americanism."

"But frankly, won't you confess that for Americans, if for no other national group, art must be eclectic, cosmopolitan?"

"I know so little—please—" was Mr. Rachmaninoff's plea. It seemed to imply an unshaken adherence to his nationalistic creed. A polite impulse to make that firm creed as kind as possible to American art was perhaps responsible for his adding, "But this I can say, that any nation which has *des chants populaires* is bound to develop a worthy musical art."

"But we Americans don't have folk-songs. There are the Negro songs, of course."

"Some of them I have heard. They are lovely."

"And they have inspired a few fine works. But it is only through the Southern regions that these Negro folk-songs are part of the life of the people, and that composer of ours who comes most quickly to mind as having used them is a Southerner. Whatever else we have in the way of folk-music has been brought here by immigrants, and is an echo of the folk-music of the countries from which they came. The hope you hold out for us is no hope at all. What then is to be done?"

"I will believe the situation to be bright until I have definitely informed myself to the contrary. At present, how can I possibly say anything? I am looking forward to Hofmann's all-American recital; perhaps I shall learn something from that. Meanwhile, however little art-music you may have and however little you may have of folk-music, which I mentioned as a fertile soil for the more sophisticated sort, you Americans have at least the heart in the right place. And when we reiterate that the heart is the animating force in music, do we not say that the hope for the future must be great?"

And thus the conversation ended on the note of romanticism, for Mr. Rachmaninoff was at this point called away to attend to some of the multitudinous arrangements for his concert appearances, the first of which is to occur on the fifteenth of December in Boston, the very citadel of American eclecticism.

"National and Radical Impressions in the Music of To-Day and Yesterday,"
The Etude 37/10 (October 1919): 615–16

An Interview Secured Expressly for THE ETUDE with the Eminent Russian Composer, Pianist, Conductor, Sergei Rachmaninoff.

[EDITOR'S NOTE. —Not since the days of the triumphs of Rubinstein in America, has any Russian pianist-composer achieved such success as has Mr. Rachmaninoff. In Russia he is equally famed as a conductor. Although best known through his famous Prelude in C♯ Minor, he is equally the most renowned of the living Russian composers in a more deeply serious vein. A comprehensive biography of the Russian master, written by a leading Russian critic, appears elsewhere in this issue. This biography has been authenticated by the composer, and it is accurate in every particular. Rachmaninoff, like all men of real greatness, is exceedingly simple, wholly sincere, and deeply in earnest. To him music is truly linked with the eternal soul of humanity. Though not wanting in humour, he finds little time for the merely trivial. It is a fine commentary upon the musical receptivity of America, that this master has met with such enthusiastic welcome everywhere. The following interview was secured especially for this issue of THE ETUDE designed to honor our distinguished Russian guest. It is interesting to note that during the interview the composer repudiated the story that the famous Prelude was written about a legend. It is no program music in any sense of the word.]

Music's Link with Folk Music of the Past

It must be quite clear to American musicians that the link between the music of many of the greatest European masters and the folk music of the lands of their birth is a close—a most intimate association. Not that the masters make a practice of taking folk themes bodily and transplanting them to their own works (although this occurs repeatedly in many masterpieces), but that they have become so saturated with the spirit of melodies common to the native people that all their compositions thereafter produced have a flavor as readily distinguished as the characteristic taste of native fruit or wine.

Take such a work as Rimsky-Korsakoff's best known operatic composition, *"Le Coq d'Or"* (The Golden Cock). It is strongly flavored with the Russian folk song spirit, and is distinctly Russian—Russian and nothing else. Rimsky-Korsakov, whom I knew very well indeed, worked carefully to preserve the Russian folk song flavor in it. Indeed, with the exception of a few modernists, all of the latter-day Russian composers have been imbued with the spirit of the Russian peasant song. Rubinstein, it is true, had a decidedly German complexion in much of his work, but nevertheless, there are many Russian suggestions in his music. Tschaikovsky, who, I understand, is thought by some critics in America to have followed German or continental methods and models, more than native Russian modes, used Russian themes freely and adhered to the national flavor as much as his period would permit.

Glinka is given the reputation of being the first of the Russians to introduce Russian themes. Tschaikovsky said about him that he was to be compared to the seeds of an oak tree which laid the foundation for greater strength to come.

Melody Supreme

Composers of experience take into consideration first of all that melody is the supreme ruler in the world of music. Melody is music—the integral foundation of all music, since a perfectly conceived melody implies and develops its own natural harmonic treatment. Schopenhauer has phrased this idea wonderfully when he said: "Music—that is, Melody—and words thereto—ah, that is the whole world!" Melodic inventiveness is, in the highest sense of the term, the vital goal of the composer. If he is unable to make melodies which command the right to endure he has little reason to proceed with his studies in musical composition. It is for this reason that the great composers of the past have shown such intimate respect for the peasant melodies of their respective countries. Rimsky-Korsakoff, Dvořák, Grieg, and others, have turned to them as the natural springs of inspiration.

The Futurists, on the other hand, openly state their hatred for anything faintly resembling a melody! They clamor for "color" and "atmosphere," and, by dint of ignoring every rule of sane musical construction, they secure efforts as formless as fog, and hardly more enduring.

By the word "modern" I do not refer to the Futurists. I have little regard for those who divorce themselves from Melody and Harmony, for the sake of reveling in a kind of orgy of noise and discord for discord's sake. The Russian Futurists have turned their backs upon the simple songs of the common people of their native land, and it is probably because of this that they are forced, stilted, not natural in their musical expression. This is true not only of the Russian Futurists, but of the Futurists of almost all lands. They have made themselves outcasts, men without a country, in the hope that they might become international. But in this hope they reason amiss; for if we ever acquire a musical Volapuk or Esperanto, it will be not by ignoring the folk music of any land, but by a fusion of the common musical languages of all nations into one tongue; not by an apotheosis of eccentric individual expression, but by the coming together of the music of the plain people of every land, as "the voice of many waters" from the seven seas of the great world.

The composer who has doubtless employed Russian folk themes the most is Rimsky-Korsakoff, although the music of Moussorgsky is continually imbued with the Russian spirit. Borodin, Moussorgsky, and many others, are characteristically Russian. On the other hand, Scriabin is quite un-Russian. His early compositions are Chopinesque, many of them exquisitely beautiful. His later compositions, however, belong to a musical "No man's land," and, while they have added notably to his reputation for eccentricity they have not enhanced his repute for true musical constructiveness. Some shortsighted critics have had the impudence to point to Moussorgsky as a composer whose works have but few melodies, whereas he abounds in lovely melodies of rare and exquisite originality, although he employed somewhat elaborate means of bringing them out. It is my earnest belief that the works of the Futurists, with a few possible exceptions, will not endure. Futurism is a kind of fungus growth, with little solidity, to withstand the test of time. It is not because the adherents of this school are modern, in the common acceptance of the word, the works of such a composer as Medtner (who unfortunately is little known in America) are wonderfully fresh and modern, yet there is no suggestion of the Futurist about his music. Indeed Medtner detests the Futurists. America must learn more about the works of this truly great composer. Russia is beginning to realize that he has already taken a place among our immortals. Strauss, Schoenberg, Reger, and others have been widely heralded in America—why Medtner has been ignored I am at a loss to understand.

Variety of Material in Russia

The variety of folk song material in Russia is almost boundless. The immense dimensions of the country make it quite naturally a collection of diverse peoples—many of them totally and absolutely different from people in other parts of the land. They have diverse languages and different folk songs. The peasant music of the Caucasus and the Crimea, for example, are hardly Russian at all. They are Oriental. Borodin recognized this, and he has used them in some of his works with Oriental settings with wonderful effect.

Probably the best known and most used folk songs are those of Middle Russia—the region of the Volga. Although Russia has a territory of eight million square miles, not all of this is distinctively Slavic. The reason for this is that, in times past, the country has been overrun by many different races—Goths, Huns, Avars, Bulgarians, Magyars and Khazars—all leaving their impression in a way, but never wholly eradicating the strong Slavonic mold which marks the Russia of today, and is so characteristic of the significant music of the great Russian masters.

It has, for some time, been my impression that those countries which are the richest in folk song are naturally the ones to develop the greatest music. I am surprised to learn that Spain, which has so much wonderful folk music, has developed so few composers of international renown. But, on the other hand, consider the remarkable literary masterpieces that Spain has produced from the time of Cervantes down to the present day. On the contrary, a little group of countries, such as Scandinavia, with a comparatively sparse population, has produced, in music, men like Grieg, Svendsen and Sinding.

Russian Music of Yesterday and To-Morrow

There seems to be an impression that the Russian Church has made a profound impression upon Russian music. This is not exactly true. The composers for the Church, however, have resorted to collections of ancient melodies for use in their religious music. On the whole, I think that the influence of the Church is overestimated in the consideration of our music. I am sometimes asked whether I feel that the momentous change in regime in Russian affairs at the present time is likely to affect the future of Russian music. For the time being the unrest of conditions certainly impedes all creative work. It will take Russia some time to stagger out from the confusion resulting from the world war. I am firmly convinced, however, that Russia's musical future is limitless. The Czars did little that was of moment to aid the development of musical expression in Russia. This may be understood, when it is remembered that most of the great modern musicians of Russia were forced to make an avocation of music, and to earn their living through other occupations. The late Czar Nicholas was rarely seen at a concert, and he had little or no interest in the great musical achievements of his country. Indeed, his musical status may be estimated by the fact that his chief musical pleasure was found in the band of Ballalaika players conducted by Andreieff. This organization of well-drilled native players was creditable, but as circumscribed in its field as might be an American mandolin or banjo club compared with one of your great Symphony Orchestras.

The American composer, it seems to me, should find his outlet in music of a cosmopolitan type, rather than seek to evolve a purely national type. America is young, but as time goes on it will gradually acquire its own folk songs, and until this comes about the natural expression of its music will be as many-tongued as the sum of the various nationalities who are finding a home here. I recently attended a concert—a very successful one—given by Mr. Josef Hofmann, whose program was entirely of American composers. The compositions were very creditable, but—I did not hear American music. It was French music, German music, Italian music, just as surely as if it had been made in those countries.

There is a strong national characteristic in America, a characteristic born of her broad Democracy, the gathering together of many nations, a cosmopolitan note which your composers must catch and write into your music. How it will be done, or when, or where, no one knows. I am convinced, however, that the plan of taking Indian themes, and Negro themes, is scarcely likely to produce the great, distinctive American music, unless, indeed, these themes are developed by Indian composers and Negro composers. The highest quality in all art is sincerity.

MacDowell Popular in Russia

MacDowell is, as yet, the only American composer known to any extent in Russia, and some of his compositions are very popular there, as they deserve to be. He had a beautiful melodic sense, and he treated his material in a very musicianly manner. On the other hand, I am in America at present for the reason that nowhere else in the world is there such music as there is in America now. You have the finest orchestras, and the most musically appreciative people, and I have more opportunity to hear fine orchestral works, and more opportunity to play. Take the Philadelphia Orchestra, for instance. The development of the body and of its leader, Mr. Stokowski, has not been mere leisurely progress—it has been a vital leap ahead! All musical conditions in America have advanced so markedly in the past ten years that I can hardly realize it possible.

American students are deprived, in many cities, of one opportunity which seems to be the common and accepted right of musical students in Russia. Orchestral concerts are expensive, and few students can afford to buy tickets for them. In America, I understand, the concerts are sold out so far in advance that only the few can attend them. In Russia, on the contrary, if a student shows the slightest signs of ability above the average, that student is recommended to the director of the Conservatory as deserving the privilege of attending the final rehearsals of orchestral concerts. Upon this recommendation, the student is admitted to all rehearsals without cost. In Russia there are usually at least three rehearsals, and the last is virtually a finished performance. Think how advantageous this would be to American students. Why cannot American Conservatories arrange such a plan?

I am asked whether it is my opinion that the interest in the piano is likely to become dulled. Why ask such a question? The mastery of the piano is always a matter of keen, artistic interest to all concerned in music. To my mind, no pianist of the present day approaches the playing of the great Rubinstein, whom I heard many times. The possibilities of the piano are by no means exhausted, and until this is achieved, the pianists of to-day and to-morrow have a great goal before them in striving to equal the art of

Rubinstein and other great masters of the piano. It is true that the standard of piano playing has advanced wonderfully. This was the case, even in the time of Rubinstein. And this fact reminds me of a remark of the master, not untinged with satire. When Rubinstein played in Moscow "everybody was there," and the concert was sold out weeks in advance. Shortly afterward Rubinstein went to hear a new pianist—who had already made quite a name for himself by reason of his talent—at a recital which was rather sparsely attended. When he was asked after the recital what he thought of the newcomer's playing, Rubinstein wrinkled up his heavy brows and then said earnestly, "Oh! nowadays everybody plays the piano well." That was the point. "Everybody plays the piano well!" But how few—how very, very few—even approach the greatness of Rubinstein?

Basanta Koomar Roy, "Rachmaninoff Is Reminiscent," *The Musical Observer* 26/5 (1 May 1927): 16 and 41

Among composers, Rachmaninoff looms large. While it seldom transpires that one gains equal distinction as a composer, and a pianist, yet this may be said of Rachmaninoff. In the course of the next hundred years or so the excellence of his piano playing will no doubt have become mythical, but the message of his musical compositions for the orchestra, for the voice and for the piano will still remain as cherished treasures of mankind.

One fine morning not long ago, I found myself, by appointment, in the spacious studio of Rachmaninoff overlooking the Hudson. In this quiet and contemplative room where the master did much of his composing, we talked of many things. In the course of our conversation I asked the master musician from Moscow how he first gained recognition as a composer, for this is one of the most difficult things a young composer has to contend with.

"When I was studying piano at the Moscow Conservatory of Music, I felt within myself the impulse to compose," said Rachmaninoff reminiscently. "So I studied the science and art of musical composition with Professors Tanieiev and Arensky. And during my year of postgraduate work, composed my first opera, Aleko. I was very much encouraged by Tschaikowsky. He was so kind and helpful to me as a composer that he even came to the rehearsals of Aleko to assist with his vast store of wisdom, knowledge and experience. Aleko was first produced in April 1893 at the Grand Theatre of Moscow. I was then twenty years old. With Aleko I made my bow to the world as a composer. It was well received by the critics and the public. This gave me the incentive to continue with my composition.

"And under the incentive provided by that early appreciation for my opera, I composed during the summer of that same year The Rock (an orchestral fantasy); The Prayers of the Ever Watchful Mother of God (a choral work); Six Songs, one violin piece, and my first Suite for two pianos. Tschaikowsky died in October of that year and my deep sense of bereavement moved me to write my Trio Elegiaque (op. 9, a la memorie d'un grand artiste) for piano, violin and cello. So you see the year of my debut as a composer was rather a strenuous one. I composed several serious things after this, but strange to say, a small piano piece, the C Sharp Minor Prelude, made me known in many lands."

"Some people would like to call you Mr. C Sharp Minor," I said. The master laughed. This was the first time that I found the melancholy musician could laugh so heartily.

Finding him in such a mood I was encouraged to ask him how he got his inspiration for the C Sharp Minor Prelude as well as the various sources from which he derives inspiration.

"One day the Prelude simply came and I put it down," he said. "It came with such force that I could not shake it off even though I tried hard to do so. It had to be—so there it was. And I also remember that I received only $20.00 for it. The piece was printed and sold in large quantities throughout the world but I never received any further compensation. The recognition which the piece brought me, however, was worth considerable.

Source of Inspiration

"It is most difficult to analyze the source of inspiration for compositions. So many factors work together in a creative work. Love is certainly a never failing source of inspiration. Love inspires as nothing else does. To love is to gain happiness and strength of mind. It is the unfoldment of a new vista of intellectual energy. The beauty and grandeur of nature helps. Poetry inspires me much. Of all the arts I love poetry the best after music. Our Pushkin I find admirable. Shakespeare and Byron I read constantly in the Russian. I always have books of poetry around me. Poetry inspires music—for there is so much music in poetry. They are like twin sisters.

"Everything of beauty helps," said Rachmaninoff with a smile that lingered in the corners of his mouth. "A beautiful woman is certainly a source of perpetual inspiration. But you must run away from her, and seek seclusion, otherwise you will compose nothing—you will accomplish nothing. Carry the inspiration in your heart and mind; think of her, but be all by yourself for creative work.

"Real inspiration must come from within. If there is nothing within, nothing from outside can help. The best of poetry, the greatest of painting, the sublimest of nature cannot produce any worthwhile result if the divine spark of creative faculty is lacking within the artist."

"How does painting affect you?"

"After music and poetry, I like painting the best."

"I know painting was responsible for your symphonic poem, The Island of the Dead. Where did you see the painting first?"

"I first saw only a copy of the famous painting of Boeklin at Dresden. The massive architecture and mystic message of the painting made a marked impression on me, and the tone poem was the outcome. Later I saw the original painting in Berlin. I was not much moved by the coloring in the painting. If I had seen the original first, I might not have composed my Island of the Dead. I like the picture best in black and white."

"This tone poem was my first acquaintance with you as a composer," I interposed. "I admired it so much that Mr. Stransky was gracious enough to play it a second time the same season, only at my most humble request. It stirred something within me. I wish I could hear it played once by Stokowski with his Philadelphia Orchestra. At times he accomplishes such uncanny feats through his orchestra. And this is an uncanny piece of music born of an uncanny painting. By the way, what about other noted composers in Russia today?"

"The Russian school of music is one of great significance. The world is slowly waking up to the fact, too slowly, it seems to me. The boycott of German music during the war, a thing quite injurious in itself, has, however, helped people to seek and find classical music beyond the borders of Germany and Austria. Besides others we have today Medtner and Glazounoff. They are well worthy of consideration. During my lifetime we have lost Tschaikowsky, Rimsky-Korsakoff and Scriabine. I told you before that after the death of Tschaikowsky I composed my Trio Elegiaque. After the death of Scriabine I toured all over Russia playing his compositions as my humble homage to that great master of music. And as for Rimsky-Korsakoff I tell you that when I was obliged to leave my home and my beloved Russia after the Bolshevik revolution, I was allowed to take with me only 500 roubles each for my family of four, and of all the music I had, I chose to carry with me only the score of Rimsky's Coq d'Or.

Russian Music

"It is true," continued the master pianist, "that Russian music is very little known in America, but its influence is felt all over Europe. Take Debussy, for instance. He is intensely influenced by Rimsky-Korsakoff. It is not plagiarism in the case of Debussy, for he was a musical genius himself—it was only influence. Just as a poet is influenced by another poet. Perhaps Tagore has influenced many young poets in India."

"Yes, influenced quite a few, not only in writing verse, but also in the dressing of their hair."

"That's exactly what I mean by influence."

"Many of our artists have gone through various vicissitudes of fortune before they arrived. I am wondering what has been your lot in this respect."

"I had my full share of sorrows, sufferings and privations," he went on. "Though born in a wealthy family I soon discovered that I had to support and educate myself. Something went wrong with our family fortunes. So trouble began. As a boy I made good progress in music and began giving lessons in piano when I was only sixteen years old. It was necessary for me to earn money by this means in order to continue my musical education. I charged seventy-five cents an hour. And in the first month I earned about fifty roubles. I was glad for this teaching experience. In order to be able to teach conscientiously I had to know much more than my pupils, and I learned how to solve many problems of technic. My forced pedagogy was certainly a blessing in disguise in my development. For I am proud to say that I am a self-made musician. So after much trial and tribulation, when appreciation came I was happy. My second opera, The Miser Knight, gave me the first real start in life.

"But whenever I think of my career as a musician I cannot forget the patronage of Tschaikowsky. He thought I had talent; so he encouraged me and helped my development. At the premiere of my first opera, Aleko, he desired that his one act opera, Iolanthe, might be produced along with my first attempt. I was indeed proud of the compliment thus bestowed. You really cannot realize what it meant to me then. The great Tschaikowsky, our national musical hero, wished that his opera might be produced with mine. I was simply intoxicated with joy. And I tell you that patronage from such a great musical figure certainly did help me in carving out a career for myself. Tschaikowsky was a dynamic personality, even as Chekov."

"You have raised a question by the use of the word personality," I said, "about which there is much diversity of opinion. It is claimed in certain musical quarters that the personality of a musician has little to do with his success. What is your opinion?"

"The personality of a musician has a great deal to do with it. If personality does not count, then why not listen to the phonograph or radio? Why go to concerts at all? Take one concrete example. Mr. Kreisler has a tremendous personality. He comes on the stage, he plays and he conquers. You know the way he conquers. Now suppose at one of his concerts he played from behind a curtain. Do you think the audience would enthuse as much as is usually the custom?"

"No, I don't think so."

"Then you agree with me. The personality of a musician influences the audience, consciously or unconsciously, in the appreciation of music. In the enjoyment of music human hearts play a more important part than human brains."

"Do you think you would have been a success as a pianist if you were handicapped by some physical deformity, even though your playing remained the same?"

"Under such conditions I would have been a dismal failure even if I played a hundred times better than I do today. Take the case of an actor like Stanislavsky, the founder of the Moscow Art Theatre. If he had a deformed body and yet acted much better, he would have been a failure just the same. As for composers and dramatists it is quite different. If I were deformed and could not play the piano in concert, I might have composed greater symphonies, greater operas and greater concertos. There are always compensations. That's why I insist that personality has a great deal to do with the success of a musician who appears in public."

Musical Future of America

While talking about America I asked this distinguished Russian what he thought of the musical future of this country.

"America has a great future musically. Today we see only the beginning of a new musical age here. All great musicians from Europe are coming here and contributing their share for the advancement of music in this country. It is a misfortune for Europe, but it is a great thing for America. Perhaps a greater music is to be born in this country, where they manufacture such excellent pianos. But I am sorry to say that there is not an organized national effort to co-ordinate America's musical forces for the highest good of the land.

"The first thing I would do were I in a position of authority, would be to establish a National Conservatory of Music in a building quite in keeping with the financial resources and international dignity of this country. Then I should make that the radiating center of the highest and the purest in music. For three years as the Vice-President of the Imperial Russian Music Society, I did similar work in Russia."

Rachmaninoff lives a very quiet and simple life. He shuns luxury and costly habits in every shape and form. He is absorbed in his art and devotes much time to reading, playing and gardening in the summer time. He is seldom seen at concerts. But when his old friend Chaliapin sings, or when Medtner plays, it is hard to keep him away.

He is very devoted to the theatre. In his youth he was a great admirer of Chekov. He is a friend of the players of the Moscow Art Theatre. I remember what a stimulating sight I saw one afternoon in the Artists' room after a Rachmaninoff concert at Carnegie Hall, New York. There stood in a corner a huge glittering laurel wreath in green, gold and white, presented to the master pianist with the cordial greetings of the Moscow Art Theatre. The actors and actresses from the greatest theatre of the world led by stalwart and handsome Stanislavsky, almost surrounded him. Some of the men kissed him, and he them in real Russian style. They exchanged a few words in the tempo of a chant before an altar. Then for a minute or two they spoke not a word. The Moscow players simply looked at the great Moscow musician in reverent silence. Such devotion, such poise, such childlike sincerity, I never saw before, even on the stage of the Moscow Art Theatre. The actors surpassed themselves. Then they gently walked away one by one, like so many children, sad at parting from their playmate. The master's gaze was fixed on them, and he waved at the last actor who looked back as he went out of the door. I watched this bit of drama in life with breathless wonder, and I am not ashamed to admit that the sanctity of the scene moved me to tears. And from the quick movement of his eyelids I could notice that the master's eyes were not altogether dry either.

I shall never forget this one act play of the Moscow Art Theatre, Rachmaninoff playing the part of the hero. It was more than a play, it was a sacrament. I was doubly happy to see the dramatic mightiest in Russia paying homage to the musical mightiest of Russia in such a solemnly unique way. It was certainly a fitting tribute most worthily paid to the maestro of Moscow.

David Ewen, "Music Should Speak from the Heart: A Conference with Sergei Rachmaninoff, the World-Famous Composer-Pianist," *The Etude* 59/12 (December 1941): 804 and 849

The name of Sergei Rachmaninoff requires very little introduction to readers of THE ETUDE. In the triple rôle of composer, conductor, and concert pianist he has acquired a position of unequalled importance in the music of our times. Although he is generally accepted as one of the world's greatest pianists, Rachmaninoff is more likely to be honored by future generations for his work as a composer. Already, his piano concertos and symphonies, as well as an entire library of songs and smaller piano pieces, have become permanent fixtures on concert and symphony programs, and are likely to become among the most important contributions of our generation to the literature of music.—EDITOR'S NOTE

Composing is as essential a part of my being as breathing or eating; it is one of the necessary functions of living. My constant desire to compose music is actually the urge within me to give tonal expression to my feelings, just as I speak to give utterance to my thoughts. That, I believe, is the function that music should serve in the life of every composer; any other function it may fill is purely incidental.

No Sympathy for Modern Music

I have no sympathy with the composer who produces works according to preconceived formulas or preconceived theories. Or with the composer who writes in a certain style because it is the fashion to do so. Great music has never been produced in that way—and I dare say it never will. Music should, in the final analysis, be the expression of a composer's complex personality. It should not be arrived at mentally, tailor-made to fit certain specifications—a tendency, I regret to say, all too prevalent during the past twenty years or so. A composer's music should express the country of his birth, his love affairs, his religion, the books which have influenced him, the pictures he loves. It should be the product of the sum total of a composer's experiences. Study the masterpieces of every great composer, and you will find every aspect of the composer's personality and background in his music. Time may change the technic of music, but it can never alter its mission.

From all this you can gather that I have no warm feeling for music that is experimental—your so-called "modern music," whatever that may mean. For, after all, is not the music of composers like Sibelius or Glazunov *modern* music, even though it is written in a more traditional manner? I myself could never care to write in a radical vein which disregards the laws of tonality or harmony. Nor could I learn to love such music, if I listened to it a thousand times. And, I say again and again, that music must first and foremost be loved; it must come from the heart and must be directed to the heart. Otherwise it cannot hope to be lasting, indestructible art.

Yet I must add, I can respect the artistic aim of a composer if he arrives at the so-called modern idiom after an intense period of preparation. Stravinsky, after all, did not compose *Le Sacre du Printemps* until he had had an intensive period of study with a master like Rimsky-Korsakoff, and until he had composed a classical symphony and other works in the classic forms. Otherwise, *Le Sacre du Printemps*—for all its boldness—would not have possessed such solid musical merits in the form of imaginative harmonies and energetic rhythms. Such composers know what they are doing when they break a law; they know what to react against, because they have experience in the classical forms and style. Having mastered the rules, they know which can be violated, and which should be obeyed. But, I am sorry to say, I have found too often that young composers plunge into the writing of experimental music with their school lessons only half learned. Too much radical music is sheer sham, for this very reason: its composer sets about revolutionizing the laws of music before he learned them himself. Whatever a composer's goal as an artist may be, he can never dispense with thorough technical training; a complete scholastic training is indispensable, even with all the talent in the world. There is a famous Russian painter by the name of Vroubel, who paints modernistic canvases. But, before he strove for a new and radical expression, he mastered the old rules and acquired a formidable technic. There is a valuable lesson in this for every young composer who wants to speak a new language. You cannot explore a new world, without first becoming familiar with the old one. Once you are in the possession of technic, once you have learned your classic rules well, you are so much the better equipped to set out in your own direction as a composer.

Know the Old Methods

And there is always this possibility: if you insist on becoming intimately acquainted with the old world before venturing upon a new one, you may very well discover that there is room enough for you in the former—that there is no need for you to seek new paths. I frequently have the feeling, in listening to the radical works of many younger men, that they go in all directions, harmonically and contrapuntally, in their music, because they are not sufficiently well instructed in the old methods to make them pliable tools for their ideas. It is my own pet belief that, if you have something important to say, you don't need a new language in which to say it. The old language is sufficiently rich and resourceful. The young composers make the mistake of believing that you achieve originality through *technic*. Actually, the only originality worth achieving is that which comes from *substance*. A composer can use all the accepted tools of composition and produce a work far different in style and subject matter from any ever produced, because he has put into the music his own personality and experiences.

In my own compositions, no conscious effort has been made to be original, or Romantic, or Nationalistic, or anything else. I write down on paper the music I hear within me, as naturally as possible. I am a Russian composer, and the land of my birth has influenced my temperament and outlook. My music is the product of my temperament, and so it is Russian music; I never consciously attempted to write Russian music, or any other kind of music. I have been strongly influenced by Tschaikowsky and Rimsky-Korsakoff; but I have never, to the best of my knowledge, imitated anyone. What I try to do, when writing down my music, is to make it say simply and directly that which is in my heart when I am composing. If there is love there, or bitterness, or sadness, or religion, these moods become a part of my music, and it becomes either beautiful or bitter or sad or religious.

When composing, I find it of great help to have in mind a book just recently read, or a beautiful picture, or a poem. Sometimes a definite story is kept in mind, which I try to convert into tones without disclosing the source of my inspiration. By that I do not mean that I write program music. Since the sources of my inspiration are never revealed, the public must listen to the music absolutely. But I find that musical ideas come to me more easily when I have a definite non-musical subject to describe. This is particularly true in writing a shorter piece for the piano.

Young composers are often apt to look condescendingly upon the smaller forms of music, and to expend all of their energy and devotion to the greater forms of the symphony and the concerto. This is a mistake. A small piece can become as lasting a masterpiece as a large work. As a matter of fact, I have often found that a short piece for the piano has always given me much more pain, and has presented to me many more problems, than a symphony or a concerto. Somehow, in writing for the orchestra, the variety of colors provided by the instruments brings me many different ideas and effects. But when I write a small piece for the piano, I am at the mercy of my thematic idea which must be presented concisely and without digression. In my concertos and symphonies, there are frequent times when I can write fluently. But every small piece I have produced is the result of great care and hard work. For, after all, to say what you have to say, and to say it briefly, lucidly, and without any circumlocution, is still the most difficult problem facing the creative artist. The artist learns, after long experience, that it is more difficult to be simple than to be complicated. The young composer should bear this in mind.

Glenn Quilty, "Rachmaninoff—The Last Romantic Composer," *HiFi Review* 3/4 (October 1959): 26 and 28

Rachmaninoff represents the final flowering of the romantic movement in music, which started with Beethoven early in the nineteenth century. Yet those of us who knew him, recall a master essentially modern, whose evaluation of his own work was unique. It is not, however, in dynamic aspect of his tonal language that we find the timelessness of the man, but rather in his melodic line with its suggestive philosophy. Here he was one of a kind; his music reflects his highly emotional feelings. There is a pictorial audio-visuality present in his music that is missing in music of the more abstract composers.

Although the great Russian did not care to teach, he did have a number of protégés. In my youth, I was one of the fortunate few who came to his notice as a composer and concert pianist. In later years, when I had become a music critic and a musicologist, I interviewed him a number of times. It was at these sessions that I fully came to realize his place in the history of music. I believe also that he was more frank with me than with other writers because of my concert and compositional career. I had, in fact, dedicated my *Victorian Concerto* to him and had played his works on many of my programs in America and Europe.

At one of the interviews in his suite at the Ansonia Hotel in New York, Rachmaninoff had seated himself in a throne-like chair near a window, his countenance, creased and lined like a map of rivers and tributaries, was filled with a sad benevolence. Only his dark, sparkling eyes lived in that face. They burned with a fierce penetration that projected power and authority. Now and then, as he talked, a wise leprechaun expression was apparent that at times would melt into a grandfatherly smile. (This was the period toward the end of his career.)

"I have watched you come on stage many times," I began, "and each time you enter with a calm, impersonal expression. Your face seems encased in its lines and wrinkles. Yet after the first group you are pink and less lined, and at the encores you appear young, rosy and unlined."

"Yes, I know. I am intoxicated with the power that pours through me from the source. And who can say what and where it is? Nevertheless, all creative people draw from this essential reservoir throughout life; each one is born with the ability to turn on and off an immortal fountain."

"My readers often write and ask what to listen for in your music—"

"Tell them that all music is best heard at maximum benefit if the listener is *historically* aware of its message and content; it is wise to know the political, economic and social scene of the composer's life in order to evaluate him."

"And in your own case?"

"I reflect the philosophy of old Russia—White Russia—with its over-tones of suffering and unrest, its pastoral but tragic beauty, its ancient and enduring glory. With this comes my own personal feeling. I am a Victorian-Edwardian—actually the last of the romantic composers."

"In no way modern?"

"Not in my harmonic arrangements and tonalities. They are in the genre of flowing, lush effects and illuminated vistas viewed from a romantic point. I like to unfold pictures in sound. But my melodic line is quite up-to-date if you analyze it and realize its declaration and spartan economy. Sibelius has this also. But Schönberg and Hindemith have an entirely different approach."

"How so?"

"They are more incisive; they declare themselves in shorter phrases; there is a sharpness and a decided strong accent felt throughout. My 'genie' would not permit this, excellent as it is for them. I prefer to evolve my thematic material slowly without over-aggression or over-emphasis. I don't dramatize. I invite the listener to dramatize in his mind with enfolding color. This is particularly true of my *Etudes-Tableaux*, my songs, my *Second Concerto*."

"How would you place yourself with composers past and present?"

"I am not an intellectual composer, rather an emotionalist. I do not deal in abstractions or cerebral torturings and posturings. I utilize musical narrative, telling a story in musical terms as writers do in words. I wish to encompass the listener in warmth, and to reveal and open to him rich landscapes, to transport him to an ideal planet. Not utopia, for there is an undercurrent of sorrow in my work. But a place where suffering and peace are transcended into a healing whole."

"Would you compare your music to any paintings?"

"I am fond of the paintings of Ingres and Turner and there may be a parallel here to my work. An impressionist like Monet is related to a composer like Debussy, Stravinsky to Picasso."

"Please tell me what the average listener should seek in your work."

"He should concentrate on the themes, the solo voices. These are interspersed with bridges of harmonic material leading to the next individual melody. I alternate theme and bridge with frequent modulations to sustain aural interest. Each theme, solo, or melody unfolds from the foregoing one, like petals from the same flower, only the petals are different colors and shapes in this case."

"What is the future of romantic music as against the atonal harshness of extreme modern examples?"

"The public will always understand and love romantic music. The bitter tonalities of today will vanish eventually. True, they reflect our times, but they don't reflect the warmth and depth of compassion in human nature which is timeless."

As the interview drew to a close, Rachmaninoff seated himself at the piano and played some of his compositions to me. As he played I felt the room fill with his glowing rich harmonies until the walls were pushed out of sight and our spirits were soaring away from the building and New York itself. But I seemed to sense a sorrowful philosophy enacted here, a dramatization of the spirit of man going forward endlessly; so with a gesture of thanks to the composer, I quietly withdrew.

The music of the last romantic composer followed me down the hall. Reaching the street, it came faintly down to me from above, and, as I walked on, it merged with the roar of the city.

NOTES

1. "S. V. Rakhmaninov ob Amerike," *Muzïkal'nïy truzhenik* 7 (1910): 18–19, at 18.

2. Rachmaninoff to Emil Medtner, 1/14 April 1910, in S. Rakhmaninov, *Literaturnoye naslediye*, ed. Z. A. Apetyan, 3 vols (Moscow: Sovetskiy kompozitor, 1978–80), 2:7. At this time, Medtner was close to the Symbolist poet Marietta Shaginyan, whose "musico–psychological study" of Rachmaninoff's music appeared in a short–lived modernist periodical with links to Medtner. See Marietta Shaginyan, "S. V. Rakhmaninov (muzïkal'no–psikhologicheskiy etyud)," *Trudï i dni* 4–5 (1912): 97–114.

3. "Ob odnom nashumevshem interv'yu: Pis'mo v redaktsiyu," *Russkiye vedomosti*, 14 November 1910, reproduced in Rakhmaninov, *Literaturnoye naslediye*, 1:24–27.

4. See, for instance, V. Ya. [Yakovlev], "S. V. Rakhmaninov," *Russkaya starina*, 148/12 (1911): 515–20. Rachmaninoff provided the biographical details used in this article and wrote to thank the author when it eventually appeared in print. See letter of 6 January 1912, in Rakhmaninov, *Literaturnoye naslediye*, 2:40.

5. Iwan I. Ostromislensky, Sergei Rachmaninoff, and Count Ilya L. Tolstoy, "Tagore on Russia: The 'Circle of Russian Culture' Challenges Some of His Statements," *New York Times*, 15 January 1931.

6. Rachmaninoff to Sofiya Satina, 24 August 1933, in Rakhmaninov, *Literaturnoye naslediye*, 2:359.

7. In his 1950 biography of the composer, Victor Seroff recalled that Rachmaninoff asked him to remove some critical comments about his American contemporaries from the interview he gave for *Vogue* magazine in 1943: "My words . . . in reference to the American composers, are the holy truth. I do not want to substitute a lie for the truth. But as the truth is *unbearable*, I prefer to say nothing at all. Therefore, please omit the four lines. Please do this for me. Everything else is acceptable." See Victor I. Seroff, *Rachmaninoff* (New York: Simon and Schuster, 1950), 230. Seroff's interview was published, just a few days after Rachmaninoff's death on 28 March, as "The Great Rachmaninoff," *Vogue*, 1 April 1943, 43 and 88.

8. Basil Maine, "Conversation with Rachmaninoff," *Musical Opinion* 60/709 (October 1936): 14–15, at 14.

9. Important, if incomplete, bibliographies of Rachmaninoff's interviews can be found in Robert Palmieri, *Sergei Vasil'evich Rachmaninoff: A Guide to Research* (New York and London: Garland Publishing, 1985); and Robert E. Cunningham, Jr., ed., *Sergei Rachmaninoff: A Bio-Bibliography* (Westport, CT, and London: Greenwood Press, 2001).

10. A large number of interviews are included—in Russian translation—in Rakhmaninov, *Literaturnoye naslediye*, 1:62–148; and feature prominently in Sergei Bertensson and Jay Leyda, *Sergei Rachmaninoff: A Lifetime in Music* (Bloomington: Indiana University Press, 2001). Originally published in 1956, Bertensson and Leyda's account—effectively authorized by the composer's heirs and family—has been extensively mined by subsequent biographers.

The Eighteenth Variation

STEVE SWAYNE

The year is 1987. The place is the Kennedy Center in Washington, D.C. The president of the United States is in the audience along with all the cultural elite from the area. The occasion is a concert by Sparky, an eight-year-old wunderkind from just outside Pittsburgh. He is in the nation's capital to conduct and perform the *Rhapsody on a Theme from* [sic] *Paganini* by "Rachmanioff." He gives the downbeat, and he and the orchestra play the *Rhapsody* from its beginning to the end of Variation V, whereupon the music segues to the second iteration of Variation XVIII and then to the coda. This is the climactic performance in the animated cartoon *Sparky's Magic Piano*; soon afterward we find out that the flawless Chopin, Mozart, Beethoven, Brahms, Grieg, Liszt, Schumann, Gottschalk, and Rachmaninoff that we have heard in the 48-minute cartoon are products of Sparky's dream of a piano that could play anything Sparky could imagine.[1]

The year is 2021. I enter the search terms "Rachmaninoff Rhapsody" at a website for sheet music. I find arrangements of the eighteenth variation for all manner of forces and abilities: organ, easy piano, early advanced piano, intermediate piano, advanced piano, piano duet, viola and piano, cello and piano, violin and cello, string trio, string quartet, strings and piano, string orchestra, flute and piano, horn and piano, woodwind quartet, saxophone quartet, brass quartet, handbells, orchestra at various difficulty levels, and as part of *A Rachmaninoff Rhapsody* for concert band. The variation also appears in numerous anthologies for piano, including *World's Greatest Wedding Music* (easy piano), where the *Rhapsody on a Theme of Paganini*—actually, just the eighteenth variation—lives alongside *As Time Goes By*, *The Rose*, and *You Raise Me Up*.[2]

It is not difficult to understand how evocative words—*Rhapsody on a Theme of Paganini*—serve as a synecdoche for everyday ones; peacock phrases are more attractive than peahen ones. But how and why the eighteenth variation came to occupy such a commanding perch in the musical aviary merits its own story. It is a colorful one, timebound and timeless at the same time.

Three Little Words

Let us start by acknowledging that we are talking about a *moment* in music, not even a complete movement, let alone an entire piece. Bo Widerberg's 1967 film *Elvira Madigan* caused the slow movement of Mozart's Concerto No. 21 in C Major, K. 467, to acquire the stage name of the circus performer whose nobleman/cavalry-officer lover murdered her before taking his own life in 1889, all because the movement appears throughout the movie. (Vivaldi's *Le quattro stagioni* also appears in the film, but no one I know of refers to the "Elvira Madigan" *Four Seasons* the way they speak of the "Elvira Madigan" Concerto.) A less checkered notoriety befell both Johann Pachelbel's non-canonic Canon when it appeared in the 1980 American film *Ordinary People*—you'll need to keep reading to find a connection between Pachelbel and Rachmaninoff—and Scott Joplin's *The Entertainer*, often mistakenly called *The Sting* after the 1973 film of that name brought a new audience to Joplin's music. But the Joplin and the Pachelbel are whole pieces. More apposite to my thoughts is how the fourth-movement Adagietto from Mahler's five-movement Symphony No. 5 became attached in many people's minds to Luchino Visconti's 1971 adaptation of Thomas Mann's *Death in Venice*.

So allow me to recount the oddities again. "Elvira Madigan" and Pachelbel's Canon and *The Sting* and the Adagietto all have a specificity about them that the eighteenth variation does not. The eighteenth variation of what, precisely? Does anyone ever refer to any variation from any other set of variations by its number in its larger sequence? There is the reference to "Notte e giorno faticar" in Beethoven's *33 Variations on a Waltz by Anton Diabelli*, Op. 120. Might someone talk about the *Don Giovanni* variation? Maybe. Would they say "the Twenty-second Variation"? Probably only those who study or play the set. And who among us calls the ninth variation from Elgar's *Enigma Variations*, Op. 36, "the Ninth Variation"? No one I know, even as I suspect that some of you reading this have intuited which variation is the ninth and have started humming or singing to yourself "Nimrod" (and again, note the nomenclatural specificity here that is lacking in the Rachmaninoff—and note further how the structure of "Nimrod" eerily mirrors the structure of our eighteenth variation).

And yet, as this essay will show, a lot of people know the "Eighteenth Variation" without knowing the eighteenth variation, or even the whole work from which it came. How did this come to be?

Rachmaninoff and Variations

The *Rhapsody on a Theme of Paganini*, Op. 43 (1934), happens to be the last full set of variations that Rachmaninoff composed. Immediately preceding the *Rhapsody* were the *Variations on a Theme of Corelli*, Op. 42, which he completed in the summer of 1931.[3] But the genesis of the eighteenth variation and the *Rhapsody* may predate the Corelli, so a quick look at two other sets of variations will set the stage for what Rachmaninoff did with—and to—Paganini's caprice.

Rachmaninoff composed three sets of variations altogether. In addition to the Paganini and the Corelli, there are the *Variations on a Theme of Chopin*, Op. 22 (1902–1903). Given our focus here on one particular variation from a larger set, suffice it to say that in the Chopin variations—a work ostensibly in C minor—one of the most lyrical variations is the penultimate one (out of a total of twenty-two), and it is in D-flat major, the same key as our eighteenth variation, which is an odd key for a work in C minor (the Chopin variations) as well as for a work ostensibly in A minor (the *Rhapsody*).[4] But as we shall see, D-flat major is the tonal area in which Rachmaninoff routinely gave voice to some of his most melodic and passionate passages in works that are not in that key.[5]

It is another "set" of variations that may tell us the most about how Rachmaninoff came to construct a combination of variations and fantasy. The central section of the third movement of his Concerto No. 3 in D Minor, Op. 30 (1909) features a set of four variations that embroider the second theme from the first movement of the work. This set of variations arrives less than four minutes into a 14-minute movement and takes up more than a third of the movement. A similar puckishness will find a home in the scherzo section of the *Rhapsody* (Variations XIII–XV), and the backward glances to earlier moments in the concerto—the opening theme from the first movement is also recalled—seem intent on reminding the listener of the lyricism of earlier moments that, surprisingly, the third movement is short of otherwise. But it is the coda of the fourth variation that prefigures our eighteenth variation. The orchestra is silent, and the solo piano concludes this E-flat major incursion in an ostensibly D-minor movement by, among other things, throwing a chromatic and coloristic chord into the mix that seems slightly out of place in what is a primarily diatonic close. Let us call it a "stinger chord" for now, a term I will further define as we go along.

While Rachmaninoff's portfolio of compositions shows a relative paucity of variations in comparison to other pianist-composers, his performing repertoire as a pianist and conductor features numerous sets of variations, including the "changing background variations" found in Glinka's *Kamarinskaya* and Tchaikovsky's Second and Fourth symphonies, all of which he conducted. He also performed sets of piano variations by Beethoven, Handel, Haydn, Mendelssohn, Schubert, and Schumann.[6] Most notable for our purposes is the fact that in 1928 Rachmaninoff added to his repertoire the sixth of Liszt's *Grandes études de Paganini*, the etude that is a set of variations on the same caprice that Rachmaninoff would use for his *Rhapsody*. Whereas Liszt wrote eleven variations and a coda, Rachmaninoff set himself the task of writing twenty-four variations, in keeping with the Paganini caprice itself being the last of Paganini's twenty-four Caprices, Op. 1.

The entire *Rhapsody* merits its own study. Take, for example, its architectonic structure: a three-movement construction where a central slow movement (Variations XI–XVIII) incorporates a scherzo (XIII–XV). This structure—which one finds in Tchaikovsky's Concerto No. 1 in B-flat Minor, Op. 23, a work in Rachmaninoff's repertoire and one he must have known from his youth—is also found in the Second and Third concertos and the Third Symphony. Or consider its tonal movement from A minor (I–X) through a fantasy of sorts (XI) to F major via D minor (XII–XV), then to D-flat major via B-flat minor (XVI–XVIII), and then back to A minor (ending, presumably, in A major: XIX–XXIV)—in other words, a rotation of major thirds that is reminiscent of *Parsifal*, which Rachmaninoff saw at Bayreuth in 1902. (Amfortas's Leitmotif is built around the augmented triad, signifying his uneasy place within the Knights of the Holy Grail and sounding in contradistinction to Parsifal's unassailable triadic harmonies.) Or note how one of the most rhapsodic variations—XXII—is the exact double of the first variation that escapes the confines of the foursquare Paganini (XI). But let us leave these other fascinating variations—by Rachmaninoff and others—to focus on that eighteenth variation.

Rachmaninoff and Inversion

A sketch for the eighteenth variation appears in a notebook that Rachmaninoff used for the Fourth Concerto, Op. 40 (1926), and the *Three Russian Songs*, Op. 41 (1927). Although it is tempting to posit that the sketch for the eighteenth variation dates from as early as 1927, the notebook also contains sketches for the *Symphonic Dances*, Op. 45 (1940), so it might be safer to argue that Rachmaninoff turned to this particular notebook because it had blank pages to work out ideas for works that were completed after 1927.[7]

A look at the sketch (Rachmaninoff's original pencil sketch is given in Figure 1; Example 1 provides the author's transcription) reveals that four features of the eighteenth variation were fixed in Rachmaninoff's imagination at the time: 1) the tonality of D-flat major (or at least D major); 2) a metrical organization in $\frac{3}{4}$ instead of the $\frac{2}{4}$ of the Paganini; 3) a structure of at least two iterations, with one ending on the dominant and the second ending on the tonic; and, perhaps most strikingly, 4) its status as an *inversion* of the original caprice, which Rachmaninoff first sketched in A major and then

Figure 1. Rachmaninoff's original pencil sketch, giving details of the Paganini theme and its manipulations.

transposed to D-flat major.[8] Neither of the two major sets of variations of this Paganini caprice prior to Rachmaninoff's—the Liszt mentioned above, and Brahms's two books of fourteen variations each (Op. 35)—features an inversion of the Paganini. One might have expected inversion in the Brahms; his facility with canon, fugue, and other contrapuntal legerdemain placed him in a special category among Romantic-era composers.[9]

How did this inversion come to be? Let us first place to the side Nicolas Slonimsky's assertion that the "Big Tune" is "the precise reproduction of a passage from William Byrd's *Credo* in the Mass for three voices with the words 'non erit finis,' which Rachmaninoff happened to have heard in March 1934."[10] While the voices at this moment in the Byrd (mm. 200–210) share the same melodic contour as the first four notes of the eighteenth variation, the downward leap at the end of the figure is not fixed: it is as small as a minor third and as large as a perfect fifth—the same as the downward leap in the Rachmaninoff. Furthermore, Slonimsky neither provided evidence of wheher or where Rachmaninoff heard the Byrd, nor explained why Rachmaninoff did not see the possibility of inversion prior to hearing the *Credo*, especially since his sketch shows Rachmaninoff inverted the entire caprice and not just the first five notes of the Paganini. The extant evidence suggests that Rachmaninoff came upon the idea of inverting the caprice on his own, though he may have been familiar with Max Reger's *Variations on a Theme of Mozart*, Op. 132 (1914), a once-popular orchestral composition that features the inversion of the theme in its second variation.[11]

Example 1. Transcription of Rachmaninoff's original sketch.

Inversion was in the air when Rachmaninoff was writing his *Rhapsody*, though not for the kind of music he was writing. The year 1923 saw the publication of Arnold Schoenberg's Suite for Piano, Op. 25, the first of his compositions where serial procedures determined all the pitch materials. Schoenberg limited his choices to eight tone rows: P–0 and P–6 (*P* stands for prime), their inversions (I–0 and I–6), and the retrogrades of these four rows.[12] Whatever musical exposure Rachmaninoff may have had to Schoenberg's excursions into dodecaphony, the talk among musicians of prime, inversion, retrograde, and retrograde inversion—at times in awe but often in mockery—would have been hard to escape.

Thus it is worth considering that, in finding his way to an inversion of the Paganini and in using it in three variations—the scherzando fourteenth and fifteenth variations as well as the eighteenth—Rachmaninoff was obliquely addressing the new music around him through an inside musical joke. Just as Leonard Bernstein could write a twelve-tone fugue subject in *West Side Story* and label it "cool," so, too, could Rachmaninoff manipulate musical material more than two decades earlier in ways that followed Schoenbergian procedures, but with results that were vastly different and popular: warm to the point of risking being overripe.[13]

There are also some numerological considerations that may be in play. Another one of Schoenberg's twelve-tone compositions—the Variations for Orchestra, Op. 28 (1926–28)—has twelve movements and positions the theme after an introduction. If Schoenberg was composing twelve movements as a covert reflection of dodecaphony, perhaps Rachmaninoff composed twenty-four movements as an overt homage to Paganini's having positioned his A-minor caprice in the twenty-fourth slot of his own composition. Certainly no other composer who has varied this caprice has felt compelled to ring this many changes on the original, so Rachmaninoff's design can look both backwards to Paganini and forwards to Schoenberg. As speculative as parsing the reasons for twenty-four variations might seem, it feels like more than a happy coincidence that the *Rhapsody*'s most melodic and most memorable variation is identified with the same number—18—as Rachmaninoff's most melodic and most memorable piano concerto: the Concerto No. 2 in C Minor, Op. 18 (1901). By the time of the *Rhapsody*'s premiere, the concerto had achieved and maintained its status as Rachmaninoff's most famous concerto, and that work was poised to have even greater double exposure just two years after Rachmaninoff's death in 1943: first, as the soundtrack to David Lean's 1945 film *Brief Encounter*; and second, in Buddy Kaye and Ted Mossman's hit song of the same year, *Full Moon and Empty Arms*, based on the second theme from the concerto's third movement (which, at its second iteration, is heard in the key of D-flat major).[14]

Rachmaninoff and Commerce

The hyper-romanticism of the eighteenth variation—what I have characterized as its overripeness—was deliberate on Rachmaninoff's part. The composer-pianist could easily be caricatured, both in his supposedly epigonal music and his physical appearance, the classic putdown being Stravinsky's remark that Rachmaninoff was a six-and-a-half-foot scowl.[15] In the eighteenth variation, Rachmaninoff provided a parody of his own melodic efflorescence, something that critics argued had waned ever since the Second Concerto. In writing this hypermelodic melody, itself an overturning of the Paganini and a possible sly reference to Schoenberg, Rachmaninoff anticipated the hyper-romanticism that would become the calling card for Hollywood film score composers such as Erich Wolfgang Korngold, Max Steiner, and others. In short, he wrote music for Hollywood before Hollywood was asking for such music, and he did so with a twinkle in his eye.

Pianist Vladimir Horowitz was in on the joke at the time Rachmaninoff was composing the *Rhapsody*:

> In Lucerne, Horowitz reveled in his close proximity to Rachmaninoff and was flattered when the older man would consult him on a work-in-progress. For instance, in 1934, when composing his *Rhapsody on a Theme of Paganini*, Rachmaninoff telephoned him nearly every day: "I have a new variation to play for you," he would announce. The composer's caustic humor about his own works endlessly amused Horowitz. "I have composed this one for my manager," he joked about the eighteenth variation. "Well, maybe this will save the piece."[16]

Or *was* it a joke? Horowitz told the same story another time to the same person, but with a different ending:

> I remember when we were in Switzerland, during one summer when he was composing the *Rhapsody on a Theme of Paganini*, a terrific piece. A little more modern-sounding, difficult, too, but not so many notes as the Third Concerto. Rachmaninoff played it the best.
>
> Each day, Rachmaninoff would call me over, and he would play for me his newest variation. At the No. 18 Variation, I say to him, "Oh, this sounds like the older Rachmaninoff," and he tells me, "Yes, I compose this variation for my manager. Maybe it will save the piece." You know that Rachmaninoff suffered that the critics didn't like his music? He tried to change his style a little. They always said he composed like Tchaikovsky, he's not of our century. This hurt Rachmaninoff very much.[17]

Although the eighteenth variation can be both heartfelt and ironic at the same time, the evidence of the *Rhapsody* as a whole and the structure of the variation suggest that raillery was always an aim. The opening and closing gestures that bookend the work feature a quiet cadence in the home key, something unexpected in a concerto for large forces and certainly uncommon as a final gesture, which itself is ambiguous as to whether the major or minor mode is indicated. The only other quiet ending I can think of is Berg's Violin Concerto, and there the affect is worlds removed from Rachmaninoff's conception, even though the works are separated by only a year. Meanwhile, the variation itself, with its piling on of instruments and volume and its literal raising of the stakes to a fever pitch in the third iteration, seems calculated not simply to tug at heartstrings but to yank them to the breaking point. Indeed, as the third iteration unfolds, the music begins to collapse back upon itself, as if to say that sustaining emotion at such a high level is exhausting and unsustainable. As with the last of the four variations in the Third Concerto, so too here does the orchestra drop out and the pianist is left alone to bring the proceedings to a quiet close.

This ending features chains of unresolved chords that, often as not, stand outside of what might be considered standard harmonic practice, which is one way that Rachmaninoff maintained dramatic tension in this coda. Before the orchestra dies out, the downbeats of this third section are harmonically unstable and resolve on the subsequent beat. Then, with the orchestra tacit, the piano weaves chains of augmented chords that waft upward, their trajectory anchored by the low D♭ in the left hand while at the same time resisting establishing a clear harmonic direction. These chords are sonic fog, atmospheric mist that trails off, only to have the piano emphatically conclude by repeating the opening of the variation, one octave lower from where it all began, a solemn valedictory to a moment of emotional seism and purgation.[18]

I linger on these amorphous chords, because Rachmaninoff throughout the *Rhapsody* rang the changes on the one moment in the original caprice that momentarily disrupts the common harmonic progression of Paganini's day of tonic-dominant and the circle of fifths. In the parlance of music theory, the antepenultimate harmony in the caprice is identified as an augmented sixth chord, so named because of the interval between the lowest note and what often is the highest note. (It may seem strange to some to speak of "harmony" in the caprice, given that it is a single-line composition with no other supporting voices, but nearly all monophonic music from Bach to Bartók contains harmonic implications in how the line unfolds.)

The augmented sixth chord's piquancy meant that composers would use it sparingly, lest it lose its aural sapor, and one often finds it in this antepenultimate position, where it is followed by the dominant and then the final tonic (see Example 2).

A look back to Rachmaninoff's sketch for the eighteenth variation reveals that this piquant moment was also imagined from the start, with the only accidentals in the inversion occurring in the same antepenultimate location as in the caprice. And that momentary rupture of the music's "normal" harmonic flow grabs the listener's ears by virtue of its violation of the harmonic "norms" from what standard harmony—even late Romantic era harmony—might predict. It is an auditory paroxysm, a sonic *frisson*, an overly fecund three seconds of musical bliss.

If the prose above sounds over the top, I have meant it that way, because this variation and this one chord sound over the top—Rachmaninoff out-Rachmaninoffing himself, giving not just his manager something to sell but the audience something to buy and the critics something to bay over. This melody, with its pungent reinterpretation of the augmented sixth chord, repulses some and enraptures many, many more. As Horowitz said, the old Rachmaninoff is back, but the sly and wry Rachmaninoff is also present, the one whose technical polish, in this moment, packaged emotional sincerity as a commodity.

Before we think more fully of the eighteenth variation as a commodity to be bought and sold, the antepenultimate chord, which I have suggested permeates the entire *Rhapsody*, deserves a bit more unpacking. The opening introduction to the work is a "variation" on this chord, sending

Example 2. Niccolò Paganini, Caprice in A Minor, Op. 1, No. 24. Augmented sixth is shaded.

it through various permutations and ending with a final, crunching, *Sacre du printemps* dissonance, followed by the dominant and tonic harmonies. This is Rachmaninoff's augmentation of Paganini's augmented sixth chord. I have already limned the sonic fog at the end of the eighteenth variation, which is, again, an outworking of the same chord. Indeed, in Rachmaninoff's hands, this sonority is the functional equivalent of a "stinger chord": a trope in film music that is meant to command the attention of the viewer.[19] As these examples from the *Rhapsody* suggest, stinger chords need not always be loud and highly dissonant; what they are meant to do is to trouble the mood of the moment by means of introducing a sonic disjuncture of some kind—of volume or timbre or, typically in the *Rhapsody*, harmony. In the case of the eighteenth variation, the stinger chord intensifies the moment by means of its harmonic displacement and, hence, surprise. And appearing as it does late in Rachmaninoff's career, when dodecaphony and neoclassicism were becoming the reigning ideologies of musical commerce in the rarefied world of art music, the red-blooded and unapologetic Romanticism of the eighteenth variation is Hollywood *avant la lettre*. Rachmaninoff, like the film score composers who followed him, engaged in the business of making money.

Indeed, Rachmaninoff was not being completely tongue-in-cheek with Horowitz about the role the eighteenth variation might play in making the *Rhapsody* programmable on his tours. A compendium of all of his performances has yet to appear, but by 1934 only the second of his four piano concertos had caught fire with audiences and other pianists. The First, both the 1891 original version and the 1917 revised version, received few performances beyond those by the composer himself; the Third—whose slow movement is in D-flat major—was premiered in 1910 but failed to achieve a firm toehold during Rachmaninoff's lifetime in the repertoires of other performers (its dedicatee, Josef Hofmann, never performed it; Horowitz would win for it a permanent place in the repertoire); and there are no performances by Rachmaninoff of the Fourth between 1930 and 1940, the year of its revision.[20] If the *Rhapsody* was going to succeed, Rachmaninoff thought, its success would rise or fall on the appeal of the eighteenth variation.

His hunch paid off. Between its premiere in late 1934 and his death in early 1943, Rachmaninoff performed the *Rhapsody* on no fewer than thirty-nine occasions; in contrast, he performed the Second Concerto thirty-seven times in that same period.[21] And evidence that the eighteenth variation was propelling the popularity of the *Rhapsody* can be located in the music publishing industry. His American publisher, Charles Foley, came out with a two-piano version of the eighteenth variation in the same year as the entire *Rhapsody* appeared, something that required little additional typesetting given that the two-piano version of the *Rhapsody*, instead of the orchestral score, is the version most pianists would purchase. Foley published piano solo and violin and piano arrangements—both in D major—in 1953, the same year as *The Story of Three Loves*, and the arrangements have mushroomed ever since.[22]

Perhaps the only thing that has kept the eighteenth variation from being even more commercially available is that the work remains under copyright in the United States and thus requires licensing at the present time. How else to explain Eric Carmen's failure to set the *Rhapsody*'s "Big Tune" to words in the way he had done with the slow movements of the Second Concerto (*All By Myself*, 1975) and the Second Symphony (*Never Gonna Fall In Love Again*, 1976)?[23] But words or no, the eighteenth variation has become one of Rachmaninoff's most played compositions on the ice rink, with no fewer than twenty-eight ice-skating and ice-dancing routines set to its music since 1986. Here again it rivals the Second Concerto, which accompanied at least twenty-six ice-skating and ice-dancing routines in the same period.[24]

Rachmaninoff and Time

Commerce, the ice rink, and romance meet in the movies. The eighteenth variation has appeared in at least five commercially available films: *The Story of Three Loves* (1953), *Somewhere in Time* (1980), *Singapore Sling* (1990), *Groundhog Day* (1993), and *Ronin* (1998). This last movie references Alfred Hitchcock's 1956 suspense thriller *The Man Who Knew Too Much*, where an attempted assassination occurs during a climactic moment in an orchestral performance. In *Ronin*, the successful assassination takes place as the fictional figure skater Natacha Kirilova (played by German skater Katarina Witt) performs a routine to the eighteenth variation. The continuity of the music is constantly disrupted, and it is unclear whether Kirilova skated to the variation as a continuous composition. Indeed, the entire sequence in the film lasts just over five minutes, so either some repeat of the variation was worked into the routine or the cinematic time does not match musical time. Whichever the case, the emotional weight of the music and the slow unfolding of the violent murder, committed indirectly by Kirilova's Mafioso boyfriend, work in tandem to reinforce the heightened mood of the moment.

Three of the other films that deploy the eighteenth variation play upon the notion that its music is of another time, functioning as an aural wormhole. These three deal with love in some fashion: unconsummated love in *The Story of Three Loves*, rom-com love in *Groundhog Day*, and everlasting love in *Somewhere in Time*. The latter has led to the eighteenth variation being adopted as a potential wedding staple, but all three deal with the ephemeral nature of time, of love lost in one point in history and possibly regained in another. The eighteenth variation buttresses the films' stance that no hardship or tragedy can displace true love.

The first of the trilogy of stories in *The Story of Three Loves*, "The Jealous Lover," recounts the death of Paula Woodard (played by Scottish ballet dancer and actress Moira Shearer). Paula is an aspiring ballerina who discovers that she suffers from some undisclosed condition that makes a career in dance life-threatening. The discovery of the malady occurs after a rehearsal of a new work being choreographed by Charles Coudray (James Mason), during which she faints in front of Coudray and the others. (Frederick Ashton was the choreographer for the dance sequences; in 1980 he would create the ballet *Rhapsody*, using the entire Rachmaninoff.) Paula attends the premiere of the work, and after everyone has left, she finds her way to the stage where she moves to the music in her head. Coudray sees her and insists that she has captured the spirit of the music better than he has. He demands that she come to his house where she will dance for him as he makes notes. As she contemplates which outfit Coudray has made available for her, we hear the climactic cadenza of Variation XXII on the other side of the door: a stinger chord of sorts, as it startles Paula (and us). We cut to Coudray at the gramophone, who fields a phone call asking him why he's not at the post-premiere party: "Tell them I'm finding something really worth celebrating!" Paula emerges from the other room in an elegant white gown with matching tiara and toe shoes, and the music segues from the end of

Variation XXIII to Variation XII as Paula lithely begins her interpretation of the *Rhapsody*. Coudray encourages her improvisation. She stops when the variation ends, but Coudray insists that she continue. Variation XVI ensues, a transition to truncated renditions of Variations XIX and XX, and then a second transition incorporating the introduction to Variation XVI that takes us to the eighteenth variation, which is performed in its entirety (and includes a third D-flat major piano chord at its end). Coudray is enraptured by Paula, and, with the eighteenth variation as underscoring, he pleads with her not to leave him and speaks of how she will now become his muse: "I want us to be together. I want us to do these things together. I want you to be with me always." Paula promises, "I will be with you," and they kiss. (You can guess which part of the variation accompanies their kiss, and you would guess correctly.) She retreats to change out of her costume, and Coudray sings to himself snippets of the eighteenth variation, but she surreptitiously leaves without Coudray making the connection between her and the girl who collapsed: "I don't even know your name." Paula returns home, where her Aunt Lydia (Agnes Moorehead) asks her about the premiere. Paula relates the story of what happened at Coudray's home ("I danced! Darling, I danced!"), much to Lydia's consternation. Lydia tells Paula that the two of them can discuss these matters further in the morning, and Paula retreats up the stairs and out of view, only to come tumbling down to the landing. Lydia gathers her in her arms as Paula utters her final words: "I promised to be with him." And then, after Lydia's sobbing has subsided—the climax of the eighteenth variation.

At this distance, the interposition of the Rachmaninoff sounds like a miscalculation, as if it derides the nearly impossible (and likely exploitative) love between two unequal partners. But in the wake of *Brief Encounter*, the music appears to signal the intensity of the love that Coudray did have for Paula, as the scene returns to the ocean liner where the story began and where we see Coudray refuse to tell an adoring fan why he permanently removed the work from his repertoire. Now, at the end of what has been a flashback, Coudray looks poignantly into the distance as the eighteenth variation continues and the film segues to the next *Three Loves* story. Time, for Coudray, has temporarily stood still, and the eighteenth variation has haunted him and will haunt him forever.

A different kind of enchantment occurs in *Groundhog Day*, the story of meteorologist Phil Connors (Bill Murray) getting stuck in a time loop in Punxsutawney, Pennsylvania. Groundhog Day (February 2) endlessly repeats until the spell is broken by Phil persuading his producer, Rita Hanson (Andie MacDowell), that he truly is in love with her, and Rita surrendering to his advances by returning with him to his hotel room.

The moment that convinces Rita that Phil is a catch comes at a dance sponsored by the townspeople at which Phil is the keyboardist for the dance band. Phil had never played piano before, but the constant repetition of the same day leads him to sign up for piano lessons in an attempt to better himself. (It is not explained how each day can be a repeat and some events reoccur each day all while Phil makes progress as a pianist.) The piece he eventually masters: the eighteenth variation. And when Rita enters the ballroom, he signals the band to stop, whereupon he plays, solo, the first four measures of the variation (in the key of D major and in $\frac{3}{4}$). He then invites the band to rejoin him in a $\frac{4}{4}$ jazz version of the variation, complete with the stinger chord and ending with a blues oscillation followed by downward Jerry Lee Lewis glissandi on the keyboard to bring the hot rendition to a close. (Rita: "I didn't know you could play like that!" Phil: "I'm versatile.") So here the time it takes Phil to learn the Rachmaninoff is immaterial, but its role in helping to cinch his amorous intentions is of a piece with how the variation functioned for Charles Coudray in *The Story of Three Loves*: it is the sonic representation of timeless love, albeit a more modern kind of timeless love.

As important as the eighteenth variation is for *Groundhog Day* and *The Story of Three Loves*, it found its popular zenith in *Somewhere in Time*. Rather than a flashback, the movie's plot revolves around time travel. Richard Collier (Christopher Reeve) is an up-and-coming playwright whose new play, *Too Much Spring*, is premiered in a Millfield College Workshop performance on 19 May 1972. At the reception following the premiere, Richard is startled by a well-dressed elderly woman (Susan French), who takes his right hand, places an elaborate pocket watch in it, closes his hand, enfolds his hand in both of hers, and tells him in a whisper: "Come back to me." The woman's age and appearance mark her literally as living outside the time and place of Richard's friends, who ask him who she is. Richard: "I never saw her in my life." We then see the woman being driven home in an older British automobile—the chauffeur is on the right side of the vehicle—and returning her to her dwelling, which is a suite in a grand old hotel situated near a body of water. Another woman, whom we later discover is her housekeeper and companion, greets her upon her return, but the elderly woman does not acknowledge her. Instead she enters the living room, closes the door behind her, and places a London/ffrr (full frequency range recording) LP on the turntable.[25] As she looks at the playbill and stares off into the distance, we hear the eighteenth variation. We see her tear-stained face as she stares out to the water, and then, as she sits in a rocking chair with the playbill in her hand and a model of the hotel to her left, she brings the playbill to her chest and slowly rocks back and forth as the Rachmaninoff plays in the background.

The music continues as a crossfade takes us to Chicago eight years later. We are now in Richard's home office, where he is trying to write a new play. The camera pans across windows overlooking the Chicago skyline to the office wall, where a playbill for *Too Much Spring* hangs on the wall in a framed triptych of his works, and then to Richard, who is gazing out the window in a distracted fashion. By this point, we have passed the climax of the third iteration, and the music is winding down. A cut reveals a wide shot of the office, where Toby Cole's 1961 anthology, *Playwrights on Playwrighting*, is open and lying flat on the desk, and a 1972 recording of Mahler's Tenth Symphony with the New Philharmonia Orchestra conducted by Wyn Morris leans against the stereo system, which has a turntable on top playing the Rachmaninoff. Richard moves away from the window and returns to his desk, where there is a piece of paper in his IBM Selectric typewriter. He goes to make a phone call but places the receiver back on the cradle before dialing. He yanks the paper out of the typewriter, balls it up, throws it on the ground, and gets up to remove the tonearm from the LP just as the chain of upwardly wafting indeterminate chords are heard. In other words, there is no cadence as Richard interrupts the music—and, potentially, its meaning for him.

How the eighteenth variation unites the two is revealed when Richard, having stumbled upon the grand hotel, enters its Hall of History, and reads a newspaper clipping hanging on the wall. He stops in his tracks, and the audience hears the eighteenth variation. We discover that he is reading about Elise McKenna, an actress who lived at the hotel and died the day after the premiere of *Too Much Spring*. He sees a photo of her at the end of the room and is entranced, something the audience can intuit because of the Rachmaninoff playing in the soundtrack. He tracks down the housekeeper, discovers that the model of the hotel is a music box that plays the eighteenth variation, which he calls his favorite piece, and learns that the pocket watch he received had gone missing at the time of McKenna's death. Then, after having learned about time travel through one of his former professors, he wills himself back to 1912 and the same hotel, where he meets Elise (Jane Seymour)—again!—and where they fall in love.

During a moment where the two are rowing across the lake, Richard starts humming the eighteenth variation.

> Elise: "It's beautiful! What is it?"
> Richard: "It's Rachmaninoff . . . from the *Rhapsody*." [Which we know was not yet composed in 1912]
> Elise: "Hmm. I saw him with the Philharmonic once. I love his music, but I've never heard this piece."

Richard: "Really? Well, I'll introduce it to you sometime."

As it happens, Richard isn't able to introduce Elise to the *Rhapsody*. In showing off a coin pocket in his circa 1900 suit, he extracts a 1979 penny. In a daze he reaches for Elise, who is screaming his name as Richard is cast back to the present, where he soon dies of despair at the hotel. Why a 1934 composition did not thrust him back is left unexplored. But clearly Elise did hear the Rachmaninoff and knew it was the same piece that Richard had hummed to her in 1912. She, too, made it her favorite piece because it reminded her of Richard. And while we do not hear the Rachmaninoff during the denouement, when they are reunited in the after-life, we do hear John Barry's title theme, with its surging strings and rippling piano accompaniment, a more popular companion to the eigh-teenth variation.

Despite its poor showing at the box office in 1980, *Somewhere in Time* found an audience when it appeared on cable television the following year, and the title track and the Rachmaninoff both went on to become wedding staples. In this, they compete in the marriage market with Pachelbel's Canon, which was featured in *Ordinary People*, also released in 1980. How that film about a profoundly dysfunctional family begot wedding music is a mystery; how *Somewhere in Time* also conquered the marriage market is overdetermined, given its message of finding one's true love no matter what. And the variation's association with the film can help explain its prominence on the ice from 1986 forward as well as its pivotal role in *Groundhog Day*, *Sparky's Magic Piano*, and other post-1980 films and television shows that employ the variation.[26]

Conclusion

The year is 2013. The eighteenth variation is featured prominently in the launch trailer for the release of the video game *Gran Turismo 6*. The first solo piano iteration features images associated with the legendary Brazilian racing driver Ayrton Senna and the Instituto Ayrton Senna, dedicated to helping foster the human development of young Brazilians and founded shortly after Senna's fatal crash in 1994. When the orches-tra enters for the second iteration, the video switches to designers of the video game, showing the care and precision they put into physical and digital models and renderings. Then, halfway through the video and at the moment where the harmonically unstable augmented chords hang in the air, the music of video game composer Daiki Kasho takes over with its pounding drums, prominent bass, and synthesized voices as it accom-panies short clip after short clip of race cars of all vintages screaming and screeching across the screen. Both the Rachmaninoff and the Kasho signify passion: the eighteenth variation, the old-school craft of beautiful artistry; the Kasho, the testosterone-driven world of the racetrack and the muscle car.

And yet the presence of the eighteenth variation in a video game trailer feels apropos. The music conjures a bygone era, which it did at the time of its premiere. It is music of its time and out of time, legible—audible—across generations and populations. It is classic and popular at the same time, not unlike Formula One cars and vintage Jaguars. Its outsized impact was designed deliberately to express and impress—to express Rachmaninoff's aesthetic and to impress those exposed to it:

> I do not deal in abstractions or cerebral torturings and posturings. I utilize musical narrative, telling a story in musical terms as writers do in words. I wish to encompass the listener in warmth, and to reveal and open to him rich landscapes, to transport him to an ideal planet. Not utopia, for there is an undercurrent of sorrow in my work. But a place where suffering and peace are transcended into a healing whole.[27]

Rachmaninoff ascribed visual imagery to his creative process, yet few of his instrumental works have names that identify imagery (compare the titles for the four movements of the Suite No. 1 for Two Pianos, Op. 5; and *Isle of the Dead*, Op. 29). Perhaps he felt, after having provided in January 1930 "secret explanations" of five of his *Études-tableaux* to assist Ottorino Respighi in his orchestrations only to sour on Respighi's work, that the less he divulged about what a piece evoked in his mind, the better.[28] Certainly the ad men would have loved a nickname for the eighteenth variation to include in their marketing campaigns, something akin to the "Creme de Menthe" designation that Rachmaninoff bestowed upon the final variation.[29]

But we know the eighteenth variation today simply as "the Eighteenth Variation"—a musical moment that, in some way, needs no additional signifier. It has a prehistory: it was concretized in 1934 and can be traced back to sketches and the Paganini. And it has a reception history. But in some ways, the Eighteenth Variation has always been a part of us, whether we knew it or not, whether we know it or not: unnamed, faintly familiar, ever elusive, nearly always welcomed.

NOTES

I would like to thank my colleagues in Dartmouth's Society of Fellows for their input to a presentation on these ideas that I gave in spring 2021. I would also like to thank Richard Beaudoin, Will Cheng, and Rowland Moseley for their insights and suggestions. The editor of this volume, Philip Ross Bullock, has been immensely helpful and supportive to a relative newcomer in this musicological subfield. This article is dedicated in gratitude to Richard Taruskin, who led me to reaffirm my love of late Rachmaninoff.

1. *Sparky's Magic Piano*, dir. Lee Mishkin, 1987, is an animated expansion of the Capitol 1947 record of the same name. The voice actors for the animated cartoon include Vincent Price, Coral Browne, Tony Curtis, Cloris Leachman, Josh Rodine, Mel Blanc, and William Schallert, and Lalo Schifrin conducts the Paris Philharmonic Orchestra, with Leonard Pennario as the pianist.

2. Dan Fox, arr., *World's Greatest Wedding Music: 50 of the Most Requested Wedding Pieces* (Van Nuys, CA: Alfred Music, 2007).

3. Barrie Martyn, *Rachmaninoff: Composer, Pianist, Conductor* (Aldershot, UK: Scolar Press, 1990), 315.

4. Martyn considers the sixteenth variation in the Chopin variations "the lyrical equivalent in this work of the famous eighteenth variation in the *Paganini Rhapsody* more than thirty years later, whose D-flat tonality, despite the key signature, it shares" (146). While there is a passage in the sixteenth variation in which D-flat major is tonicized, the variation is in F minor, which the key signature clearly indicates and the final cadence confirms. In contrast, the twenty-first variation is unmistakably in D-flat major, which may reflect the importance of the root-position Neapolitan chord in Rachmaninoff's source material, namely, the C-minor Chopin prelude.

5. For D-flat major "as a key area, as a concept . . . [of] special significance in Rachmaninoff's oeuvre as a whole" and of the *Rhapsody*'s particular place in that oeuvre, see Blair Allen Johnston, "Harmony and Climax in the Late Works of Sergei Rachmaninoff" (PhD diss., University of Michigan, 2009), 236–53.

6. Beethoven, 32 Variations in C Minor, WoO 80; Handel, "The Harmonious Blacksmith," the final movement from Suite No. 5 in E major, HWV 430; Haydn, Variations in F Minor, Hob. XVII:6; Mendelssohn, *Variations sérieuses*, Op. 54; Tausig, two-hand arrangement of the Andantino varié from Schubert's four-hand *Divertissement über französische Motive*, D. 823; and Schumann, *Etudes symphoniques*, Op. 13. Martyn, *Rachmaninoff: Composer, Pianist, Conductor*, 418–35.

7. The notebook—a Christmas 1922 gift to Rachmaninoff from Eugene Somoff—is in the Russian National Museum of Music, Moscow (inventory number F18.1424). As David Butler Cannata writes, "Previous scholars have only identified this source as containing material used for the *Fourth Concerto* and the *Three Russian Songs* . . . However, in this document Rachmaninoff also recorded materials for both the *Rhapsody on a Theme of Paganini* and the *Symphonic Dances*. On f. 32r we find Rachmaninoff's initial manipulation of the Paganini theme. . . . The many sketches for the *Fourth Concerto* and the *Three Russian Songs* that appear before f. 32r indicate that Rachmaninoff had this book handy between 1923–6." See Cannata, *Rachmaninoff and the Symphony* (Innsbruck: Studien Verlag, 1999), 55–56.

8. Cannata reproduces the sketch in *Rachmaninoff and the Symphony*, 57, making a number of editorial additions, such as clefs, key signatures, time signatures, and accidentals that are not present in the original.

9. Brahms inverted the fugue theme in his Variations and Fugue on a Theme by Händel, Op. 24, but inversion in fugues is not uncommon. In Brahms's first book of the Paganini variations, the figures in the right hand of Variation 1 reappear in the left hand of Variation 2, but the caprice itself is not inverted.

10. Nicolas Slonimsky, *Supplement to Music Since 1900* (New York: Charles Scribner's Sons, 1986), 264. Cannata dismisses Slonimsky's suggestion (*Rachmaninoff and the Symphony*, 56n1), and Slonimsky failed to account for the presence of inversion in XIV and XV. Short of having Rachmaninoff's account of the sketch, we cannot be certain where the inspiration lies.

11. See Reinhold Brinkmann, "A 'Last Giant in Music': Thoughts on Max Reger in the Twentieth Century," *The Musical Quarterly* 87 (2005): 643.

12. For more information on serial composition, see Dave Headlam, Robert Hasegawa, Paul Lansky, and George Perle, "Twelve-note composition," *Oxford Music Online*, https://doi.org/10.1093/gmo/9781561592630.article.44582.

13. Rachmaninoff spoke to the difference between his aesthetic and Schoenberg's: "My melodic line is quite up-to-date if you analyze it and realize its declaration and spartan economy. Sibelius has this also. But Schoenberg and Hindemith have an entirely different approach. They are more incisive; they declare themselves in shorter phrases; there is a sharpness and a decided strong accent felt throughout. My 'genie' would not permit this, excellent as it is for them. I prefer to evolve my thematic material slowly without over-aggression or over-emphasis." Glenn Quilty, "Rachmaninoff—The Last Romantic Composer," *HiFi Review* 3/4 (October 1959): 26.

14. For more on the Lean film, see Richard Dyer, *Brief Encounter*, 2nd ed. (London: Palgrave, 2015), esp. 22–23. For more on Mossman, see "Full Moon & Empty Arms," *Time*, 23 June 1947, http://www.time.com/time/magazine/article/0,9171,798001,00.html.

15. Igor Stravinsky, in Robert Craft, *Conversations with Igor Stravinsky* (New York: Doubleday, 1959), 42.

16. Glenn Plaskin, *Horowitz: A Biography of Vladimir Horowitz* (New York: Quill, 1983), 186.

17. David Dubal, *Evenings with Horowitz: A Personal Portrait* (New York: Carol Publishing, 1991), 181.

18. In Elgar's "Nimrod" variation, the beginning of this "fourth iteration" is marked *fortissimo* with a crescendo; in the Rachmaninoff, the beginning of the "fourth iteration" is marked *piano*.

19. For more on stinger chords, see David Neumeyer, "Film Music Analysis and Pedagogy," *Indiana Theory Review* 11 (1990): 1–27, at 4n6; and Claudia Gorbman, *Unheard Melodies: Narrative Film Music* (Bloomington: Indiana University Press, 1987), 88–89.

20. For Rachmaninoff's concerto repertoire, see https://www.rachmaninoffdiary.com/category/diary-entry/solo-pianist-with-orchestra/. For Hofmann, see Martyn, *Rachmaninoff: Composer, Pianist, Conductor*, 216.

21. The figures for all five concerted works between 1934 and 1943, with Rachmaninoff as soloist: the First (13 performances); the Second (37 perf.); the Third (18 perf.); the Fourth (6 perf., all of the 1940 revised version); and the *Rhapsody* (39 perf.). See https://www.rachmaninoffdiary.com/category/diary-entry/solo-pianist-with-orchestra/.

22. The arrangement for piano was adapted for piano solo by Hermene W. Eichhorn and first appeared in 1943, the year of Rachmaninoff's death; the one for violin and piano was arranged by Fritz Kreisler.

23. Carmen is American, and these two Rachmaninoff works, unlike the *Rhapsody*, were not under copyright in the United States in the 1970s. Carmen settled with the Rachmaninoff estate once his songs became international hits. See "How It Works: Music Copyright for International Use," *Music Mayhem Magazine*, 20 May 2021, https://musicmayhemmagazine.com/how-it-works-music-copyright-for-international-use/.

24. For the use of the *Rhapsody* in figure skating routines, see https://figure-skating.fandom.com/wiki/Rhapsody_on_a_Theme_of_Paganini and https://figure-skating.fandom.com/wiki/Piano_Concerto_No._2_(Rachmaninoff).

25. The performance of the eighteenth variation in *Somewhere in Time* features Lynda Cochrane, piano, with the Royal Scottish National Orchestra, John Debney, conductor. There is a 1972 recording of the *Rhapsody* on London, with Vladimir Ashkenazy, piano,

with the London Symphony Orchestra, André Previn, conductor, making it a new release when we see it on the turntable on 19 May 1972 (London CS 6776) It is a "full frequency range recording."

26. The deployment of the eighteenth variation in movies and television shows since 1980 often draws upon the legacy of *Somewhere in Time*, which perverted the music's use as a romantic theme. In *Singapore Sling* (dir. Nikos Nikolaidis, 1990), the variation underscores the climax of the film: a double homicide between two individuals who had been engaged in sadomasochistic sex for much of the film. We witness both characters succumb to the attacks they committed against each other: the woman, sliced open through her genitals by the man, bleeds to death; and the man, shot twice by the woman, falls into an open grave he had dug earlier. A different form of perversion occurs in the short Croatian comedy-romance *Nikolina & Tomislav* (dir. Marin Mandir, 2013). The two title characters accidentally meet as they search for their exes, who happen to have the exact same first and last names. At the end of the film, the new couple sees their exes, paired up and arguing. It is unclear whether this sighting is real or imaginary, yet it does not appear to matter. They shrug, and as they walk off into the distance holding hands, the eighteenth variation starts at its second iteration and continues over the credits. In "Winning Ugly," an episode of television's *The Good Wife* (dir. Rosemary Rodriguez, 12 April 2015), a flowery title card announces "A Romantic Interlude," which is followed by (male) actors in directors' chairs reading sexy emails. Framing the video is this explanatory text: "A pair of highly talented thespians lend their divine talents to the latest modern love story: The Tale of Saint Alicia Florrick [the central character in *The Good Wife*] and her Recently Deceased Employer. Truly the love story of our time. Sit back, pour a fine drink, and take in the sensual yet delicate words of the email romantics." The eighteenth variation plays throughout the scene, which cuts to a commercial at its conclusion. For other references to the eighteenth variation in film and television, see imdb.com/name/nm0006245/.

27. Quilty, "Rachmaninoff—The Last Romantic Composer," 28.

28. For the "secret explanations," see Serge Bertensson and Jay Leyda, *Sergei Rachmaninoff: A Lifetime in Music* (Bloomington: Indiana University Press, 2001), 262–63; for his disappointment in the Respighi orchestrations, see Martyn, *Rachmaninoff: Composer, Pianist, Conductor*, 314–15.

29. "In 1934 Rachmaninoff played the world premiere of his now celebrated *Rhapsody on a Theme of Paganini* with the Philadelphia orchestra. A few days before the performance, at a New York dinner party, he confessed to me that he was nervous about the opening event. 'I wrote the Variations down,' he said, 'and it looked good. Then I went to the piano and tried it, and it sounded good, but now when I am practicing it for the concert, it all goes wrong.' The composer was especially concerned about a series of excruciating chord jumps in the twenty-fourth of the Variations. Just then a butler entered the room with a tray full of liqueurs. Rachmaninoff, a teetotaler, refused. 'Why Sergei Vasilievich,' I urged, 'you *must* have a glass of Creme de Menthe. It is the best thing in the world for jumps.' 'Do you mean it?' he asked seriously. 'Definitely!' I assured. Whereupon he called the butler back and helped himself to a generous quaff of the emerald cordial. Afterwards, in the drawing room, he gave a faultlessly executed preview of his new composition. Eye-witnesses testify that before the performance in Philadelphia, Rachmaninoff downed another large Creme de Menthe and that, following the spectacular success of the Rhapsody on that occasion, he never failed to have a Creme de Menthe in the greenroom before playing the work publicly. On the score of the Paganini Rhapsody inscribed to me, the twenty-fourth Variation is plainly marked in the composer's hand: 'The Creme de Menthe Variation.'" Benno Moiseiwitsch, "Reminiscences of Rachmaninoff," *Music Journal* 21/1 (1963): 20–21 and 68, at 21.

"One of the Outstanding Musical Events of All Time": The Philadelphia Orchestra's 1939 Rachmaninoff Cycle

CHRISTOPHER H. GIBBS

> To make records with the Philadelphia Symphony Orchestra is as thrilling an experience as any artist could desire. Unquestionably, they are the finest orchestral combination in the world: even the famous New York Philharmonic, which you heard in London under Toscanini last summer, must, I think, take second place. Only by working with the Philadelphians both as soloist and conductor, as has been my privilege, can one fully realise and appreciate their perfection of ensemble.

Thus spake Sergei Rachmaninoff in an interview with *Gramophone* in 1931.[1] This was just one of many instances, over many years, in which he expressed enduring admiration for the Philadelphia Orchestra, "the best of the best."[2] He was willing to alienate other eminent orchestras with famous conductors—such as Toscanini, with whom he never performed—by going on record. Pun intended: the Philadelphia Orchestra accounts for all of Rachmaninoff's recordings as a concerto soloist and as a conductor. It was the ensemble that gave the world premieres of all of the concerted and orchestral pieces he composed in America during his last quarter-century.

The Philadelphia Orchestra became his sonic ideal, what he heard in his inner ear. Music director Eugene Ormandy remembered Rachmaninoff addressing the orchestra at the final rehearsal for the premiere of the *Symphonic Dances*, his last composition:

> When I was a young man, I idolized Chaliapin. He was my ideal, and when I thought of composition I thought of song

and of Chaliapin. Now he is gone. Today, when I think of composing, my thoughts turn to you, the greatest orchestra in the world. For that reason I dedicate this my newest composition to the members of The Philadelphia Orchestra and to your conductor Eugene Ormandy.[3]

The special relationship between Rachmaninoff and the Fabulous Philadelphians (as they came to be known) is explored in this essay, focusing on a particular occasion. During two weeks in late 1939 the orchestra mounted a "Rachmaninoff Cycle," or "Festival," of three concerts in New York and five in Philadelphia to mark the thirtieth anniversary of his American debut.[4] Rachmaninoff appeared as soloist with Ormandy and he conducted the final program himself. The Festival was billed as "one of the outstanding musical events of all time." Publicity hype to be sure, but also revealing of the composer's stature, the culmination of his career as pianist, conductor, and composer. In anticipation of the event, Rachmaninoff wrote to a friend: "This *Festival* seems to be, for some reason, a 'totaling of the sum.'"[5]

The claim about the outstanding historic moment serves as the header for a four-page brochure (see Figure 1) that included two further personal tributes to the Philadelphia Orchestra:

> Philadelphia has the finest orchestra I have ever heard at any time or any place in my whole life.

> I don't know that I would be exaggerating if I said that it was the finest orchestra the world has ever heard.

The brochure lists the three Festival programs (later somewhat modified) and makes the pitch that few composers have ever enjoyed such "worldwide acceptance" during their lifetime and that few performers have sustained such "front rank box-office appeal for half a century." Yet Rachmaninoff, "probably alone in the history of music," has been able to accomplish both these feats. Moreover, "with a shyness characteristic of so many truly great men, Rachmaninoff has never before lent himself to the presentation of a 'festival' or 'cycle.'" The reason he agreed to do so in this instance was because of "his intense admiration for the Philadelphia Orchestra, so often expressed, and his high regard for Eugene Ormandy as a conductor and interpreter of his works."

The extraordinary collaboration between Rachmaninoff and the Philadelphia Orchestra is so well known that it may obscure some of its

PRESENTING THE **RACHMANINOFF** CYCLE
ONE OF THE OUTSTANDING MUSICAL EVENTS OF ALL TIME . . .

WITH
● SERGEI RACHMANINOFF
● EUGENE ORMANDY
● *AND THE* PHILADELPHIA ORCHESTRA

Three Consecutive Sunday Evening Concerts — NOVEMBER 26th,
DECEMBER 3rd, DECEMBER 10th, *at eight forty-five,* Carnegie Hall, New York

Figure 1. Cover page of the brochure for the Rachmaninoff Cycle.

special features. One could argue that their relationship was the closest
that any major composer had with a single orchestra until that time, with
the possible exception of Felix Mendelssohn and the Leipzig Gewandhaus
Orchestra, although they premiered surprisingly few of his major works.
Any vague notion of Mozart or Beethoven collaborating with the Vienna
Philharmonic—or with some putative precursor—is a fantasy. That august

ensemble was founded only in 1842 and did not have as close a relationship as some might think with later composers. The Vienna Philharmonic premiered Brahms's Second and Third symphonies, but only a few of Bruckner's and only Mahler's Ninth (posthumously). Perhaps most comparable, both as conductor and composer, is Edward Elgar's engagement with the London Symphony Orchestra. Another parallel is with Dmitry Shostakovich. He had many fewer options open to him in the Soviet Union, but nonetheless the Leningrad Philharmonic premiered his first six symphonies, albeit under four different conductors; the Beethoven Quartet premiered all but the first and last of his fifteen string quartets. Important composer/performer relationships more often were on a personal level, such as those the eminent violinist Joseph Joachim had with Brahms, Dvořák, Schumann, Bruch, and others. As Rachmaninoff acknowledged, he had enjoyed this with Chaliapin. During his American years his relationship was not with a single musician—that with the violinist Fritz Kreisler came closest—but with what he called the "best orchestra in the world."

The First Thirty Years

Rachmaninoff's bond with the Philadelphians began during his first trip to America in 1909–10, when he conducted the ensemble. Between 1919 and 1936, Leopold Stokowski conducted the premieres, concerto appearances, and recordings, and from January 1937 until their final concert in May 1942 they were led by Ormandy.[6] As we will see, Rachmaninoff continued to conduct the orchestra himself, for recordings in 1929 and 1939, as well as during the Festival. Table 1 lists key events in this long collaboration and Table 2 the repertory that he performed and recorded with the orchestra, all of it his own music except for twice conducting Musorgsky's *Night on Bald Mountain* and once playing Beethoven's First Piano Concerto. The relationship represented a series of firsts in the orchestra's history: the first star soloist to record with them, the first guest conductor to record, and the first composer to record his own music.[7]

There is some irony in the fact that even though Rachmaninoff's initial appearance with an American orchestra took place in Philadelphia, it was not with the hometown band. He began his 1909 visit by giving a recital at Smith College on 4 November and four days later commenced an extended tour with the Boston Symphony Orchestra, conducted by Max Fiedler, playing his Second Piano Concerto at the Academy of Music.[8] As Rachmaninoff would recall thirty years later, Boston "was America's best orchestra then. Today it is still wonderful. But today the Philadelphia Orchestra is the finest in the world."[9] His debut with

Table 1. Timeline of Key Events of Rachmaninoff and the Philadelphia Orchestra 1909–42; 1919–36 conducted by Leopold Stokowski and 1937–43 by Eugene Ormandy

26–27 Nov. 1909	Debut conducting Musorgsky's *Night on Bald Mountain* and Second Symphony
March–April 1919	Performances of Piano Concertos Nos. 1 (revised version) and 2
Feb. 1920	Performances of Piano Concerto No. 3 and U.S. premiere of *The Bells*
April 1921	Performances of Piano Concerto No. 2
Dec. 1923–Jan. 1924	Recording of the Piano Concerto No. 2 (only movements 2 and 3 released)
March–April 1927	World premieres of Piano Concerto No. 4 and *Three Russian Songs*
April 1929	Rachmaninoff conducts recordings of *The Isle of the Dead* and "Vocalise"
April 1929	Recording of Piano Concerto No. 2
7 Nov. 1934	World premiere of *Rhapsody on a Theme of Paganini*
Dec. 1935	Performances of *Rhapsody on a Theme of Paganini*
13 Jan. 1936	Benefit performance of *Rhapsody on a Theme of Paganini*
6 Nov. 1936	World premiere of Symphony No. 3
Jan. 1937	Performances of Piano Concerto No. 2 and *The Bells*
23 Oct. 1937	Benefit performance of Piano Concerto No. 1
Oct. 1938	Performances of Piano Concerto No. 1 with revised Symphony No. 3
8 Nov. 1938	Performance of Beethoven's Piano Concerto No. 1 at Carnegie Hall
Nov.–Dec. 1939	Rachmaninoff Festival (see Table 2)
Dec. 1939	Rachmaninoff conducts recording of Symphony No. 3
Dec. 1939–Feb. 1940	Recordings of Piano Concertos Nos. 1 and 3
Oct.–Nov. 1941	Performances of Piano Concerto No. 4 (premiere of revised version)
3 Jan. 1941	World premiere of the *Symphonic Dances*
Dec. 1941	Recording of Piano Concerto No. 4 (revised version)
9 May 1942	Final appearance playing Piano Concerto No. 2 in Ann Arbor

Table 2. Rachmaninoff's Repertory as Pianist and
Conductor with the Philadelphia Orchestra 1909–42

Listed in order of first performance, followed by the number of total performances; an
asterisk indicates repertory Rachmaninoff recorded with the orchestra. All pieces are by
Rachmaninoff unless indicated.

Symphony No. 2	(2)
Musorgsky, *Night on Bald Mountain*	(2)
*Piano Concerto No. 1	(8)
*Piano Concerto No. 2	(12)
*Piano Concerto No. 3	(5)
*Piano Concerto No. 4	(11)
The Isle of the Dead	(recording only, in 1929)
*"Vocalise"	(recording only, in 1929)
Rhapsody on a Theme of Paganini	(6)
Beethoven, Piano Concerto No. 1	(1)
*Symphony No. 3	(3)
The Bells	(3)

the Philadelphians came later that month when he conducted Musorgsky's
Night on Bald Mountain, his own Second Symphony, and played three of
his preludes.[10]

Rachmaninoff's first trip to the United States was packed with a diz-
zying schedule of recitals and orchestral appearances, twenty-six in all,
that gave him an initial impression of the country, its audiences and halls,
and experiences with some of its leading orchestras.[11] On 28 November,
a day after conducting his second Philadelphia concert, he gave the world
premiere of the Third Piano Concerto with Walter Damrosch leading
the New York Symphony Orchestra; he repeated the work the following month with the Philharmonic Society of New York under its new
music director Gustav Mahler.[12] (These competing orchestras merged in
1928 to what we now know as the New York Philharmonic.) In December
Rachmaninoff played the Second Concerto with the Chicago Symphony
Orchestra under Frederick Stock (and himself conducted *The Isle of the
Dead*) and the next month performed the same concerto with Stokowski
leading the Cincinnati Symphony Orchestra, their first collaboration.[13]
His final appearance in New York City was on 27 January with the Russian

Symphony Orchestra when he again conducted *The Isle of the Dead* and played the Second Concerto under Modest Altschuler.[14]

Rachmaninoff and his family returned to America in November 1918, arriving just before Armistice Day, now an exile who sought extensive performances to rebuild his financial fortunes. His international renown was split among profiles as composer, pianist, and conductor. An observation he made to Oskar von Riesemann in *Rachmaninoff's Recollections* was recycled in the American press: "I have 'hunted three hares.' Can I be sure that I have killed one of them?"[15] This reference to an old Russian proverb points to his worries about spreading himself too thin. He was an unusually accomplished performer in two domains when there was at the time an ever-increasing separation between performers and composers.

During Rachmaninoff's first trip to America he had been offered the music directorship of the Boston Symphony Orchestra and now Boston asked him to conduct 110 concerts in thirty weeks.[16] The Cincinnati Symphony proposed a two-year contract. He declined both offers, perhaps feeling that his repertory of orchestral pieces was small (and usually restricted to a single performance); in Russia he had concentrated on conducting Russian opera and his non-Russian orchestral experience was limited. Rachmaninoff's profile as a conductor pretty much disappeared when he came to America and is documented only by three recordings he made with the Philadelphians in 1929 and 1939. He conducted just five more public concerts during his life, three for the Festival and two with the Chicago Symphony Orchestra for its golden jubilee in 1941, all with the same program: the Third Symphony and *The Bells*.

Rachmaninoff now supported his family, and generously helped many individuals and causes, through a grueling schedule as a recitalist and concerto soloist in both America and Europe.[17] His demanding tours were not just for the income, but also borne of his often expressed desire to connect with the public. In order to make it to his next engagement, he would sometimes take a night train immediately after a performance, albeit usually in the considerable comfort of a private wagon and then staying in a fine hotel.[18] His orchestral appearances sometimes featured him performing two concertos on the same program, usually two of his own or paired with repertory such as Liszt's First Piano Concerto and *Totentanz*, Schumann's Piano Concerto, or Beethoven's First Concerto.

Rachmaninoff's first orchestral appearance upon his return to America was playing his Second Piano Concerto on 12 January 1919 with Damrosch and the New York Symphony.[19] The Philadelphia Orchestra relationship was renewed in March with the newly revised First Piano Concerto.[20] Next season Rachmaninoff performed the Third Concerto in a concert that included the American premiere of *The Bells*, billed at the time as his Third Symphony (6 and 7 February 1920).[21] For the occasion Stokowski wrote a program note that concluded: "The symphony speaks eloquently for itself, without analysis, because, although it is music of great complexity, it is organized and ordered, and the richness of details is always in relationship to the great architectural plan."

After playing the Second Concerto with Stokowski again in April 1921, Rachmaninoff did not perform in public with the Philadelphians for six years, although in late December 1923 and early January he recorded that concerto.[22] The public collaboration resumed on 18 March 1927, when Stokowski conducted the double world premiere of the Fourth Piano Concerto and the *Three Russian Songs*, Op. 41.[23] These premieres proved disappointing in their critical reception, especially of the concerto, which he stopped playing until revising it years later.[24] The day before Stokowski had written to Rachmaninoff:

> You have made me very happy by offering to dedicate the score of your three Russian Songs to me. The more I am able to penetrate into the inner spirit of your new Concerto and these Russian Songs the more I love this music. For me they are two of the finest of all your creations, and I am very proud to be associated with their performance, and to have the dedication of the Russian Songs, which have so much of the beautiful old simple poetic spirit of Russia which I love and admire so much.[25]

There was now another long gap in Rachmaninoff's public performances with the Philadelphians, until November 1934 when Stokowski and the orchestra gave their third Rachmaninoff world premiere: the *Rhapsody on a Theme of Paganini*. Throughout both these long stretches in which Rachmaninoff did not perform, the Philadelphians of course continued to program his music and to engage other soloists for his concertos. As during the first hiatus, the second was punctuated by a recording reunion, a particularly noteworthy one as it entailed Rachmaninoff's reemergence as conductor. He had not led any orchestra in twelve years, since his final appearance in Moscow in January 1917.[26] In April 1929 he recorded the *Isle of the Dead* and his string orchestra arrangement of the "Vocalise," as well as the Second Piano Concerto.[27]

Here it is worth noting the important role both Stokowski and Ormandy had in the early history of orchestral recordings and of which Rachmaninoff was a beneficiary. Although recording technology went back to the late nineteenth century, early acoustic recordings favored the voice (such as Enrico Caruso's) and solo instruments, such as violin or piano. The first recording of a symphony came in 1910, an abridged Beethoven Fifth. The advent of electronic recordings in 1925 proved a great advance in which Stokowski and the Philadelphians were at the forefront. The young Ormandy, as music director of the Minneapolis Symphony (now the Minnesota Orchestra), released an unexpectedly large number of recordings in 1934 and 1935, including Rachmaninoff's Second Symphony, because favorable union rules made for inexpensive costs.[28] Rachmaninoff said on several occasions how pleased he was to be able to document his interpretations through recordings, although he was extraordinarily demanding in what he approved for release and was adamant in not allowing any live broadcasts on the radio (his Philadelphia recordings would usually be played to fill the time).[29]

Rachmaninoff's 1929 recordings aside, there was a seven-year hiatus before his next public appearances with the Philadelphians, premiering the *Rhapsody* in Baltimore on 7 November 1934.[30] That event proved a considerable critical as well as popular success, which got a further boost five years later when the choreographer Mikhaíl Fokine premiered his ballet *Paganini* at London's Covent Garden. Yet Robert A. Simon, critic for the *New Yorker*, continued what was a long tradition of looking down on Rachmaninoff's music while making an argument about its popular appeal, a theme to which we will return: "The Rhapsody isn't philosophical, significant, or even artistic. It's something for audiences, and what our orchestras need at the moment is more music for audiences. More music for audiences means more audiences for music, and with this sage apothegm, I conclude another salute to Mr. Rachmaninoff."[31]

Over the course of two seasons starting in 1936, the Philadelphia Orchestra began a gradual transition of music directors, from Stokowski to Ormandy.[32] Stokowski, born in 1882, had become the orchestra's third conductor in 1912, immediately after leaving his post in Cincinnati. Ormandy, nearly twenty years younger, was initially appointed co-conductor, inaugurating a dual leadership that lasted for five seasons as Stokowski's appearances dwindled. Ormandy assumed the title (and authority) of music director in September 1938 with a five-year contract, and in 1941 Stokowski severed his ties completely, not conducting the orchestra again until he returned as a guest in 1960.

Rachmaninoff had already performed in 1932 with Ormandy and the Minneapolis Symphony. On 9 April 1936 Ormandy wrote to him looking forward to collaborating again during the coming season, now for "five times in front of the great Philadelphia Orchestra." He related that the orchestra's

Figure 2. Rachmaninoff rehearsing the Philadelphia Orchestra for the Festival.

manager had informed him of Rachmaninoff wanting him to conduct *The Bells*, but tells the composer he has not yet seen a score. Ormandy continued by floating an idea that would finally be realized in the Festival three years later: "If you prefer to conduct it yourself, I shall be more than delighted to greet you as conductor of this work." (Figure 2) He writes that the concert will be an all-Rachmaninoff program featuring whichever concerto Rachmaninoff wishes to play and the Second Symphony.

Ormandy wrote to Rachmaninoff again on 3 May that he had still not seen the score for *The Bells* and repeated his request: "I really would like to see you conduct it yourself." He also boldly broached another matter, which must have been delicate as his senior colleague Stokowski had conducted all the previous Philadelphia premieres of the composer's music—he asks whether Rachmaninoff has finished his new symphony: "I would feel honored if I could give its world premiere. As a matter of fact, I am planning to make your appearance with the Philadelphia Orchestra an All-Rachmaninoff Festival. I would greatly appreciate your suggestion for a program." Rachmaninoff responded a few days later, saying that he hopes the new symphony will be ready in the winter. He relates that he would be "only too happy to have its world premiere given by the Philadelphia Orchestra. I believe Mr. Foley [Rachmaninoff's manager] has already mentioned this to Mr. Stokowski and I am not sure whether he made any promise to Mr. Stokowski with regard to the first performance. This, however, can be adjusted between Mr. Stokowski and you." Ormandy responded on 16 May (writing in German) that he was trying to arrange to conduct the premiere as part of a "Rachmaninoff Festival." Having now received the score to *The Bells*, he again asks about which concerto (or the *Rhapsody*) Rachmaninoff wants to play, and wonders what else might be programmed since the concert should not contain more than about eighty minutes of music.[33]

These exchanges, just before Ormandy assumed his post in Philadelphia, show his interest in having Rachmaninoff conduct the orchestra, the early use of the word *Festival*, and his own ambition to conduct the next world premiere. In a letter of 11 July Rachmaninoff inquired whether Ormandy, who was then in Europe, might come to Lucerne to help with bowings for the piece. In the end, Stokowski enjoyed the honor of giving the orchestra's fourth Rachmaninoff premiere, on 6 November 1936. Rachmaninoff reported to his friend Vladimir Wilshaw that the Third Symphony "was played wonderfully. . . . Both audience and critics responded sourly. Personally, I'm firmly convinced that this is a good work."[34] The critical response was indeed tepid, with *Time* magazine calling the work "disorganized," and quoting two New York critics. Lawrence Gilman, in the *New York Herald Tribune*, wrote that "it has much of his familiar quality—his blend of somber brooding and lyrical expansiveness and defiant gaiety. But the eminent Russian has said most of it before, in substance, and has said it with more weight and felicity and salience." Olin Downes of the *New York Times* asked: "Would not a pair of shears benefit the proportions of this work?"[35]

Rachmaninoff's first Philadelphia collaboration with Ormandy came on 5 January 1937, with a performance in New York of *The Bells* and the

Second Concerto.[36] Early the next season, on 23 October, they presented the First Piano Concerto at a benefit concert in New York. During the summer of 1938, two months before Ormandy officially became music director, he wrote to Rachmaninoff about the upcoming season in which he would be the first soloist: "Your appearance with our orchestra is the highlight of the season." He asked which concerto he wanted to play and whether the orchestra should program his Second or Third Symphony. Ormandy returned to his request of two summers before: "At any rate, how would you react to my suggestion of conducting your own symphony? I know that you are a great conductor and believe that the public would enjoy seeing you lead your own work." Rachmaninoff replied that he could not conduct the Philadelphians that season, but these repeated inquiries may have laid the groundwork for the 1939 Festival in which the composer finally returned to the podium for his first public concerts in twenty-two years.[37]

Ormandy's all-Rachmaninoff program early that season, on 21 and 22 October, opened with orchestrations of three preludes by Lucien Cailliet (the orchestra's bass clarinetist), followed by the First Piano Concerto, and concluded with the Third Symphony, that piece switched at the last minute from the planned Second so as to give Rachmaninoff the chance to hear the revision he had worked on over the summer. The following month, on 8 November, Ormandy conducted the symphony at Carnegie Hall, although the rest of the program was different, now ending with Strauss's *Don Juan* and with Rachmaninoff playing not his own concerto but rather Beethoven's First Concerto. This is a surprising substitution of Beethoven for just one performance (which required at least some rehearsal) and was the only occasion in which Rachmaninoff and the Philadelphians performed a concerted work by another composer.

The transition in leadership from Stokowski to Ormandy went quite smoothly, although there was a rocky patch when Stokowski returned in March 1939 after a fifteen-month break. He had not conducted concerts anywhere during that time. His fame was at its height, he was beginning the fruitful association with Hollywood and with Walt Disney, and his name was linked romantically to Greta Garbo.[38] The orchestra players, audiences, and critics welcomed him back to Philadelphia with open arms: Stokowski was a brilliant showman as well as a superb musician and audiences adored him. The inevitable comparisons made to Ormandy's stewardship, to the younger conductor's disadvantage, prompted Stokowski to step in with public statements supporting his colleague.[39]

When Stokowski next returned, in November just before the Rachmaninoff Festival, he again sparked attention for his latest experiment: a radical reseating of the orchestra with the woodwinds just in front of him, the brass instruments on either side, and the strings behind them all. The much-discussed but short-lived scheme drew in both Ormandy and Rachmaninoff, who when asked his opinion was noncommittal but pointed out that Stokowski's earlier reseating of the violins en masse to the left of the conductor and cellos to the right had since been adopted by many orchestras. Ormandy discontinued the controversial experiment, which endeared him to change-resistant Philadelphia audiences as well as to the orchestra. This time when he returned after Stokowski's visit the "audience left no doubt of their pleasure at seeing Dr. Ormandy back again" and "his first appearance on the stage was greeted by a burst of affectionate applause which grew to ovation proportions and in which the orchestra joined."[40]

The Planning of the Festival

Rachmaninoff now had thirty years of significant collaborations with the Philadelphia Orchestra, which brings us to the "outstanding musical event" that was the Festival. The claim in the publicity brochure that he had not allowed such things in the past is consistent with his well-known dislike of anniversaries, public birthday celebrations, testimonials, and honors.[41] The 1939 Festival was different, however, honoring his special relationship with the Philadelphia Orchestra. Its timing allowed him to dispel rumors that he would retire "next season." The press seems to have come to this idea because of a reporter misunderstanding Rachmaninoff's dry sense of humor. When asked on a trip to Minneapolis whether he was retiring, he replied: "Certainly I will retire, this trip has been exhausting," and then he went off to bed. Just before the Festival Rachmaninoff told the press that talk of his retirement was "a fairy tale composed by the reporters. At the end of a concert season I am tired, not retiring."[42] Furthermore, although all-Rachmaninoff concerts had long been common in Philadelphia, and were often presented by other prominent American orchestras, an intensive cycle for a living composer offering such a broad chronological range of works was unique. The Festival offered the chance for Rachmaninoff to present what he wanted, how he wanted, and not have to worry about having to play the ubiquitous Prelude in C-sharp Minor that so dogged his recitals.

Rachmaninoff let his trusted representatives, Charles Foley and Marks Levine, handle the negotiations. Foley was his manager, publisher, and good friend. Charles O'Connell, who produced recordings for RCA Victor, recalled that Rachmaninoff's "business affairs were invariably handled by the lovable Charlie, who drove a hard bargain; the artist himself never, ostensibly at least, entered into such matters. I came to know Mr. Rachmaninoff too well, however, not to understand that he was the will which dictated his affairs to the minutest detail."[43] Levine, although born in New York City, grew up in Russia. From 1930 to 1941 he managed the concert division of NBC Artists Service and was later the director of the Rachmaninoff Memorial Fund.[44] NBC Artists Service carefully tended to Rachmaninoff's publicity and crafted his image through elaborate press packages containing detailed background information.[45]

Most of the initial correspondence planning the Festival was between Foley or Levine and Reginald Allen, the Philadelphia Orchestra's manager.[46] In late 1938 Allen broached the idea of mounting a celebratory festival in New York and Philadelphia that would feature Rachmaninoff as both pianist and conductor and be devoted entirely to his own compositions.[47] From the start, the focus was on what to present at Carnegie Hall as the hometown concerts would be part of the regular subscription series. The Philadelphia Orchestra, founded in 1900, had made its Carnegie Hall debut in November 1902, and started to give a series of five concerts there each season in 1918–19, which had increased to ten Tuesday evenings by 1921–22. (The orchestra also had shorter-run series in Baltimore and Washington.) The 1939–40 Carnegie season would feature thirteen concerts rather than ten because of the three Rachmaninoff events on Sunday evenings.

In fact, the initial plan was to give fourteen concerts with four added evenings (19 and 26 November, 3 and 10 December), the first three featuring Rachmaninoff as soloist in his four concertos and the *Rhapsody* as well as a group of solo piano pieces. Rachmaninoff would conduct the final concert and "not play the piano unless he wished, but would conduct 'The Bells' Symphony with first-class soloists and a chorus arranged by Dr. Harl McDonald." Allen suggested that Rachmaninoff could decide the rest of the program, conducting either his own compositions or whatever he wanted.[48]

The ambitious first iteration for a four-concert Festival featured not only all five of Rachmaninoff's concerted works, the Second and Third symphonies, and *The Bells*, but also *The Rock*, *The Isle of the Dead*, the cantata *Spring*, *Three Russian Songs*, and some orchestral songs and solo piano works. It is striking that at this late date Rachmaninoff still wanted to present such early works as *The Rock* (1893) and *Spring* (1902), which were virtually unknown in America.[49] By early 1939 the plans had changed. Allen eliminated the first concert scheduled for 19 November and revised the repertory by cutting *The Rock*, *The Isle of the Dead*, the Fourth Piano Concerto, *Three Russian Songs*, orchestral songs, and solo piano works. The final concert would be priced higher because, Allen wrote, it is "safe to say that there is little likelihood of Mr. Rachmaninoff's

Table 3. Programs for the 1939 Rachmaninoff Festival at Carnegie Hall

Original Plan	Announced	Actual Festival
19 November		
Symphony No. 2 Piano Solos Concerto No. 1	Concert eliminated	Concert eliminated
26 November		
The Rock *Paganini Rhapsody* *Three Russian Songs* Concerto No. 3	Symphony No. 2 Concerto No. 1 *Paganini Rhapsody*	Symphony No. 2 Concerto No. 1 *Paganini Rhapsody*
3 December		

Isle of the Dead
Concerto No. 4 or
  solo piano
Group of songs
  (voice and orchestra)
Concerto No. 2
	Concerto No. 2
	Spring
	Concerto No. 3
		Concerto No. 2
		Isle of the Dead
		Concerto No. 3

10 December		
Symphony No. 3 *Spring* *The Bells*	Symphony No. 3 *The Bells*	Symphony No. 3 *The Bells*

conducting again in New York and to the best of my knowledge this will be the first time he has conducted there for at least a very long while."[50] Five weeks later, on 23 February, Allen related information that shows Stokowski was in the picture even though he now conducted the Philadelphians only a few weeks each season: "I received a typical equivocal letter from Mr. Stokowski in which he said he would love to conduct the first Rachmaninoff Festival program, but that I had better plan the thing without him. This leaves us exactly where we were at the beginning." He told Foley that he was moving forward with Ormandy.

There were three basic iterations of the Festival programs: the original four-concert plan from November 1938, a three-concert version that was announced to the public in the summer of 1939, and what actually took place that November and December (see Table 3). The five concerts at the Academy of Music in Philadelphia were programmed differently except for the final program, which Rachmaninoff conducted. The First Piano Concerto, *Paganini Rhapsody*, and *Isle of the Dead* were not performed there. Allen initially hoped that Rachmaninoff could perform both the

Second and Third concertos in Philadelphia before playing them on program two at Carnegie Hall. He explained that this was desirable so there would "be no additional rehearsal demand on him and he will have the opportunity to polish both concertos with two public concerts before the New York performance." The plan did not work out in the end and the Second Symphony was paired with the Third Concerto on the first and second of December and with the Second Concerto on Monday 4 December. This nonetheless remains a remarkable feat: at age sixty-six Rachmaninoff played both the Second and Third concertos on the same concert; it would have been nearly impossible to do that four nights in a row.[51] Rachmaninoff's endurance puts into context the frequent comments about the "tired" Russian. Few commentators were aware of the exhausting schedule he maintained and how especially intense the two weeks of the Festival were, what with travel, rehearsals, and performances of so many pieces both as pianist and conductor.

A major challenge in planning the Festival was arranging the chorus and vocal soloists for the proposed second and third concerts, which eventually led to further repertory changes. In the earliest iteration of the programs three works involved a chorus: *Three Russian Songs*, *Spring*, and *The Bells*. The last was Rachmaninoff's favorite work, as recounted by Riesemann and reaffirmed during the Festival by Rachmaninoff, who replied to a reporter's inquiry on his favorite, "Never ask a composer that, he's always wrong," but admitted it was *The Bells*. In the end, it was the only vocal piece to remain, concluding the Festival under his direction.

Despite the proposal that Rachmaninoff conduct *The Bells* "with first-class soloists and a chorus arranged by Dr. Harl McDonald" (who had prepared Ormandy's January 1937 performance of the work), the plan was to engage the Art of Musical Russia Chorus, which was a subsidiary of the Musicians Emergency Fund, Inc. Rachmaninoff wanted to work with a Russian-language group and the Art of Musical Russia Chorus toured the country presenting Russian operas.[52] Allen negotiated with its executive director Yolanda Mero-Irion, who also suggested soloists for *The Bells*, proposing the organization's president Ivan Ivantzoff (tenor), Vladimir Zorin (baritone), and Jeanne Palmer (soprano). Foley's reaction to Allen on these suggestions was "Confidentially the tenor, Ivan Ivantzoff . . . belongs to the 'World of Yesterday.'" He said he did not know Zorin, commenting that if he is really good someone other than just Irion "should have heard of him." But there was still a chance for "a home run by engaging a tenor on the style of [Beniamino] Gigli, a baritone like [Lawrence] Tibbet [*sic*] . . . and a soprano on the order of [Kirsten] Flagstad." Foley was aiming high. Allen expressed the hope that

Jan Peerce might be available but was "not even sure he sings in Russian and I hate to offer him so little."

Another complication arose in late March when Reginald Allen resigned as the orchestra's manager, effective the first of June. Rachmaninoff wrote to Levine on the second of May after learning the news: "The idea and the arrangements of the Festival were due to his initiative. I do not know who the next manger will be, or how he will deal with the Festival." He wondered whether it might not be best to postpone decisions until a new manager was chosen "so that, in the event of unsatisfactory developments, cancellation may be effected without undue unpleasantness." Rachmaninoff was also concerned about the advertising campaign, which was to have started on the first of April but had yet to happen. Levine followed up noting that "naturally he [Rachmaninoff] is unduly disturbed but I have to answer to his satisfaction" and proposed that Allen send Rachmaninoff a letter reassuring him that everything was set and furthermore that the new manager would also write "a letter expressing his enthusiasm for this particular Festival" as well as providing details about its promotion.

Rachmaninoff may have been heartened when he learned that the new manager would be Harl McDonald, a composer, conductor, educator, and administrator who already had a long association with the orchestra and would remain the manager for the next sixteen years, until his death at age fifty-five. Although now a forgotten figure, McDonald was at the time a widely performed composer, writing in a conservative style not unlike Rachmaninoff's. Both Stokowski and Ormandy recorded his works—indeed, to this day the Philadelphia Orchestra has given more world premieres of his music than of any other composer. McDonald himself conducted and recorded with the orchestra. He had been the chair of the music department at the University of Pennsylvania, and led the University of Pennsylvania Choral Society as well as other choruses, including the Mendelssohn Club. He had also been a member of the orchestra's board of directors and had recently become the business manager.[53] McDonald followed Foley's suggestion, writing to Rachmaninoff on 17 May to assure him that "during the past year of close association with Mr. Allen, I have been very happy to learn of his plan for the Rachmaninoff Festival for next season . . . bright spots of our season's plan . . . will be carried forward with all my enthusiasm and ability."

One of McDonald's first headaches came when Irion informed him that the Art of Musical Russia Chorus would not be available because members could not be compensated during the summer, as had happened in the past, and they were unwilling to learn the music. The brochure had already announced their participation and that *Spring* and *The Bells* would be sung in Russian. McDonald immediately reached out to Dr. John Williamson, director of the Westminster Choir in Princeton, New Jersey. Williamson responded they would be happy to participate and noted that the chorus had performed before in phonetic Russian to good reviews.

Before committing himself, Rachmaninoff wanted to hear some recordings. By the end of the summer Levine wrote to Ormandy: "In view of the uncertainty about the chorus, he [Rachmaninoff] feels (and I agree with him) that it would be best to limit the choral part of the Festival to 'The Bells,'" which meant changing *Spring* to "an orchestral work. He suggested *The Isle of the Dead*." In the end the Westminster Choir performed with 222 singers. After all the concern about Russian diction, *The Bells*, based on Edgar Allan Poe's poem, was "sung in an English translation of the German translation of the Russian translation of the original, the text has gone all around Robin Hood's barn in getting back to Poe." But for this critic, Oscar Thompson, it "scarcely mattered last night since none of the soloists—much less the chorus—could make the words understood."[54] The vocal soloists were a trio of American singers: Susanne Fisher (1903–1990), Jan Peerce (1904–1984), and Mack Harrell (1909–1960), the last particularly lauded in reviews.

The Rachmaninoff Festival

The Philadelphia Orchestra's 1939–40 season featured twenty-eight Friday–Saturday pairs, supplemented by an additional ten Monday evening performances, most of them conducted by Ormandy.[55] The Rachmaninoff Festival was the highlight: the "first series of concerts in many years in which an orchestra of the first rank has devoted itself to the exclusive exploitation of a living composer."[56] The politically fraught context of World War II weaves in and out of the press coverage of the season, beginning with reports that three of the orchestra's members could not make it back from Europe. (They arrived in time for the first rehearsal.) A looming question concerned the programming of German and Russian music as well as featuring more American composers. Ormandy opened the season with an all-German program (Bach, Beethoven, Wagner, and Brahms) followed by an all-Russian one (Musorgsky, Prokofiev, Scriabin, and Stravinsky), which he took to New York. Ormandy felt strongly about the issue and argued:

> We must not permit ourselves to be led into the folly of 20 years ago when Wagner and Strauss were cast out of our concert halls merely because they were German. That is cutting off the nose to spite the face. In such tragic times as these we

need all the solace that great music can bring us. A composer is to be measured only by artistic standards. The place of his birth does not make his music great. . . . It is the color of a composer's orchestrations that we are concerned with, not the color of his skin. It does not matter what church he goes to, or if he goes to any. Perhaps if we can all steep ourselves in the universal harmony that is music we can sooner restore harmony among the warring nations.[57]

Politics arose when Rachmaninoff talked to reporters on 30 November. The *Philadelphia Inquirer* stated that "Soviet bombs bursting over Finland yesterday shook loose Sergei Rachmaninoff's last hope of returning to his native Russia" and declared that he had been "staatenlos" for the past twenty-one years. One frequently quoted remark, mentioned in *Time* magazine, was his response when asked what kind of government he would like to see in Russia: "A better one!"[58] A Philadelphia press conference just before the Festival also touched on topics such as his attraction to fast American automobiles, the way he cut his cigarettes in three pieces so as to cut down on smoking, and a telling response when asked about his favorite modern composer: Francis Poulenc, who "seems to me to be the most sincere."[59]

Most of the information about the success of the Festival comes from the press coverage, although Rachmaninoff gave a typically low-key account in a letter: "The cycle was rather successful. . . . We are well, although I am very tired."[60] He made a lot of money: the financial records of the Philadelphia Orchestra show payments to him of $1,619 and $9,704, an extraordinary sum in those days.[61] Critics had the unusual chance to present a more comprehensive overview of Rachmaninoff's career and achievement than on any previous occasion. The inclusion of a large number of his most important orchestral and concerted works invited discussion about the evolution of his musical style, as well as larger assessments of their value.

The quantity of reviews is quite large, although some particularly prominent critics who had reviewed Rachmaninoff through the years were now retired or dead, figures such as Henry Krehbiel, James Huneker, and W. J. Henderson.[62] The most significant voice was that of Olin Downes, chief critic of the *New York Times*. Downes wrote about Rachmaninoff often, beginning in the *Boston Globe* during the 1909 visit, and had favorably reviewed his most recent Carnegie Hall recital just six weeks earlier. In 1943, upon Rachmaninoff's death, he penned a long tribute in which he lamented "a poignant loss" and praised the "sincerity and greatness of his spirit," commenting that "no virtuoso ever dominated his audience by such purely musical means."[63] Downes's reviews of the three Carnegie Hall concerts deserve detailed consideration because of the prominence of the venue, their length, and the level of their critical insight.[64] Other articles are best viewed topically, as common themes run through them, from Rachmaninoff's imposing physical appearance, performing style, and audience appeal to essentializing remarks about his Russianness and melancholy sensibility. About the music, many commented on his debts to earlier composers, particularly Tchaikovsky, and remarked on his conservative style in contrast to the leading modernists of the day. That his music was untimely yet somehow timeless accounted for much of its appeal, but about this many critics were ambivalent. It was easier to praise his performances exorbitantly while loftily looking down (or at least snidely sideways) on the compositions.

Downes began his review of the opening Carnegie Hall concert by noting that "the dimensions and demonstrations of the audience gave proof of the exceptional hold that Mr. Rachmaninoff has upon the public of this day. This influence is due to his unique abilities as a creative and interpretive musician, his impressive personality, and his prowess as a virtuoso; and it holds because of his gifts and his sincerity as an artist." He pointed out that the programming of the First Piano Concerto, Second Symphony, and *Rhapsody* provided an overview of the composer's first, second, and third periods, with only the *Rhapsody* evincing "a distinctly modern stamp, and even so a stamp of character and purpose rather than any revolutionary idiom." Like other reviewers, Downes observed that Rachmaninoff had thoroughly revised the concerto decades after its premiere, but nonetheless he found it "essentially of an old-fashioned and drawing room character" and "the weakest part of last night's offering, and it is reasonable to assume that its hearty reception by the audience was due principally to the brilliance of the composer-pianist's performance. Its essential interest, one would say, was historic."

The composer's middle period, represented by the Second Symphony, "is distinguished by the full flowering of Rachmaninoff's lyrical style, his authoritative handling of the orchestra and treatment of the form, and the graceful Slavic sensuousness, depth of color and rhythmic swing which continue to fascinate most of us whenever this excellent symphony is played." Downes broached an issue he would come back to in subsequent reviews, namely whether the piece is "modern," and suggests that those who judge a work according to that yardstick, be it atonal, neoclassical, or other "prevalent hall-marks of the post-war period . . . these people may not be stirred by the symphony." He says that he approaches pieces with fewer preconceptions and that it is full of ideas, which are handled masterfully and with luxuriant invention, and feeling. It has a fine line and exceptionally coherent structure. It bears inalienably the stamp of a creative personality. A very few measures, and you say, "Rachmaninoff!" This cannot be said of some very smart scores that very smart neo-classicists and internationalists of music turn out today. What a real and eloquent piece of music! What an organic form!

Downes found the *Rhapsody* "a very brilliant and ripe piece" and given the masterful performance,

> hardly necessary to say, it brought down the house. That, however, was only the logical conclusion to the evening. When Mr. Rachmaninoff appeared for the first time on the stage to play his concerto most of the audience rose in his honor, from those on the floor to those near the roof. Their admiration for him and their enjoyment of his music were more evident there than words can make them here. The occasion was a memorable tribute to a great artist.

Downes thus began and ended his review by focusing on the audience response, a topic to which we will return.

Downes again raised the issue of musical style concerning the second concert, featuring the Second and Third concertos and *The Isle of the Dead*. He wondered how "a denizen of the League of Composers" would react to the program:

> As an alleged modernist, such a person must have felt like a fish out of water. What was modern here? The music, where idiom was concerned, could all have been written before 1900. The concertos are derived from those of Rubinstein and Tchaikovsky and, especially in the case of the Second, they have a spaciousness, and stride, and splendor, which, in the hand of such a performer, are stupendous. . . . Even when it is not in its most distinguished vein, when it verges perilously on the sentimental or indulges in Chekhovian melancholy, it makes very much of the other music of our day appear puny, dully costumed and undernourished. This is all splendor, spaciousness and stride. It harks back to palace and steppe, saber and spur, and you think of the old

Russia, its opulence and pomp and ceremony. No doubt this is a ruinous confession in these times of social and economic change. Unfortunately, the later day has not equaled the earlier one either in fertility of invention or in breadth of design or nobility of gesture—qualities inherent in Rachmaninoff's representative music.

He went on to describe Rachmaninoff's physical appearance, the "prodigious élan" of his playing, and reported that the Third Concerto "did not overwhelm the audience as did the Second." Downes concludes with an enthusiastic account of *The Isle of the Dead*, "his masterpiece."

About the final concert, Downes felt "it was a pity that it was necessary to wait so long" to hear him conduct:

> For Mr. Rachmaninoff, on the rare occasions when this writer has heard him lead an orchestra, has proved as masterly in his control, musicianship, and projective power as he is when he plays the piano. And the styles of the pianist and of the conductor are of a piece. There is the same lack of ostentation, the same dignity and apparent reserve, the same commanding, evocative power. . . . In fact, there were places last night when Mr. Rachmaninoff, the conductor, outshone in significance the composer of the music.

Downes thought this particularly so with the Third Symphony, a piece he did not "find to be a sustained flight of inspiration or sufficiently novel in its manner of statement to stand forth as a towering peak among Rachmaninoff's symphonic creations." Although he did not consider *The Bells* among his "most original creations, there is much which is distinctive in it, as for example the magnificent scoring. . . . The bell resonances obtained from the orchestra are ingenious." Downes concludes, "At the end, Mr. Rachmaninoff was bowing, without the apparent change of a feature, to an audience that was noisily demonstrative, loathe to part with either the man, or, temporarily, his music."

Downes's repeated references to the extraordinarily enthusiastic audience responses at the sold-out concerts were echoed by the press in both cities. Philadelphia critics mentioned Rachmaninoff's special relationship with the hometown orchestra: "The audience responded with an ovation that spoke of the highest esteem and also of the personal affection which has for so many years existed between Mr. Rachmaninoff and his Philadelphia audiences" and "a very large and exceptionally enthusiastic audience gave Mr. Rachmaninoff an ovation both upon his appearance on the stage and at the close of the concert which has rarely been tendered any artist in this city."[65]

The lavish praise of Rachmaninoff's performances as pianist is consistent with countless reviews over his career. Nor is it surprising that critics would comment that "as an expounder of his own music, Mr. Rachmaninoff still has no peer" or that "there is probably no piano concerto of modern times that has enjoyed greater popularity than the C Minor, and perhaps none that has a more secure claim to permanence. Certainly Mr. Rachmaninoff stands alone as an interpreter of his work."[66] The enthusiasm evinced in the first two programs, when he was piano soloist, continued with the final one he conducted: "So far as the results indicated, he might have been a regular practitioner, however, and the audience gave him the greeting usually reserved for Toscanini."[67] These reviews are of interest as there is so little else written about his conducting. It too was highly praised, with the *New York Post* noting "it may be said at once that the sincerity and simplicity that characterize Mr. Rachmaninoff as pianist marked his leadership of the Philadelphia Orchestra." Henry Pleasants, in Philadelphia's *Evening Bulletin*, observed that "Rachmaninoff was more the careful, studious musician functioning in a supervisory capacity than the virtuoso conductor. His beat is clear and he makes his authority and insight felt." Linton Martin wrote in the *Inquirer*: "Grave, scholarly, earnest and utterly devoid of any ostentation or excesses on the podium, the tall, intense Russian gave his cues yesterday in clear-cut fashion, using score throughout in his own music."

Many critics mentioned Rachmaninoff's debt to Tchaikovsky. Edwin H. Schloss commented in the *Philadelphia Record* that the Second Symphony and Third Piano Concerto "are early Rachmaninoff, written 30 years or more ago and both, in form and spirit, are tributes to the great P. I. Tchaikovsky who was the idol of Rachmaninoff's youth." The symphony captures "all of his master's merits and a few of his faults. There is the same love of yearning melodic line, and the same tendency to hang on to it once it is established; there is the same preponderance of suspicious sentimentalism and lack of dramatic conviction. But on the other hand there is also the same gift for melodic invention, warmly felicitous orchestration, and charming use of pseudo-folk material. And there is no doubt that for yesterday's audience the credits outbalanced the debits." In a later review the same critic said that the Third Symphony

> finds the composer rather more fully weaned from the
> Tchaikovskian breast than his Second, heard here last week.

Though the Third is music of uneven inspiration, it is a score to be heard with respect and admired for its musicianly writing and occasional moments of charm rather than criticized for what it is not. It was, of course, played with great authority and virtuosity. The audience was enthusiastic at all times during the afternoon, and Rachmaninoff was recalled for repeated acknowledgements.

As a result of the programming of the second and third concerts, which respectively paired the Second and Third concertos and the Third Symphony with *The Bells*, Rachmaninoff competed not only against other composers, but also against himself, with his later pieces suffering in comparison with their younger siblings. Jerome D. Bohm in the *New York Herald Tribune* stated:

Although the third piano concerto was composed about a decade after the second, the two works are essentially alike in style. Both owe much to Tchaikovsky, although Rachmaninoff, even when he recalls his predecessor to mind, is not mere imitator; the sincerity of his lyricism is unquestioned. It is Russian to the core, and its sentimentality, which might be questioned if it emanated from another source, is so unaffected that one cannot fail to be touched by the honesty of the emotional impulse behind it.

The *New York Sun* preferred the Second Concerto for its "greater authenticity and scope. . . . Especially when it is performed with the vitality and eloquence that Mr. Rachmaninoff can impart to its patterns, this is a heart-warming experience, belonging to an age of musical thinking and feeling which no longer exists."

After mentioning Rachmaninoff's personal fondness for *The Bells* and praising Rachmaninoff's conducting, the critic for the *New York World Telegram* asked, "Still, how many would agree with the composer in preferring it to any other of his scores?" Miles Kastendieck, in the *Brooklyn Eagle*, noted that "not often does it happen that a composer conducts two of his own symphonies in a single program at Carnegie Hall. . . . It was a sombre evening, for the predominating mood was that of melancholy brooding quite in keeping with the Slavic temperament and Rachmaninoff in particular." The *New York Post* critic wrote that "there is little to be said at this date about the two symphonies heard last evening. They are, like most of the composer's music, romantic expressions of an individual and a country whose nobly sensuous and often melancholy lyricism is a thing of the past. It is not the less treasurable." Writing in the *Inquirer* about *The Bells*, Linton Martin argued:

> Certainly it is a work vastly more vital than the later, and purely orchestral, Third Symphony, which was played first yesterday. Unfortunately, this Third Symphony does not improve on further acquaintance. It has some captivating cantilena passages, especially in the first movement. But hearing the work yesterday confirmed earlier impressions that it is at once pretentious and banal, almost entirely empty of inspiration and spontaneous musical speech. Its throes of creation seem achieved by the light of midnight oil and not the morning sun. But it was played for all it was worth—and possibly, one suspects, for a little more than it was worth.

The Bells also elicited a rare mention of the political situation when Francis D. Perkins in the *New York Herald Tribune* commented on the third movement: "The potent communication of the overwhelming terror and despair of the brazen warning of fire and of 'warring desolation'—this last an all too timely subject now."

Few critics had much good to say about the Third Symphony, Rachmaninoff's most recent piece. Oscar Thompson wrote in the *New York Sun*:

> The tall figure on the podium went easily and naturally about the projection of the A minor symphony. This did not impress the reviewer as a work that went much beyond resourceful craftsmanship when Leopold Stokowski introduced it in the same surroundings on November 30, 1936. The composer's own "reading" of it left the earlier opinion unchanged. The symphony has Rachmaninoff's individual voice. There are fine pages, including some stirring climaxes. But at its best it repeats the essence, if not the notes, of the composer's earlier works.

By contrast, the *Rhapsody* continued to be Rachmaninoff's most widely hailed work. Kastendieck said the "work is ingenious and rightly takes its place among the very few symphonic variations in the concerto style." Thompson wrote "This is a technical masterpiece of the first order. It gains steadily in re-hearings. One wonders what the meaning is of the composer's recurring use of the 'Dies Irae.' Is there a hidden program? Certainly there is bitterness in this work, as there is diablerie."

Rachmaninoff recorded the Third Symphony in Philadelphia the day after the last Festival concert at Carnegie Hall.[68] Ormandy and the orchestra were back in New York two days later for their next concert in the Tuesday night series. (Kastendieck commented, "The Philadelphians must be well qualified to rank as America's No. 1 commuting orchestra.") During the following two and a half years Rachmaninoff made six more appearances with the Philadelphians, five performances (and recording) of the Fourth Concerto in late 1941, and then giving a one-off final appearance playing the Second Concerto in Ann Arbor, Michigan, on 9 May 1942, his forty-third time as soloist.[69]

Greatness, Sincerity, and Success

Over his long career, Rachmaninoff weathered some brutal criticism of his compositions, beginning with the devastating reception of the First Symphony in 1897 that derailed him for several years. The success of the 1939 Festival may have proved something of an oasis in that respect, leading as it did to his last major composition and fifth Philadelphia world premiere: the *Symphonic Dance*s. Rachmaninoff started writing it during the summer and played the piece through for Ormandy in late August. A surreptitious homemade recording exists from mid-December that provides extraordinary aural documentation of another run-through just two weeks before the premiere on 3 January 1941.[70] Despite the dedication of the *Symphonic Dances* to Ormandy and the orchestra, the conductor responded tepidly to the piece.[71] He programmed it just once more during the composer's lifetime, on the final Ann Arbor concert in May 1942, a performance that Rachmaninoff did not think went well.[72] A letter from Ormandy to Rachmaninoff the previous month shows that a recording conducted by the composer was being scheduled for shortly before the concert, but that plan fell through.[73]

Rachmaninoff died less than a year later, on 28 March 1943. Ormandy sent a telegram to his widow: "Members of the Philadelphia Orchestra and I wish to extend to you and your family our deepest sympathy in your great loss. The world has lost one of the greatest musicians in the history of music making and our orchestra one of its greatest and most sincere friends." A few days later he conducted *The Isle of the Dead* as a memorial tribute and gave a short speech before.[74]

There is no doubt that the Rachmaninoff Festival was an enormous critical success for Rachmaninoff the performer as well as a considerable one, if more mixed, for him as composer. Critics were for the most part kinder about his music around this special anniversary event celebrating a grand old man than they were during most of his American years. Even as they continued to comment on Rachmaninoff's conservative musical language, one begins to perceive his vindication as a late great Romantic composer writing music that to this day remains a vibrant part of the active concert repertory. Perhaps it is not surprising that Philadelphia audiences and their orchestra, a great ensemble in a genteelly conservative city, so readily embraced his music, as they did that of Jean Sibelius and native son Samuel Barber. While Stokowski promoted these composers, he also challenged audiences and musicians alike by premiering and championing thorny scores by cutting-edge figures. Many modernist composers have faded from the concert hall even as they continue to enjoy academic prestige. These illustrious figures include Varèse, Cowell, and Schoenberg, not to mention the totally forgotten likes of Werner Josten, whose *Jungle* Stokowski chose to perform (twice!) to end the opening concert of the 1932–33 season.

Depending on how one does the calculation, Rachmaninoff was the most successful composer of the 1930s and particularly so if measured in terms of a combination of the quantity of performances, audience adoration, and financial rewards.[75] Virgil Thomson, who just a few months after the Festival assumed the powerful post of music critic for the *New York Herald Tribune*, made many snide comments about Rachmaninoff over the years. But he too recognized his formidable talent, training, and performing genius. In 1950 Thomson remarked that "the only kind of success he never enjoyed was that of intellectual distinction." Downes and other critics likewise referred to Rachmaninoff's lack of elite intellectual acceptability, claiming that his musical language was old-fashioned and derivative rather than new and innovative. But for Rachmaninoff, comparisons to Tchaikovsky were a compliment, as he proudly sought to uphold a glorious Russian musical tradition. He acknowledged the influence but said he "had never, to the best of my knowledge, imitated anyone."[76] Thomson was fair enough to add that "it is not possible, I think, to withhold admiration for the sincerity of the sentiments expressed or for the solid honesty of the workmanship." He then gets to the heart of the matter when he acknowledges:

> Success was his in a way that musicians seldom experience it. It came to him in his own lifetime, moreover, and through the practice of three separate musical branches. As a composer, as a conductor, and as a touring virtuoso of the pianoforte he received world-wide acceptance and acclaim.[77]

These comments from an antagonistic critic resonate with Rachmaninoff's reception through the decades, not just with the claim in the Festival brochure about his unique living stature, but even more with his own concern about having three different musicianly profiles, having "hunted three hares." Even as he juggled these profiles, it may now, some eighty years later, be more productive to realize the enormous success he won in his own time as well as over time, the proverbial last laugh from a supposedly gloomy person, "a-six-and-a-half-foot scowl" as Stravinsky notoriously called him.[78] What vexed Rachmaninoff's contemporary critics as well as many historians ever since is reconciling a figure who enjoyed such popular appeal with historical imperatives that most value novelty and innovation, themselves a Romantic concern.

And this is where Rachmaninoff's personal values, combined with his extraordinary work ethic and determination to regain the financially privileged life into which he had been born, helped to forge an extraordinary career and artistic legacy. The Festival's claim to offer "one of the outstanding events in music history" may not seem so far-fetched. Perhaps it is best to trust Rachmaninoff, who throughout his career let audiences decide. That strategy served him well both as performer and composer, and listeners over time are still siding with him. Summing up his popular success at the Festival, Miles Kastendieck wrote of the final concert: "There was much applause for the man responsible for the entire evening's performance. Admiration was expressed without stint for a prodigious task. And this Rachmaninoff cycle will go down on the record as one of the big events of this and many seasons."[79] If this does not live up to the brochure's promise it nonetheless registers what we know mattered most to Rachmaninoff, what energized him, and what ultimately vindicates his achievement.

Rachmaninoff's connection with his public in live performances accounts for his intense aversion to radio with its unseen listeners: "I cannot conceive of playing without an audience. If I were shut up in a little 'cigar-box' of a room and were told my audience was listening somewhere outside I could not play well. The most precious thing for me when I play is the feeling of contact established with my audience. Anticipation of this contact, on days when I play, gives me the utmost pleasure."[80] This resonates with many similar statements he made. *Newsweek* said, during the Festival, that "after a concert, he defers to the masses, not to the critics. 'Taken individually,' he says, 'the people in the audience may all be poor critics of music, but as a complete body the audience never errs. It is never wrong in its reaction to a performance.'" The magazine further reported that in a recent CBS poll surveying which living composers would be remembered in a hundred years, "the public gave Rachmaninoff third place on a list of ten names. Only Jean Sibelius and Richard Strauss were ahead of him: ones after him included Stravinsky, Prokofieff, and Shostakovich." Now that that hundred years has almost passed, the list holds up pretty well while many of the high-minded modernists of the time are shunned in the concert hall and relegated to history books. For as Richard Taruskin has recently argued, historians have largely ignored or dismissed Rachmaninoff's "enormous historical significance" and thus widened "the embarrassing gap between the academic canon and the performing repertory."[81]

As a composer and performer, Sergei Rachmaninoff respected his audiences. There is no indication of him selling out. He calculated, to be sure, as most musicians do (just read Mozart's letters), but not cynically, and with a good bit more humor than might be expected from an allegedly melancholic Russian—note his famous quip in a letter to Nikolai Medtner about omitting parts of the Corelli Variations depending on how much the audience was coughing.[82]

To conclude: we have seen the word *sincere* often used with regard both to the man and to his music, from Downes's memorial tribute praising his "sincerity and greatness of spirit" to the orchestra's telegram to his widow, and even to the grumpy Virgil Thomson. Rachmaninoff used the word as well—it was what he admired in Poulenc. Although greatness, sincerity, and success are usually terms of abuse for a modernist mindset, these values align well with Rachmaninoff's personal integrity, family values, spiritual convictions, and artistic goals. John Williamson, who had prepared the Westminster Choir for *The Bells*, wrote Rachmaninoff a letter after the Festival that also counters many of the clichés about his image and offers yet another indication of the unusual nature of his great and sincere success. The young musicians

> fell in love with you as a man. This sounds rather funny, I know, but they all say you are the sweetest person they have ever met. Perhaps you have never had young people use that adjective before, but they so fell in love with your absolute sincerity, with your simplicity and your great honesty, and they used the word "sweet" in its right meaning, not any sentimental meaning.[83]

NOTES

This project was born from my having served as the program annotator and consulting musicologist for the Philadelphia Orchestra since the 1999–2000 season. Preparing for a series of Rachmaninoff concerts in 2017 provided the impetus to delve deeper into his relationship with the orchestra. This was made much easier because of the extraordinary preparation for an earlier festival undertaken by the orchestra's consulting archivist, Jack McCarthy. When in 2019 the Bard Music Festival decided to explore Rachmaninoff and his world for the 2021 season (ultimately delayed a year because of the COVID-19 pandemic), I wondered how I might write about the unusual relationship for this book. I made a preliminary trip to Philadelphia to work in the orchestra's archives. Jack McCarthy generously shared scans he had made from the Library of Congress and the University of Pennsylvania. The pandemic then made travel more difficult and the orchestra's archives were being packed for transfer to the University of Pennsylvania, which made them inaccessible within the time frame of this project. I offer this explanation because normally I would have been able to provide more precise references to some primary documents. All of the documentation I use here is drawn from the Philadelphia Orchestra archives or is part of the University of Pennsylvania's collections relating to Leopold Stokowski and Eugene Ormandy. Further documents are part of the Sergei Rachmaninoff Archive at the Library of Congress. Unless otherwise noted, reviews of the Festival are from a scrapbook of press clippings in the Philadelphia Orchestra archives and cover the last four months of 1939; the publication and author (when signed) are given in the narrative, but not always the date. This essay would not have been possible without materials provided by Jack McCarthy and the enormous help of my editor at the orchestra for all these years, Darrin Britting. I am grateful for my time as a Fellow at the American Academy in Berlin to finish this project.

1. Sergei Rachmaninoff, "The Artist and the Gramophone," *Gramophone*, April 1931, 525–26, at 526.

2. Sergei Bertensson and Jay Leyda, *Sergei Rachmaninoff: A Lifetime in Music* (Bloomington and Indianapolis: Indiana University Press, 2001), 353.

3. This account by Ormandy is included in the liner notes for the orchestra's Columbia Masterworks recording of Rachmaninoff's Third Symphony and "Vocalise" (ML 4961).

4. The brochure and much of the publicity refer to the event as a "Cycle," whereas most of the correspondence and reception call it a "Festival"; the names will be used here interchangeably.

5. Letter to Vladimir Wilshaw on 26 July 1939; Bertensson and Leyda, *Rachmaninoff*, 353.

6. During his American years Rachmaninoff performed with some thirty different conductors, most often with Ormandy, then with Damrosch and Stokowski. See Robin S. Gehl, "Reassessing a Legacy: Rachmaninoff in America, 1918–43" (PhD diss., University of Cincinnati, 2008), 322–29.

7. Richard Freed, "The Living Legacy," in *The Philadelphia Orchestra: A Century of Music*, ed. John Ardoin (Philadelphia: Temple University Press, 1999), 61.

8. The performances in Boston came later as Rachmaninoff and the BSO played in many American cities over several months, ending in Buffalo on 31 January 1910. Rachmaninoff conducted *The Isle of the Dead* with the BSO on 17 and 18 December in Boston.

9. Arthur Bronson, *Philadelphia Record*, 1 December 1939.

10. The concerts were on 26 and 27 November. As originally announced, the orchestra's conductor, Carl Pohlig, was to open the evening with Tchaikovsky's 1812 Overture, but a notice was inserted in the program that "Mr. Pohlig has decided to give the entire

Programme at this week's Concerts to SERGEI RACHMANINOFF," and the Tchaikovsky was omitted, making it an all-Rachmaninoff concert. The composer played his preludes in D major, G minor, and C-sharp minor.

11. This information comes from the performance list in the Sergei Rachmaninoff Archive at the Library of Congress. During the 1909–10 American tour he gave eight recitals, appeared eleven times as a concerto soloist, and seven times as a conductor and also playing. He conducted the Philadelphia Orchestra, Chicago Symphony Orchestra, Boston Symphony Orchestra, and Russian Symphony Orchestra.

12. Oskar von Riesemann, *Rachmaninoff's Recollections*, trans. Dolly Rutherford (London: George Allen & Unwin, 1934), 158–59.

13. Oliver Daniel, *Stokowski: A Counterpoint of View* (New York: Dodd, Mead, 1982), 67–68.

14. Rachmaninoff had known Altschuler since their student days at the Moscow Conservatory, and the conductor was his earliest orchestral advocate in America. The Russian Symphony Orchestra's inaugural concert had featured the American premiere of *The Rock* in 1904; two years later Altschuler tried to arrange an America tour for Rachmaninoff. In January 1909 he led the orchestra in the first American performance of the Second Symphony.

15. Riesemann, *Rachmaninoff's Recollections*, 205–6.

16. Bertensson and Leyda, *Sergei Rachmaninoff*, 161 and 212.

17. Rachmaninoff helped with the Philadelphia Orchestra's deficit in 1938. The *Washington Daily News* of 26 October 1938 published a photograph of him handing Ormandy a check to help, as he remarked, "We all should do our part to assist such wonderful musical organizations." Concerning his charitable activities, see Gehl, "Reassessing a Legacy," 158–81.

18. Of Rachmaninoff's 992 concerts during his American years, 194 were with an orchestra. New York was the city he appeared in the most (115 times), followed by Philadelphia and Boston in second place (54 times). Ibid., 54–56.

19. Bertensson and Leyda, *Sergei Rachmaninoff*, 217.

20. Altschuler had given the premiere of the revised version of the First Piano Concerto on 28 January 1919 in New York; see Max Harrison, *Rachmaninoff: Life, Works, Recordings* (London: Continuum, 2005), 221. The Philadelphia performances were on 28 and 29 March, followed on 8 April with a performance of the Second Concerto for a benefit concert at the Metropolitan Opera House in New York.

21. Stokowski conducted *The Bells* in New York on 10 February but Rachmaninoff did not appear on that concert, rather Stokowski's wife, Olga Samaroff, played Beethoven's Choral Fantasy. Walter Damrosch announced that Rachmaninoff would appear in April with the New York Symphony as composer and soloist in the Second Concerto, and conductor of *The Bells*, but that piece was replaced by the cantata *Spring* because of problems getting the music. There was a last-minute announcement that a medical problem prevented Rachmaninoff from playing and conducting in the same evening. See Bertensson and Leyda, *Sergei Rachmaninoff*, 221.

22. Rachmaninoff approved only the second and third movements for release. The rejected first movement was recorded on 22 and 24 December, and the others on 31 December, 3 January, with a reduced orchestration. Barrie Martyn, *Rachmaninoff: Composer, Pianist, Conductor* (Aldershot, UK: Scolar Press, 1990), 441.

23. The concerts were given in Philadelphia (twice), New York, Washington, and Baltimore. For the Carnegie Hall concert on 22 March the *Three Russian Songs* were replaced with Beethoven's *Egmont* Overture and Symphony No. 8.

24. Some of the critical reception is in Bertensson and Leyda, *Sergei Rachmaninoff*, 248–52.

25. This letter and others concerning the premiere are in the Sergei Rachmaninoff Archive at the Library of Congress.

26. The last concert Rachmaninoff conducted in Russia was in Moscow on 7 January 1917, a one-off event; he had not conducted since October 1914.

27. The orchestral works were recorded on 15 and 20 April, and the concerto on 10 and 13 April. Martyn, *Rachmaninoff*, 479.

28. Herbert Kupferberg, *Those Fabulous Philadelphians* (New York: Charles Scribner's Sons, 1969), 119.

29. His recorded legacy is discussed at length in Martyn, *Rachmaninoff*, Harrison, *Rachmaninoff*, and in Gehl, "Reassessing a Legacy," 129–56. See also Rachmaninoff's interview with *Gramophone*, 525–26.

30. The concert was repeated the next day in Washington, but Philadelphia did not get to hear the work until over a year later, on 13 and 14 December 1935.

31. Bertensson and Leyda, *Sergei Rachmaninoff*, 309.

32. Kupferberg, *Those Fabulous Philadelphians*, 100, 121–26. Stokowski supported Ormandy's appointment, as did Rachmaninoff.

33. These letters are in the Sergei Rachmaninoff Archive at the Library of Congress, and some abridged versions appear in Bertensson and Leyda, *Sergei Rachmaninoff*, 318–19. On 18 July Rachmaninoff wrote in a letter to Wilshaw that he had given its first performance, "as usual, to my favorite orchestra, in Philadelphia" (ibid., 321).

34. Bertensson and Leyda, *Sergei Rachmaninoff*, 330, 343.

35. *Time*, 23 November 1936.

36. The concert was repeated in Philadelphia, Washington, and Baltimore. On this occasion the work was sung in English by the University of Pennsylvania Choral Society prepared by Harl McDonald.

37. Bertensson and Leyda, *Sergei Rachmaninoff*, 330.

38. According to Oliver Daniel, Stokowski explored the possibility of Rachmaninoff being part of *Fantasia*; see Daniel, *Stokowski: A Counterpoint of View*, 383–84.

39. See Daniel, *Stokowski*, 372–74; and Kupferberg, *Those Fabulous Philadelphians*, 121–22.

40. Rachmaninoff's view is reported by Henry Pleasants, *The Evening Bulletin*, 30 November; Edwin H. Schloss, *Philadelphia Record*, 2 December.

41. The fortieth anniversary of his 1892 public debut in Moscow was marked by a surprise ceremony at a New York Philharmonic concert in 1932 and the next year he confronted recognitions surrounding his sixtieth birthday. See Bertensson and Leyda, *Sergei Rachmaninoff*, 291–98.

42. Bertensson and Leyda, *Sergei Rachmaninoff*, 355; and Arthur Bronson, *Philadelphia Record*, 1 December 1939.

43. Charles O'Connell, *The Other Side of the Record* (New York: Greenwood Press, 1970), 165.

44. See the obituary for Levine in the *New York Times*, 29 May 1971.

45. See Gehl, "Reassessing a Legacy," 50–54; Appendix C gives all the press material for the 1932–33 season, 235–51.

46. Kupferberg, *Those Fabulous Philadelphians*, 99, 123, 128.

47. Correspondence for planning the Festival is in the archives of the Philadelphia Orchestra. Much of the material concerns practical issues around publicity, pricing, press accommodations, orchestral rental fees, and so forth.

48. This original plan is outlined in a letter from Allen to Foley on 16 November 1938. Allen later proposed that the Festival "open with Mr. Rachmaninoff's best-liked symphonic work, the Second Symphony," believing that a concerto to start would be less effective. Allen also outlined the financial scheme for the New York concerts, which was somewhat complicated because not all the choral works would be performed in

Philadelphia as part of the regular season. The projected receipts of nearly $16,000 were only off in the end by $154, although some costs were higher than anticipated.

49. Rachmaninoff had conducted *The Rock* on his last Moscow concert in 1917, but never in America. The Philadelphians did not perform the piece until 1991. They first performed *Spring* in Saratoga on 11 August 1984. Charles Dutoit conducted and recorded both works with the Philadelphians. The *Three Russian Songs* were first performed in 1973.

50. Allen to Foley, 14 January. This information was inaccurate, although widely reported, as he had conducted *The Isle of the Dead* in January 1910.

51. Rachmaninoff had only performed the two concertos on the same concert one previous time, in 1921, with Damrosch.

52. The chorus had collaborated with the Philadelphia Orchestra during the 1935–36 season in performances of Borodin's *Prince Igor* and Rimsky-Korsakov's *The Invisible City of Kitezh*.

53. Kupferberg, *Those Fabulous Philadelphians*, 128.

54. *New York Sun*, 11 December. The English translation, by Fanny S. Copeland, was thus quite different from Poe's original poem.

55. Ormandy conducted twenty of them, Stokowski four, Rachmaninoff one, with the remaining performances led by associate conductor Saul Caston and Edwin McArthur, who was Kristen Flagstad's accompanist.

56. *Philadelphia Record*, 18 October 1939.

57. *Washington Times-Herald*, 26 November 1939.

58. *Time*, 31 October 1938.

59. *Evening Ledger*, 30 November 1939.

60. From a letter to Arthur Hirst in Bertensson and Leyda, *Sergei Rachmaninoff*, 357.

61. I am grateful to Jack McCarthy for sharing his discovery of this information with me. Concerning Rachmaninoff's considerable wealth, see Gehl, "Reassessing a Legacy," 57.

62. Mark N. Grant, *Maestros of the Pen: A History of Classical Music Criticism in America* (Boston: Northeastern University Press, 1998).

63. Olin Downes, *Olin Downes on Music: A Selection of His Writings During the Half-Century, 1906–1955*, ed. Irene Downes (New York: Simon & Schuster, 1957), 20–21 and 314–17.

64. The reviews appeared 27 November, 4 December, and 11 December.

65. Henry Pleasants in *Evening Bulletin*, 2 December; and Samuel L. Laciar in the *Evening Ledger*, 4 December.

66. Jerome D. Bohm in the *New York Herald Tribune*, 4 December, and *Musical America*, 24 December.

67. *Evening Bulletin*, 11 December.

68. During the Festival, on 4 December, they had recorded the First and Third Piano concertos, supplemented by a later session on 24 February 1940. Earlier plans to record the Third Symphony in London in September 1937 had fallen through. See Harrison, *Rachmaninoff*, 319.

69. The performances of the Fourth Piano Concerto were in Philadelphia, Washington, Baltimore, and New York, with the recording made in December.

70. The home recording was made on 21 December 1940 and released as *Rachmaninoff Plays Symphonic Dances*, Marston Records, 53022-2.

71. Ormandy confessed in a letter to Olin Downes that it "is dedicated to our orchestra and myself, but in all honesty I doubt whether this is his best work although he told me he felt it was. However, we know so well that composers are not always the best judges of the merits of their works." Quoted in Richard Taruskin, "Rachmaninoff Plays *Symphonic Dances*: Newly Discovered 1940 Recording," CD liner notes to *Rachmaninoff Plays Symphonic Dances*, Marston Records, 53022-2.

72. Ormandy next conducted the work sixteen years later, in April 1958, followed by a recording in 1960 for Columbia. He gave another Rachmaninoff American premiere in March 1948 of the rediscovered First Symphony.

73. Ormandy to Rachmaninoff, 8 April 1942. According to Charles O'Connell various things prevented this from happening and when the possibility later emerged for the Chicago Symphony to do it, "Rachmaninoff was not at all enthusiastic." Learning that Frederick Stock would conduct it, he became "actively resentful and things were rather uncomfortably between us for a time." O'Connell, *Other Side of the Record*, 168. An earlier plan to record *The Bells* also did not materialize; Rachmaninoff wrote to John Williamson on 4 September 1941 that should it happen he would want to use the Westminster Choir. The letter is in the Sergei Rachmaninoff Archive at the Library of Congress.

74. Bertensson and Leyda, *Sergei Rachmaninoff*, 355. The concert was on 2 April 1943. A recording of that performance of *The Isle of the Dead*, including Ormandy's opening remarks, is available on Marston Records, 53022-2.

75. Although the data are incomplete, the principal source for statistics about the repertory of American orchestras is Kate Hevner Mueller, *Twenty-Seven Major American Symphony Orchestras: A History and Analysis of Their Repertoires, Seasons 1842–43 Through 1969–70* (Bloomington: Indiana University Press, 1973).

76. Bertensson and Leyda, *Sergei Rachmaninoff*, 369.

77. Virgil Thomson, Foreword to Victor I. Seroff, *Rachmaninoff* (New York: Simon & Schuster, 1950), xi–xii.

78. Igor Stravinsky and Robert Craft, *Conversations with Igor Stravinsky* (New York: Doubleday, 1959), 42.

79. *Brooklyn Eagle*, 11 December.

80. *New York Times*, 11 December 1932; also in Bertensson and Leyda, *Sergei Rachmaninoff*, 290–91.

81. Richard Taruskin, "Not Modern and Loving It," in *Russian Music at Home and Abroad* (Oakland: University of California Press, 2016), 120–33.

82. Martyn, *Rachmaninoff*, 320.

83. Bertensson and Leyda, *Sergei Rachmaninoff*, 356–57.

"The Case of Rachmaninoff":
The Music of a White Emigré in the USSR

MARINA RAKU

TRANSLATED BY JONATHAN WALKER

In 1956, *Spring on Zarechnaya Street* appeared on Soviet cinema screens. Since the production team consisted almost entirely of newcomers and the film had been shot at the provincial Odesa film studio, expectations were low. And yet, by the end of that same year, it had been seen by no less than 30 million viewers, and today, over six decades later, its popularity remains undiminished. The director Marlen Khutsiyev, the cameraman Pyotr Todorovsky, and the leading actor Nikolai Rybnikov all entered the annals of Soviet cinema, and the film, released just three years after the death of Stalin, inaugurated the era of the Khrushchev Thaw.

The film is about a straightforward lad with a job at a steelworks and, in particular, his unrequited love for a new teacher at the local "evening school for the educational improvement of young workers." In addition to this touching story line, the score also contributed to the film's swift ascent. The song "When Spring Comes," with lyrics by Aleksey Fatyanov and music by Boris Mokrousov, and performed by the leading man, Rybnikov, became a popular favorite in its own right. As a kind of leitmotif for the protagonist, it is transformed over the course of the film from its original presentation with a rather artless guitar accompaniment to a powerful rendering in orchestral clothing. The scoring clearly acquires its own semantic layer as the plot develops. The guitar is used to characterize the drab life of the workers, periodically relieved by boisterous winter feasts or summer picnics. The sound of the orchestra carries the film's climactic scene at the steelworks with a symphonic rendering of the song: reflected in the lava of burning metal, the workers' rustic features are transformed into something heroic, and the inner beauty of the students is now revealed to the young teacher (among them, the young man whose love she has rejected). The symbolic moral victory of learning (in the form of art music) over everyday life (in the form of the guitar song) is driven home in the film's final frames, when the leading man confronts a vulgar and dirty gossip, and shoves him, together with his "philistine" guitar, into a muddy pond.

Between these two semantic poles of the song's presentation is an episode that provides the key to the film's musical drama. The steelworker approaches the teacher on the pretext that he needs to consult her about a literature class. She asks him to wait a few minutes to listen to some music on the radio, which she had requested. The presenter duly announces Rachmaninoff's Second Piano Concerto, and the powerful chords of the main theme fill the teacher's room. The young woman is entirely immersed in the depths of the music, leaving the young man to come to terms with the great cultural gulf that lies between him and his beloved. He now understands that his feelings for her are futile.

When the film's creators looked for a musical symbol that could represent an unattainable spiritual absolute, why did they choose Rachmaninoff? There was actually another instance in the same year of 1956, when Asaf Messerer's choreographic miniature *Spring Waters* had its premiere at the Bolshoi. Here, the score was an orchestral arrangement of a celebrated Rachmaninoff song with the same title (Op. 14, No. 11). The subject matter of the ballet (and song) was the Russian thaw at the beginning of spring, when the icy landscape runs with water again, and this vigorous, life-affirming piece became a popular favorite on the ballet stage, serving as an artistic symbol of the incipient Khrushchev Thaw. Even so, how could the still heavily censored Soviet art of this period suddenly take up the work of an émigré artist who had been staunchly anti-Soviet and use it for this purpose?

Answering this question is not a simple matter, and draws us into the wider topic of "Rachmaninoff in the Soviet Union," which is still a subject of debate in the composer's homeland and beyond.[1] It is widely thought that his music was not given a platform in Russia during the interwar period until he provided significant material assistance to the Red Army in its struggle with Nazi Germany.[2] The composer's great-great-granddaughter, Susan Sofia Rachmaninoff Volkonskaya Wanamaker, for example, stated in an interview with Radio Liberty that "Rachmaninoff fled persecution after the 1917 Revolution . . . and by way of reprisal, the Russian authorities banned his music for decades."[3] Not only bloggers and journalists, but sometimes even Russian musicologists maintain this narrative.[4] It would seem timely, then, to submit the Soviet reception of Rachmaninoff's work to a more rigorous examination.

Departure: Circumstances and Reasons

Rachmaninoff left Russia on 23 December 1917, taking advantage of a surprise invitation to perform in Stockholm, which he received "some three weeks after the Revolution."[5] On his departure, Rachmaninoff was not registered as an émigré and, according to both contemporary and biographical accounts, had merely received a Swedish visa valid for two months.[6] To all appearances, the celebrated artist was simply embarking on another of his tours. However, as his sister-in-law Sofiya Satina recollected, Rachmaninoff made no plans to return, since he expected nothing good to come of the situation in Russia.[7] He and his family stayed on in Scandinavia for most of 1918, since he had managed to arrange a busy concert schedule. Finally, on 1 November 1918, they set out from Norway aboard a transatlantic liner to New York.

Satina thought that the exit permit "was obtained without too much effort or bother,"[8] but this is difficult to credit, given the collapse of the bureaucracy across state institutions during the transfer of power in November and December 1917. Additionally, Sweden had tightened its passport controls: "Beginning in 1917, Sweden's borders became very difficult for foreigners to cross. . . . Controls were especially strict for Russians; for example, the Swedish envoy in Petrograd, General Edward Brandström, deemed it necessary to consult with the Minister for Foreign Affairs himself on the subject of transit visas for Russian citizens."[9] The problem was all the more acute because of Sweden's decision to close its Russian border after the October Revolution, and no new visas were to be granted. In December, those traveling from Russia first had to pass through Finland (now independent from Russia) to reach any border crossing to Sweden. To date, we have no record of the difficulties the composer must surely have faced in order to obtain the requisite documentation. All we can say is that Rachmaninoff's near-miraculous emigration took place at an opportune moment, perhaps thanks to some bureaucratic loophole. An explanation may lie in the recognition that the composer had received across Europe—his prestige might have opened doors that were closed to others.

In contemporary memoirs and in Rachmaninoff's own correspondence we find sufficient explanation for the composer's departure. As Satina recalled: "The February Revolution of 1917 was generally received with delight in Russia, and for Rachmaninoff, it was certainly a joyful occasion. It was not long, however, before joy gave way to anxiety, which deepened as events unfolded. Rachmaninoff was eventually led to despair by the inertia and impotence of the Provisional Government."[10] The October coup finally convinced him that there was no longer any possibility that he might return to his work and former way of life in Russia.[11] Unlike many Russian émigrés abroad, Rachmaninoff preferred to avoid any public declarations regarding his political position, at least in the early years. Although his public activity among émigrés amounted to no more than charity, the Soviet authorities could still view it as support for the "White emigration," which for them covered all social strata of Russians abroad (not merely those who had fought against the Bolsheviks). In 1921, he began to work with the Committee for the Education of Russian Youth in Exile, which had been founded in Boston but soon established branches in Europe. News of the composer's involvement appears to have reached the Soviet plenipotentiary in Italy, Vatslav Vorovsky, an Old Bolshevik and now a statesman of the new Russia. When Rachmaninoff's sister-in-law and her parents left the Soviet Union in the spring of 1921, Vorovsky wrote indignantly to Vyacheslav Menzhinsky, chief of the Cheka's Secret Operational Directorate: "The family of the composer Rachmaninoff (as I read in the newspaper) has been released from Moscow. I hope you realize that Rachmaninoff is one of the most vicious counter-revolutionaries and haters of Bolshevism."[12] Vorovsky cited Rachmaninoff's case to warn against the granting of such exit permits in future. Nevertheless, on 21 August that same year, Fyodor Chaliapin also received a permit allowing him to leave on a business trip (supposedly to return afterward); this left him free to emigrate and join his old friend Rachmaninoff.

Rachmaninoff's Music in the Soviet Union During the 1920s
For all that, Rachmaninoff's prestige back in Russia remained unshakable. Over the course of the 1920s, his music was programmed without hindrance in orchestral concerts, to be heard alongside many other pieces by pre-Revolutionary Russian composers.[13] Nothing published for Soviet concert audiences gave them any reason to believe that Rachmaninoff was politically incorrect,[14] and the new philharmonic societies even dedicated whole concerts exclusively to his works. Nor was Rachmaninoff the only émigré composer performed on the Soviet stage. At the beginning of the decade, the music of Stravinsky (who had settled in the West before the Revolution) was also performed, although much less frequently; a Russian monograph on Stravinsky finally appeared in 1929, written by the prominent Soviet musicologist Boris Asafyev (under his pseudonym Igor Glebov). Concert halls and theaters also took great interest in programming the work of Sergei Prokofiev.

In 1923, Rachmaninoff's fiftieth birthday was widely celebrated in Russia, drawing greater attention to the composer and his music. The composer and choir director Aleksandr Kastalsky wrote to an American contact:

> All over Moscow, seven-foot high posters are being pasted up: On 4 June, on the occasion of S. V. Rachmaninoff's fiftieth birthday, a concert will be held in which all three of his piano concertos are to be performed: a) the First Concerto, in a new edition, will be performed for the first time by Goldenweiser, b) the Second Concerto by Igumnov, and c) the Third Concerto by Feinberg. . . . I don't know how things are abroad, but here, the posters often say: "Concert of works by S. V. Rachmaninoff" (whether songs, piano pieces, or orchestral pieces). Generally speaking, Moscow cannot be accused of amnesia.[15]

Nor could Petrograd be accused of "amnesia." Rachmaninoff's operas returned to the stage there during the 1920–21 season. On 10 April, at the State Academic Theater of Comic Opera (formerly the Mikhailovsky Theater), *Aleko* was performed with Chaliapin in the title role, and on 20 May, *The Miserly Knight* was also performed there.[16] Chaliapin tried to make his Aleko resemble Pushkin's, and this drew some criticism from the press (although Chaliapin had already done the same in some pre-Revolutionary productions). *The Miserly Knight*, on the other hand, had a very favorable critical reception. Both of these productions were revived in the spring of 1923, and performed together for the composer's fiftieth-birthday celebrations, and even the city's leading Communist paper saw fit to announce the performance (this was the organ of the Leningrad City Committee of the All-Union Communist Party of Bolsheviks and the Leningrad Council of Workers, Peasants, and Red Army Deputies).[17] The event was also recorded in the national press.[18] The critics were generally unimpressed by the level of the performances, comparing them unfavorably to the performances at the Comic Opera two years earlier.[19] Rachmaninoff's one-act operas continued in the repertory through to the end of the following season (although they were performed in combination with one-act operas by other Russian composers).[20] In the second half of the decade, the composer's name no longer appeared on theater posters, not because of any hostility toward him, but rather because of the avant-garde turn in Leningrad's artistic life during those years (the city was renamed in 1924, shortly after the death of Lenin).

Aleko was given a prestigious staging in Moscow in 1925, at the Moscow Art Theater Music Studio under the direction of Vladimir

Nemirovich-Danchenko as part of a Pushkin triptych, together with *The Fountain of Bakhchisarai* by Anton Arensky and *Cleopatra* by Reinhold Glière.[21] The triptych was then taken on tour in the United States, and in the summer of 1928 brought to Leningrad. Soviet reviewers thought that the union of these three disparate works under the name of Pushkin was rather perfunctory,[22] but singling out *Aleko*, they showed "a clear sympathy for Rachmaninoff's first opera."[23] The public was evidently won over, since *Aleko* was then brought to the amateur stage, for example by the Moscow Kukhmisterov Railway Workers Club in 1927 and the Perm Railway Workers Club in 1935.[24] *Aleko* was also staged in 1929 by the opera class at the Moscow Conservatory.[25] It was even broadcast on radio, bringing the opera to a wider audience than ever before (Soviet state radio was established in 1924).[26] These performances met with the approval of critics in the central Party press and in the organ of RAPM (Russian Association of Proletarian Musicians).[27] The choice of opera raised questions, but these were not strongly ideological:

> The production of *Aleko* by the Kukhmisterov Railway Workers Club, as far as the performance and staging are concerned, is an unqualified triumph for the choral circle. . . . The only debatable element is the choice of repertory. When making their selection, why did the choir circle settle on the opera *Aleko*? It would seem that the decision to put *Aleko* on the club stage was not entirely successful as far as the content is concerned. If the opera group is to reveal its strengths and capabilities, they would do better if they concentrated on excerpts from classical examples. They could select tableaux from *Prince Igor, The Maid of Pskov, Mazepa, The Tsar's Bride*—these are operas with a historical plot, and with original and striking music—and they would also be more appropriate and beneficial for the club's stage.[28]

The 1929 repertory guide, issued by the Central Repertory Committee, included a section on Russian opera, where all three of Rachmaninoff's operas were endorsed for performance. The Committee placed them in category "B," denoting works that were of the "second rank" but nevertheless "ideologically acceptable and posing no obstacle to widespread performance."[29]

Most remarkably, even Rachmaninoff's sacred works still featured in Soviet musical life of the 1920s. In Moscow, for example, there were performances of the complete *All-Night Vigil*, as well as extracts including the Six Psalms (*Shestopsalmiye*) and "Nunc Dimittis" from the *Vigil*, and "To Thee We Sing" and "The Mercy of Peace" from the *Liturgy of St. John Chrysostom*.[30] The performances took place in cathedrals and concert halls, from the Cathedral of Christ the Savior to the Great Hall of the Conservatory, and often featured excellent musicians. In one case, the event was presided over by the Great Patriarchal Archdeacon Konstantin Rozov, with leading soloists and the choir of the Bolshoi Theater under the direction of Nikolai Golovanov. There were also performances with choirs under the direction of Kastalsky, Pavel Chesnokov, and others. Petrograd/Leningrad had a similar spread of sacred works through to the end of the 1920s, with some outstanding performances by the soloists and the choir of the former Mariyinsky Theater and the State Academic Capella under the direction of the leading choral conductor Mikhail Klimov. Rachmaninoff's sacred music was heard in the provinces as well. The composer, we know, was aware of at least some of these performances; he was informed, for example, about a performance of the *Vigil* in Kazan in 1922.[31]

But it was not just Rachmaninoff's sacred music that attracted church musicians in this period, and several other liturgical composers were more popular. We have an objective measure for interest in the performance of Rachmaninoff's sacred music in the 1920s, namely the payment of royalties by Dramsoyuz, an organization set up to protect copyrights. Rachmaninoff's name appears only in eleventh place on the list for performances in churches.[32] Admittedly, this was partly due to the scoring of these works, which required a body of performers beyond the norms of liturgical singing. Still, the very fact that Rachmaninoff's music was so often performed for liturgical purposes in the Soviet Union of the 1920s is in stark contrast to the present situation, where Rachmaninoff's sacred music has become the preserve of the concert halls.

The saturation of the aural environment of the 1920s with the music of Rachmaninoff found an echo in the fiction of the time. In 1920, a socio-philosophical fantasy titled *My Brother Aleksey's Journey to the Land of the Peasant Utopia* was published by the leading Soviet economist and agriculturalist Aleksandr Chayanov (under the pseudonym Ivan Kremnyov).[33] Chapter 12 "describes significant improvements in Moscow museums and amusements," as the subtitle tells us, and in the middle of that chapter is a portrayal of one remarkable Moscow "amusement," which is witnessed by the main characters (some are participants in the event):

> When they came out into the street, there were dense crowds
> flooding the squares, parks, and gardens all along the banks

of the Moscow River. Aleksey, receiving the program in his hands, read that the Aleksandr Smagin Society, to celebrate the end of the harvest, was inviting the peasantry of the Moscow Region to come and hear the following music, which was to be performed on the Kremlin bells, assisted by the bells of other Moscow churches:

Program
1. Chimes (Rostov, sixteenth century)
2. Rachmaninoff, *Liturgy*
3. Chimes (Akimovsky, 1731)
4. Chimes (Yegorevsky, with changes)
5. Scriabin, *Prometheus*
6. Chimes (Moscow)

A moment later, the heavy tolling of the Polyeleos bell swept over Moscow, and the Kadashi, the Great Cross of Nicholas, and the Monastery of the Conception echoed it at the octave, and the Rostov peal rang out over Moscow. The sounds of bronze falling from on high upon the heads of the rapt crowd were like the flapping wings of some unknown bird. The Rostov chimes, once they had come full circle, slowly ascended into the clouds, and the Kremlin bells launched into the stern scales of the Rachmaninoff liturgy.[34]

Chayanov's fictional utopian society reflected his own views on how Russia should evolve into a "peasant paradise." Rachmaninoff's liturgy is presented within a historical series—and it is no coincidence that the musical society performing the concert takes its name from an outstanding bell ringer of the second half of the nineteenth century. Rachmaninoff's music is therefore consigned to the past, while Scriabin's *Prometheus* symbolizes the future. Even then, Rachmaninoff belongs to a kind of "past in the future" within Chayanov's vision of the coming utopia.

Rachmaninoff's sacred music was often presented in a similar manner during this period. In 1926, for example, the Capella of the Leningrad State Academy, under the direction of Mikhaíl Klimov, gave a cycle of choral concerts: the first of these was devoted to Russian folk music, and the second was a performance of Rachmaninoff's *Vigil*, and the third was Stravinsky's *Les Noces*. This attempt to reclassify sacred works as a kind of "musical archaeology" did not, however, deceive the vigilant censors of Soviet culture. From 1922, the regime sought to strengthen anti-religious

work in an organized form, and in 1925, this led to the emergence of the
Union of Militant Atheists, headed by the Old Bolshevik and prominent
Party journalist Yemelyan Yaroslavsky. This organization started to introduce bans on concert performances of sacred works of various periods
and national schools. At the beginning of 1927, concert performances
of Rachmaninoff's *Vigil* were banned, alongside classic Western sacred
works by Bach, Handel, and Mozart.[35]

The atmosphere of the era is conveyed in an episode recorded in the
diary of Nikolai Zhegin, director of the Tchaikovsky House Museum at
Klin. On 6 May 1924 he describes a concert given in Moscow by the baritone Sergei Migay:

> Finally, Migay came on with Kramarev [his accompanist] and
> devoted the entire first half to Rachmaninoff. He sang mar-
> velously. I do not know who wrote the words for "Christ Is
> Risen." but the song is completely counterrevolutionary by
> today's standards, and its performance would not be permit-
> ted in Klin.[36]

A little over a week later, however, on 14 May, his diary contains this new
entry:

> Migay's mother telephoned; she sounded worried, and
> revealed that Sergei Ivanovich was in Leningrad and that he
> had been sent a summons from the GPU [the Soviet secret
> police], requiring him to present himself and explain why he
> had performed a particular song at his last concert. It concerns,
> of course, Rachmaninoff's "Christ Is Risen," which he sang at
> Medea Figner's concert. I laughed at this point, as a police offi-
> cer who was at the concert had applauded him enthusiastically.[37]

The affection in which Rachmaninoff's music was held by both Russian
musicians and a broad swath of the ordinary Soviet public was seriously
tested around this time.

Rachmaninoff as a "Composer of the Past"
In early Soviet culture, Rachmaninoff was consistently discussed as
a relic of the past. For some, this was a reason for rejecting his music,
whereas for others it was an occasion for regretful nostalgia. Two normally opposing camps, the Russian Association of Proletarian Musicians
and the Association for Contemporary Music, were united in viewing

Rachmaninoff as the very personification of conservatism, whether on ideological or aesthetic grounds. The musical conflict of these years was outlined in Leonid Sabaneyev's *Music After October*:

> In the early part of the post-revolutionary era, almost all composers of the past had labels attached to them, announcing categorically, more or less, where they stood in relation to the supposed art of the proletariat. . . . The "bourgeois" composers included Tchaikovsky, Rachmaninoff, Debussy, Chopin, and Schumann, and the revolutionaries included Scriabin, Musorgsky, Bach, Beethoven, Wagner, etc.[38]

In this context, labeling art as "bourgeois" did not yet imply that such art bore any "class hostility" toward the new society; the champions of a revolutionary proletarian music used the label, rather, to draw attention to what they saw as the limitations of this art. Although Sabaneyev, as a modernist, was in an opposing camp, he arrived at a similar assessment:

> We have a tragedy of whiners (Tchaikovsky, Rachmaninoff, and now Myaskovsky), this weak and pitiful tragedy of outcasts that gives us a salon, or a nightmare, or a hermetic ethnographic nationalism. What we do not have is heroic tragedy and majestic valor, but this is just what we need now, when we should no longer be speaking to the exquisite salon-goers, but rather to the masses, who are waiting for a heroic leap forward.[39]

Another leading "contemporary music" figure, Vyacheslav Karatygin, voiced the same ideas, classifying Rachmaninoff, along with Tchaikovsky, as a "poet of the average man's soul."[40] Artists of this kind could thus be ranked not only as bourgeois but even as philistine. However, in the absence of a new generation of young Soviet "revolutionary composers" of "heroic personality" to rival Rachmaninoff and Tchaikovsky, the disgruntled had to tolerate the lingering presence of these artistic conservatives on concert posters.

Such declarations were all very well, but they could have little effect on the practices of both concert venues and composers. Rachmaninoff was much loved by audiences and performers, but also, more surprisingly, by such people as the rising young modernist Dmitry Shostakovich. In 1927, with the internationally celebrated First Symphony already behind him, Shostakovich named Rachmaninoff as a composer who was,

DSCH

Example 1. Dmitry Shostakovich, Suite for Two Pianos, Op. 6, movement 2, mm. 44–73.

DSCH

Example 1, continued.

Example 2. Dmitry Shostakovich, Suite for Two Pianos, Op. 6, movement 4, mm. 212–21.

for him, one of music's leading lights.[41] This admiration had already been confirmed in his Suite for Two Pianos, Op. 6 (1922), the most monumental work of the aspiring composer prior to his symphony, and remote in style from the avant-gardist works of a few years later. The resemblance to Rachmaninoff is not accidental, and it provides us with the clue we need to trace the Suite back to its conception in the composer's mind. It was prompted by two of Rachmaninoff's works for the same scoring, both under the same title, namely the First and Second Suites (1893 and 1901 respectively). On a biographical level, Shostakovich's Suite is dedicated to the memory of his father, who had died in 1922, still in his forties. Little attention has been paid to this, one of Shostakovich's earliest major works, and for this reason, musicologists have missed the composer's quotation from Rachmaninoff's famous G-minor Prelude, Op. 23, No. 5: its motto, including the harmony and grim character, and its relentless rhythmic ostinato, which serves as a symbol of doom in both works (see mm. 58–70 of the second movement, Example 1). There is an echo of the same rhythm, imposed on a harmonic sequence from Rachmaninoff's Prelude, that appears several times toward the end of the Suite, with one particularly expressive quotation in the coda (see mm. 212–21 of the fourth movement, Example 2). Rachmaninoff's *Aleko* also influenced the younger composer, who planned in the early 1920s to write an opera called *The Gypsies*, based on the same poem by Pushkin, but using its original title. The precise chronology of this opera's composition has not been established. Apart from a few individual numbers, the work was destroyed by the composer in 1926.

The Attitude of the Soviet Press in the 1920s to Rachmaninoff's Emigration

The authorities did not block the performance of Rachmaninoff's music during the 1920s, an attitude that was characteristic of Soviet cultural politics when it came to the question of émigrés more generally. The official view of Rachmaninoff's departure at this time can be gleaned from the afterword to Viktor Belyayev's "Rachmaninoff: Characteristics of His Artistic Activity, and a Sketch of His Life" (1924). The booklet begins and ends with the contention that Rachmaninoff is internationally recognized. Rachmaninoff's substantial trips abroad prior to the Revolution are all listed, with a description of how their artistic fruits enriched Russian culture. Belyayev closes his essay with the following words: "In January 1918, Rachmaninov set out on a concert tour to Sweden, and from there he traveled on to England. He currently resides in New York, and enjoys the loftiest reputation as a pianist in America and Europe."[42] And, of course, whatever cavils there were regarding Rachmaninoff the composer, his authority as a performer (both pianist and conductor) was beyond all contention. Moreover, his reputation as a humane and generous individual only developed during his émigré years, thanks to the unfailing assistance he provided to Russian musicians in need, both Soviet citizens and émigrés.[43] Apart from the wealth of evidence in letters to and from the composer, one colorful token of gratitude for his charity appears in the form of a cantata for choir and piano by Glière to words by Vladimir Wilschau, "From Your Distant Homeland." The score was posted to Rachmaninoff in the United States in time for Russian Christmas, 7 January 1923:

We send you greetings and our love	С далекой родины твоей
From this your homeland far away!	Тебе мы шлем привет все разом!
With heart and soul we wish to say	И сердцем, и душой мы скажем
"Long live Sergei Rachmaninoff!"	Да здравствует Рахманинов Сергей!

Nineteen professors of the Moscow Conservatory saw fit to attach their signatures to this musical message.[44]

Articles and columns about Rachmaninoff appeared regularly in the press at this time, along with accounts of the composer in various memoirs, all attesting to the contribution he had made to music, both in Russia and internationally. For example, the artistic director of the former Mariyinsky, Vasily Shkafer, in an interview for the anniversary of the Bolshoi Theater (where he had previously worked), spoke of Rachmaninoff as an artist who had ensured the superiority of the Mamontov Private Opera over the Bolshoi.[45] After the death of Vladimir Telyakovsky, the last pre-Revolutionary director of the Imperial Theaters, a fragment from his memoirs was published, in 1926, titled "Why Rachmaninoff and Koussevitzky Are Gone." The fragment discusses strife among the artists of the Bolshoi Theater, from which the two famous émigrés extricated themselves, and it closes with the following lament: "In Russia, generally speaking, there is nothing feared more than outstandingly talented people—this disease is rife, from top to bottom."[46] The implication is that those reproaching Rachmaninoff and Koussevitzky for their departure should consider instead the responsibility of Russian society, or indeed the musical community, for driving them away (that is, they were not blaming the two musicians themselves, and could hardly lay the blame on the October Revolution).

The Soviet press kept readers abreast of new developments in Rachmaninoff's life abroad. In 1924, there were reports that he had composed an opera based on "The Fugitive," Lermontov's "mountain legend" poem.[47] There is no such opera, of course, and biographical sources provide no evidence that such a project was ever in the composer's mind.[48] As it happens, Rachmaninoff later mentioned that in the first decade of the century, he had contemplated writing an opera based on a different Lermontov work, "Bela," the first story in *A Hero of Our Time* (to a libretto by Anton Chekhov).[49] The first negative press coverage Rachmaninoff received in the Soviet Union was in reaction to the announcement that he had (allegedly) been made "an honorary citizen of an American city."[50] This brief news item, published in 1925, was sardonically titled "American Generosity," and it is the first time in the Soviet press that any noticeable tension arises in connection with Rachmaninoff. In July of that year, Boris Krasin tried to arrange a meeting with Rachmaninoff in Paris. Krasin had recently become the head of the All-Russian Philharmonic, and his task at this juncture was to persuade significant émigré musicians to cooperate with the Soviet regime. According to Prokofiev, Rachmaninoff "avoided any meeting, and said 'I know they will summon me to Russia, but I have made a vow that I would not go, so there is nothing to discuss.'"[51]

It was not until the beginning of the 1930s that official hostility was displayed toward émigré artists such as Rachmaninoff. The reasons for emigration were not primarily political, but terms such as "emigration" and "non-return" began to take on the sense of an accusation in Soviet legal practice, escalating to "treason to the Motherland." The foundations of the new policy were laid in 1929 by a decree of the Presidium of the Central Executive Committee of the Soviet Union: "On the Outlawing of Officials—Soviet citizens abroad who have flown to the camp of enemies of the working class and the peasantry, and who refuse to return to the Soviet Union." The decree was prompted by the many cases of state employees leaving their posts in Soviet organizations abroad and defecting to their host countries. This was in fact the origin of the term "defector" in Soviet official parlance. At this stage, it was applied only to "unfaithful servants of the regime."[52] The annual rate of such defections more than doubled over the course of the 1920s. In 1930, there were already 277 cases by 5 June, thirty-four of whom were even Party members.[53] The punishments that awaited them back in Soviet Union were harsh: under their outlaw status, all their property was confiscated, and on the occasions when the offender was captured, execution followed within twenty-four hours. The law was also applied retroactively.

Initially, there were only sporadic cases of officials leaving their posts abroad, but the rash of defections rose steeply in 1925 after the arrest in London of a prominent Old Bolshevik, Aleksandr Kvyatkovsky. Over the following months, there were twenty-four defections. Further momentum came in 1929, when an avalanche of defecting officials was triggered by Stalin's policy of "the great turning point" (*velikiy perelom*). The Sixteenth Party Congress, in the summer of 1930, discussed the problem and expanded the scope of the term "defector." By 1931, Rachmaninoff's name was being discussed in this context.

Around *The Bells:* The Boycott of 1931–32

One ubiquitous feature of the literature on Rachmaninoff is the trouble surrounding a 1931 performance of *The Bells* in the Great Hall of the Moscow Conservatory by the choir and orchestra of the Bolshoi Theater under the baton of Alfred Coates. The work was subsequently banned from further performance. The official public signal that Rachmaninoff was no longer to be tolerated was a review of the concert, published 9 March in the newspaper *Vechernyaya Moskva*. Curiously, this response to the concert appeared belatedly. The concerts had been held on Thursday and Friday, 5 and 6 March, but *Vechernyaya Moskva*, which was a daily newspaper, published its review of the concerts on the following Monday. The delay was perhaps due to preparations at the paper for one of the major festivities of the Soviet calendar, International Women's Day. The article began thus: "So you enter the concert hall, you take your seat, and you start listening to the music. Church choral singing, one moment savagely pagan, the next moment eerie and mystical."[54] A description of all the cantata's movements followed. The absurdity of the review is already clear from the opening, which characterizes this "savagely pagan" music as a kind of "church choral singing." The author is not in the least worried by the "devilry" that he detects in this supposed "church liturgy," as he falsely terms it in his review. It is all too clear that the article is made-to-order, and the writer reveals his hand in his closing paragraphs:

> You look around in surprise. Yes, we are surrounded by an audience that is very strange indeed, with some old men in long frock coats, some old women in old-fashioned silks smelling of mothballs, there are bald skulls, quivering necks, swollen eyes, long gloves, and lorgnettes. Who is the author of this text, who is the composer of this mystical music?
>
> The music is by an émigré, that ardent enemy of Soviet Russia, Rachmaninoff. The words (based on Edgar Allan Poe) are by the émigré mystic Balmont. The concert was directed by Albert Coates, formerly the conductor of the Mariyinsky Opera House, who left Russia in 1917 and is now invited back on a foreign passport.

Bell-ringing, liturgy, devilry, cries of horror at some natural calamity—this is all of a piece with the old order that had rotted away well before the October Revolution. Is it not clear for whom this concert was intended? Isn't it for all the flotsam and jetsam of pre-revolutionary Russia, whose cries of horror are embodied in the text and music? Wouldn't it be interesting to know whether the creators of this concert recognized what they were presenting to their audience? Ultimately, it would be interesting to know the names of these organizers.[55]

And so this official organ of the Moscow Soviet signaled the all-clear for other publications to do likewise. A fortnight later, *Literaturnaya Gazeta* published an article by Daniel Zhitomirsky, later to become a respected musicologist, but at that stage of his career, a RAPM activist. According to his account, "Onstage, there is a symphony orchestra, a choir, and some distinguished soloists. They are performing the famous 'Bells,' a truly Russian piece, as they say. This is no mere symphony—it is a full mystery-play of bells."[56]

Zhitomirsky is more outspoken even than the author of the first review, and he reveals the true reason for the sudden appearance of these indignant Soviet reviews aimed at Rachmaninoff. The new hostility stemmed from the publication of an open letter by Rachmaninoff and two other Russian émigrés in the *New York Times* of 15 January 1931. The poet Rabindranath Tagore had already appeared in the paper with an account of his stay in the Soviet Union, in which he had shared his positive impressions of the growth of culture and education in the country. The response from Rachmaninoff and his co-signatories took Tagore to task for using his public prestige to lend "strong and unjust support to a group of professional murderers."[57] The other signatories were the chemist Ivan Ostromyslensky, who was well known in scientific circles but not to the wider public, and Ilya Tolstoy, who was not famous in his own right but only as the son of the novelist Lev Tolstoy. Only Rachmaninoff's name carried real weight for the average reader. The letter was not published in the Soviet Union, and Zhitomirsky summarized it as a rant "about GPU torture" and "forced labor," and condemned it as "vile beyond comparison." He went on to recall that "the pest Chayanov took a fancy to the chimes of Rachmaninoff's *Bells* in his book 'My Brother Aleksey's Journey,'" and quoted a passage from an article of a year earlier by Yaroslavsky, who was in charge of anti-religious propaganda: "The Chayanovs of the world are impatient for a day when the masses listen to concerts featuring *The Bells* of Rachmaninoff's liturgy, when Scriabin's *Prometheus* will become the national anthem."[58] Zhitomirsky disappointedly concluded, "We must admit that some among the masses have waited for just this."[59]

The campaign against Rachmaninoff's *Bells* became a kind of background theme of this campaign to achieve "the defeat of the anti-Soviet opposition." A political show trial was held in Moscow (1–9 March) to coincide with the Fifteenth All-Russian Congress of Soviets (ending 5 March 1931). This was the case of the "Union Bureau of Mensheviks," treated by the press as a sequel to the trial of the "Industrial Party," which had finished the previous December. These were reprisals against the overt political opposition, and against engineering and scientific "specialists" who were, rightly or wrongly, associated with it. To these categories were added the "agrarianists," because the OGPU (successors to the Cheka) was engaged in fabricating a case against a "Labor Peasant Party"; the indictment was issued by Menzhinsky at the end of September 1931. Chayanov, who had now been arrested, was regularly featured in the press in this period, with scathing references linking him to Rachmaninoff's *Bells*. These years were marked by an ever more intense anti-religious campaign to stifle any residual opposition from Orthodox Christians. In 1929, there was talk of a "centralized plan of religious activities by the Union of Militant Atheists as part of the general economic plan,"[60] and in 1932, an "Atheist Five-Year Plan" was announced, with the aim of eradicating religion in the USSR by 1937. The campaign's daily newspaper, *Bezbozhnik* (The Atheist), enjoyed a circulation of 75,000 copies in 1929, which more than doubled over the following year to 170,000, and in 1931, it had soared to 400,000 (by way of comparison, Moscow City Council's *Vechernyaya Moskva* had a circulation of only 135,000 at the time). Plans were even made to increase the print run of *Bezbozhnik* to one and a half million copies.[61]

The very name of Rachmaninoff's cantata came to be interpreted as a symbol of religious opposition to the regime when, in the years around 1930, the campaign for the destruction of churches reached its peak. This strange treatment of what was, after all, a secular work, not only had ideological motivations, but some very practical economic motivations. The accelerated industrialization of the country undertaken during the first Five-Year Plan was hampered by serious shortfalls of both human and material resources. The opposition within the Party, whose leader, Trotsky, was now in exile, pointed to the lack of copper in particular:

> It is out of the question that the five-year plan can be fulfilled within four years. . . . 47,000 tons of copper were smelted

during 1929–30; in 1931, 48,000 tons, which was only one-third of the planned target. In the current year (1932), the plan has been reduced to 90,000, but less than 30,000 tons was actually smelted over the course of eight months. It is hardly necessary to spell out the implications for mechanical engineering in general, and electrical engineering in particular.[62]

Rudmetalltorg, the Soviet administrative body responsible for trade in metals and minerals, proposed a solution: a special five-year plan for the delivery of bronze from bells. The proposal was accepted, and its implementation did indeed provide the country with all the non-ferrous metal needed for the dozen years that elapsed before the war: "Inspired by the center, local authorities, labor collectives, and factories resolved to prohibit bell ringing and hand over bells to the industrialization fund."[63] A significant number of church treasures, including unique bells, were sold abroad (since their sale value exceeded their value as metal).[64] A secret decree of the Council of People's Commissars of the Russian Soviet Federative Socialist Republic, dated 14 November 1930, marked the beginning of the anti-bell campaign, launched without warning, and lasting for the next two or three months. All "unnecessary bells" were to be confiscated to meet "the needs of our industry."[65] The destruction of church property was presented by the press as a "demand of the working people," and the teams who removed and broke up the bells received good pay for their work. In newspaper articles of the time, a standard literary image was the opposition of the dying tradition of bell-ringing to the life-affirming hum of cars. This was the perspective from which the press consigned the performance of Rachmaninoff's *Bells* to the art of a "decaying" past, the musical manifesto of a hidden "enemy not yet killed."

Just as the removal of church bells was declared to be "the will of the people," so the 1931 ban on the performance of Rachmaninoff's music was presented as if in answer to public demand. Instead of an officially promulgated decree from above, it was announced that "a public boycott" of Rachmaninoff's music had begun. The announcement was made by the Party, and by the Komsomol (Communist Youth League), together with the students and teachers of the "F. Kon Higher Musical School" (as the Moscow Conservatory was called from 1929 to 1932). Yet the scandals of the open letter to the *New York Times*, or the Easter performance of *The Bells*, were not featured on the pages of the main Party organs, *Pravda* and *Izvestiya*, which focused on much grander events that were taking place across the country.

The resolution adopted at the Conservatory restated ideas that had already been aired in the reviews by Zhitomirsky and the unnamed author of *Vechernyaya Moskva*, and might even have been penned by the same authors. Zhitomirsky was not only a leading light in the Conservatory's branch of the Komsomol, but he also sat on the editorial board of *Proletarskiy muzïkant*.[66] This journal covered the meeting at the Conservatory, and in the same issue there was another, more detailed article on the same topic, whose author, Nikola Vygodsky, a pianist and organist, was a young teacher at the Conservatory, and a member of the Russian Association of Proletarian Musicians. He wrote:

> Both concerts consisted of two major works: Rachmaninoff's *Bells* and Holst's *Planets*. The common theme, looking "heaven-ward," surely ought to cause some concern. The names of those who created the works are an aggravating factor: Rachmaninoff and Balmont, the gods of the decadent pre-revolutionary bour-geois intelligentsia of the salons, who are now white émigrés; Holst, that flatterer of today's European-American imperial-ist bourgeoisie; and finally, a favorite of European fashionable society, the former conductor at the Mariyinsky Theater, Mr. Coates, who departed from Russia in 1917.
>
> Our concerns are only heightened when we see the audi-ence, redolent of the priests and pogromists, for whom such concerts are intended. They fill the Great Hall to capac-ity and give the music a thunderous ovation. Of course, the applause was simultaneously conveyed to the Bolshoi Academic Theater, the organization that took upon itself the task of organizing a mass for the "great Lenten fast." . . . And where did we end up? At a memorial service, a black mass, a séance, or a spiritual concert? Where do all these mystic horrors come from? . . . The performance of such a program during "Lententide" and the Menshevik sabotage process underlines the political character of these concerts as an exhibition of hostile class forces.[67]

The Leningrad press reacted oddly to events in Moscow. Leningrad City Council's newspaper, *Vechernyaya Krasnaya gazeta*, published an item headed with the directive: "Boycott Rachmaninoff!"[68] Leningrad's princi-pal arts magazine, *Rabochiy i teatr*, reported that the Moscow Conservatory resolutions were supported by the Leningrad Conservatory staff, and that "they were joined by industrial workers who were taking music education courses in the amateur music workshop of the Second Muztechnikum" (at the Leningrad Conservatory).[69] Whereas in Moscow the reason behind the boycott was disguised as a response to performances of *The Bells*, Leningrad presented the matter bluntly: the boycott was needed because of "Rachmaninoff's anti-Soviet attack on the subject of forced labor in the Soviet Union." Revealingly, only a few months later, the same magazine published an item calling for the formation of theater groups in forced labor camps, thereby confirming the existence of the camps that were previously presented as mere fictions of White Guard propaganda.[70] Yet the Leningrad press seems to have enjoyed greater latitude at this juncture, since the same journal that had announced the Rachmaninoff boycott published a sympathetic review, in the following issue, of Albert Coates's touring performances with the Mariyinsky, concluding with warm wishes for the future: "It is quite obvious how beneficial it would be for Coates to give further performances in Leningrad."[71]

For Rachmaninoff's music, however, the message in Moscow and Leningrad was the same. Strict instructions for the implementation of the boycott were sent to all the relevant bodies: "The general meeting calls on all music educational institutions, concert and publishing organizations to follow the example of the Kon Higher School of Music [Moscow Conservatory] and to cease performance and publication of the works of that inveterate enemy of Soviet power, namely the White Guardist Rachmaninoff."[72] Muzgiz, the state music publishing house, reacted swiftly, advertising its compliance immediately after Moscow Conservatory's resolution: "Due to the appearance of the composer Rachmaninoff's counter-revolutionary tract in the American press, the board of Muzgiz has resolved to stop reprinting Rachmaninoff's works and to withdraw from sale all mass-published editions of his works."[73] Leningrad's "workers" were supposedly roused to action against the "petty-bourgeois and salon creativity of Rachmaninoff." According to *Rabochiy i teatr*:

1. Rachmaninoff's works are not to be performed.
2. Explanatory work should be carried out in production units on the boycott of Rachmaninoff's works, with the demand that his works should no longer be published or sold, that Soviet stages should be free of all performance of his works, and that his works should be withdrawn from all music libraries.[74]

We have no information about the withdrawal of scores from libraries, but the publication of Rachmaninoff's works did indeed come to a halt in the Soviet Union.

It is instructive to review interest in Rachmaninoff between the Revolution and the boycott. In 1918 and 1919, references to his music in the press were sporadic, but the civil war would naturally account for this. As Bolshevik victory drew close in 1920, about fifteen scores were in print, including *The Bells*. In 1921, the numbers fell, with only half the number of new editions as in the previous year. It was very different in 1922, with around forty new scores appearing; these notably included the *All-Night Vigil* and a song, "Christ Is Risen," to words by another "White émigré," Dmitry Merezhkovsky. The composer's fiftieth birthday in 1923 was marked by fifty publications; these were of small-scale works, suitable not just for concert performance but also for amateur music making. The year 1924 saw another eighty or so publications, but there was a steep decline in 1925, when only three new items are to be found in library catalogues. The "defectors" controversy arose in that year, and may have had repercussions for the publication of an émigré composer, but we cannot be sure of this, and other factors may have been at work. In 1926, there was an improvement, with well over twenty new items. In 1927 and 1930, there were over ten each, and in the intervening years of 1928 and 1929, over twenty each. In early 1931, several piano miniatures were published (including some transcriptions), but then the boycott struck, and there were no publications of the composer's work in 1932. It was not long, though, before the force of the ban began to dissipate, and several vocal miniatures were published in 1933.

In the spring of 1931, Prokofiev received a letter from Mikhaíl Druskin, a young Leningrad pianist, who would later go on to become a renowned Soviet musicologist. In it, Druskin reports on the campaign against Rachmaninoff's *Bells*. He was able to speak openly because at the time, he was writing from Berlin, and hence his letter was not subject to inspection by Soviet censors. Prokofiev replied with equanimity: "I heard about the boycott of Rachmaninoff, but history teaches us that in such cases, the results are often the opposite of what is intended."[75] Prokofiev was right: audiences and performers responded to Rachmaninoff's disgrace in silent protest, which soon overcame all of the obstacles which had been put in the way of his music. If there was an official termination date for the boycott, it must be 11 December 1932, when a concert at the Bolshoi, under the baton of its chief conductor, Nikolai Golovanov, was devoted exclusively to Rachmaninoff. His music had already begun to resurface during the preceding months. On 30 September 1932, for example, Heinrich Neuhaus performed two Preludes (D major and G-sharp minor), and three of the *Etudes-Tableaux*, Op. 39 (C minor, A minor, and D major) in the Small Hall of the Moscow Conservatory.[76] In November, several of his works were included in concerts given by graduates of the Moscow Conservatory.[77] From then on, the composer's place in

Russian concert life was restored to the *status quo ante*. The formerly vindictive authorities were now prepared to overlook not only his open letter about the camps, but also his signature (in March 1931) on an appeal for a public boycott of Soviet goods,[78] as well as a *New York Times* interview of 20 March 1931, in which he stated that the Soviet regime's anger toward him was a matter of personal pride.[79] For another decade, up to the outbreak of the war, a steady stream of Soviet publications continued, numbering ten to twenty each year, and Rachmaninoff's music returned both to the concert platform and to the conservatory classroom. As Tatyana Naumenko notes:

> Documents in the Russian State Archive of Literature and Arts on the Moscow Conservatory during this period paint a tranquil picture, remote from the actual dramatic events. Throughout the 1930s, not only did graduates of the Conservatory's piano department *not* boycott Rachmaninoff's works, but on the contrary, they invariably played them, and even chose to include them in the program for the state exam in their special field. On the basis of the minutes of graduation performances at the Moscow Conservatory, the students engaged with the entire heritage of Rachmaninoff's piano literature.[80]

Naumenko also points out that the first (undergraduate) thesis on Rachmaninoff was completed in 1939, titled "Stylistic Features in Rachmaninov Piano Works," by E. Tsfas. The examiners passed the thesis at the viva voce presentation without impediment:

> The examiners were Dmitry Kabalevsky and Grigory Kogan. Their comments are remarkable: Kabalevsky records that the choice of topic and the approach to the research were highly successful; he praises the thorough review of press coverage, and the analysis of the clash between Scriabin's and Rachmaninoff's followers. In an aside, Kabalevsky indicates that the significance of Rachmaninoff's music is exaggerated, but he still calls him "a major figure in our country's past." The pianist Kogan objected to Kabalevsky's remark, holding that Rachmaninoff's high standing as a composer was quite appropriate; he praises the subtlety of the stylistic analysis, especially in the area of rhythm. Among his reservations, he notes that the Western European context is not supplied, and that the description of the composer's "second period" (prior to his emigration) is not entirely successful: "Comrade Tsfas,"

the examiner noted, "points out that there is a trend toward gloomy colors. But the epithet 'tragedy' is not appropriate here. In Rachmaninoff's output, this is a period that is bright, blossoming, and fragrant." The graduate was passed with a mark of "excellent," and recommended for graduate school.[81]

Some later developments are already well known. The help Rachmaninoff provided in wartime to the Red Army redeemed him completely in Soviet propaganda, and he was added to the ranks of the official "Russian patriots," now a term of approbation in Soviet rhetoric. The composer's death at the height of the war, separated from loved ones and far from his blood-soaked homeland, lent him a tragic aura. Marietta Shaginyan responded to news of his death in the manner of an appeal to the composer's compatriots:

> Rachmaninoff was a deeply Russian person. . . . But he was fated to die and be buried in a foreign land. I am certain that Rachmaninoff yearned for his homeland, and suffered greatly because of his separation from her. And it is my hope that the young generation of musicians will further enrich Soviet musical culture by assimilating his precious legacy, the spirit of his music, the lessons to be drawn from his compositional mastery, the brightness and sweetness of his image as a musician, and the enormous demands he placed on himself.[82]

In the years that followed, this compact was fulfilled, and every vestigial suspicion that Rachmaninoff's music was alien to Soviet listeners was eradicated. Even amid the hardships of the Second World War, the number of publications of his music often rivaled those of the prewar years. After the war, a complete edition of his piano works was launched, and by 1948, the first two volumes (of an eventual four) were already in print, edited by Pavel Lamm and Konstantin Igumnov. And of course one of the most significant events in the postwar reception of Rachmaninoff's music in the USSR was the reconstruction of his First Symphony on the basis of the surviving orchestral parts by Aleksandr Ossovsky, Boris Shalman, and Aleksandr Gauk. Performed by the State Symphony Orchestra of the USSR and conducted by Gauk himself, the symphony was heard in the Main Hall of the Moscow Conservatory on 17 October 1945, almost fifty years after its disastrous premiere in March 1897.

Up to this point, all of the Soviet publications of Rachmaninoff's music had featured his pre-Revolutionary works, but 1953 (with Stalin dead) finally witnessed the appearance of a major work of his émigré years: the *Symphonic Dances* (reprinted in 1962). The publication of the composer's second version of the Fourth Piano Concerto came in 1956. Finally, in 1957, for the first time in decades, *The Bells* came back into print. Further publications, performances, and recordings marked the 1960s as the decade when Soviet musicians and listeners finally absorbed Rachmaninoff's émigré compositions.

Why did Rachmaninoff's music embed itself so deeply in Soviet culture, despite the composer's political stance? What distinguished him from his colleagues? Some comparisons will be helpful. Prokofiev, for example, actually reconciled himself to the Soviet regime and returned to his homeland, but even then there were obstacles to the performance of various works. Stravinsky was not even an émigré in the same sense as Rachmaninoff (he had left long before the Revolution), and he was not given to making public political statements, yet his music disappeared from the concert halls and theaters in the early 1930s. Stravinsky was even pursued by the writers of textbooks on Russian music, who discussed him in the most unflattering terms and accused him of "formalism." The contrast between the treatment of Rachmaninoff and Stravinsky is encapsulated by two Soviet films—lovingly in *Spring on Zarechnaya Street*, as mentioned at the beginning of this essay, and negatively in *Rimsky-Korsakov* (1953), in which the young composer Gleb Ramensky, clearly representing Stravinsky, is portrayed as a "prodigal son" who turned his back on his great teacher and homeland.[83] Ramensky is shown returning from Paris, having picked up all the latest musical novelties there, and in front of Rimsky-Korsakov, mounting a dissonant assault on the piano. The audience has already heard the older composer's "realistic" music, and can therefore draw its own conclusions about the ungrateful upstart. An indignant Rimsky-Korsakov scolds Ramensky: "It lacks melody, there is just dissonance. Thoughtless! Mere fashionable pranks! Decadence!"

In this imaginary battle of émigré composers in the Soviet cultural arena, Rachmaninoff undoubtedly emerges the victor. Since Rachmaninoff's politics should have placed him at a disadvantage to Stravinsky, and especially Prokofiev, we are forced to turn to the character of his music alone. In the musical hierarchy that was laboriously constructed by Soviet cultural ideologists, Rachmaninoff's music gradually made its way from mere "conservatism" to "classic" status, his works joining the undisputed masterpieces of the past. Soviet composers, ideally, were to strive to create a body of "Soviet classics" during the 1930s, 1940s, and 1950s, and in the later part of this period Rachmaninoff's pre-Revolutionary music turned out to be among the best models, even if younger Soviet composers had great trouble using the model to create classics of their own. The slogan that artists should look back to the classics emerged in the mid-1930s, and during the 1948 campaign against "formalism" in music, the epithet "Russian" was added to the slogan.[84] This clearly pointed toward Rachmaninoff as a composer who continued in the traditions of Tchaikovsky and the *moguchaya kuchka* (or Mighty Handful), which to the end of his career he never renounced. As ever, Asafyev expressed this most memorably in the best-known passages from his article of the late 1940s on Rachmaninoff:

> Rachmaninoff's greatest merit lies in his highly lyrical melodies. . . . Rachmaninoff's melodies always steal in, like a path through the fields, unpremeditated and unobtrusive. . . . In an era when the melodic principle that structures music is progressively choked off, his talent always flourished purely through melody. . . . The Russianness of Rachmaninoff's music, in the fabric of the melodies, was something he absorbed from all his beloved Russian surroundings, from Russian reality.[85]

All the appropriate stresses—at least for the purposes of Socialist Realism—are placed here with utmost precision: Rachmaninoff is a melodist, a realist who escaped the lure of avant-gardist fashions, and a composer who was thoroughly Russian. Accordingly, Asafyev now found it possible to speak of *The Bells*, the *All-Night Vigil*, and even the works of the émigré period, whose place in the composer's development is summarized thus: "Rachmaninoff's Third Symphony adheres to the best traditions of the Russian symphonic classics."[86]

Even so, Rachmaninoff's style still had to be "adjusted" when it was absorbed in the symphonic, piano, vocal, or cinematic music of Soviet composers from the 1940s to the 1960s. In *Spring on Zarechnaya Street* the Second Piano Concerto could be played on a radio in the teacher's room, but it could not serve as an accompaniment to the scenes of Soviet industrialization that followed. Here the score certainly strives for the scope, power, and pathos of Rachmaninoff, but ultimately it speaks in a different language about a different world. Rachmaninoff, the "Russian classic," might well have become the ideal Soviet composer, were it not for one problem: the meaning and inner narratives of his works, in which the theme of fate, Russia's tragic destiny, and the bittersweet beauty of its lost world remain unchanged. Were it not for the bells, whose manifold voices always formed an accompaniment to his music.

NOTES

1. "Kto i kogda v SSSR zapreshchal S. V. Rakhmaninova," https://alexfisich.livejounal. com/759257.html.

2. Svetlana Zvereva, "Sergei Rakhmaninov: Posledniye godï," *Yezhegodnik Doma russkogo zarubezh'ya imeni Aleksandra Solzhenitsïna* 4 (2014): 437–51.

3. "V Rossii ne uvazhayut Rakhmaninova-cheloveka," https://www.svoboda.org/a/27202 842.html.

4. T. I. Naumenko, "Rakhmaninov i rannesovetskoye muzïkovedeniye," in *Muzïkal'nïy mir S. V. Rakhmaninova na rubezhe XX–XXI vekov: Problemï dialoga kul'tur*, ed. E. V. Kiseyeva and A. V. Krïlova (Rostov-on-Don: Izdatel'stvo RGK im. Rakhmaninova, 2017), 9–22.

5. Sergey Bertensson and Jay Leyda, *Sergei Rachmaninoff: A Lifetime in Music* (Bloomington and Indianapolis: Indiana University Press, 2001), 206.

6. Ibid.

7. S. A. Satina, "Zapiska o S. V. Rakhmaninove," in *Vospominaniya o Rakhmaninove*, ed. Z. Apetyan, 5th ed., 2 vols. (Moscow: Muzïka, 1988), 1:12–115, at 48.

8. Ibid.

9. A. A. Borovskaya, "Russkaya emigratsiya v Shvetsii: Problemï vzaimootnosheniy diasporï, gosudarstva i obshchestva (1918–1940)" (PhD diss., St. Petersburg State University, 2017), 72.

10. Satina, "Zapiska o S. V. Rakhmaninove," 47.

11. For further details of Rachmaninoff's attitudes toward the Revolution, see Vera Val'kova, "S. V. Rakhmaninov i russkaya revolyutsiya," *Uchyenïye zapiski RAM imeni Gnesinïkh* 2 (2018): 27–41.

12. Vorovsky to Menzhinsky, 10 June 1921, in *Bol'shaya tsenzura: Pisateli i zhurnalistï v Strane Sovetov 1917–1956*, ed. A. N. Yakovlev and L. V. Maksimenkov (Moscow: MFD "Materik," 2005), 22.

13. Pauline Fairclough, *Classics for the Masses: Shaping Soviet Musical Identity Under Lenin and Stalin* (New Haven and London: Yale University Press, 2016), 54 and 59–60.

14. See, for example, program notes for symphony concerts on Lyadov, Stravinsky, Taneyev, Arensky, Vasilenko, Glière, and Rakhmaninoff, 24 September to 5 October 1919, Rossiyskiy gosudarstvennïy arkhiv literaturï i iskusstva (RGALI), f. 2658, op. 1, yed. khr. 231; program notes on Tchaikovsky, Rakhmaninoff, Liszt, and Glazunov, 12 June to 15 September 1921, RGALI, f. 2659, op. 1, yed. khr. 240.

15. *Russkaya dukhovnaya muzïka v dokumentakh i materialakh* (Moscow: Yazïki slavyanskoy kul'turï, 1998–), vol. 5: Aleksandr Kastal'skiy, *Stat'i, materialï, vospominaniya, perepiska*, ed. S. G. Zvereva (2006), 738–39. (Aleksandr Goldenweiser, 1875–1961, Russian pianist and composer, professor at the Moscow Conservatory from 1906; Konstantin Igumnov, 1873–1948, Russian pianist, professor at the Moscow Conservatory from 1899; and Samuil Feinberg, 1890–1960, Russian pianist, professor at the Moscow Conservatory from 1922. —Trans.)

16. N. Strel'nikov [N. M. Mezenkampf], "'Groznïy muzh i tsar' Groznïy," *Zhizn' iskusstva* 724–26 (1921): 1; Georgy Nosov, "Skupoy rïtsar'," *Zhizn' iskusstva* 818 (1921): 3.

17. "Akademicheskiye teatrï," *Yezhenedel'nik Petrogradskikh akteatrov* 25 (1923): 11. See also K. A. [A. P. Koptyayev], "K 50-letiyu S. V. Rakhmaninova," *Yezhenedel'nik Petrogradskikh akteatrov* 33–34 (1923): 10.

18. "Oznamenovaniye 50-letiya so dnya rozhdeniya Rakhmaninova v b. Mikhaylovskom teatre," *Izvestiya VTsIK i Mossoveta*, 29 April 1923.

19. DEM [D. N. Mazurov], "K pyadesiteletiyu S. V. Rakhmaninova," *Vechernyaya Krasnaya gazeta*, 5 May 1923.

20. Ye. Yantaryov, "'Aleko' i 'Iolanta,'" *Muzïka i teatr* 9 (1924): 3–4; "'Aleko' i 'Iolanta,'" *Zhizn' iskusstva* 11 (1924), 3–4.

21. Vladimir Nemirovich-Danchenko, 1858–1943, Russian theater director and playwright, in 1898 cofounded the Moscow Art Theatre together with Konstantin Stanislavsky. —Trans.

22. S. Bugoslavskiy, "Pushkinskiy spektakl'," *Zhizn' iskusstva* 26 (1925): 15; V. Ya., "Pushkinskiy spektatkl' Muzïkal'noy studii im. Vl. I. Nemirovicha-Danchenko," *Muzïka i revolyutsiya* 11 (1926): 32.

23. Ye. V. Varvatsi, "Operï Rakhmaninova na sovetskoy stsene," in *S. V. Rakhmaninov: Sbornik statei i materialov*, ed. T. E. Tsïtovich (Moscow: Muzgiz, 1947), 173–190, at 188.

24. Ibid.

25. Marian Koval', "'Aleko' v Mosk. gos. Konservatorii," *Proletarskiy muzïkant* 3 (1929): 35.

26. Vs. Lyutsh, "'Aleko' Rakhmaninova, 'Payatsï' Leonkavallo," *Radioslushatel'* 48 (1929): 7.

27. See, for example, G. Polyanovskiy, "Opera v ispolnenii khorkruzhka," *Pravda*, 8 February 1928.

28. G. Polyanovskiy, "'Aleko' Rakhmaninova v klube im. Kukhmisterova," *Muzïka i revolyutsiya* 12 (1927): 27. (The operas mentioned here are by Borodin, Rimsky-Korsakov, Tchaikovsky, and Rimsky-Korsakov respectively. —Trans.)

29. See Ye. S. Vlasova, *1948 god v sovetskoy muzïke* (Moscow: Klassika–XXI, 2010), 47 and 68.

30. See the section on sacred music concerts in the 1920s in *Russkaya dukhovnaya muzïka v dokumentakh i materialakh* (Moscow: Yazïki slavyanskoy kul'turï, 1998), 9/1; *Russkoye pravoslavnoye tserkovnoe penie v XX veke: Sovetskiy period, 1920-ye–1930-ye godï*, ed. M. P. Rakhmanova (2015), 576–606.

31. S. Rakhmaninov, *Literaturnoye naslediye*, ed. Z. A. Apetyan, 3 vols. (Moscow: Sovetskiy kompozitor, 1978–80), 2:443.

32. M. P. Rakhmanova, "'Ya ne sluzhitel' religioznogo kul'ta, a chlen Profsoyuza . . .' (Delo Dramsoyuza)," *Iskusstvo muzïki: Teoriya i istoriya* 7 (2013): 23–46, at 38–40.

33. Ivan Kremnyov [A. Chayanov], *Puteshestviye moyego brata Alekseya v stranu krest'yanskoy utopii* (Moscow: GIZ, 1920). Chayanov (1888–1937) was a professor at the Timiryazev Agricultural Academy in Moscow, where he worked until 1930. He was the founder and director of the Institute of Agricultural Economics (1922–28), the first such institution in the country. He was later accused of anti-Soviet activity and executed.

34. V. P. Shestakov and G. I. Dzyubenko, eds., *Vecher v 2217 godu: Russkaya literaturnaya utopiya* (Moscow: Progress, 1990), 208.

35. Pauline Fairclough, "Don't Sing It on a Feast Day: The Reception and Performance of Western Sacred Music in Soviet Russia, 1917–1953," *Journal of the American Musicological Society* 65/1 (2012): 67–111.

36. Diary of N. T. Zhegin, Tchaikovsky State House Museum, Klin, p. 1, no. 205, l. 35. I am grateful to A. V. Komarov for providing this information. The words of the song are by Dmitry Merezhkovsky.

37. Ibid., l. 39.

38. L. Sabaneyev, *Muzïka posle Oktyabrya* (Moscow: Rabotnik prosveshcheniya, 1926), 20.

39. Ibid., 160.

40. V. Karatïgin, "Chaykovskiy i Rakhmaninov," *Zhizn' iskusstva* 40 (1923): 10.

41. "Shostakovich o sebe i o svoikh sochineniyakh: Anketa po psikhologii tvorcheskogo protsessa," in *Dmitriy Shostakovich v pis'makh i dokumentakh*, ed. I. A. Bobïkina (Moscow: GTsMMK im. M. I. Glinki, 2000), 475.

42. V. Belyayev, *S. V. Rakhmaninov: Kharakteristika yego tvorcheskoy deyatel'nosti i ocherk zhizni* (Moscow: Khudozhestvennaya pechat', 1924), 24.

43. See N. Yu. Tartakovskaya, "'Pis'ma, kotorïmi tï menya baluyesh'...' Iz perepiski Vladimira Vil'shau s Sergeyem Rakhmaninovïm," in *Novoye o Rakhmaninove*, ed. I. A. Medvedeva (Moscow: GTsMMK; Deka-VS, 2006), 67–98.

44. http://www.muzcentrum.ru/radio-old/programs expomusic/2810-blagodarstve nnaya-kantata-sergeyu-rakhmaninovu.

45. "K 100-letiyu Bol'shogo teatra: Mamontovskaya opera i Bol'shoy teatr (Beseda s upravl. Akoperoy V. P. Shkaferom)," *Zhizn' iskusstva* 5 (1925): 12.

46. V. Telyakovskiy, "Pochemu ushli Rakhmaninov i Kusevitskiy," *Zhizn' iskusstva* 38 (1926): 12–13. Telyakovsky's complete memoir was later published as V. A. Telyakovskiy, *Vospominaniya* (Leningrad and Moscow: Iskusstvo, 1965).

47. "Teatral'naya khronika," *Vechernyaya Krasnaya gazeta*, 26 November 1924.

48. See V. I. Antipov, ed., *Tvorcheskiy arkhiv S. V. Rakhmaninova: Ukazatel' proizvedeniy, sbornik statey* (Tambov: Izdatel'stvo Pershina R.V., 2013), 42. I thank Vera Valkova for her help in ascertaining this fact.

49. Oskar von Riesemann, *Rachmaninoff's Recollections*, trans. Dolly Rutherford (New York: Macmillan, 1934), 151. Von Riesemann erroneously suggests that Rachmaninoff completed the libretto for an opera on "Bela." The idea of writing an opera on this story was also considered by Chekhov and Tchaikovsky in 1889, although it was never realized.

50. "Amerikanskaya shchedrost'," *Vechernyaya Krasnaya gazeta*, 17 May 1925.

51. Sergey Prokof'yev, *Dnevnik*, 2 vols. (Paris: sprkfv, 2002), 2:346, entry for 27 July 1925.

52. See more on this in V. L. Genis, *Nevernïye slugi rezhima: Pervïye sovetskiye nevozvrashchentsï (1920–1933), opït dokumental'nogo issledovaniya*, 2 vols. (Moscow: n.p., 2009).

53. V. Genis, "Nevozvrashchentsï 1920-kh—nachala 1930-kh godov," *Voprosï istorii* 1 (2000): 46–82, at 46.

54. D. G., "Kolokola zvonyat (ob odnom kontserte v konservatorii)," *Vechernyaya Moskva*, 9 March 1931. I have been unable to establish the identity of the author behind this pen name.

55. Ibid. The full text of this article is reprinted in Sergey Rakhmaninov, *Vospominaniya, zapisannïye Oskarom fon Rizemanom*, trans. and ed. V. N. Chemberdzhi (Moscow: AST, 2016), n124.

56. D. Zhitomirskiy, "O chyom zvonyat kolokola?," *Literaturnaya gazeta*, 24 March 1931.

57. Iwan I. Ostromislensky, Sergei Rachmaninoff, Count Ilya L. Tolstoy, "'Tagore on Russia: The 'Circle of Russian Culture' Challenges Some of His Statements," *New York Times*, 15 January 1931.

58. Yem. Yaroslavskiy, "Mechtï Chayanovïkh i sovetskaya deystvitel'nost'," *Pravda*, 18 October 1930.

59. Zhitomirskiy, "O chyom zvonyat kolokola?"

60. "Bezbozhnaya pyatiletka," in *Pravoslavnaya entsiklopediya* (Moscow: Tserkovno-nauchnïy tsentr "Pravoslavnaya entsiklopediya," 2000–), 4:443–44, at 443.

61. Ibid., 444.

62. L. Trotskiy, "Sovetskoye khozyaystvo v opasnosti! (Pered vtoroy pyatiletkoy)," *Byulleten' oppozitsii (bol'shevikov-lenintsev)* 31 (1931): 3.

63. V. F. Kozlov, "Gibel' tserkovnïkh kolokolov v 1920–1930-ye godï," http://www.zvon.ru/zvon7.view2.page12.html#1. "One of the first Soviet decrees was to prohibit alarm bells, in order to exclude these as a means to signal an uprising against the Bolsheviks."

64. Ibid. "This is why in 1930–31 a unique set of bells from the Monastery of the Meeting of the Lord [*Sretenskiy*], exceptional in their musical qualities and weighing around 400 puds, was saved from being melted down. . . . It seems that if these bells were sold in England, and today their wonderful sound is to be heard in Oxford."

65. V. S. Batchenko, "Slomit' religioznost' dervni, slomav kolokola: Antikolokol'naya sostavlyayushchaya v bor'be s religiyey na rubezhe 1920–1930-kh godov (na primere zapadnoy oblasti)," in *Kul'turnaya pamyat' i kul'turnaya identichnost'* (Yekaterinburg: Izdatel'stvo Uralskogo universitata, 2016), 241–46, at 243.

66. "Protiv propagandï beloemigrantskogo tvorchestva," *Proletarskiy muzïkant* 2 (1931): 42.

67. N. Vïgodskiy, "Nebesnaya 'idilliya' ili fashizm v popovskoy ryase (K kontsertam A. Kouts 5 i 6 marta 1931 goda)," *Proletarskiy muzïkant* 2 (1931): 27–28.

68. "Boykot Rakhmaninovu," *Vechernyaya Krasnaya gazeta*, 16 March 1931.

69. "Rabochiy otvet kompozitoru–beloemigrantu," *Rabochiy i teatr* 10 (1931): 22.

70. "Teatr dlya mest zaklyucheniya," *Rabochiy i teatr* 7 (1931): 22. The renaming of "concentration" camps as "correction-by-labor" took place in the summer of 1929.

71. A. S., "Al'bert Kouts," *Rabochiy i teatr*, 1 April 1931, 23. On these tours, he conducted three operas: Bizet's *Carmen*, Rimsky-Korsakov's *The Tale of Tsar Saltan*, and Wagner's *Götterdämmerung*.

72. "Protiv propagandï beloemigrantskogo tvorchestva. Khronika," *Proletarskiy muzïkant* 2 (1931): 42.

73. "V MUZGIZ'e: Khronika," *Proletarskiy muzïkant* 2 (1931): 43.

74. "Ravochiy otvet kompozitoru-beloemigrantu," 22.

75. L. Kovnatskaya, "Chto Vam pishut iz SSSR? Mne—malo...," *Muzïkal'naya akademiya* 2 (2000): 203–16, here 213–14.

76. See the collections of the Russian National Museum of Music (RNMM, Inv. 23138/X). I am grateful to A. V. Komarov for sharing this information with me.

77. RNMM, f. 161, programs, nos. 3893 and 3894.

78. V. Bryantseva, *S. V. Rakhmaninov* (Moscow: Sovetskiy kompozitor, 1976), 537.

79. "Albert Coates in Moscow," *New York Times*, 29 March 1931.

80. Naumenko, "Rakhmaninov i rannesovetskoye muzïkovedeniye," 13.

81. Ibid.

82. M. Shaginyan, "S. V. Rakhmaninov (Prilozheniye k pis'mam)," *Novïy mir* 4 (1943), 110–13.

83. *Rimsky-Korsakov*, Lenfilm, 1931, script by Anna Abramova and Grigory Roshal, directed by Gennady Kazansky and Grigory Roshal. The role of Ramensky was played by Bruno Freundlich.

84. See more on this in Marina Raku, *Muzïkal'naya klassika v mifotvorchestve sovetskoy épokhi* (Moscow: Novoye literaturnoye obozreniye, 2014).

85. B. V. Asaf'yev, "S. V. Rakhmaninov," in *Izbrannïye trudi*, 5 vols. (Moscow: Izdatel'stvo Akademii nauk SSSR, 1952–57), vol. 2 (1952), 289–305, at 294.

86. Ibid.

Aesthetic Ambition and Popular Taste: The Divergent Paths of Paderewski, Busoni, and Rachmaninoff

LEON BOTSTEIN

Almost eighty years have passed since the death of Sergei Rachmaninoff. His fame is undiminished, though he remains an elusive and controversial figure. In his lifetime, he was routinely regarded as the greatest pianist of his time by audiences and journalists as well as by colleagues.[1] Rachmaninoff left a comparatively generous legacy of recordings of his own works as well as standard piano repertory; it has helped keep undisturbed the posthumous aura surrounding Rachmaninoff as pianist.[2]

Rachmaninoff rose to prominence as a composer relatively quickly, bolstered by the patronage of Tchaikovsky and Sergei Taneyev. But the young Rachmaninoff encountered serious setbacks, the most significant of which was the disastrous premiere of his First Symphony in 1897. But after a three-year struggle, during which he made an unusual choice for the time—psychological treatment—he resumed composition at a remarkable pace. By 1917, the year the Revolution broke out, Rachmaninoff had written most of the works he is known for today. Three compositions, each of them involving the piano, stand apart in terms of broad familiarity and popularity: the legendary and ubiquitous C-sharp Minor Prelude from his Opus 3, the C-minor Piano Concerto, Op. 18, and the "Vocalise," Op. 34, No. 14.

Despite this early achievement, by 1914, one year after the notorious Paris premiere of Stravinsky's *Rite of Spring* and a year before the unexpected death of Scriabin, Rachmaninoff's standing in Russia as a composer appeared unsettled; his music, although popular, seemed complacent, old-fashioned, and behind the times. Vyacheslav Karatygin, the Russian critic, observed in 1913, "The public worships Rachmaninoff because he has hit the very center of average philistine musical taste."[3] In contrast, Scriabin's late works promised a new music that could lead to a mystical quasi-religious renewal—music with a high ethical and spiritual purpose that transcended the inherited canon of musical beauty to which Rachmaninoff's music remained committed.[4] And Stravinsky, following the path charted by Rimsky-Korsakov, had opened up a new world of contemporary music derived from a reimagining of an archaic Russian tradition. Rachmaninoff himself was most discouraged by the enthusiasm for that "wretched" Scriabin, whom he accused—despite genuine admiration for his earlier music—of "demoralizing" the public with his "crazy music."[5]

Rachmaninoff left Russia keenly aware of the critical ambivalence toward his music and the widening gap between his conservatism and bolder modernist trends in music. Once safely abroad, he found himself cut off from the key Russian sources of his creativity; his home and the landscape he cherished were gone. The social, cultural, and professional circles that had nurtured him had been dispersed. As Rachmaninoff recalled in 1934, "When I left Russia, I left behind me my desire to compose: losing my country I lost myself also. To the exile whose musical roots, traditions, and background have been annihilated, there remains no desire for self-expression."[6] And the new Bolshevik regime promised little encouragement with respect to sustaining the aristocratic habits and tastes dear to Rachmaninoff the man and musician. Although there was an "official" effort in the 1920s to make the case for the music of Rachmaninoff's beloved mentor Taneyev, it was linked entirely to Taneyev's influence on Scriabin and new directions in music.[7]

Economic necessity as well as spiritual and social dislocation gave Rachmaninoff the impetus to shift his center of gravity toward performance. Rachmaninoff's reputation as a conductor, despite his relatively limited experience, was high enough to get him offers from Boston and Cincinnati at the start of his exile. But he feared the burdens of a music directorship and the enormity of the repertoire he would have to learn. Despite his frequent complaints, he was relieved to reinvent himself as a performer, a piano virtuoso, and acknowledge a dignified practical reason—money—to set composition to the side.[8]

In the interwar years, Europe witnessed an explosive burst of aesthetic innovation that celebrated an overt break with past practices and challenged the entrenched tastes and traditions of prewar art and culture. This further isolated Rachmaninoff's music. It seemed out of step not merely with new Russian music but with European and American trends in contemporary music; it suggested a nostalgic attachment to a largely reactionary pre-revolutionary Russia, a regime now judged severely, whose culture and society were viewed with critical skepticism. The nadir of Rachmaninoff's standing as a composer among a significant and influential part of the community of musicians and critics—but not the music-loving public—was reached after his death—coinciding, particularly in the West, with the Cold War.[9]

However, as Richard Taruskin has argued, notably in his essay "Not Modern and Loving It," the history of music in the twentieth century cannot be said to have vindicated the assumption that animated those for whom Rachmaninoff became and remained anathema. Modernists of varying persuasions may have once been confident that a new musical culture would thoroughly supplant the traditions and habits bequeathed by the nineteenth century. But continuity rather than a sharp break between past and future can be said to have triumphed in Russia, as evidenced by the link between Mahler and Shostakovich, in America by the place the music of Copland and Gershwin has maintained in the repertory, and in German-speaking Europe by the emergence of Richard Strauss as the twentieth century's most important composer.[10] Celebrated names once thought to embody the unique character of twentieth-century music— Boulez, Stockhausen, Sessions, Carter, Wuorinen, Babbitt—have receded into the shadows in terms of today's concert life and the vibrant world of new music in the twenty-first century.

Indeed, since the collapse of the Soviet Union, attitudes toward Rachmaninoff the composer have improved dramatically in America and Western Europe, buffeted by the reconsideration of three major works written in exile (the *Rhapsody on a Theme of Paganini*, the Third Symphony, and the *Symphonic Dances*) and a change in musical taste and judgment. New music took unexpected directions at the end of the twentieth century, as composers rejected what appeared to be an academic orthodoxy about the qualities contemporary music ought to have, and began to re-embrace tonality and ideals of expression associated with late nineteenth-century Romanticism. The premium on a formalist view of the aesthetics of music suspicious of expressiveness, lush textures, repetition, continuity, predictability, and evocative melodic lines gradually receded. Whether modernists liked it or not, in recent decades composers have pursued an eclectic search for strategies that could achieve broad comprehensibility and elicit enthusiasm at first hearing from listeners who had grown up with attachments to folk music, as exemplified by Bob Dylan, and a variety of staggeringly successful forms of popular music, not to speak of music for films and television. Rachmaninoff's music was well suited for an improbable comeback even within the increasingly rarefied world of musicians, critics, and scholars.

The persistent popularity of Rachmaninoff's music after the First World War galled the partisans of constructs of a progressive and distinctly twentieth-century anti-Romantic aesthetic in music. This critical contempt of the music as sentimental, too easy to listen to, and without any critical or provocative edge never had much impact on concert audiences. Public enthusiasm for Rachmaninoff's music, both during his lifetime and posthumously, became a source of envy and resentment. It inspired snobbery greater than that once directed at Tchaikovsky, Rachmaninoff's idol, precisely because it challenged modernity's demand for an arresting discontinuity and the unprecedented in musical art.

Rachmaninoff's works were seen not only as retrograde and oblivious of history, but as indulgent, inauthentic, and manipulative. In 1941, a year and a half before the composer's death, a leading Chicago critic, commenting on the Third Symphony and the Fourth Piano Concerto, called the nearly seventy-year-old Rachmaninoff "one of the leading talents of the nineteenth century" and predicted that his music, with "its overstuffed melodies, the drugged lyricism and brief military passages marcato," would be forgotten in twenty years.[11]

Twenty years later, in the early 1960s, at the height of the prestige of radical musical modernism, Gunther Schuller, the eminent composer, musician, and champion of new modernist music, recorded a conversation with the pianist Russell Sherman.[12] The subject was Sherman's mentor, the pianist Edward (originally Eduard) Steuermann, an émigré to America and onetime student of both Ferruccio Busoni and Arnold Schoenberg. Steuermann, legendary for his collaboration with Karl Kraus, the Viennese satirist and critic and hero to modernist writers and philosophers, was an inspiring teacher and a fierce advocate of the high musical modernism of the mid-twentieth century. According to Sherman, Steuermann did not particularly like Rachmaninoff's music and "decried" Rachmaninoff's "popularity," but he had to admit, "with a slightly grudging admiration," that Rachmaninoff wrote "just those tunes one can never get out of one's head.'"[13]

Sherman added to Steuermann's unexpected confession by reminding Schuller of a concert at the New England Conservatory from the year 1908. It included works by Webern, Debussy, and Rachmaninoff (his symphonic poem *The Isle of the Dead*). Rudolf Kolisch, the violinist, teacher, and doctrinaire champion of the aesthetics of the Second Viennese School (he was Schoenberg's brother-in-law) happened to be in the audience. Sherman recalled that when "Rudi came out from that concert—he didn't care about Webern or Debussy, but Rachmaninoff." "What a composer!" he exclaimed. "He was just amazed."[14]

The Piano, America, and the European Tradition

The defiant and uninterrupted popularity of Rachmaninoff's music, from the turn of the century to the end of the Cold War, would be unthinkable without the central place played by the piano in the musical culture of the first half of the twentieth century. And even during the 1950s and

1960s, as piano playing and piano instruction declined in America and the piano receded in importance, Rachmaninoff's accessible, expressive, and virtuosic realization of the instrument's unique musical qualities sustained the piano in the popular imagination as an indispensable protoganist of beauty and feelings communicated through music. The piano entered the twentieth century as the decisive and exemplary instrument of musical culture. Rachmaninoff the composer became inseparable from the prestige of the piano. Rachmaninoff the pianist wrought from the keyboard unequaled intimacy, beauty, and intensity and represented the pinnacle of virtuosic dexterity and refinement.

It is no surprise that Rachmaninoff's career from its start in Russia to its close in America, coincided with the expansion in the market and demand for pianos, particularly in America. When Rachmaninoff was born, in 1873, there were 156 American piano manufacturers producing slightly over 24,000 instruments a year in a nation with nearly 50 million inhabitants. In 1909, when the thirty-six-year-old Rachmaninoff made his first tour of the United States, 294 piano manufacturers produced 374,000 instruments in a nation of 92 million. Between 1919 and 1929, when the composer was based mostly in America, piano production kept steady around 300,000, only to collapse by two thirds in 1929. By the time of Rachmaninoff's death in 1943, the industry had recovered somewhat, with an annual output of 160,000 instruments in a country with a population of over 132 million people.[15]

The correlation between Rachmaninoff's fame and popularity and the prominence of the piano as a consumer item in America can be measured by the fortunes of America's most successful popular publication about music, *The Etude*. Founded in 1883, the monthly began with print runs of under 5,000. During Rachmaninoff's first American tour in 1909, its circulation was slightly over 130,000. By the end of the First World War, the magazine boasted nearly 218,000 subscribers. Between 1920 and 1940, when Rachmaninoff was most active as a virtuoso performer, readership hovered between 120,000 and 170,000, only to plummet to under 50,000 by the time it ceased publication in 1957.

The Etude magazine's core readership consisted of amateurs and teachers. Each issue was dominated by subjects about piano music and playing (including sheet music of short pieces of medium difficulty). Next in line in terms of editorial priority were the organ, and then the voice and singing, followed, as a close fourth, by violin and string playing. Each issue contained innumerable advertisements for teachers, schools, publications, and concerts. Not surprisingly, Rachmaninoff was not only a frequent subject but also an occasional contributor.[16]

The piano was the leading engine of the democratization of musical culture in America before the First World War; its commercial progress paralleled that of America's industrial power. From the 1870s on, America increasingly provided the stage on which fame and fortune could be won by composers and performers from Europe, particularly virtuoso pianists. But America's influence on musical life was not defined only by the magnitude of the concert audience. From the 1860s onward, American piano manufacturers—notably Steinway in New York, Chickering and Mason & Hamlin in Boston, and Knabe in Baltimore—led in the technological development of the instrument. American pianos set the international standard for what the instrument should sound like, especially concert-quality pianos.

Anton Rubinstein, whom Rachmaninoff repeatedly identified as the greatest of all pianists after Liszt, was among the first to demonstrate, in the 1872–73 season, the financial and reputational significance associated with gaining a following in America by exploiting the corporate sponsorship of a leading piano manufacturer. Steinway promoted itself by assisting Rubinstein to cultivate an audience throughout America, not only in New York and Boston, but across the nation. He gave 215 concerts in 239 days during his tour.[17]

The landmark year in terms of America's indispensability to the careers of European keyboard virtuosi was 1891. It was then that Steinway arranged for Ferruccio Busoni (1866–1924) to teach at the New England Conservatory and pursue a concert career.[18] In November 1891, the Polish pianist Ignacy Jan Paderewski (1860–1941) arrived in New York for his first tour of the United States. Paderewski would become the most widely known virtuoso performer from Europe. His fame as a charismatic performer was unmatched, bolstered by his looks and his mannerisms, captured in daily newspapers, photographs, and caricatures.[19] No one who followed in his path ever rivaled Paderewski's notoriety in America, even though most if not all of his competitors, including Rachmaninoff, were regarded as vastly superior pianists and musicians.[20]

The money that could be made by a successful virtuoso pianist was astounding, and after the war, America became even more economically essential for artists from Europe.[21] Busoni, Paderewski, and Rachmaninoff, however, developed an ambivalence toward their dependence on their careers as performers. All three had ambitions to succeed as composers, not only of piano music for their own use, but of music for the stage and orchestra. Paderewski, Busoni, and Rachmaninoff (as well as perhaps Ernö von Dohnanyi) were in fact the last major virtuoso pianist-composers in a historical line that included Mozart, Beethoven,

Chopin, Liszt, von Henselt, Anton Rubinstein, Moritz Mozskowski (who refused to concertize in America), and Eugen d'Albert. For all of them composition took precedence over performance. What set Paderewski, Busoni, and Rachmaninoff apart from the group of predecessors (except for Rubinstein) was the shared encounter with the scale, character, and tastes of the American public. Their experiences and reactions—each distinct—contributed to the way in which the musical culture of the nine-teenth century made a transition to the twentieth in Europe and America.

The careers of Paderewski, Busoni, and Rachmaninoff (the youngest of the three) were carried along by the emergence of a mass public nur-tured by journalism and marketing strategies that had helped spawn a moneymaking cultural industry. Each sought to reconcile his exceptional popularity as performer with his aspiration as composer. How they did so revealed the connection (or lack thereof) between exploding forms of pop-ular music at the turn of the century (all dependent on the piano) and the continuing traditions of "classical" music. The tension between the virtuoso performance of historic repertoire and the writing of new music high-lighted contradictions between late nineteenth-century musical practices and the political, social, and economic realities that prevailed after the "long nineteenth century" came to its decisive close at the end of the First World War. Before the war, New York's notorious 1913 Armory Show had made it apparent that the present moment was considered the start of a new age that demanded a new art, in all its manifestations.[22] That conviction deep-ened in the aftermath of the war. Its horrors challenged the culture and mores that had failed to prevent it, and justified the effort to realize a radical aesthetic agenda on behalf of a progressive postwar modernity.

For many Europeans, America was the harbinger of the future. Of the three composer-pianists under discussion, Busoni remained the most criti-cal and the least sympathetic. "I hold no brief for its cultural ascent," he wrote. He predicted that the "average" would triumph in America. He mis-trusted its Protestant heritage. New York made a "barbaric" impression, tempting him "to return home on the next boat." He described America as a land of misplaced conceits, where the individual was devalued in favor of a community devoted to practicality, exaggeration, publicity, sensation-alism, and quantity over quality. The ideal of success was anything within "the reach of all, even the lowest."[23] For Busoni, America's nonchalance toward the fatal illness of Mahler in 1911 and the quick elevation to star status of Theodore Spiering, the concertmaster who stepped in to com-plete the season, seemed typical.[24]

Rachmaninoff was more circumspect. His attitude fluctuated between gratitude, high praise, reserved optimism, and residual skepticism. In a short piece for the May 1923 issue of *The Etude*, Rachmaninoff observed: "American audiences seem to be more rational, more clearly appreciative of the substantial and beautiful elements in the art of music than are many European audiences." Europe was "suffering" from a "contagious mania for cacophony."[25]

Paderewski's love affair with America exemplified most vividly the spirit and extent of America's romance with the piano and the virtuoso pianist. Like Busoni and Rachmaninoff, he played mostly a historical repertoire, from Bach, Mozart, and Beethoven to works by some contemporaries, including his young countryman Karol Szymanowski. Paderewski, at a gala Chicago World's Fair concert with Theodore Thomas, playing a Chopin Concerto, gained particular notoriety by defying a ban on using a Steinway (a retaliation against Steinway's decision not to exhibit its instruments at the fair). Paderewski delighted in the affection of the American audience. He recalled that at one 1895 concert in Kansas City, "several hundred people arrived from Texas. . . they stood in line at the box office—all with their music in hand." That same year, in Los Angeles, "people came even from Phoenix, Arizona," and in Salt Lake City, "a train full of music lovers, young students from far away Montana, came to the concert." A blizzard had delayed them and Paderewski postponed the start of the concert until their arrival.[26]

All three composer-pianists—even Paderewski, who basked in America's adulation—resented the stress, pressure, and demands of the American public. But unlike Busoni, Rachmaninoff and Paderewski could and would not abandon intense concertizing as virtuosi, and they were more successful at it. Paderewski was best known for one short hit, the Minuet in G, a piece Rachmaninoff also performed, perhaps as an expression of sympathy with his own inability to shake off the insatiable public demand for his C-sharp Minor Prelude, arguably the most popular single piece of piano music in music history.[27] Paderewski became exceptionally indebted to America and transferred his popularity as a performer to his role as the most prominent spokesman for the independence of Poland. His success in marshalling popular and political American support for Polish national aspirations before America's 1917 entrance in the war was the result of his fame as a virtuoso.

The rage for the piano and its music was not limited to New York, Boston, and Philadelphia. Americans, no matter where they lived, were not as philistine and uneducated as many Europeans believed, Rachmaninoff noted in 1923.[28] In 1910, after his first tour, Rachmaninoff had written that the "mission" of the virtuoso was "to educate the public." But, at the same time, the virtuoso had the right to expect "a certain grade of musical taste, a certain degree of musical education." The virtuoso was at the top of a musical hierarchy of professionals whose obligation was the "education of the great musical public," which meant avoiding "musical trash."[29]

The self-sufficiency of the modern piano as a musical instrument became apparent in the late nineteenth century. Its capacity to realize a multi-voiced work of music and plausibly reproduce orchestral and operatic music helped define the aesthetic norms of the musical experience for the wider public. It became popular as a device for solitude and intimacy in the home as well as a vehicle of public theatricality and spectacle. The American audience saw the piano—apart from its character as an enhancer of unpretentious social entertainment like dancing—as a vehicle of art and elevated taste tied to a grand historical tradition, and as purveyor of sentimental expressiveness, clarity of mood, elegance, and charm. The comprehensible and the profound were not at odds. Repetition and contrasts in sonority, when clearly laid out, made listening an adventure in the construction of subjective narratives. Piano music, historical as well as contemporary music modeled on past practices, was not trivial. It offered a nonverbal opportunity for the construction of personal narratives and sequences of daydreaming and visualization; sounds were silently translated into private feelings, words, and pictures that could be experienced, without embarrassment, in public.

The connection between the virtuoso on stage and the listening audience, in America as well as Europe, mirrored that of a sports professional and the onlooking crowd of spectators. The crowds included a range of amateurs and afficionados, many of whom had tried their hand at playing. In the 1937 British film *Moonlight Sonata*, in which Paderewski starred, the opening scene is a recital. As the camera pans through the rapt audience, it lingers briefly on a man, a standee, who moves his fingers along with the music Paderewski is playing. The cinematic representation of Paderewski's audience confirmed Rachmaninoff's conviction that the piano held the "greatest appeal for the amateur" and was the ideal instrument for the beginner. The piano was the "door" to all "musical literature" because it contained "treble, bass and all inner voices" and all "the tones are already made at the keyboard," making it less difficult than other instruments, such as the violin, that require the student to locate pitches and make them sound.[30]

This enthusiastic and large middle-class and aristocratic public developed an allegiance to the expressive and sentimental character of music. The audience was armed with varying degrees of familiarity with an established piano repertory from the past whose currency was further enhanced by the brief but spectacular popularity of the "automatic piano," the sales of which rose to more than half of all pianos sold between 1919 and 1925.[31] That allegiance contributed to the public resistance to aggressively adventuresome twentieth-century music. The modern piano not only required little maintenance and was durable, it was also affordable in its upright forms. It held its tune for large stretches of time. Its format was standardized. As Rachmaninoff recognized, it was relatively easy to teach and required no particular innate musicality. The piano encouraged an attachment to tonality, and put a premium on consonance and an inherited ideal of beauty audible in the comprehensible shape of melodies. The piano's technological character and musical potential as a percussion instrument, a feature Percy Grainger would highlight in a 1913 essay, remained in the background.[32]

The automatic piano, in its various incarnations as player piano (or pianola), underscored the function already provided by the modern piano as the protagonist of a musical past and its aesthetic norms. The automation of piano playing through piano rolls realized the inherently reproductive character of the conventional piano as a machine, a sort of musical typewriter that enabled the user to produce a comprehensible text without requiring him or her to possess serious literacy or understanding. The automatic piano bypassed the need to learn how to play the piano and brought the greatest artists from the public arena into one's living room to play the audience's favorite pieces.

The player piano was expensive to build and keep up, however, and it remained a luxury item. It fell prey to its natural, logical, and cheaper technological successor, the gramophone. As the sound of recorded music improved, the gramophone displaced completely the automatic piano and permanently weakened the market for all pianos. Paderewski, in his characteristically optimistic manner, welcomed "sound-producing machines" precisely because they helped to honor the past. They would "carry masterpieces to thousands" otherwise excluded from access to the traditions of music and strengthen "the demand for musical instruction."[33]

Rachmaninoff agreed and embraced the gramophone, but famously refused to participate in the subsequent technological advance, the radio broadcast.[34] Radio transmissions were fleeting events in time, like concerts. They left no sound residue. The concert required attendance and a focus on the music, making the concert hall a secular church with a single altar and a ritual of sorts, whereas the radio sullied the listening experience, permitting music to be heard but also ignored as other activities took place in the home during a broadcast.

The gramophone, in contrast, returned control into the hands of the listener, who chose when and where to listen. Further, the recording was a permanent record of an artist's achievement and demanded the artist's approval. As an exemplary musical realization, it could be played repeatedly and therefore could inscribe familiarity and affection for music in the absence of access to concerts. It could also compensate for the lack of anything approximating a good musical memory. The gramophone record became the efficient, low-cost heir to the reproductive function assumed by the mass-produced modern piano. It exponentially expanded the reach of musical culture by ending the monopoly of live concerts and, more radically, overriding distinctions in innate musicality in the general population far more than the piano ever had. It rendered musical literacy more dispensable and consequently damaged, in Rachmaninoff and Paderewski's lifetimes, the commercial viability of music publishing, a thriving industry before the advent of the long-playing record and the compact disk.

The fundamental issue at the core of the questions about the contemporary character and meaning of music as an art form, particularly after 1918, was: What sort of music should a composer write, for whom, and how might music be adequate to the present yet relate to an inherited cultural tradition? What justified music as a vital constituent of public and domestic culture? What was music's purpose and its rightful place in a new world that appeared, on the surface, radically discontinuous with history? Although Paderewski, Busoni, and Rachmaninoff were each cognizant of their success, particularly its American incarnation, and their dependence on their performing careers, they answered these question by pursuing divergent paths as composers of new music for an audience attached to the allure of the piano.

For all its eagerness to acquire the trappings of culture from Europe, the American audience was comparatively without pretentions and easy to please. It was quite different from the public of Rachmaninoff's youth and early career, before the 1917 Russian Revolution. The pianist, composer, and critic Leonid Sabaneyev, a contemporary of Scriabin and Rachmaninoff, noted the acute awareness in the Silver Age among Russian middle-class and aristocratic audiences of the spiritual and intellectual currents in poetry, painting, and music.[35] The public Rachmaninoff first encountered as a composer in Russia, Sabaneyev argued, was possessed of an "overrefined, bourgeois aestheticism" that was "Janus-faced," with one side focused intensely on the present and the other only on the past.[36]

Rachmaninoff assumed the mantle of the past, and the eccentric and ambitious Scriabin and the younger radicals Prokofiev and Stravinsky stood for the future. Interest in Rachmaninoff as composer may have waned in Europe after 1918, but Rachmaninoff's aesthetic conservatism was understood by the American public as emotionally generous, and a sophisticated modern affirmation of tradition. The music conveyed clear and comprehensible musical values that Americans, who were proud of their status as citizens of a democracy, were eager to appreciate and understand, and if they could, replicate. The works Rachmaninoff composed before his exile affirmed their newly acquired status as patrons and participants in a world of established and valid norms of culture and art. In 1919, in response to a young American's question of whether popularity was compatible with "real genius" and "profundity of feeling," Rachmaninoff replied, "Yes, I believe it is possible to be very serious, to have something to say and at the same time be popular."[37]

The American public Rachmaninoff came to know did not have a dominant context of a nationally distinctive classical musical heritage; its concert music culture had been imported during the nineteenth century from Europe, especially from Germany, and that which did exist was dominated by urban centers such as Boston, Philadelphia, and New York. The prestige and enthusiasm for American concert music were relatively novel. As Rachmaninoff put it, in an article that appeared in *Good Housekeeping* in 1922, "America is young; she has, as yet, no music tradition and her composers, in my opinion, must express themselves in music of a cosmopolitan order. Much creditable composition is being done in this country, but it is not American music. It is cosmopolitan, and this is natural, for you have here the peoples of every country in the world."[38]

The appropriated historical European musical tradition became a dimension of contemporary culture, an emblem of the present rather than the past. Music's long history blended together for Americans into a coherently reconfigured, unified, and imported foundational synthesis for a new, acquired American sensibility. Classical music functioned much like the European masterworks and architectural artifacts wealthy Americans brought over and installed in their homes during the Gilded Age. The sharp differences between American Wagnerians and anti-Wagnerians, for example, did not fracture the shared acceptance of the European musical heritage. America emerged as a major international center of art and culture between the 1890s and 1914. Yet music as an art had not given voice to a distinctive American national ethos and identity. The currents coming from Europe, before and after the First World War, were met with curiosity, tolerance, indifference or, in the worst case, an undercurrent of mistrust.

When Scriabin arrived in America for a tour in December 1906, he came primarily as a composer. The response was respectful, muted, and, with regard to *The Divine Poem*, an example of Scriabin's later music with which Rachmaninoff was not in sympathy, bemused. *The Divine Poem* was thought "extremely modern," a "program symphony" that "pursued the ugly and the painful"; it was the work of a "neurotic," "a pretentious and amazing phantasmagoria of tone" that had "impressive passages" of "harmonic richness and poignancy" as well as "unashamed sentimentality." Scriabin seems to have been pleased by his reception. "America has a great future . . . there is a very strong mystic movement there," he observed.[39]

During the 1920s circumstances with respect to a distinct American musical voice began to change. The virtuoso pianists who decisively popularized the European musical heritage carefully distanced themselves from the emergence of a unique American music. Busoni wrote two works based on Native American materials in 1915, the *Indian Fantasy* and four piano studies titled *Indian Diary*, but his overriding ambitions were centered on the future of music in Europe.[40] Paderewski had been exceptionally generous as a philanthropist to America and American musicians before the First World War, but from 1910 on he turned gradually from music to the political future of Poland.

Rachmaninoff, however, became a regular and visible presence in interwar America's musical scene. He ultimately acquired citizenship. But for all his appreciation, dependence, and gratitude toward the United States, the home he eventually built that was evocative of the one he lost in Russia was in Switzerland, not America. As a composer he resolved to remain on the periphery of the development, during the 1920s, of American politics and a new American music. He admired Paul Whiteman, George Gershwin, and Ferde Grofé.[41] To the end of his life, he considered himself a loyal citizen of a regime that had vanished and a member of a community that had been dispersed. He was irrevocably tied to its diaspora and a world that lived only in recollection. Rachmaninoff remained Russian through a form of creative nostalgia defined by the astonishingly rich "local" cultural landscape of the first forty-four years of his life. Influences from the new musical environment of his exile, particularly its American base, make their appearance in four major works from the last years of his life, but they are deftly integrated into a normative aesthetic framework to which Rachmaninoff remained loyal.[42]

Paderewski

Of the three contemporary keyboard virtuosi who sought to establish themselves as composers, Paderewski was, in terms of posthumous reception, the least successful.[43] Yet his compositions should not be dismissed entirely. Though slight in comparison to the works of Busoni and Rachmaninoff, his works include a full-length opera, *Manru* (1901), a Piano Concerto in A Minor (1888), and the 1893 *Polish Fantasia*, as well as the gargantuan 1908 Symphony in B Minor, "Polonia." Most of

Paderewski's music, however, was written for piano alone. It is dominated by short solo pieces, transcriptions, and adaptations of and variations on Polish folk material. Paderewski seems to have published no music after 1917 and left a variety of unfinished large-scale projects. The output is amazing given his punishing schedule as a piano virtuoso. Unsurprisingly, much of Paderewski's music is designed to foreground him as a virtuoso.

But Paderewski the composer harbored a greater ambition. He sought to use music to communicate the character of the modern Polish spirit, its virtues and culture. His musical evocation of Poland was consistent with the work of two older contemporaries, Poland's leading historical painter, Jan Matejko (1838–1893), and Poland's most famous novelist, Henryk Sienkiewicz (1846–1916). The ideology and images in Sienkiewicz's historical novels from the 1880s, all set in the seventeenth century, shaped Poland's self-image at the turn of the century. National character and destiny were seen as legacies of lost glory, victimization, and suffering. Poland, once a powerful monarchy dominated by the idealistic leadership of a chivalric noble class, had been betrayed, dismembered, and subjugated, beginning in the 1770s and for good in 1795. Chopin's piano music became the voice of the Polish national cause after the uprising of 1830, and Paderewski sought to sustain the symbiosis Chopin forged between music and patriotism. His objective was to emulate Chopin and employ music to deepen internal and international sympathy with Poland's historic plight and its claim to political independence.

Paderewski's music sought to project a mythical historic unity between the noble landowner and peasant through the sentimentalized transformation of folk material into dramatic piano pieces, songs, and short lyrical vignettes. A routinized version of a common-folk culture was rendered compatible with the heroism and patriotism of the noble class, the *szlachta*. In Paderewski's music, just as in Matejko's carefully staged historical scenes and Sienkiewicz's prose epics, this synthetic construct of the national was dependent on the use of a well-understood late nineteenth-century rhetorical arsenal that favored realist illusionism. Chopin had provided the sounding musical representation of the Polish national character. In their separate domains all three artists—Matejko, Sienkiewicz, and Paderewski—clung to historical models and practices and vigorously opposed deviations from the reigning taste. Challenges in music, painting, and literature to this patriotic realism, already apparent in the 1890s, were condemned as nihilistic decadence, irresponsible aestheticism, and a pessimistic attitude to human nature and the possibilities of progress.

Paderewski's adherence to qualities closely identified with late nineteenth-century Romanticism in music for the piano—sentimentalized expressiveness, ease of recognition, surface refinement, and decorative elegance—is the thread that connected his success and aura as a public performer (his mannerisms, the manipulation of image and personality, itself a harbinger of the celebrity culture of the twentieth century), his efforts in composition, and his unique achievement in politics. Only *Manru* and the symphony give glimpses of an effort to push form and content beyond the confines of charm and the reliance on predictable correspondences between feelings and music.

Paderewski's effort to appropriate Wagner (particularly in the symphony) into his musical evocation of the Polish spirit was understandable. But the contrast between Wagner and Paderewski as advocates of the national is instructive. Wagner sought to use music in a new way to reinvigorate and reinvent "Germanness" and therefore redefine what being German meant. This involved a confrontation with inherited aesthetic tastes, practices, and reigning conventions. His innovations—leitmotifs, and the use of harmony and orchestral color to sustain motivic repetition—accelerated the accessibility and democratization of musical experience. But his attack on inherited aesthetic tastes aligned with his vision of the future of Germany and his assertion of its superior national culture and destiny. By the time Paderewski came of age in the early 1880s, Wagner had captured a rapidly growing audience with new music and a new politics. Paderewski sought to do for Poland what Wagner had done for Germany.[44]

But for all his patriotism, Paderewski's dependence on the piano and his skillful utilization of conventional strategies associated with the aesthetics of piano music falsified the character and potential of modern Poland. The political cause was sentimentalized, as if it were mere drawing-room or theatrical entertainment. Precisely this got under the skin of Karol Szymanowski, the most significant Polish composer of the early twentieth century. Paderewski, Szymanowski argued, misunderstood Chopin and his achievement as a "Polish" composer and his historic contribution to the formation of a national cultural consciousness.

Paderewski cloaked the "true objective value" of Chopin by perceiving it "through a black veil of mourning," thereby trivializing it. Using his magnetic personality, his "mystery of gesture," Paderewski made Chopin's music an emblem of "commonplace patriotism." Paderewski over-sentimentalized Chopin in performance and tied the essence of his music all too readily to "melancholy." The habit of inserting routine expressions of melancholy, loss, and sorrow as distinctive markers of the national culture into Poland's folk music heritage erected a false barrier; the Romantic musical tradition became an obstacle to art playing its rightful role in fashioning a modern and progressive Polish identity. In order to take its place as an equal among nations, Polish national art and culture had to be cosmopolitan, like Chopin, not reductively provincial, exclusionary, or exotic.[45]

Chopin's true achievement, according to Szymanowski, had been to elevate a distinctly Polish ethos and identity through his novel, innovative music. Chopin integrated a unique Polish sensibility into the great European and universal traditions of culture. Through Chopin, Polish music assumed world-historical significance alongside the music of Bach, Mozart, Beethoven, and Wagner. In contrast, the music Paderewski promoted as Polish adhered to a reductive retrospective aesthetic, a formulaic and sentimental evocation of Poland's past greatness and sufferings. When Szymanowski heard Paderewski's explicitly nationalist symphony in November 1911, he declared it a "stupendous abomination" and observed that "patriotism in the artistic field, for us in particular, is an impossible absurdity. This hideous symphonic buffoonery has harmed us all exceedingly."[46] Paderewski's grandiose pseudo-Wagnerian gestures mirrored the elegant but superficial imitative expressiveness of his piano music. This retrospective historicism did nothing to spark a contemporary musical equivalent to Chopin. Modern Poland needed to contribute in a distinct manner to humanity. Music's role was to deepen national pride through art that resisted xenophobia and broke down artificial barriers among nations.

Paderewski's use of folk melodies and dances struck Szymanowski as an act of essentialist exoticism: the romantic simplifications and decorations delivered music that eviscerated the authentic expressive potential of premodern Polish folk idioms. The determination to rid Poland of the melancholy sentimentality of Paderewski's patriotism inspired Szymanowski's own use of Polish folk idioms in the 1931 stage pantomime-ballet *Harnasie*. It offered a modern patriotic alternative to the anti-cosmopolitan (and often anti-Semitic) romantic expression of Polish nationalism that flourished before 1918 and later in interwar Poland.[47]

The image of Poland so successfully promoted by Paderewski throughout America and at the Peace Conference at Versailles (at which he was a signatory) was as romantic as it was reactionary and regressive, and bore an uncanny resemblance to Paderewski's contributions as a Polish composer and pianist. Paderewski's skill in communicating sentimental simplifications to a mass public from the keyboard made it possible for him to achieve a political prominence unlike any other musician in modern history. He attained a visible and important role in Poland's interwar reemergence as an independent nation. He served as prime minister of Poland for much of 1919 under Józef Pilsudski, as well as Minister of Foreign Affairs. At the end of his life, during the first two years of the Second World War, he was Chief of the National Council of Poland.[48]

A remarkable irony of history did not escape Szymanowski. The true heirs of Chopin's greatness as composer, whose primary vehicle was the piano, were Rachmaninoff, Medtner, and above all, Scriabin, leading composers from Russia, Poland's most hated occupying oppressor.[49] Their music extended Chopin's revolutionary use of harmony, form, and melodic construction into a contemporary musical language suggestive of melancholy and interiority to listeners all over the world, without shedding its Russian character. Their music transcended narrow nationalism without denying its national origins, just as Chopin's had in the 1830s and 1840s.

The essential weakness of Paderewski's music, even in his finest achievement, the opera *Manru,* stemmed from the comfort and success provided by his concert audience; he manipulated the reigning tastes of not only "90 percent of the elite of Polish intelligentsia and culture," as Szymanowski observed in 1910 at the centenary celebration of Chopin's birth, but also of the tastes of the concert-going public generally, particularly in America.[50] As Paderewski himself claimed, for all but the very gifted destined to become professionals, learning to play the piano opened the individual to the acquisition of a pleasing cultural heritage and its attendant values. The past defined the present. "The actual study of music," he wrote, "results in almost limitless gratification in later life in the understanding of great musical masterpieces."[51]

In this way musical culture, acquired through the piano, helped secure the mission of middle-class self-improvement in the early twentieth century. This affirmation of conservative and anti-cosmopolitan constructs of the social and political order inspired by a mythical past buttressed a regressive ideal of national homogeneity and grandeur that dominated Polish politics between the wars. Paderewski was certainly not as much of a chauvinist and nationalist as his opponents on the political right were during the 1920s. He had absorbed too much of America's democratic culture and remained exceptionally admiring and fond of America. Yet the musical aesthetic Paderewski promoted and popularized in Poland and internationally on behalf of an idealized Poland—a myth to which the musical culture centered on the piano gave credence—also affirmed a contrasting national self-image in America: its sense of itself as a land of opportunity. As one Paderewski biographer noted, "Paderewski and America responded to each other perfectly . . . his personality and attitude were irresistible to most Americans. He quickly became a figure to be pointed out . . . to illustrate the possibilities of the American dream."[52]

Busoni

The contrast between Busoni and Paderewski is stark. Busoni was an exceptional virtuoso who communicated intensity and spontaneity at the keyboard. He, like Paderewski, exhibited a vast freedom in interpretation. Unlike Paderewski, however, Busoni did not exploit the theatricality of public performance. Rather, his playing had an exceptional authority, an astonishing command of color and sonority, and an unerring sense of form. The range of his repertoire was boundless. What made this possible and set Busoni apart was his originality as composer, improviser, and thinker. As Landon Ronald, the British conductor, commented in 1923, "The pianist Ferruccio Busoni has one of the most remarkable musical brains of living musicians." He was also a remarkable writer, and his influence, given the highly peripatetic nature of his career, was astounding. It extended to Sibelius, Varèse, and Weill, among many others.[53] By the First World War, and certainly during his last decade, Busoni focused increasingly on his work as a composer, writer, and teacher. The pressure to satisfy the public—concert-goers, amateurs, teachers, and critics—grated on him. Paderewski, on the other hand, reveled in the democratization of concert and classical music and the public acclaim it brought him. It made his political career possible.

Busoni harbored no political ambitions, but was persuaded that arts and ideas were decisive forces in history. Leading artists had the obligation to sustain and advance a vibrant aesthetic culture. Busoni suspected that the era he was living in was facing a dangerous debasement of tastes and standards. The glorious tradition in the arts exemplified by Bach and Cervantes, by Liszt and Goethe, was threatened by the cheapening of standards. The transformation of society through industrialization and technological innovation at the end of the nineteenth century may have led to the expansion of the public sphere, but not necessarily for the better. For Busoni, "The artist exists only for artists . . . the public, the critics, the schools, and the teachers are nothing but stupid and harmful parasites."[54]

Busoni's encounter with America seemed to vindicate his fears. Contrary to common prediction, Europe, not America, held the greatest promise for an advance in art and culture adequate to the modern world, particularly the advances in commerce and technology.[55] Therefore, in the aftermath of the First World War, art and culture in Europe needed to be protected from the threat of American efficiency, materialism, and utilitarianism. In 1919, Busoni lamented the influence of Americans on postwar Paris: "One sees a great many American soldiers with insolent and expressionless faces . . . they walk along . . . without talking or laughing. . . . People do not like them."[56] Only Boston, owing to its more externally European character, appealed to Busoni.

Busoni feared most that the individual, and therefore the ideal of the exceptional person, was being subordinated to communal and commonplace group values. Despite having valued American colleagues and students, memorable experiences as a teacher and performer, and success and recognition (including a well-publicized recital at the White House), Busoni was deeply concerned:

> Indeed I am beginning to have my doubts about the "future" of America and the development of the nation in the sense of the blossoming of the arts in the "old" world. During my ten years' absence there has been no change—the American way of life was formed virtually at a stroke from a brilliantly practical idea and has remained so—imagination seems only to run to the superlative fulfilment of community needs.
> Let me summarize this in the following sections:
> The means of transport aim for speed and comfort;
> Domestic comforts are practical, but neither aesthetic nor poetic; i.e.: elevators from kitchen to the dining room, bathrooms adjoining the bedroom, recessed cupboards and similar tomfoolery.
> Thirdly: the patenting of inventions for practical and domestic life, mechanical kitchen gadgets, pressure cookers, powders for polishing metals and shoes, etc.
> Fourthly: *publicity*, pushed to its limits, the importance of the press (for this sole reason), its impudence towards any possible rivals, its exaggeration, untruthfulness, "*sensationalism*." The *result: success* (a concept which has a purely financial meaning here.) And now success has to be mass-produced, thus the object of any sort of success must be such that it can be *within the reach of all*, even the lowest.
> The outcome: success and the means of achieving it can be the subject of an exchange of ideas of a conversation between persons superior and inferior (at least in rank), without any difference of intellect becoming apparent.
> All America has founded its ideal on
> Quantity
> and not on quality, about which everyone is in perfect agreement.
> It seems to me that the American character is now completely formed and has perhaps arrived at a point of stagnation. The Americans have learned *everything* from Europe, but they are convinced they have surpassed it in everything. This conviction

has a fatal influence on development and could have serious consequences. In fact it seems to me that even in those things which one could call American *specialties*, Europe is beginning to leave them behind. French automobiles, the underground railway in London, the electric train at Zossen, the factories of Essen and Stettin have already overtaken the wonders of the United States. As for the Untergrundbahn in Berlin, an American could never have dreamed of finding such an elegant way of combining technology with aesthetics.[57]

Busoni came from German and Italian ancestry. He was a genuine cosmopolitan. His identity was that of a European. He saw himself as a member of an international aristocracy of artists, musicians, writers, and thinkers. Busoni resisted the cultural chauvinism that flourished during the First World War. He was a man of learning who pursued writing, and was an ardent bibliophile. He was obsessed with *Don Quixote*, studied the life and work of Leonardo da Vinci, Dante, E. T. A. Hoffmann, and, like his contemporary Richard Strauss (whose intelligence he admired but whose music, he felt, was too reliant on skillful effect), Goethe. Busoni was interested in architecture, drawing, and painting. He absorbed the prejudices of the late Nietzsche, including skepticism about Wagner and his influence. Busoni, like Nietzsche, admired Bizet; he was also a lifelong enthusiast of Saint-Saëns as composer and performer.

Busoni assumed the real and symbolic status as the most influential proponent of new and experimental music in the twentieth century. The eclectic and shifting preferences Busoni displayed in his career, both in his music and writings, reveal one key underlying conviction—that music possessed a "oneness," a unified metaphysical essence. Despite its many incarnations, music was a spiritual form of life that remained neutral in terms of meaning as defined by words and images. Even though he deeply admired Wagner, Busoni believed that in the opera theater, music should dominate all other aspects, that is, the scenic and the literary. He advocated a return to sequences of scenes, each defined by musical time and form, in contrast to the use of music to generate an illusion of continuity, as the author of a realist novel (e.g., Tolstoy) might. Busoni's formal model was Cervantes' *Don Quixote*. He was determined to complete *Doktor Faust*, his novel synthesis of the operatic tradition that went beyond Wagner and Strauss.

Melody was for Busoni the formal category that lay at the core of all music. As music's most important element, melody functioned as a dynamic and unifying force:

This "absolute" melody, at first a self-sufficient formation, united itself subsequently with the accompanying harmony and later melted with it into oneness; out of this oneness the continually progressive poly-harmony aims to free and liberate itself . . . melody has expanded continuously . . . has grown in line and in capacity for expression, and . . . must succeed in attaining universal command in composition.[58]

All pitch systems and procedures lent themselves to melody and its use in shaping musical forms of meaning and beauty. Busoni broke away, as H. H. Stuckenschmidt observed, from a model of thematic development derived from Viennese Classicism and conceded "new rights to melody" that "demanded an extremely involved polyphony."[59] This was a radical position. Beauty and meaning in music were not defined by established conventions or fixed by concrete rules; they were not realized by existing descriptive, illustrative, or didactic practices.

New scales, new sounds, new timbres, new harmonies, and a new approach to time, duration, meter, and rhythm were possible; the "oneness" in music was inexhaustible. The controversial dialectical twist in Busoni's thought was this: adherence to music's "timeless destiny" and eternal and singular character demanded different-sounding music for discrete eras in history. Music, owing to its fundamental autonomy, was a unique arena of freedom. Therefore, modernity demanded a music adequate to modern life, a music that remained faithful to music's freedom to sound differently in the "oneness" of its beauty and meaning. Paraphrasing Jean Jacques Rousseau's famous opening line in *The Social Contract*, Busoni wrote, "Music was born free," and to "win freedom is its destiny."[60] Like Rousseau, Busoni accepted the idea of the "perfectibility" of the human species.

Busoni, unlike Paderewski and Rachmaninoff, had a constructive attitude toward the aesthetic and spiritual implications of the sharp discontinuities between the mid-1890s and the years that followed the First World War. For Busoni, modernity brought more than fears; it brought unprecedented opportunities in art. The fundamental and invariant principles of art, as universal truths, could be realized anew to adequately match the distinct requirements of the contemporary historical age. The world was facing a "new renaissance" in culture that mirrored the human progress evident in the new power of machines.[61] Music and literature equal to the achievements of the past would be created in the present and future through innovation, not by reaction and resistance. In two 1925 essays on Busoni, Kurt Weill described how after Germany's defeat he and his generation had felt overwhelmed by new ideals and hopes. They did not know how to realize the promise inherent in their new freedoms now that the "chains" of the past had been broken. But then Busoni arrived in Berlin and inspired an entire generation with the spirit of his genius. He realized that Wagner had exhausted his own ideology. He introduced French musical "impressionism" and was the first to promote Schoenberg. Under his guidance, an inspiring but restrained new aesthetic was fashioned out of the divergent stylistic trends of past decades.[62]

Busoni's philosophy of history assumed the premises of German historicism. Each past age possessed a unique character; the arts and culture shaped and revealed these attributes more than politics.[63] But since an axiomatic set of aesthetic and ethical norms prevailed throughout time, the past remained indispensable to the present and future. This made Bach's music relevant to modernity. Bach could reanimate a sense of ethical and epistemological discipline and truth to the musical culture of post-Wagnerian Romanticism. Novelty itself, detached from the fundamental principles of art and an understanding of human character, was not a sufficient criterion for new music and art. But Busoni celebrated progress and the role art could play in realizing it. Humans, Busoni observed, are "obliged to look forward." In the "confused" present "it is preferable for a disturbed epoch to close in on a future order." The challenge in music was to realize "an absolute demonstrable beauty and perfection" in the face of opposition and philistinism.[64]

Busoni, who once dreamed of writing the great modern Italian national opera, feared that after the war the Italy with which he identified would develop along conservative and superficial lines of the sort Paderewski encouraged in Poland, including a debased sentimental nationalist aesthetic. His ambition ultimately became pan-European. He sought to transfigure the historic achievements of his twin cultural heritage, the Italian and German, for all of Europe. Music in Europe had to free itself from an attachment to "expressionism" in which "hysteria and temperamental gestures," including cheap sentimentality, predominated.

Germany presented a different challenge. The German public had become frighteningly "sober, sentimental and awkward," Busoni wrote in 1905. "Art may be at home everywhere," but "the German is *bourgeois*, art is aristocratic." Busoni concluded, "The free bird Music runs the risk of being shut up in a cage if it comes near the Germans. The Germans are becoming custodians of museums."[65] By "bourgeois" Busoni meant the smug uncritical German self-satisfaction toward its own cultural heritage, particularly that of Beethoven and Wagner.

The bourgeois "cage" Busoni feared for Germany was exemplified by the piano. In one of the most influential books on piano playing from the second half of the nineteenth century, *Die Aesthetik des Klavierspiels* (1876), Theodor Kullak had argued that the piano had the potential to communicate widely the "law of beauty" revealed by the masterpieces written by the great composers of the past.[66] Piano playing was a "reproductive" art, a means to cultivate the proper integration of thought and feeling. It required and promoted *Bildung*, intellectual self-cultivation. Properly used, the piano strengthened *Bildung* and cultural norms defined by and rooted in the past. At the piano, an established character of beauty—a tradition—came alive, guided by rational thought and learning; this, in turn, secured "moral idealism."

Busoni saw the matter differently. The past needed to be revisited, revised, and brought up to date, but not enshrined if decadence and decline were to be averted. The musical past Busoni thought usable for the music of the future centered not only on Bach but Mozart (*The Magic Flute*, in particular), Liszt, and Verdi. Chopin and Beethoven, central to Busoni's career as an interpreter and virtuoso, remained crucial but were treated with more ambivalence by Busoni the thinker and composer in his later years as Bach and Mozart took precedence.[67]

Music's "oneness" linked each period in history, but beauty in music was not fixed and defined by any standard stylistic convention. In the future, beauty in music would be new and different, so long as new music adhered to the axiom of music's essential unity. Unlike Scriabin, Busoni was not a mystic and did not resort to notions of an overarching spiritual mystery. At the same time Busoni shared Scriabin's belief in music's unique status as the bearer of metaphysical truth and unity. For Busoni, a generous eclecticism, even in the fashioning of melody, demonstrated the invariant and constant nature of time, and the universality of music; music reconciled permanent values with the variety of subjective experiences of time consciousness in the past and present.[68]

To locate truth and unity demanded sifting through the past to extract diverse patterns and directions for the present and future that honored music's essential nature. Each age chose different pasts as starting points. After 1918, the present and future had to reject the nineteenth century and rediscover Bach and Mozart to realize the vision of the new movement that Busoni had christened "Young Classicism." Hard as Busoni tried to underscore the generosity inherent in his advocacy for a new music, particularly after the 1906 publication of his famous essay "A Sketch for a New Aesthetic of Music," he failed to prevent the association of his name with all anti-traditional sounding new music, not all of which he held in high esteem. He became the target of vilification, notably by the composer Hans Pfitzner, an arch-conservative German chauvinist. Nevertheless, he emerged as "the leader of Germany's musical avant-garde."[69]

Part of Busoni's predicament was the fragmentary and unsystematic character of his writings. Despite his stress on music as essentially "abstract" and simultaneously "old and new," Busoni was forced to defend himself against "misleading" interpretations that charged him with promoting "formlessness," "illogical and zigzag harmony," and the "noisy expression of any blunderer."[70] Yet he pioneered in the extension of tonality and encouraged the use of pitches that did not follow standard chromatic division. Music's future could not be circumscribed by set procedures or conventions of notation. Only respect for its underlying unity, the necessity of form, and its freedom were indispensable.

Busoni's notoriety as a polemicist and his experiments in contrasting styles in his music have hampered sustained advocacy of his music. Only his magnificent Bach transcriptions for the piano have gained near universal acceptance. Other noted works, apart from the shorter piano ones, include the *Berceuse elegiaque*, Op. 42 (1909), the *Fantasia contrappuntistica* (1910), and the unfinished magnum opus *Doktor Faust*, as well as, to a lesser extent, the comic opera *Arlecchino*. Busoni's output was far more extensive than Rachmaninoff's or Paderewski's. There is a fine Violin Concerto from 1897 and two stage works, *Turandot*, from 1916, and *Die Brautwahl*, from 1905, as well as a wide, unexplored catalogue of works written before he reached the age of twenty-one.[71]

At the core of Busoni's oeuvre and reputation as composer was the piano. He wrote extensively for it. The piano, emblematic of the dangers of the democratization of music but at the same time the instrument that contained the best hope for the future, represented the essential but not limiting bridge between past and future. Music in modern times required its own "pianoforte geniuses" whose gifts were to take "a new road" and accomplish "unprecedented things." Like Liszt, Chopin, and Beethoven, such great exponents of the piano "perceived new means, solved the problems of new effects, created 'improbable difficulties' and wrote a literature of their own."[72]

The composition that represents the synthesis of Busoni's foregrounding of the piano and his ambitions as a composer of large-scale works is his Piano Concerto, Op. 39. The concerto gives voice to his command and understanding of the piano's potential and power, but its complexity, duration, and use of male chorus have impeded it from becoming a regular part of the concert repertory. The score reflects the variety and magnitude of Busoni's conception of music as an art and his commitment to the ethical advancement associated with music in the public realm.[73]

Busoni's concerto is also a near contemporary to the most popular piano concerto of the twentieth century, Rachmaninoff's Second Piano Concerto, which was premiered in November 1901. Busoni began writing his concerto in 1902, completing it in 1904, the year it received its first performance. The contrast between the two, in terms of character and reception, could not be more striking. Rachmaninoff's concerto was a runaway success. Busoni's five-movement work challenged the audience and its expectations. Much like the symphonies of Mahler, the work's unsettling demands, including its eclectic assemblage of disparate elements, baffled its listeners. Busoni integrated German references—to Beethoven, Brahms, and Wagner—alongside Italian materials, including three folksongs, and a choral finale based on the final section of a Danish play, Adam Oehlenschläger's *Aladdin*.

The text of the choral ending, which Busoni described as "representing mysticism in nature," speaks of "lifting up one's heart" to Allah, to eternity, to the relentless march of time, and to life, ecstasy, and death. The verse play suggests regeneration and praises the divine maker for the existential unity of mortality and immortality. As in Mahler, there is an unresolved tension between the rigorous musical structure and the veiled suggestion of a visual and symbolic program. Busoni, like Mahler, simultaneously honors, deconstructs, and extends the tradition of symphony and concerto, and challenges the audience's habit of locating reflexive and conventional assignments of meaning and value to music.

The piano part is relentlessly demanding and, as many have observed, Lisztian in its difficulty and character. But its sonority is consistently placed within a dominant orchestral presence. Busoni's explicit intent was to write a summation of the nineteenth century, yet strike a blow against the conventions of the virtuoso concerto, particularly those in the tradition of Beethoven and Chopin in which the piano is the protagonist in a "bravura" showpiece (a model Paderewski followed in his concerto). Busoni sought to challenge "virtuosity" as musical virtue. Virtuosity, he wrote in 1904, is "now on the downgrade." The work was designed to be an example of how by "honoring the old," the "old does not yield to the new, but to the better."[74]

Busoni fought against routine and the ordinary in musical culture. The artist's role was to elevate humanity and cut new paths that the public could follow. The historical task for art and culture in the present age was to prevent the "temple" of art and culture from being degraded into a "factory," the image Busoni conjured to describe the direction of the aesthetic consensus and tastes of his time. His concerto countered the reductive routinization of a musical expressionism inherited from the nineteenth century, including both the ossified but widely disseminated monumental music that followed in Wagner's path and the decorative and patterned elegant style that had catapulted Paderewski to fame and fortune.[75]

Rachmaninoff for his part used the form of the piano concerto to realize an alternative approach to what music might contribute to public culture at the start of the twentieth century.

Rachmaninoff

Behind the trees along all the boulevards a power stood on guard, a power terribly tried and experienced, a power which followed them with wise eyes. Art stood behind the trees, an art which discriminates so wonderfully in us that we are always at a loss to know from what non-historical worlds it has brought its skill to see history in silhouette. It stood behind the trees and bore a terrible resemblance to life, and it endured this likeness, as the portraits of wives and mothers are endured in the laboratories of the learned, those dedicated to the natural sciences, that is, to the gradual puzzling out of death.

What kind of art was this? It was the young art of Scriabin, Blok, Komissarzhevsky, Bely—the leading art, enthralling, original. And it was so astounding that not only did it not awake any thoughts of a change, but on the contrary, one wanted to repeat it and make it all the more lasting from its very beginning, only to repeat it more swiftly, more warmly and more completely. One desired to repeat it at a gulp, which would be inconceivable without passion, then passion leapt aside, and along this track something new was made. But the new did not arise from a change of the old, which is the generally accepted way of thinking, but quite the opposite, it arose from an exultant reproduction of the pattern. This was the nature of the art. And what was the nature of the generation?[76]

This passage was written in 1931 as part of an autobiographical sketch by the forty-one-year-old poet Boris Pasternak, who started out as an aspiring musician and devoted admirer of Scriabin's music and personality. Pasternak does not mention Rachmaninoff, even though he was a central figure in the world of art the poet eloquently evokes. This omission from a characterization of the great Silver Age in Russian poetry, painting, design, and music properly suggests Rachmaninoff's distance from the era's engagement with art as a spiritual force in history and its flirtation with "decadence" as a virtue.[77]

Rachmaninoff cultivated his own personal distance and individual, self-consciously Russian voice from the start of his career. He stood apart from all but his family and a close circle of friends, Feodor Chaliapin among them. He remained strikingly aloof from the tumultuous political upheavals in Russia before the Revolution, certainly the social unrest in the cities, the Revolution of 1905, the disintegration of the monarchy, the political assassinations, and the disastrous Russian experience in World War I. Unlike Scriabin, he never cultivated a cult of personality, an over-arching philosophy, or an entourage.[78] At the same time, Rachmaninoff was a shrewd man of business who understood how to get the best out of managers and publishers.

Pasternak not only challenged, retrospectively, the hopes and conceits of the Silver Age—its aestheticism and elaborations of symbolism—but also articulated, unwittingly, Rachmaninoff's particular ambition and achievement: the making of "something new" from an "exultant repro-duction of the pattern" of the "old." The Silver Age, in its aestheticism, particularly in the writings of Andrei Bely, privileged music. Chaliapin makes an appearance in Bely's 1902 *The Dramatic Symphony*.[79] In "The Forms of Art" from the same year, Bely declared, "Music is the mathe-matics of the soul . . . music influences all forms of art, but is at the same time independent of them . . . every form of art has reality for its point of departure and music, as pure movement, for its destination."[80]

Rachmaninoff shared this conviction, and accepted the idea of music as emblematic of a Russian sensibility. But his approach to the realization of this belief accepted the forms and practices of his Russian predeces-sors. In 1941 he declared, "I am a Russian composer, and the land of my birth has influenced my temperament, and so it is Russian music. . . . I have been strongly influenced by Tchaikovsky and Rimsky-Korsakov; but I have never, to the best of my knowledge, imitated anyone."[81] In 1926, writing to Nikolai Medtner, the composer and pianist with whom he was most in sympathy, he defined his achievement as distinctly individ-ual, authentic and true to the unique character of music. His music was unmistakably "serious," neither "popular" and devised for the market, nor "fashionable" and therefore intentionally "modern."[82] His evident debt to his predecessors distinguished Rachmaninoff from Scriabin. Rachmaninoff shared the opinion of Yury Sakhnovsky (1866–1930), an older friend and acquaintance, who wrote, in 1911, that Scriabin's music was "decadent and degenerate." Nonetheless, Scriabin understood Rachmaninoff's intent to use music to express his Russian sensibility and personality. "You want Russian music?" Scriabin asked Boris Asafyev (1884–1949). "Then don't look for Russian peculiarity or exoticism. Take the notes of something by Rachmaninoff."[83]

The "better" that ultimately emerged from Rachmaninoff's pen, particularly during his last years of exile—the *Paganini Rhapsody*, the Third Symphony, and the *Symphonic Dances*—reveals rhythmic ingenuity, references to contemporary sonorities and styles, and despite the composer's imaginative use of tonality and traditional structures, a harmonic individualism that emerges not out of "preconceived formulas nor preconceived theories" but out of a dialectical exchange with the patterns of the past driven by the desire to reinvent them and not reject them.

The C-minor Piano Concerto, Rachmaninoff's most popular major work, exemplifies this. The work was both "new" and clearly indebted to the old—among others to Schumann, Grieg, and Tchaikovsky. It does not attempt to offer a grand summation and formal critique of a tradition.[84] But it steps back from decorative virtuosity as an autonomous element of the form. The piano retains its role as a protagonist of lyricism and achieves, in a manner different from Busoni, the subordination of mere virtuosic pianistic display. Rachmaninoff does not indulge in excessive fireworks to sustain the listener's attention or complete the formal structure. Even Rachmaninoff regarded the work not quite pianistic enough, and some pianists complained that the ending failed to give the piano its proper due. Throughout the work, Rachmaninoff, somewhat like Busoni, assigns the orchestra a crucial function in setting the mood, elaborating the material, and establishing the formal logic and impact of the composition. But it is the piano that leads first-time listeners to sense the interrelationships between the musical materials in all three movements.[85] The overriding impression is one of lucid and distinctive lyric intensity contained within a poised formal design. An endless fabric of slowly unfolding long melodies is underpinned by alluring harmonies. Rachmaninoff's genius for creating melodies of an unashamed beauty and originality that transcended the sentimental or conventional yet were immediately comprehensible and memorable, is in full flower in the concerto.

Rachmaninoff's revered teacher, Sergei Taneyev, who was known for his uncompromising critical opinions, admitted to having been in tears during the second movement at the work's rehearsal for its premiere. He considered the concerto a work of "genius."[86] Medtner declared the "soul" of the famous opening theme to be quintessentially "Russian"; the listener could feel "the figure of Russia rising up to her full height." Rachmaninoff, however, achieved this spiritual evocation of Russianness without any reference to folk materials or, as Medtner put it, any "decking out in national dress."[87] Moods and sentiments linked to the landscape and history of Russia were transformed into a highly personal but accessible musical style that captivated the non-Russian public as expressive not merely of the narrowly national, but of the human.[88]

The Russian element, although not framed by simplistic cultural referents or rendered sentimentally, remained central to Rachmaninoff's music. It generated a distinctive melodic shape and harmonic usage that successfully reinvented the still recognizable rhetoric and gestures of late nineteenth-century Romanticism. Busoni the cosmopolitan and European developed the ambition to write a piano concerto that transcended musical nationalism. He manipulated banal and recognizable national elements, particularly evocations of the Italian, but reworked them and integrated them into the musical drama and universalist philosophical argument of his concerto.

Rachmaninoff, as an ardent spiritual patriot, transmuted his "Russianness" into a language of internal emotion that matched an interior dialogue that could counter the spiritual toll taken by the relentless regularity and passage of measured time. As a twentieth-century composer who transformed a national sensibility into an unusually accessible but distinct means of musical expression, Rachmaninoff can be properly compared to Béla Bartók. They both realized Szymanowski's ideal: they appropriated particularistic national characteristics and integrated them as novel dimensions of a modern transnational and universal musical discourse. The Russian quality in Rachmaninoff's music, particularly for the piano, was not experienced as exotic or foreign. By referencing past models—Chopin and Liszt—the music was heard as more than imitative, and serious in intent and relevant to each individual's personal sensibilities. Throughout his career, Rachmaninoff was able to sustain this by foregrounding an ideal of "beauty and truth" not tied exclusively to his native tradition. In this sense he followed the example of his mentors, Tchaikovsky and Taneyev. As Sabaneyev put it in 1927: "It was not form or harmoniousness" that characterized the Russian essence in Rachmaninoff's pursuit of a distinct compositional style, but his belief that music demanded an emotional intensity free of glibness and cognizant of sorrow. In Sabaneyev's terms this meant "passion, feeling, languor, heartache."[89]

Rachmaninoff's music met the need of modern listeners for an experience that articulated intimacy and was suggestive of interiority in ways that did not sound anachronistic or detached from contemporary life. The recurring associations left by his melodic sensibility, his use of contrast, and his undulating harmonic textures were those of melancholy and loss, of nostalgia, and of an awareness of mortality that did not sound superficial or out of a distant past.

What distinguished Rachmaninoff's "exultant reproduction of past patterns" from the aesthetic complacency of Paderewski and the elegant music of other piano virtuoso composers, such as Moritz Moszkowski's E-major Piano Concerto, Op. 59 from 1898, was the foregrounding of melodies with unusual and extended trajectories, the deliberate slowing down of time within compositional frameworks, and an inventive chromaticism, rhythmic texture, and counterpoint. The awareness of structure emerged from the unfolding of musical lines and harmonic shifts.

Rachmaninoff preserved surface clarity, transparency, and comprehensibility but eschewed, for the most part, the suggestion of an explicit literary or visual program. The early tone poems for orchestra had titles and references, but the connection and their function remained ambiguous. The same can be said of the link between the natural landscape and music. An explicit reliance on a visual or literary narrative was absent from the symphonies, concerti, variations, and works for piano solo. The listener's sense of an "argument" was consistently tied to the linear evolution of melodic elements and did not suggest a close correspondence with a story line or picture.

Yet Rachmaninoff never entirely abandoned the link between music and the visual, between listening and seeing. The visual maintained its impact in music that bypassed the use of words, even when the voice is employed—as in his "Vocalise" and in the opera *Francesca da Rimini*. Visual dreaming and inspiration lent themselves readily to music in nineteenth-century practice, notably in Liszt's opera transcriptions. In a conversation with the pianist Benno Moiseiwitsch, Rachmaninoff admitted to the importance of visual images as sources for his compositional ideas.[90]

One recurrent visual impetus for Rachmaninoff was the work of the turn-of-the-century's most celebrated (and, at the time, expensive) painter, the Swiss Arnold Böcklin (1827–1901). Böcklin is linked most explicitly to *Isle of the Dead*, Op. 29. But Rachmaninoff's Prelude, Op. 32, No. 10, was inspired by Böcklin's 1887 *Homecoming*. The Etude-Tableau, Opus 33, No. 8, took its inspiration most probably from the 1880 painting *The Awakening*, or *Spring*; and the C-minor Etude Tableau from Opus 39 seems to have been motivated by one of Böcklin's paintings of mythic creatures in the sea, *In the Play of the Waves*.[91]

Böcklin provides an instructive parallel to Rachmaninoff. His debt to the painterly techniques of German Romantic landscape realism remained strong until his last, highly symbolic period. Mythic subject matter, particularly from Greek and Roman sources, gives his canvases a contemplative grandeur, a stillness, and an overarching mood of solitude and isolation strengthened by a dark, somber color palette. Background and foreground share a unified form of shapes of highly modulated color. Although his later work becomes visually more ascetic, except for the portraits, the paintings are dominated by symbolic scenes set in a stylized nature. Böcklin shared with Rachmaninoff a fascination with death and melancholy and even has an iconic painting with that title. He created a relationship with his viewers in which the onlooker is drawn hypnotically into a moment of captured visual symbolism that invites the free association of sentiments and thoughts; one is transfixed by the juxtaposition of strange isolated images within a foreboding, often wild, and sometimes frozen representation of nature. The external elements are static but the inner reaction is dynamic. Seeing becomes akin to listening, a quality that drew not only Max Reger but Johannes Brahms to Böcklin's art.

Böcklin's canvases are not illustrative in a realist manner, nor are they theatrical. Rather, they are like images in a dream—fantastic, yet comprehensible and evocative. Böcklin's idiosyncratic adaptation of the painterly conventions of landscape and historical realism creates imagery that undercuts narrative specificity. With traditional practices, both Rachmaninoff and Böcklin detach listeners and viewers from ordinary time and expand their consciousness of inner reflection. Detachment from the everyday in Rachmaninoff's shorter piano works is achieved by form and sonority. In Böcklin's paintings detachment succeeds through the juxtaposition of fantastic figurative imagery and a stylized landscape. By adapting familiar stylistic conventions associated with realism, Böcklin, like Rachmaninoff, creates an imaginary world in which the passage of time slows down to make room for rumination, introspection, and the flight of the imagination.

Rachmaninoff admired Anton Rubinstein because of his imagination as interpreter; no other pianist had inspired in his listeners as many ideas and visual images of meaning. As a pianist Rachmaninoff sought to bring color into the experience of music and to inspire a sense of meaning. Music could be understood as akin to a picture. Its content and compositional structure had to become vivid in performance. The interpreter had to locate, prepare, and execute the unique structural point that defined the sequence of events and the form of each musical work without limiting the subjective response.

Rachmaninoff's approach to musical invention as dependent on inherited traditions of tonality and pianistic sonorities cultivated in the nineteenth century defined his compositional originality. Central to his craft was the variation form: the *Variations on a Theme of Chopin*, Op. 22; the *Variations on a Theme of Corelli*, Op. 42; and, above all, the *Rhapsody on a Theme of Paganini* are testaments to this. The more "Germanic" influences encouraged by Taneyev that occupied Medtner as a composer, and the concerto and sonata models of Beethoven and Brahms had less influence on Rachmaninoff. Despite his respect for the music of Adolph von Henselt (who influenced Russian musical practice), Rachmaninoff never played or commented on his widely admired F-minor Concerto from 1847.[92] Yet its second movement can be heard as a stylistic precursor. For all his admiration of Anton Rubinstein, Rachmaninoff only performed the first movement of Rubinstein's Concerto No. 4 in D Minor, Op. 70, and then just once, when he was nineteen.

In 1932 Rachmaninoff reasserted his loyalty to the musical past. Music, as a dimension of the human condition, needed to respond to the constant existential challenges of life and the human character. In contrast to Busoni, that connection was not to be radically historicized but contained by normative practices and aesthetic criteria. Music's function as an aspect of the human was to "bring relief" by revealing "the emotions of the heart."[93] This capacity rested on "fundamentals" that all composers had to honor. Primary among these was tonality, and therefore the vast possibilities of harmony in relationship to melody. Music offered the tools by which the full range of the "emotions of the heart" could be conveyed. Rhythm and color contributed to melody's primacy in musical form. Melody could be constructed out of the widest range of tonal practice so that in the fundamentally tragic condition of modern existence, music could "rehabilitate minds and souls."

The result of Rachmaninoff's allegiance to tradition as the source of new music was his unique capacity to speak directly and clearly to his listeners. His twin vocations as performer and composer were aligned through the medium of the piano. Listeners and especially amateurs could infer and personalize at first hearing their own sense of meaning in a new composition without confronting any specific intentionality on the part of the composer. They did not need to "know" anything, follow a "program," acknowledge advances over past models, or feel obliged to read explanatory notes written by experts.

Most significantly, Rachmaninoff's music inspired in listeners the suspension of their dependence on ordinary time and the clock. The way Rachmaninoff's music unfolded succeeded in expanding the subjective consciousness of time. The deliberate pace of Rachmaninoff's melodic forms and the elongated lines all conspire to create an experience akin to dreaming and daydreaming. Through the experience of being temporarily emancipated from proper time, and by extending the sense of its temporal duration, listeners were affirmed in their sense of individual autonomy and the integrity of their private feelings—not as "educated" or "learned" individuals, but as responsive, sensitive, empathetic individuals capable of rich and deep emotions. This was, after all, the secret behind the C-sharp Minor Prelude's astonishing popularity.

The critical objection to this characterization, most eloquently articulated by Theodor W. Adorno, rests on claims that these sentiments and feelings of emancipation from quotidian time are mere illusions of autonomy and in fact reaffirm the dominance of a conformist sentimentalizing aesthetic in league with the oppressive realities of modern life. The characteristics that make Rachmaninoff so accessible affirm the powerlessness of the individual in modernity and camouflage suffering by making it seem bearable. The seductive sentimental beauty of Rachmaninoff's music deters any ambition to attain authentic freedom and fails to inspire resistance to the unjust status quo. Indeed, Rachmaninoff's explicit goal in his career as performer and composer was to provide much needed emotional relief and rehabilitation to his contemporary listeners.[94]

And every listener counted. Composers should not "reveal" meanings, Rachmaninoff declared, since "each listener should find his own meaning in music."[95] He told the young Ruth Slenczynska, "Play for the man in the last row of the gallery," but "do not waste your time with music that is trite or ignoble."[96] Rachmaninoff practiced relentlessly, determined to give his best every time, whether in a provincial town or a great metropolis. "Music, the creation of music," he declared, "was the chief thing" in his life. Rachmaninoff could not imagine life without it. His own music was designed to communicate the emotional power and true beauty of great music, old and new.[97] The intense schedule he kept was not merely an economic necessity, or a means to rehabilitate his life in exile. Despite the public forum of the concert, the experience of piano music was always private and personal. Rachmaninoff rejected the idea of retiring from the concert platform; he needed his audience. He confessed, in 1931: "The public—I love it. Everywhere and at all times it has treated me wonderfully."[98]

The act of the reproducing concert artist was therefore never considered secondary by Rachmaninoff, in part because as a composer he made no conscious effort to be fashionably "original." The mission and aesthetic criteria of all music had already been set. Playing the masterpieces of the past secured the character of the truth and beauty in music. Yet music consistently expressed each composer's particular origins, life, and influences, including "books and pictures." Each composer demonstrated the "urge to give tonal expression" to his thoughts. Music was "the expression of a composer's complex personality." As composer and performer, Rachmaninoff shared, generously and clearly, his personal emotions with the listener—his "undercurrent of suffering." Music, after all, provided "a place where suffering and peace are transcended into a healing whole."[99]

In contrast, Paderewski's music exhibited no comparable hint of introspection or the confessional. And Busoni sought to "educate," but as a prophet. His sharp rhetoric of cultural criticism directed at the materialism and philistinism of his age masked an optimism rooted in a belief in the progress of humanity and the advance of the aesthetic alongside science and technology. Rachmaninoff, a skeptic about modernity, saw music as a means of relief for the individual grappling with mortality and suffering. His music acts as a personal, quasi-epistolary communication in sound to each individual listener.

Unlike Busoni or Paderewski, Rachmaninoff was a pessimist. He evinced no confidence in the idea of progress. His primary experience was that of loss and destruction. He clung to the distinctive and rarefied values of the world in which he grew up. Rachmaninoff's world, his home until the age of forty-four, had been destroyed and the culture that nurtured him vanished. He was born with a deep allegiance to the aristocratic values of his forefathers. Although his father squandered his inheritance, the wider family still owned estates. Rachmaninoff may have been comparatively poor, but his lineage and high social status remained a source of pride. He relished being a landowner. He trained and rode horses, loved fast cars and motorboats, and had enjoyed managing the economics of his beloved estate Ivanovka.

In the rarefied and circumscribed world of his years in Russia, Rachmaninoff played for Rubinstein, met Tchaikovsky, Tolstoy, and Chekhov, a writer he and Chaliapin, in particular, venerated. The arts had long been an arena of serious endeavor within his social class. There was, consequently, no person in the cultural renaissance of the early 1900s in Russia to whom he did not have access. He set the poetry of the leading Symbolist writers of his day—including Bely, Balmont, Merezhkovsky, Blok, and Bryusov.[100] The trauma of the disastrous premiere of his First Symphony was exacerbated by the interconnected and circumscribed world of music and culture of Moscow and St. Petersburg. A close-knit cultural circle made overcoming critical failure all the more difficult. His subsequent triumphs in the same context only strengthened his attachment to pre-revolutionary Russia. The year 1917 was a personal disaster, a greater catastrophe for him than for the twenty-six-year-old Prokofiev or even Stravinsky, then thirty-five, who had recently experienced his greatest success in Paris.

The Russian exile to whom Rachmaninoff might best be compared in terms of background and outlook (apart from Ivan Bunin and Medtner) was the much younger Vladimir Nabokov, whose family was comparably ancient and distinguished but unlike the Rachmaninoffs, was fabulously wealthy.[101] Both men shared a keen sense of loss at the disappearance of the landscape and world of their youth. Nabokov, when he finally arrived in America in 1940, reinvented himself, but he kept his past alive as fragments of memory whose concrete reality could never be recovered. He created a distinct American career and identity, and integrated, with originality, eloquence, wit, and irony, his family, youth, and experiences as an émigré in Europe and America in his writings. Nabokov confronted the sense of loss and used the experience of exile as a prism through which to view modernity and human nature. But like Rachmaninoff, he kept his distance from reigning modernist enthusiasms and cultivated his own unique voice. When asked, in 1969, his opinion of living poets Nabokov replied: "I know as little about today's poetry as about new music."[102]

Rachmaninoff achieved something comparable. He reinvented himself as a virtuoso pianist, playing the standard historic repertoire. He focused on conquering the American public, and took advantage of the still novel recording industry. He became one of the first superstar performers of the mid-twentieth century, with a mass public unthinkable before modern sound reproduction. He shelved, temporarily, the identity he had cultivated before the revolution, that of composer. Unlike Nabokov, however, Rachmaninoff clung to memory and nostalgia. He never abandoned his identity as a subject of the tsar. He was unapologetic in his effort to create domestic surroundings reminiscent of his past. He retained the manners and status of a White Russian aristocrat. Having succeeded brilliantly in financial terms, he could recapture his aristocratic distance and look with disdain, without fear, and without a sense of dependence on Koussevitzky, or of envy on Stravinsky and Prokofiev.

Rachmaninoff shared with Nabokov a lifelong and intense hatred of the Soviet Union. He was withering in his critique of Bolsheviks and Bolshevism, of Trotsky and Lenin. They were brigands and mendacious criminals.[103] Rachmaninoff used his wealth to help, with elegant discretion, other émigrés. Impressed by Nabokov's poetry, written under the pseudonym Sirin, Rachmaninoff sent him money in the interwar period, first to Berlin and then to Paris. They met once, in 1940, when Nabokov went to visit the composer in New York to thank him.[104] Both lamented that the future for Russia they had once hoped for—a liberal constitutional monarchy, English-style, in which an aristocracy might survive intact—never succeeded. The memory of that failure remained with them both.[105]

Exile deepened both Nabokov's and Rachmaninoff's skepticism about the idea of art as a significant force in history. They were not protagonists of modernist utopian dreams in which art was assigned a leading role. Radical change in art could be justified merely as coincident to sharp disjunctions in history, science, technology, and politics. But there was no prescription of progress. Art possessed invariant truths regarding beauty. Rachmaninoff's conception of his vocation as a composer, conductor, and pianist had been shaped by a context in which patronage, not the commerce of the marketplace prevailed. Making art was an activity to be taken seriously, but directed at a select and cultivated public. But unlike Busoni, Rachmaninoff in exile discovered and appreciated the unique capacity of his music and piano playing to reach a far wider audience.

The years of exile only strengthened Rachmaninoff's distance from the decidedly mystical vision characteristic of the last years of Scriabin's career.[106] Before Scriabin's death in 1915, Rachmaninoff had been compared unfavorably with this contemporary and friend. Scriabin was hailed as an innovator and a visionary whose music pointed toward a new, spiritually rich future and broke sharply with the past. Scriabin's sudden death inspired Rachmaninoff to take up the cause of Scriabin's music, and it remained in his repertoire to the end. But his dislike of the *Poem of Fire*, the *Poem of Ecstasy*, and the later sonatas was rooted in a rejection of the belief in art as a transformative theurgic power and Nietzsche's privileging of the aesthetic and the artist that flourished in the Silver Age.

Music was for Rachmaninoff about personal and intimate communication—the private sphere. Rachmaninoff's outspoken rejection of modernism after 1919 led to a closer relationship with Medtner, who was, if anything, even more openly virulent in his criticism of modernism.[107] Medtner's conservatism was grounded in theory and philosophy.[108] For Rachmaninoff, and Medtner as well, the strong aversion to and rejection of modernism in music was fueled by the open alliance between modernism in the arts and radical politics in Russia that developed between 1917 and the 1920s, in poetry, graphics, painting, architecture, and music. Artists sympathetic to the Revolution and the promise of the new regime drew parallels between politics and art; they both celebrated a break with history and a new start, free of traditions.[109] All this would be dramatically reversed in the 1930s under Stalin, but the radicalism in art and poltics was not forgotten or forgiven by Rachmaninoff.

The premises behind Medtner's aesthetic conservatism, ironically, were reminiscent of Busoni. Music was about a "unity" present in all modes of being. It expressed the "inexpressible" in existential unity through "simplicity" and "coordinated complexity" using a "single" musical language.

Busoni understood this as justifying experimentalism and change. Medtner considered the normative attributes of beauty not contingent on history. The range of change in style and sound was limited. Yet both believed that all genuine authentic music was, in a formal sense, at one with itself as a single metaphysical reality.

Rachmaninoff and Nabokov both shared the Silver Age's rejection of the long-standing and critical orthodoxy that dated back to the influential literary criticism of Vissarion Belinsky (1811–1848) and, above all, Nikolai Chernyshevsky (1828–1889), who argued for the utility of art as instrument of a radical social change. The mission of literature and the arts was to foreground realism and resist the aesthetic and cultural affirmation of tsarist absolutism and social injustice.[110] For Belinsky, the primacy of social communal ideals over the celebration of individuality defined the dominant criteria of literary criticism. Although literature and painting were the primary focus of this crucial aspect of Russian letters in the nineteenth century, a comparable critical discourse was applied to music. Composers—who were far more dependent on the court, the church, and aristocratic patronage—found themselves caught in this debate, particularly on the question of "nationality."

The generation of Medtner, Rachmaninoff, and Scriabin resisted this utilitarian criticism in the arts and the application of criteria drawn from ideologies of both socialism and nationalism. They sought to restore the autonomy and primacy of the aesthetic without denying the Russian character of their art. The subordination of beauty and the pleasure and solace derived from an individual's encounter with art to the imperatives of social and political reform was challenged. For all three, music, particularly instrumental music without narrative and illustrative uses, had to break free. One source for a contemporary renewal were examples drawn from Western history, especially Bach and Beethoven. Medtner sought to reconcile his biographical and artistic allegiance to German culture in music and literature with his profound attachment to his Russian identity. Rachmaninoff, to a far lesser extent, turned to non-Russian musical models and to the poetry of Goethe and Heine within his overriding focus on Russian verse from Pushkin to Bely.

At the same time, Rachmaninoff and Medtner showed a marked reserve toward trends in post-Wagnerian German music, particularly the music of Richard Strauss and Max Reger (a disfavor shared by Busoni). They admired César Franck and Edvard Grieg. Symbolism and other departures from realism in poetry, prose, and painting, including Scriabin's aestheticized and esoteric metaphysics and mysticism, found echoes in their music, but alongside a far more restrained and philosophically conservative emphasis on expressiveness, established notions of beauty in melody, sonority, and form, and formal correspondences between poetry and music.

Rachmaninoff's ideas about music were developed well before his exile, and remained consistent to the end. Yet his music migrated successfully from an elite aristocratic culture to a commercially popular twentieth-century culture in a mass democracy. The key to this transition was the continuity provided by the piano. That continuity can be understood through the lens of Nabokov's fiction. Two of his short stories from his years in Berlin deal directly with music.[111] The first, "Bachmann," was serialized in 1924; the second, from 1932, was titled "Music."

In "Bachmann," Nabokov satirizes the modern piano virtuoso as a lionized object of public obsession. Bachmann, the madman pianist, is described physically in a manner suggestive of Medtner. His impresario, Sack, more resembles Rachmaninoff. Nabokov describes in meticulous detail Bachmann's mannerisms on stage, particularly his fiddling with the piano stool and the wiping of his hands. The story revolves around a married woman who is mesmerized by Bachmann and sits in the first row at every concert. This singular patron causes Bachmann to play with "such beauty, such frenzy" that he achieves "incomparable artistry"; he would "summon and resolve the voices of counterpoint, cause dissonant chords to evoke an impression of marvelous harmonies" and then close with a "triumphant swoop" over the theme of a "triple fugue."[112]

But Bachmann disappears after every concert and descends into the depths of depravity. The impresario and the infatuated admirer then search for him, clean him up, and get him ready for the next concert. During the three years of her faithful devotion, there is "genius" in his playing, and Bachmann composes his greatest works, including a D-minor Symphony and several "complex fugues" with "totally original . . . thematic development."[113] One night, Bachmann appears on stage to "the thunder of welcome," but his admirer is absent. He abruptly leaves the stage.[114]

Bachmann's admirer has taken ill. She is found and the two meet up in the pianist's hotel room. Nabokov writes: "I think that these two, the deranged musician and the dying woman, that night, found words the greatest poets never dreamt of."[115] After her death, Bachmann stops his music making: "Stop those sounds! Enough, enough music!" He vanishes from sight and is forgotten. The story ends six years later, with Sack noticing Bachmann from a distance in a Swiss provincial railway station throwing money, over and over, into a mechanical music box, sobbing "uncontrollably," listening to a "tinny melody." When the machine breaks down, Bachmann shakes the box, increasingly distraught, only to give up and walk away.[116]

In "Music" the scene is a drawing room salon in which a concert of piano music is underway. The story's protagonist is Victor. Apart from a few tunes, music is a foreign language to him. He struggles to pay attention, but then catches a glimpse of his former wife. Suddenly "the music had fenced them in, had become for them a kind of prison, where they were both fated to remain captive until the pianist ceased constructing and keeping up his vaults of sound." As the crowd disperses—Nabokov seizes the chance to parody the sort of talk snobs and connoisseurs indulge in after the music stops—Victor realizes that the music, which had seemed "a narrow dungeon" of "resonant sounds . . . had actually been incredible bliss, a magic glass dome that . . . had made it possible for him to breathe the same air as she." After his ex-wife leaves, Victor is approached by someone who had noticed his apparent boredom during the playing. Victor protests that he has no ear for music and inquires what had been played. The story ends with Victor's interlocutor saying, "in the apprehensive whisper of a rank outsider: 'A Maiden's Prayer,' or the 'Kreutzer Sonata.' Whatever you will."[117]

Nabokov's sardonic tales help illuminate the place of music within the world in which Rachmaninoff lived and the reasons for his extraordinary popularity. "Bachmann" puts a critical and satirical eye on the aura of the piano virtuoso and music as a public and theatrical spectacle. Yet music can fuel catastrophic illusions. Nabokov contests the conceits of aesthetes who deem the spiritual and symbolic power of art superior to the conduct of real life; he shatters the snobbish delusion of a chasm between the elevated artistic ideal and the trivial, the commercial. In "Music," Nabokov describes the contradictory but hypnotic power of music that allows the listener to experience time and memory in ways otherwise unimaginable, as both a prison and a magic dome.

Postscript

Busoni's significance to and influence on music in the twentieth century rest primarily in the many ways he used his stature as a musician—as composer, performer, and writer—to encourage experimentation and innovation. His music is eclectic, distinct, ambitious, and adventuresome. The Piano Concerto, *Doktor Faust*, and many of his pieces for piano, and orchestral and stage works are masterpieces and unique. His music deserves far more currency on concert stages and in opera houses. Paderewski the composer, on the other hand, has little presence and will remain a respectable, conventional, and characteristic voice of his era. His elegant Piano Concerto is still delightful to hear.

Of the three towering piano virtuosos and composers discussed in these pages, Rachmaninoff succeeded best to command music as an expressive medium and to capture, permanently and repeatedly, the hearts and minds of the broader public to an extent unrivaled by most of composers from his era, other than Giacomo Puccini. Rachmaninoff's "exultant" reproduction of the rhetoric and procedures of late Romanticism has come into its own in the twenty-first century. The irony in the course of twentieth-century music is that Rachmaninoff's inspired and sophisticated elaboration of tradition, his imaginative reconstruction of forms and practices drawn from Tchaikovsky and Taneyev, his engagement with Chopin and Liszt, and his allegiance to Medtner's belief in extending the past within a framework of normative musical values, has ended up at the center of a critical revision of the musical modernism of the twentieth century.

Rachmaninoff structures his music so that individual listeners sense the creation of a temporal space of their own making, in which an imaginary world of memory, aspiration, and reflection finds its expression. Time stops. It is as if the composer is inviting an act of personal, intimate communication. Sorrow and beauty find their voice in Rachmaninoff. For Rachmaninoff (as for Richard Strauss) the potential of tonality was inexhaustible and made radical modernism superfluous. Rachmaninoff provided twentieth-century music with a distinctive lyricism that transfigured the quotidian and stopped the clock, freeing the listener to find the bliss of the "magic glass dome" described by Nabokov's narrator.

The last part of the stranger's answer to Victor's question as to what had been played—"Whatever you will"—implies a work other than the two titles he suggested, "A Maiden's Prayer" or the *Kreutzer* Sonata. "Prayer," Tekla Badarzewska-Baranowska's Opus 4 from 1856, was perhaps the most widely studied and popular piano piece among amateurs; it is a cloying and predictable example of kitsch sentimentality. And the classical formal musical argument of Beethoven's *Kreutzer* Sonata, a staple of the violin repertory famously but improbably catapulted into literary history by Tolstoy who linked it to sexuality and adultery, does not invite a drifting away from the music while listening, or the slowing down of time and the experience of personal introspection. The music that might plausibly have offered Victor (and Nabokov's reader) the protected magical glass dome of "incredible bliss" associated with longing and loss, one that shut out pain and tedium and offered solace, relief from sorrow, and a temporal hiatus between past, present, and future, certainly could have been a composition by Rachmaninoff.

NOTES

1. Among those colleagues who were convinced Rachmaninoff was the greatest of all pianists were Ignaz Friedman and Josef Hofmann, also a close friend whom Rachmaninoff believed to be the leading pianist of his generation. See Allan Evans, *Ignaz Friedman: Romantic Master Pianist* (Bloomington: Indiana University Press, 2009), 93.

2. I would like to thank Byron Adams, Philip Ross Bullock, Christopher Gibbs, Richard Wilson, Irene Zedlacher, Bryan Billings, and Lesley Mirling for their assistance in preparing this essay. The main sources for the biography of Rachmaninoff used here are Sergei Bertensson and Jay Leyda, *Sergei Rachmaninoff: A Lifetime in Music* (Bloomington: Indiana University Press, 2001); Barrie Martyn, *Rachmaninoff: Composer, Pianist, Conductor* (London and New York: Routledge Press, 1990); Max Harrison, *Rachmaninoff: Life, Works, Recordings* (London: Continuum, 2005); and Ewald Reder, *Sergej Rachmaninow: Leben und Werk, 1873–1943*, 3rd ed. (Gründau-Rothenbergen: Triga, 2007). There is a touching reminiscence of Rachmaninoff by Nathan Milstein, written with Solomon Volkov, in *From Russia to the West: The Musical Memoirs and Reminiscences of Nathan Milstein*, trans. Antonina W. Bouis (London: Barrie & Jenkins,1990), 106–26.

3. Bertensson and Leyda, *Sergei Rachmaninoff*, 186.

4. For a comparable juxtaposition from the same period, see Leonid Sabaneyev, "Skryabin i Rakhmaninov," *Muzika* 75/5 (1912): 390–95. There is an excellent discussion in Rebecca Mitchell, *Nietzsche's Orphans: Music, Metaphysics and the Twilight of the Russian Empire Empire* (New Haven and London: Yale University Press, 2015), 25–103 and 137–64.

5. Hofmann's wife, Marie, quoted in Martyn, *Rachmaninoff*, 235. Rachmaninoff was Scriabin's colleague and friend rather than a rival, despite his misgivings about Scriabin's later works and lack of sympathy for his mannerisms and personality. He championed the earlier music even though his interpretations on a tour after Scriabin's death to help raise money for the family did not always please Scriabin's acolytes. Rachmaninoff retained Scriabin's music in his repertoire to the end of his career, though he was skeptical of Scriabin's turn to mysticism and the occult and his theories about sound and color. The perception of enmity seems to have been exacerbated posthumously by Koussevitzky, who championed Scriabin. See Victor I. Seroff, *Rachmaninoff: A Biography* (New York: Simon & Schuster, 1950), 71 and 158–71. Rachmaninoff also admired the early Stravinsky ballet scores, particularly *The Firebird*.

6. Martyn, *Rachmaninoff*, 26.

7. Anatoliy Lunacharskiy, "Taneyev i Skryabin," *Novy Mir* 6 (1925): 113–26. Lunacharsky, a friend of Lenin, was the first Bolshevik Commissar of Education, serving from 1917 to 1929.

8. These circumstances did not prevent even an admirer and good friend like Nikolai Medtner from accusing Rachmaninoff of "prostituting himself for the dollar." Martyn, *Rachmaninoff*, 26.

9. Rachmaninoff was sympathetic to the more liberal elements of the tsarist regime and was particularly resistant to its virulent anti-Semitism.

10. Richard Taruskin, "Not Modern and Loving It," in *Russian Music at Home and Abroad* (Oakland: University of California Press, 2016), 120–33.

11. Robert Pollak, "Rachmaninoff Plays Concert All His Own," *Chicago Daily Times*, 7 November 1941.

12. Schuller (1925–2015), gifted and versatile as a conductor, composer, and performer, was president of the New England Conservatory of Music from 1967 to 1977.

13. "A Conversation with Russell Sherman," in *The Not Quite Innocent Bystander: Writings of Edward Steuermann*, ed. Clara Steuermann, David Porter, and Gunther Schuller (Lincoln: University of Nebraska Press, 1989), 228.

14. Ibid.

15. See Cyril Ehrlich, *The Piano: A History*, rev. ed. (Oxford: Clarendon Press, 1990), 129, 131, 134; and Craig H. Roell, *The Piano in America, 1890–1940* (Chapel Hill: University of North Carolina Press, 1989), 216–17. The classic work on the piano remains Arthur Loesser, *Men, Women and Pianos: A Social History* (New York: Simon & Schuster, 1954).

16. See Travis Suttle Rivers, *The Etude Magazine: A Mirror of the Genteel Tradition in American Music* (Iowa City: University of Iowa, 1974).

17. Philip S. Taylor, *Anton Rubinstein: A Life in Music* (Bloomington: Indiana University Press, 2007), 150–55.

18. Edward J. Dent, *Ferruccio Busoni: A Biography* (London: Eulenburg, 1974), 74–75, 95.

19. Adam Zamoyski, *Paderewski* (1982; repr. Sharpe Books, 2019), 75–87.

20. See the discussion of Paderewski's playing in Kenneth Hamilton's superb *After the Golden Age: Romantic Pianism and Modern Performance* (New York: Oxford University Press, 2008).

21. A *Time* magazine article from 21 September 1942, "Music's Moneybags," lists career earnings of various musicians, with Paderewski ranked first. Only two other pianists earned over one million dollars: Rachmaninoff and Hofmann.

22. See the exhibition catalog, *The Armory Show at 100: Modernism and Revolution*, ed. Marilyn Satin Kushner and Kimberly Orcutt (New York: New-York Historical Society, 2013).

23. Antony Beaumont, ed., *Ferruccio Busoni: Selected Letters* (New York: Columbia University Press, 1987), 116, 118, 129; and Dent, *Busoni*, 98.

24. Friedrich Schnapp, ed., *Busoni: Briefe an seine Frau* (Erlenbach-Zurich: Rotapfel, 1935), 238–39.

25. Sergei Rachmaninoff, "How Russian Students Work," *The Etude*, May 1923, 298. He repeated similar sentiments in the *New York Times* of 6 January 1929.

26. Ignace Jan Paderewski and Mary Lawton, *The Paderewski Memoirs* (New York: Da Capo, 1980/1938), 275–77.

27. Stephen Kemp, "How Rachmaninoff Plays the C-sharp Minor Prelude: An Interview with Sergei Rachmaninoff," *The Musical Observer* 24/11 (November 1924): 1–2.

28. Rachmaninoff, "How Russian Students Work."

29. S. V. Rachmaninoff, "Essentials of Artistic Playing," in *Great Pianists on Piano Playing*, ed. James Francis Cooke (Philadelphia: Theodore Presser, 1917), 208–20, at 217. See also the comments in Oskar von Riesemann, *Rachmaninoff's Recollections* (London: George Allen and Unwin, 1934), 194–95.

30. Rachmaninoff "New Lights on the Art of the Piano," *The Etude*, April 1923, 223.

31. See Ehrlich, *The Piano*, 134; and Roell, *The Piano in America*, 217.

32. Percy Grainger, "Modernism in Pianoforte Study," in Cooke, *Great Pianists on Piano Playing*, 364–81.

33. Paderewski, "Breadth in Musical Art," in Cooke, *Great Pianists on Piano Playing*, 298–99.

34. Sergei Rachmaninoff, "The Artist and the Gramophone," *Gramophone*, April 1931, 525–26.

35. On Sabaneyev, see Simon Nicholls and Michael Pushkin, eds., *The Notebooks of Alexander Scriabin*, trans. Nicholls and Pushkin, Foreword by Vladimir Ashkenazy (New York: Oxford University Press, 2018), 225–29.

36. Leonid Ssabanejew, *Geschichte der russischen Musik*, ed. Oskar von Riesemann (Leipzig: Breitkopf & Härtel, 1926), 169.

37. Bertensson and Leyda, *Sergei Rachmaninoff*, 220.

38. In Elizabeth O. Toombs, "America Must Have a National Conservatory, Says Rachmaninoff," *Good Housekeeping*, February 1922.

39. Faubion Bowers, *Scriabin: A Biography*, 2nd rev. ed. (Mineola, NY: Dover Publishing, 1996), 138–64, esp. 161–62.

40. Larry Sitsky, *Busoni and the Piano: The Works, the Writings, and the Recordings* (Westport, CT: Greenwood Press, 1986).

41. On Rachmaninoff's attitude toward jazz pianists, see Evans, *Ignaz Friedman*, 130; and Harrison, *Rachmaninoff*, 246.

42. See the discussion of the Russian character of music before 1917 in Lincoln Ballard and Matthew Bengtson, with John Bell Young, eds., *The Alexander Scriabin Companion: History Performance and Lore* (Lanham, MD: Rowman & Littlefield, 2017), 59–74.

43. All three complained about the tension between a brutal performance schedule and seeking time to compose—much like Gustav Mahler, who worked in America with both Rachmaninoff and Busoni.

44. For Paderewski on Wagner, see Paderewski and Lawton, *The Paderewski Memoirs*, 62–63, 145–46.

45. For Szymanowski on Chopin and Paderewski, see "Fryderyk Chopin," in *Szymanowski on Music: Selected Writings of Karol Szymanowski*, trans. and ed. Alistair Wightman (London: Toccata Press, 1999), 177–95. See also Alistair Wightman, *Karol Szymanowski: His Life and Work* (Farnham, UK: Ashgate, 1999), 82–85.

46. Wightman, *Szymanowski*, 103.

47. Jan Steszewski, in *Karol Szymanowski in seiner Zeit*, ed. Michal Bristiger, Roger Scruton, and Petra Weber-Bockhold (Munich: Wilhelm Fink, 1984), 181–87. See also Tadeusz Andrzej Zielinski, *Szymanowski: Liryka i Ekstaza* (Warsaw: PWM, 1997), 217; Wightman, *Szymanowski on Music*, 201–2; Wightman, *Szymanowski*, 346–61.

48. See Marian Marek Drozdowski, *Ignacy Jan Paderewski: A Political Biography in Outline*, trans. Stanislaw Tarnowski (n.l.: Interpress, 1981), 144, 245–52. See also Zamoyski, *Paderewski*, 159–61.

49. For Szymanowski on Russian music as heir to Chopin, see his "On Contemporary Music in Poland," in *Szymanowski on Music*, 73–94, esp. 84–85.

50. In Wightman, *Szymanowski on Music*, 84–85. See also Wightman, *Szymanowski*, 224, on his envy of Paderewski's fame.

51. Paderewski, "Breadth in Musical Art," 290–300.

52. Zamoyski, *Paderewski*, 142.

53. See the excellent monograph by Erinn E. Knyt, *Ferruccio Busoni and His Legacy* (Bloomington: Indiana University Press, 2017). See "A Fugue While You Wait," *The Etude*, May 1923, 310.

54. Busoni made this comment in 1904, quoted in Dent, *Busoni*, 167.

55. Beaumont, *Busoni: Selected Letters*, 129, 193, 194–96, and 203. These are just a few selections from letters in which the Europe-America comparison is expressed. See also Dent, *Busoni*, 190–93, 227.

56. Dent, *Busoni*, 240.

57. Busoni to Emilio Anzoletti, 23 February 1904, in *Busoni: Selected Letters*, 69–70.

58. Ferruccio Busoni, *The Essence of Music and Other Papers*, trans. Rosamond Ley (London: Rockliff Publishing, 1957), 33.

59. H. H. Stuckenschmidt, *Ferruccio Busoni: Chronicle of a European*, trans. Sandra Morris (New York: St. Martin's Press, 1970), 212.

60. Ferruccio Busoni, *Entwurf einer neuen Ästhetik der Tonkunst* (Frankfurt: Suhrkamp, 1974), 11.

61. Beaumont, *Busoni: Selected Letters*, 30.

62. Kurt Weill, *Musik und Theater: Gesammelte Schriften*, ed. Stephen Hinton and Jürgen Schebera (Berlin: Henschel, 1990), 21, 26–28. The new aesthetic Weill was referring to was "Young Classicism."

63. See Friedrich Meinecke, *Die Entstehung des Historismus* (Munich: Oldenbourg, 1965); and Anthony Beaumont, *Busoni the Composer* (Bloomington: Indiana University Press, 1985), 29–36.

64. Busoni, *The Essence of Music and Other Papers*, 43–45.

65. Dent, *Busoni*, 118–19.

66. See Adolph Kullak, *Ästhetik des Klavierspiels*, ed. Martin Gellrich (1876; repr. Regensburg: ConBrio, 1994), 386–88. Kullak's book appeared first in 1860, its ninth edition in 1922. The original text was substantially expanded by Walter Niemann.

67. See Dent, *Busoni*, 168–70, 230, 271, 280–81, and 295. See also Busoni's writings on Bach and Mozart in *The Essence of Music*, 96–128.

68. If a moment of outlandish speculation may be permitted, the presence of an invariant constant—in Busoni's case the unity and singularity of music—can be reconciled with the validity of differentiation and subjectivity. Consider Einstein's "special" theory of relativity (published at the very same time as Busoni's "Sketch") in which the speed of light is a constant in a universe where there is no "absolute" time or space but has differing frames of reference whose vantage point are all subject to the same calculation, in a universe where none has an absolute priority. See Leon Botstein, "Einstein and Music," in *Einstein for the 21st Century*, ed. Peter Galison, Gerald Holton, and Sivan S. Schweber (Princeton: Princeton University Press, 2008), 161–75.

69. Beaumont, *Busoni the Composer*, 99.

70. Busoni, letter from January 1922, in *The Essence of Music*, 27.

71. See the excellent discussion of these works in Beaumont, *Busoni the Composer*.

72. Busoni, *The Essence of Music*, 82–83.

73. On the concerto, see Larry Sitsky, *Busoni and the Piano* (Westport, CT: Greenwood Press, 1986), 89–118; and Beaumont, *Busoni the Composer*, 61–75.

74. Busoni, in the program note to the first performance of the Piano Concerto in 1903; quoted in Sitsky, *Busoni and the Piano*, 92.

75. Busoni, "Routine," in *The Essence of Music*, 184–85.

76. Boris Pasternak, *Safe Conduct: An Autobiography and Other Writings* (New York: New Directions, 1958), 96–97.

77. See Simon Karlinsky, "Introduction," in *Dear Bunny, Dear Volodya: The Nabokov-Wilson Letters, 1940–1971*, ed. Karlinsky, rev. ed. (Berkeley: University of California Press, 2001), 22–29.

78. See the excellent discussion in Mitchell, *Nietzsche's Orphans*.

79. On Chaliapin and Rachmaninoff, see the many references in *Chaliapin: An Autobiography as Told to Maxim Gorky*, trans. and ed. Nina Froud and James Hanley (New York: Stein and Day, 1967); and the two volumes of Yu. Kotlyarov and V. Garmash, eds., *Letopis' zhizni i tvorchestva F. I. Shalyapina*, 2nd ed. (Leningrad: Muzïka, 1989).

80. Andrei Bely, *The Dramatic Symphony and The Forms of Art*, trans. Roger and Angela Keys and John Elsworth (New York: Grove, 1986), 165.

81. Quoted in Bertensson and Leyda, *Sergei Rachmaninoff*, 369.

82. Cited in ibid., 242

83. Bowers, *Scriabin*, 227.

84. See A. D. Alekseyev, *Russkaya fortepiannaya muzïka, konets XIX veka-nachalo XX veka* (Moscow: Nauka, 1969), 118–64, and on the Second Piano Concerto, 155–64.

85. On the relationship between Tchaikovsky's concerti and Rachmaninoff's (primarily the First) as well as a fine discussion of the concerti of Rimsky-Korsakov, Scriabin, and Taneyev, see Jeremy Norris, *The Russian Piano Concerto*, vol. 1: *The Nineteenth Century* (Bloomington: Indiana University Press, 1994).

86. Martyn, *Rachmaninoff*, 129.

87. Quoted in ibid., 127.

88. In the compositional output of the St. Petersburg composers, the *moguchaya kuchka*, there are few if any truly successful concertos, with the possible exception of Rimsky-Korsakov's Concerto for Piano.

89. Ssabanejew, *Geschichte der russischen Musik*, 105.

90. Maurice Moiseiwitsch, *Moiseiwitsch: Biography of a Concert Pianist* (London: Frederick Muller, 1965), 152–53; see Bertensson and Leyda, *Sergei Rachmaninoff*, 296.

91. Max Reger also used the 1883 canvas as inspiration in one of his 1913 *Four Tone Poems After Böcklin*. Rolf Andree, *Arnold Böcklin: Die Gemälde* (Zurich: Schweizerisches Institut für Kunstwissenschaft, 1977), 163, 164, 418–23, and 427; and Katharina Schmidt, ed., *Arnold Böcklin* (Basel: Kunstsammlung Basel, 2001), 260–65, 266, 280.

92. For a compelling introduction to Henselt, see the section on him in Wilhelm von Lenz, *The Great Piano Virtuosos of Our Time from Personal Acquaintance* (New York: Schirmer, 1899), 117–58.

93. Rachmaninoff, quoted in the *New York Times*, cited in Bertensson and Leyda, *Sergei Rachmaninoff*, 284.

94. Theodor W. Adorno, "Musikalische Warenanalysen," in *Gesammelte Schriften*, ed. Rolf Tiedemann, vol. 16 (Frankfurt: Suhrkamp, 1990), 285.

95. Rachmaninoff, quoted in the *World Telegram and Sun* (1940).

96. Martyn, *Rachmaninoff*, 412.

97. Ibid., 27 and 32.

98. Bertensson and Leyda, *Sergei Rachmaninoff*, 279.

99. Glenn Quilty, "Rachmaninoff—The Last Romantic Composer," *HiFi Review* 3/4 (October 1959): 26, 28.

100. See Richard D. Sylvester, *Rachmaninoff's Complete Songs: A Companion with Texts and Translations* (Bloomington: Indiana University Press, 2014). Rachmaninoff also set one poem by Ivan Bunin (1870–1953), whose social background, experience in exile, and political views were strikingly similar to his own.

101. Nabokov's grandfather and father were prominent in public life and both were remarkable for their liberal and reformist convictions, which included a rare but principled rejection of anti-Semitism.

102. Vladimir Nabokov, *Strong Opinions* (New York: Vintage International, 1990), 151. Nabokov shared the admiration for Chekhov, and for Bely, particularly his novel *Petersburg*.

103. "The Man Who Wrote the C-sharp Minor Prelude," *The Etude*, March 1919, 49.

104. The poet Khodasevich, an émigré in Berlin, was a mutual friend. Rachmaninoff subsequently sent Nabokov some old elegant clothes and tried to persuade him to translate Balmont's Russian adaptation of Poe's *The Bells* into English, a task Nabokov considered impossible. Karlinsky, *Dear Bunny, Dear Volodya*, 50–51; and David Bethea, "Introduction," in Vladislav Khodasevich, *Necropolis*, trans. Sarah Vitali (New York: Columbia University Press, 2019), ix–xxxvii. Also see Nabokov, *Strong Opinions*, 290–91.

105. Rachmaninoff also wrote letters of introduction for Nabokov upon his arrival in the United States.

106. Rachmaninoff resisted the allure of what Sabaneyev termed Scriabin's "Orphic Path," the synthesis of art and religion in which art becomes the privileged medium to reaching an all-encompassing mystic belief in the underlying unity of existence. Leonid Sabaneyev, *Skryabin* (Moscow: Skorpion, 1916), 68–69. For a sympathetic portrait of Scriabin and his philosophical and religious commitments, see Boris de Schloezer, *Scriabin: Artist and Mystic*, trans. Nicolas Slonimsky (Berkeley and Los Angeles: University of California Press, 1987). Schloezer was Scriabin's brother-in-law.

107. On Medtner, see Barrie Martyn, *Nicolas Medtner: His Life and Music* (London and New York: Routledge, 2016); and Nataliya Konsistorum, *Nikolai Karlovich Metner: Portet komozitora* (Berlin: Izdatel'stvo Henschel, 2004).

108. He delighted in Medtner's 1935 *The Muse and the Fashion*, a book published first in Russian by Rachmaninoff's own imprint and later in English, translated by their mutual friend Alfred Swan. See also Martyn, *Nicolas Medtner*, 7–10.

109. See David Haas, *Leningrad's Modernists: Studies in Composition and Musical Thought* (New York: Peter Lang, 1998), 2–4; and Larry Sitsky, *Music of the Repressed Russian Avant-Garde 1900–1929* (Westport, CT: Greenwood Press, 1994), ix–xi and 2–7.

110. The tsarist credo, formulated under Nicholas I by Sergei Uvarov read: "Orthodoxy, Autocracy, and Nationality."

111. Nabokov also wrote his finest Russian novel, *The Gift*, during that period. An extensive biography of Chernyshevsky, a figure Nabokov loathed, emerges in chapter 4 as central to the narrative. The stories are collected in Vladimir Nabokov, *Stories* (New York: Vintage Books, 1997), "Bachmann," 116–24; and "Music," 332–37.

112. Nabokov, *Stories*, 119.

113. Ibid., 120.

114. Ibid., 121.

115. Ibid., 123.

116. Ibid., 123–24.

117. Ibid., 336–37.

Index

Note: Page numbers followed by "n" indicate chapter endnotes. Page numbers in italics refer to figures, tables, and musical examples. Throughout the index, SR refers to Sergei Rachmaninoff.

Notes on the Contributors

Leon Botstein is president and Leon Levy Professor in the Arts of Bard College and Chancellor of the Open Society University Network (OSUN), as well as the author of several books and editor of *The Compleat Brahms* and *The Musical Quarterly*. The music director of the American Symphony Orchestra and The Orchestra Now, he has recorded works by, among others, Schoeck, Honegger, Szymanowski, Hartmann, Dukas, Foulds, Bruckner, Chausson, Richard Strauss, Mendelssohn, Popov, Shostakovich, and Liszt. He is co-artistic director of the Bard Music Festival.

Philip Ross Bullock is professor of Russian literature and music at the University of Oxford, and fellow and tutor in Russian at Wadham College, Oxford. He is the author of *Pyotr Tchaikovsky*, and coeditor of *Song Beyond the Nation: Translation, Transnationalism, Performance*, with Laura Tunbridge, and of *Music's Nordic Breakthrough: Aesthetics, Modernity, and Cultural Exchange, 1890–1930*, with Daniel M. Grimley. He is the recipient of the Philip Brett Award of the American Musicological Society and a former holder of the Edward T. Cone Membership in Music Studies at the Institute for Advanced Studies, Princeton.

Caryl Emerson is A. Watson Armour III University Professor Emeritus of Slavic Languages and Literatures at Princeton University. Her work has focused on the Russian classics (Pushkin, Tolstoy, Dostoevsky), Mikhail Bakhtin, and Russian music and opera. Recent projects include the modernist Sigizmund Krzhizhanovsky (1887–1950), the allegorical-historical novelist Vladimir Sharov (1952–2018), and the coediting, with George Pattison and Randall A. Poole, of *The Oxford Handbook of Russian Religious Thought*.

Peter Franklin is an emeritus fellow of St Catherine's College, Oxford, having retired as professor of music at the University in 2014. Publications include *Mahler Symphony No. 3*, *The Life of Mahler*, and *Seeing Through Music: Gender and Modernism in Classic Hollywood Film Scores*. A book based on his 2010 Bloch Lectures at the University of California at Berkeley was published as *Reclaiming Late-Romantic Music: Singing Devils and Distant Sounds*.

Emily Frey is assistant professor of musicology at Brandeis University. Her publications include articles and essays in the *Journal of the American Musicological Society*, *19th-Century Music*, *Rimsky-Korsakov and His World*, *The Cambridge History of Music Criticism*, and *Stravinsky in Context*, and she is currently finishing her first book, *Russian Opera in the Age of Tolstoy and Dostoevsky*.

Marina Frolova-Walker is professor of music history at the faculty of music, University of Cambridge, and fellow of Clare College. She is the author of *Russian Music and Nationalism from Glinka to Stalin*, *Stalin's Music Prize: Soviet Culture and Politics*, and coauthor (with Jonathan Walker) of *Music and Soviet Power, 1917–32* . In 2015 she was awarded the Edward J. Dent Medal by the Royal Musical Association for "outstanding contribution to musicology."

Christopher H. Gibbs is the James H. Ottaway Jr. Professor of Music at Bard College, co-artistic director of the Bard Music Festival, and executive editor of *The Musical Quarterly*. He edited *The Cambridge Companion to Schubert*, coedited *Franz Liszt and His World* and *Franz Schubert and His World*, and is the author of *The Life of Schubert*. He is coauthor, with Richard Taruskin, of *The Oxford History of Western Music, College Edition*. Since 2000 he has written the program notes for The Philadelphia Orchestra.

Rebecca Mitchell is associate professor of Russian history at Middlebury College. She is the author of *Sergei Rachmaninoff* and *Nietzsche's Orphans: Music, Metaphysics and the Twilight of the Russian Empire*. *Nietzsche's Orphans* was awarded the 2016 W. Bruce Lincoln Book Prize by the Association for Slavic, East European, and Eurasian Studies (ASEEES) for a first monograph "of exceptional merit and lasting significance for the understanding of Russia's past."

Simon Morrison is professor of music and Slavic languages and literatures at Princeton University. He is currently writing a history of Moscow for Random House.

Marina Raku is leading researcher at the department of music history of the State Institute of Arts Studies (SIAS, Moscow); executive scientific editor of "Dmitry Shostakovich: New Collected Works in 150 volumes" (DSCH, Moscow); scientific editor of the encyclopaedia "Tchaikovsky"; deputy chief editor of the on-line magazine *Iskusstvo muziki. Teoriya i istoriya* (www.sias.ru); and editorial board member of the magazine *Muzïkal'naya Akademiya*.

Steve Swayne is the Jacob H. Strauss 1922 Professor of Music at Dartmouth College. He is the author of *How Sondheim Found His Sound* and *Orpheus in Manhattan: William Schuman and the Shaping of America's Musical Life*. He is president of the American Musicological Society (2020–22) and the 2022 holder of the John W. Kluge Chair in Modern Culture at the Library of Congress.

Jonathan Walker is a London-based freelance writer and private teacher of advanced piano students. He is coauthor (with Marina Frolova-Walker) of *Music and Soviet Power* and *Shostakovich's Symphony No. 5*. He studied at Edinburgh University, at the Liszt Academy, Budapest, and at Queen's University Belfast, where he defended his PhD thesis on the musical-work concept. He has taught at Queen's University Belfast and Cambridge University, performed on BBC2 television, given talks for BBC Radio 4, and published translations in French and Russian.

Printed in Great Britain
by Amazon

35757277R00212